Big School of Drawing
Animals

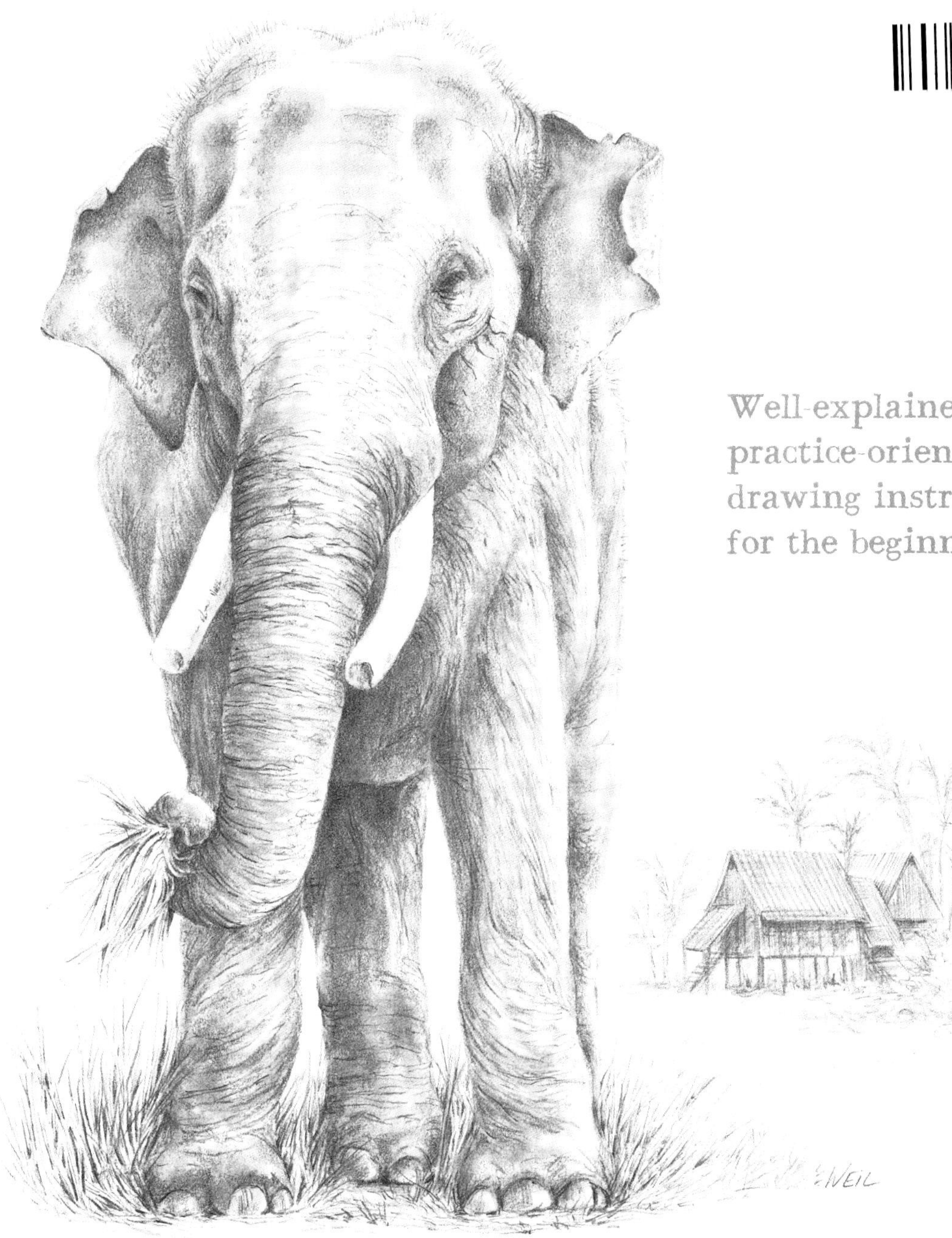

Well-explained,
practice-oriented
drawing instruction
for the beginning artist

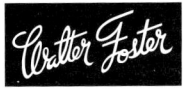
Walter Foster

Contents

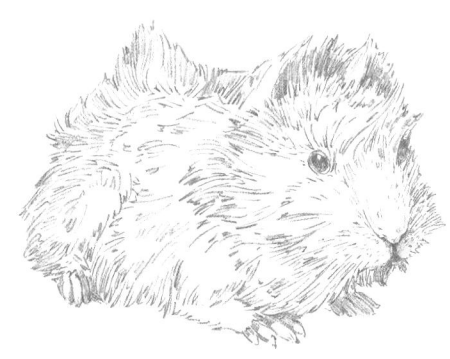

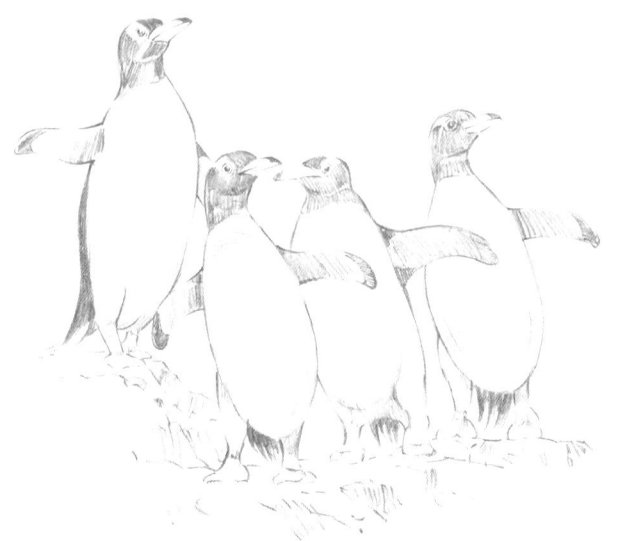

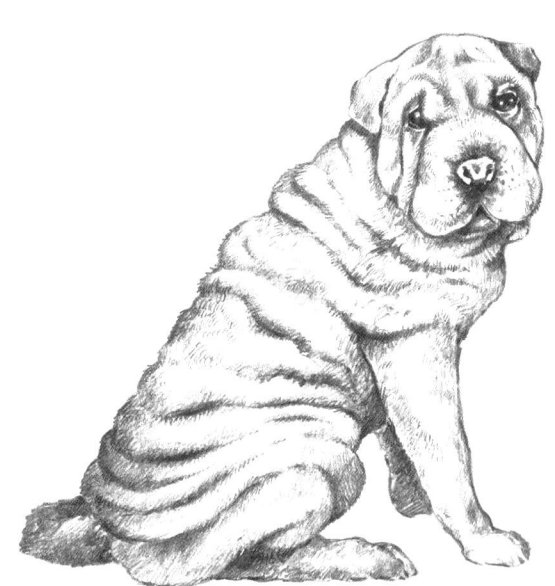

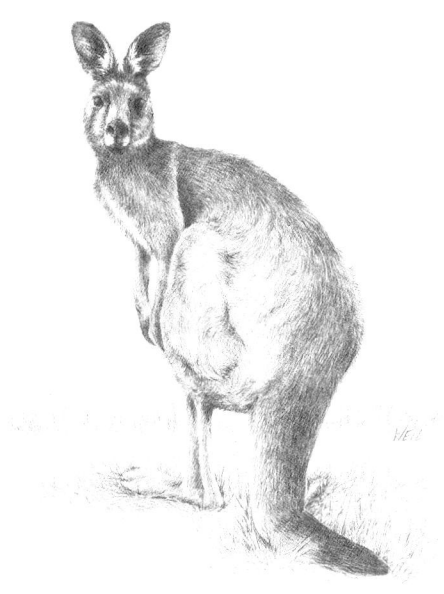

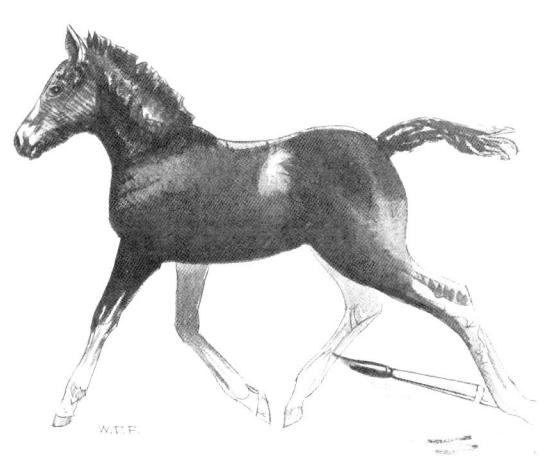

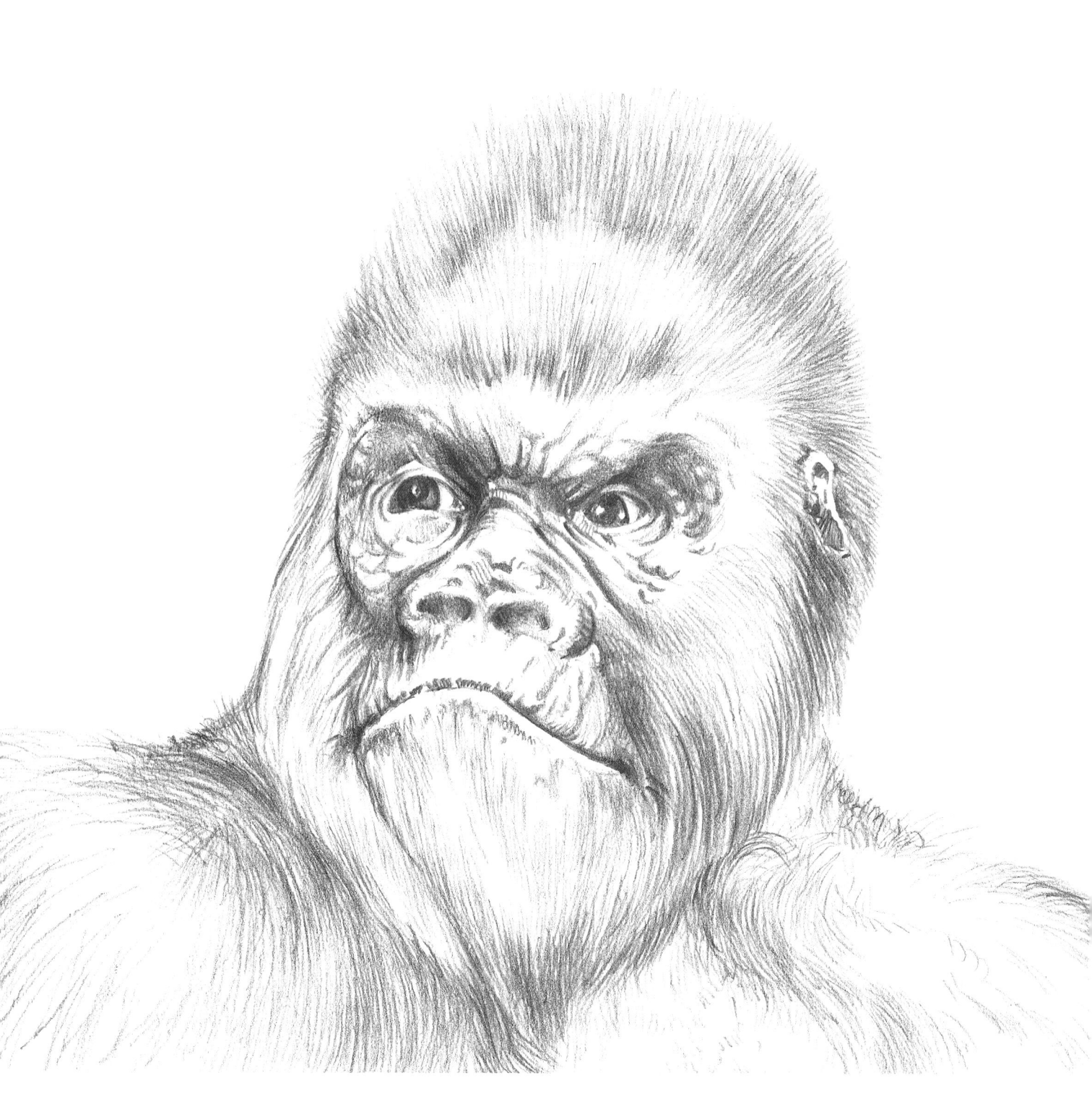

Getting Started

Animals are a source of endless enjoyment for artists because the subjects exist in a variety of shapes, textures, and personalities. From rendering the temperament of a curious kitten, to drawing the intricate patterns of a bird's feathers, each animal offers a unique opportunity for artists to learn new techniques. Whether you prefer graphite, charcoal, pen and ink, colored pencil, or a combination of these, the process of bringing these creatures to life through drawing is both fun and satisfying thanks to their many behaviors, qualities, and characteristics.

In this chapter, you'll learn everything you need to know to get started drawing right away—from tools and materials to a variety of techniques. Turn the page to get started on your exploration of animals through pencil drawing.

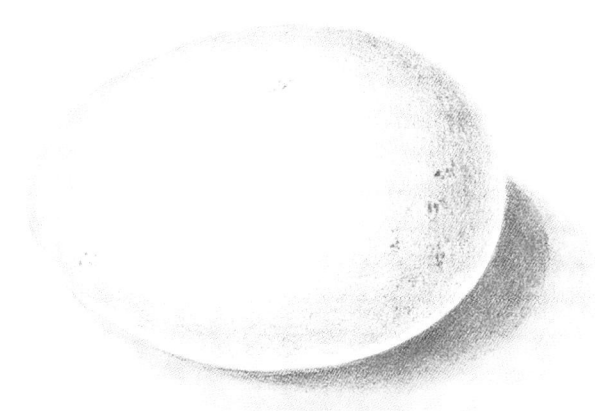

Tools & Materials

Drawing is not only fun, it also is an important art form in itself. Even when you write or print your name, you are drawing! If you organize the lines, you can make shapes. When you carry that a bit further and add dark and light shading, your drawings begin to take on a three-dimensional form and look more realistic. One of the great things about drawing is that you can do it anywhere, and the materials are generally inexpensive. Whenever possible, purchase the best materials you can afford at the time, and upgrade your supplies whenever you can. Although any tool that makes a mark can be used for drawing, you'll want to make certain your efforts will last over time. Here are some materials that will get you off to a good start.

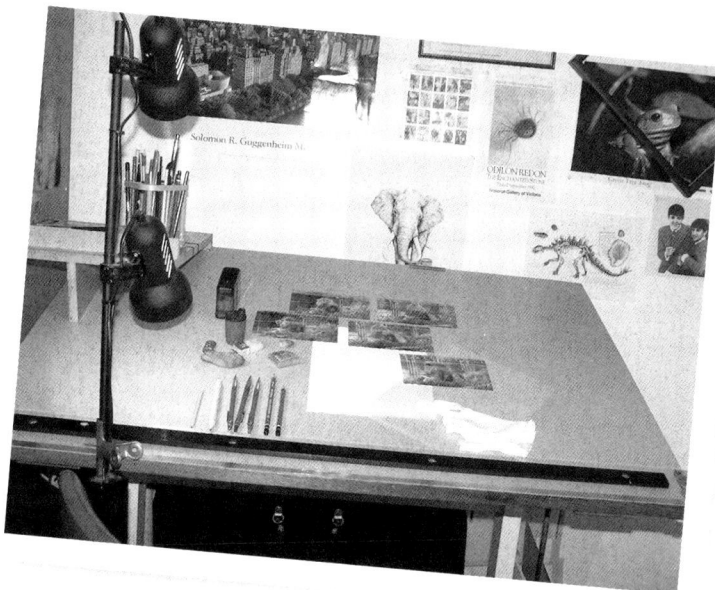

▲ **Work Station** Set up a work area that has good lighting and enough room for you to lay out your tools. A room with track lighting, an easel, and a drawing table is ideal. But all you really need is a place by a window for natural lighting. When drawing at night, you can use a soft-white light bulb and a cool-white fluorescent light so that you have both warm (yellowish) and cool (bluish) light.

◀ **Sketch Pads** Drawing pads come in a wide variety of sizes, textures, weights, and bindings. They are particularly handy for making quick sketches and when drawing outdoors. You can use a large sketchbook in the studio for laying out a painting, or take a small one with you for recording quick impressions when you travel. Smooth- to medium-grain paper texture often is an ideal choice. (The texture of paper is also known as "tooth.")

Charcoal Paper Charcoal paper and tablets also are available in a variety of textures. Some of the surface finishes are quite pronounced, and you can use them to enhance the texture in your drawings. These papers also come in a variety of colors, which can add depth and visual interest to your art.

Drawing Paper For finished works of art, using single sheets of drawing paper is best. They are available in a range of surface textures: smooth grain (plate and hot pressed), medium grain (cold pressed), and rough to very rough. The cold-pressed surface is the most versatile. It is of medium texture but it's not totally smooth, so it makes a good surface for a variety of different drawing techniques.

One of the best things about drawing with pencil is that the materials are simple and portable, so they can be taken with you in the field. As you learn to draw, you will find what works best for you, but feel free to experiment with a variety of tools, papers, and techniques. There is always more than one way to draw.

Brush This inexpensive brush (A) works well to brush away eraser crumbs and other debris from the surface of the paper.

Stick Eraser A refillable stick eraser (B) is useful for getting into tight places. You may want to use it in conjunction with the erasing shield (F).

Pencil Extender Use a pencil extender (C) to lengthen short pencils.

Blending Tools Tortillons (D), sometimes called blending stumps, are used for blending shades of graphite or charcoal and for softening edges. When the tip gets dirty, you can clean it by rubbing it on a kneaded eraser.

Kneaded Eraser A kneaded eraser (E) can be shaped to get into tight places or can be flattened to lift graphite or charcoal from the paper, and it won't damage the surface of the paper. It also doesn't leave annoying crumbs.

Erasing Shield Use this shield (F) for protecting areas that you do not want to erase.

White Plastic Eraser Useful for erasing larger surface areas, this eraser (G) does a nice job of lifting out darker values. Use it with care so you don't damage the paper.

Sharpeners Hand-held sharpeners (H) will give your pencils sharp tips. Use the fine point for thin lines and details, and use the side for shading with broad strokes.

A sandpaper block (I) gives you more control over the shape of the point. Gently roll the pencil tip over the block for a round, even point—or flatten the lead into a blunt, squared tip.

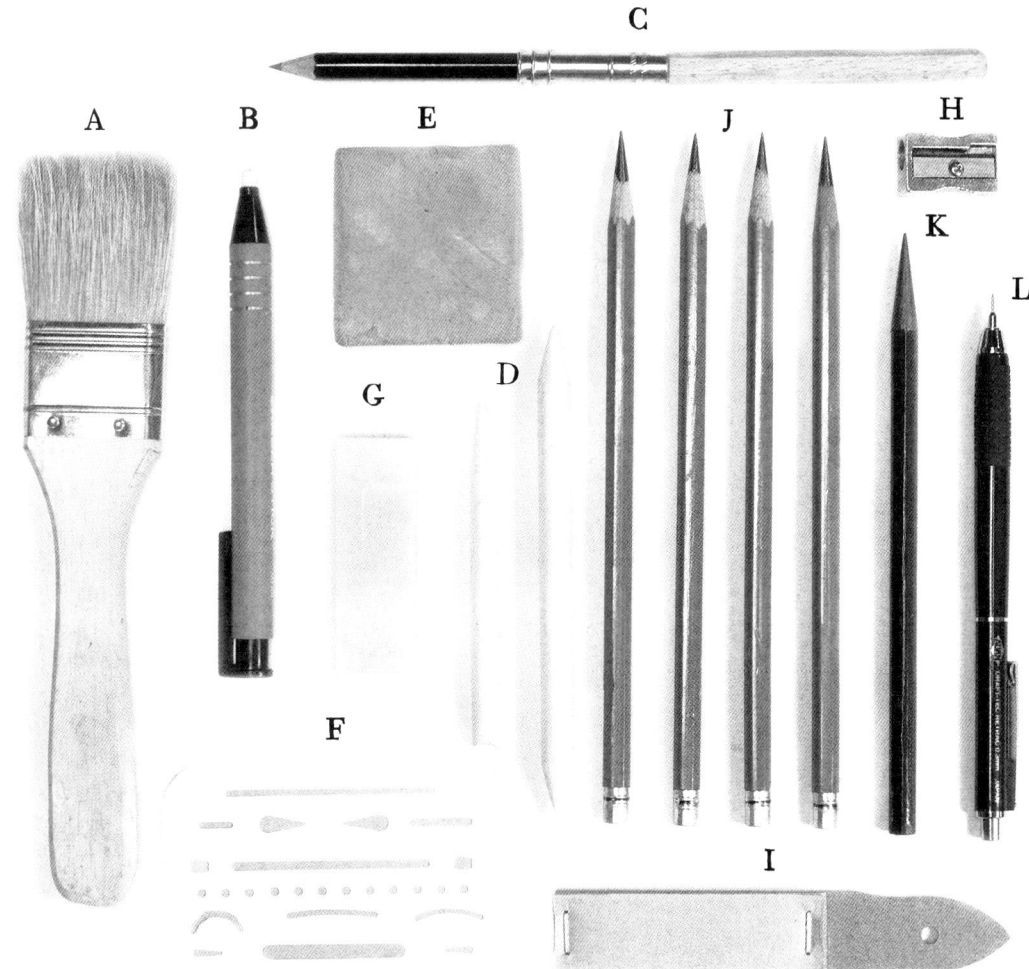

Pencils Pencils come in a vast array of options. You can try different types to find those that work best for your drawing style. Some of the types available are wood-cased (J), woodless (K), and mechanical (L). Pencils also come in varying degrees of hardness. H pencils are hard and are best for light sketches, and B pencils are softer and suitable for shading different areas of your subject. The higher the number preceding the letter, the harder or softer the pencil will be. For example, a 4H pencil is very hard and produces a light shade of graphite, whereas a 9B is very soft and yields a dark, rich mark. Note that hard pencils can dent your paper, so use them with a light hand. It's helpful to start a drawing with an HB pencil, which is equivalent to a standard #2 pencil. Commonly used pencils are HB, 3B, 4B, 6B, and 9B. They produce a wide range of values. Anything over a 6B should be reserved for the darkest areas of the image.

Additional Supplies

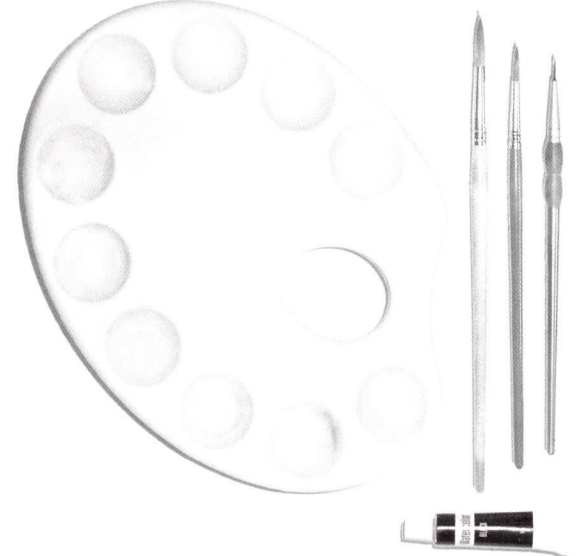

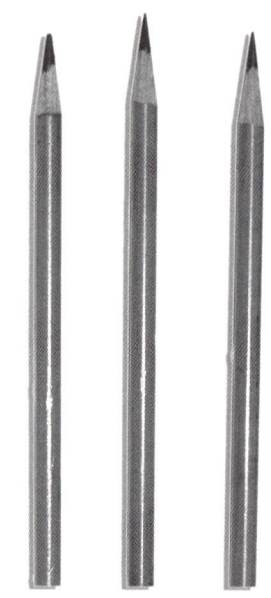

◄ **Watercolor** You may want to add simple watercolor washes (thin layers of paint) to your drawings to give them some extra pizzazz. For this, you'll just need a few paintbrushes, a tube of black watercolor paint, and a palette for mixing different values. You should also have paper towels handy for wiping excess water off the brush. You may want to try out some painting techniques on scrap paper before applying washes to your drawing.

▲ **Charcoal** Like pencils, charcoal is available in several forms. Charcoal pencils also come in varying degrees of hardness. You can also buy raw charcoal sticks. Some artists even use burnt wood scraps from their own fireplace. When blending charcoal, use the same tools you use to blend graphite.

◄ **Light Table** A light table is useful for transferring your preliminary drawing to a clean sheet of paper. You can also use it to refine your initial sketches by tracing your image onto another sheet of paper.

HOLDING THE DRAWING PENCIL

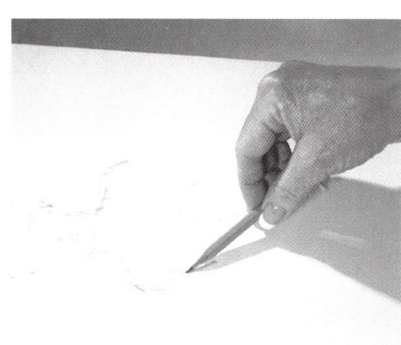

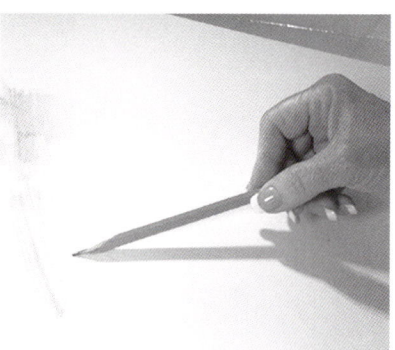

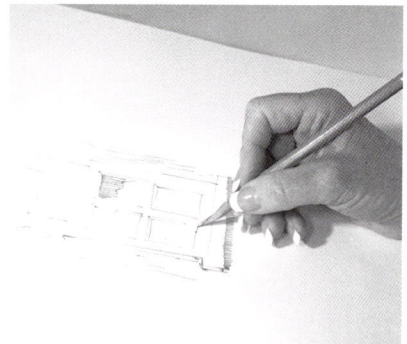

Basic Underhand The basic underhand position allows the arm and wrist to move freely, which results in fresh and lively sketches. Drawing in this position makes it easy to use both the point and the side of the lead by simply changing the angle of your hand and arm.

Underhand Variation Holding the pencil at its end allows for light strokes, both long and short. It also offers some control of lights, darks, and textures. Place a protective "slip sheet" under your hand when you use this position to prevent smudges.

Writing The writing position is the most common one, and it offers the most control for fine detail and precise lines. Be careful not to press too hard on the point, or you'll make indentations in the paper. Also remember not to grip the pencil too tightly, or your fingers may cramp.

Pencil Lines & Textures

If you're a beginner, focus on learning the drawing process rather than completing the final product for now. Hold your pencil or charcoal with a relaxed grip so that the lines flow easily. This keeps your approach simple and direct. First, make note of the overall shape of the subject, and sketch a few light guidelines from your observations. Once those are correct, make a preliminary drawing, concentrating on basic lines, angles, and shapes.

Remember that a sure pencil line doesn't just come from talent; it comes from practice. Study the various textures and strokes shown on this page, and do some practice exercises. For example, give the fish some scales, add bricks to the stone wall, or draw foliage on the trees.

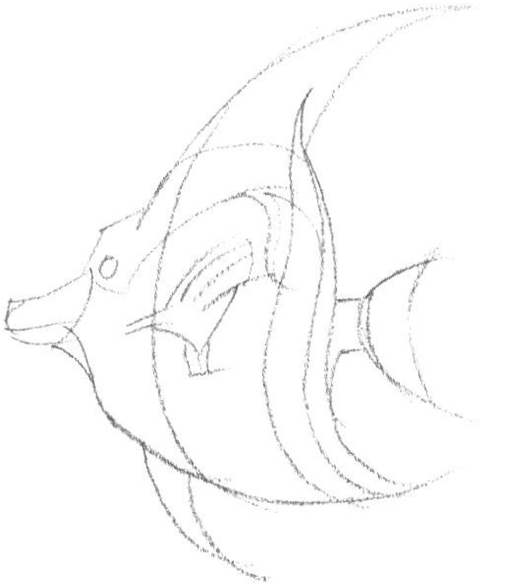

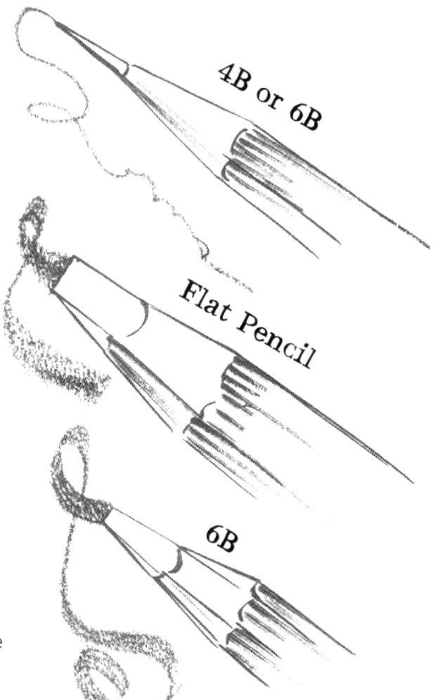

4B or 6B

Flat Pencil

6B

Notice the type of line each pencil point produces.

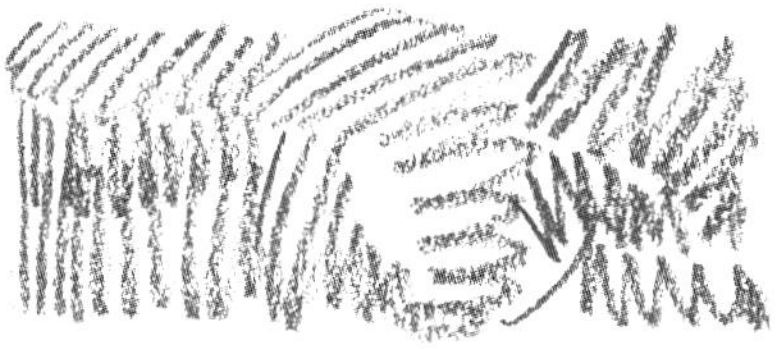

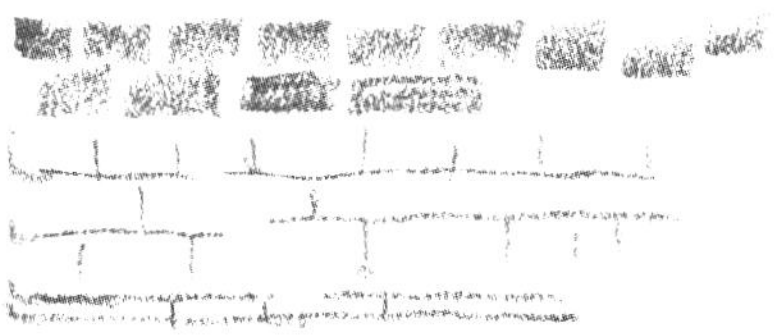

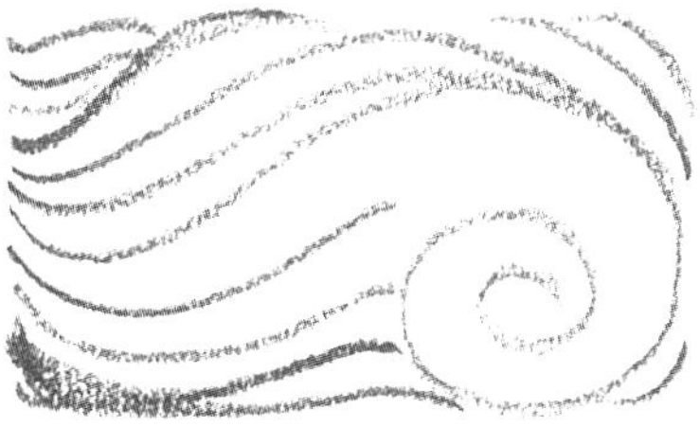

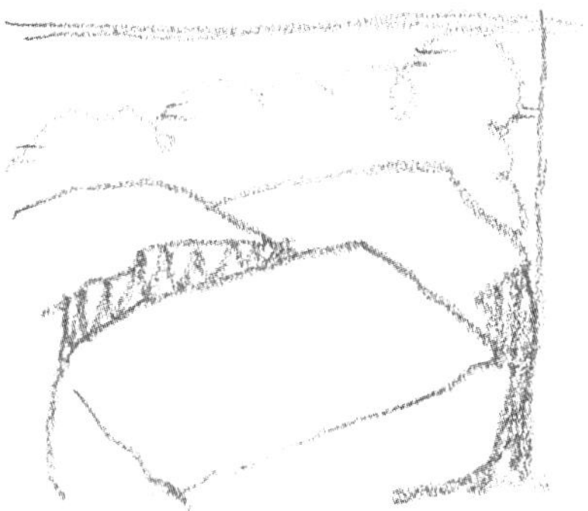

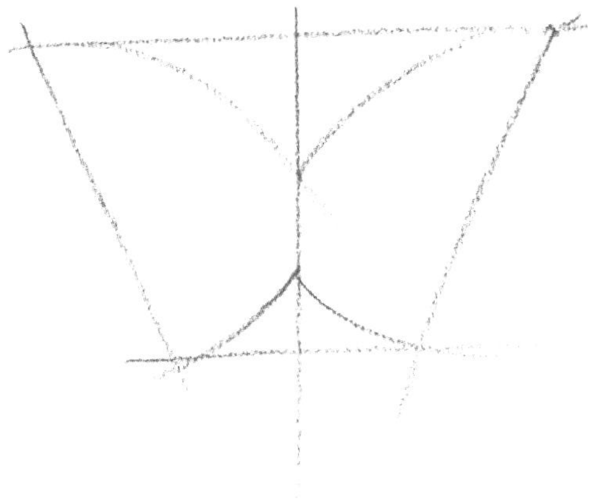

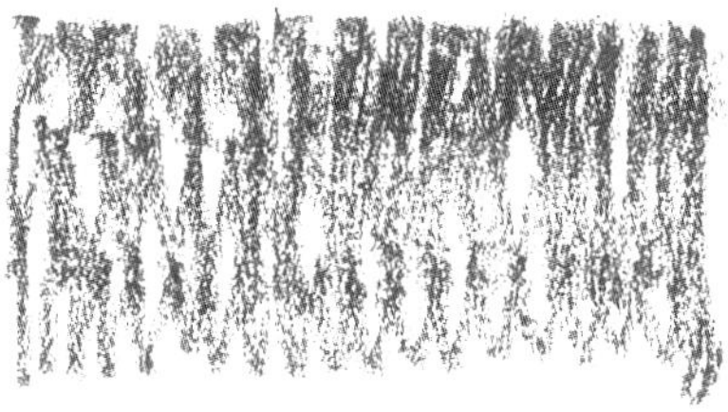

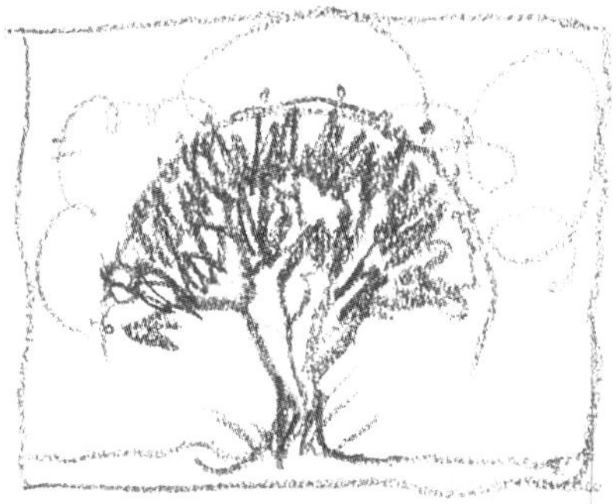

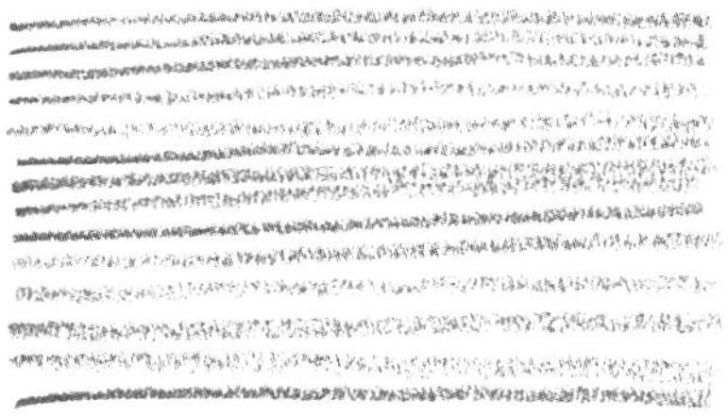

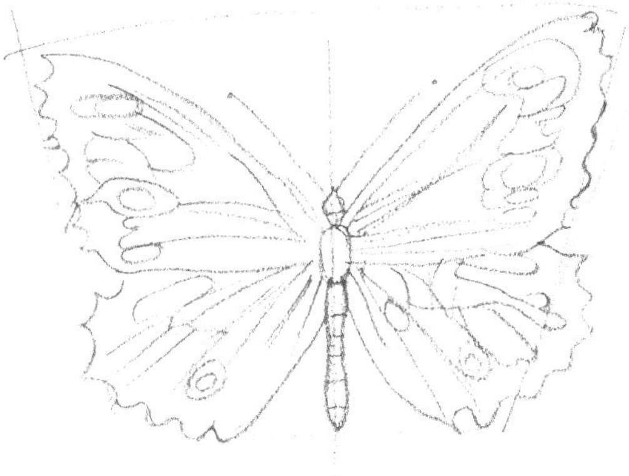

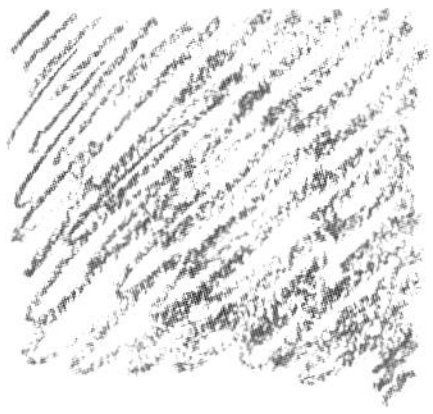

PRACTICING LINES

When drawing lines, it is not necessary to always use a sharp point. In fact, sometimes a blunt point may create a more desirable effect. When using larger lead diameters, the effect of a blunt point is even more evident. Play around with your pencils to familiarize yourself with the different types of lines they can create. Make every kind of stroke you can think of, using both a sharp point and a blunt point. Practice the strokes below to help you loosen up. Remember that even simple strokes like the ones shown below can be used to create a number of textural effects in your drawings.

DRAWING WITH A SHARP POINT

Draw a series of parallel lines. Try them vertically; then angle them. Make some of them curved, trying both short and long strokes. Then try some wavy lines at an angle and some with short, vertical strokes. Try making a spiral and then grouping short, curved lines together. Then practice varying the weight of the line as you draw. Os, Vs, and Us are some of the most common alphabet shapes used in drawing.

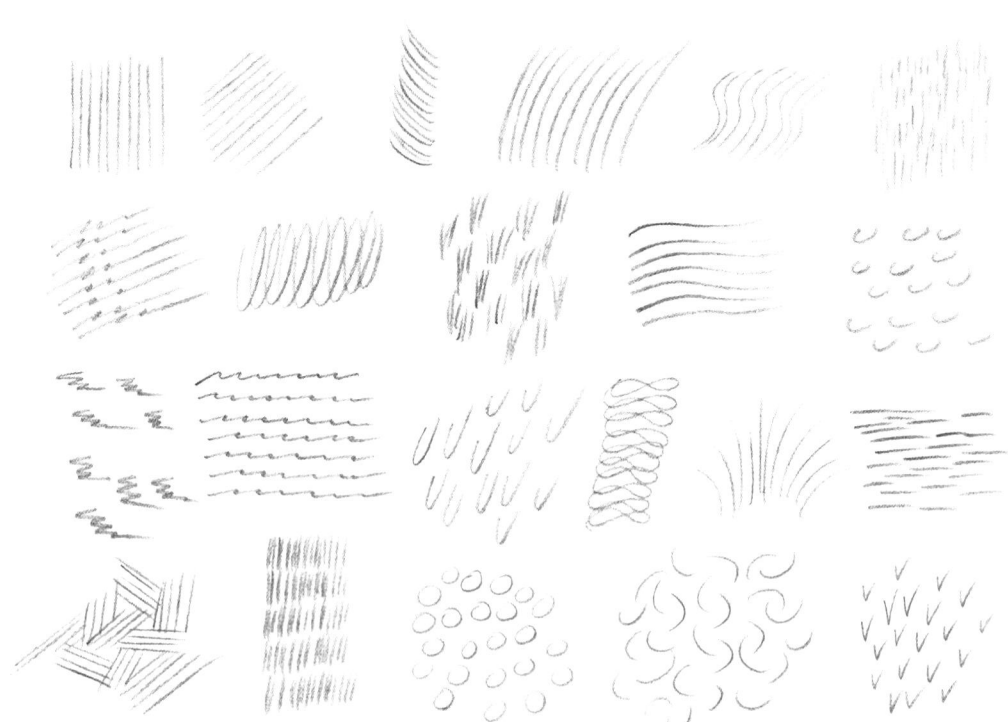

DRAWING WITH A BLUNT POINT

Now try the same exercise with a blunt point. Even if you use the same hand positions and strokes, the results will be different when you switch pencils. Take a look at these examples. The same shapes were drawn with both pencils, but the blunt pencil produced different images. You can create a blunt point by rubbing the tip of the pencil on a sandpaper block or on a rough piece of paper.

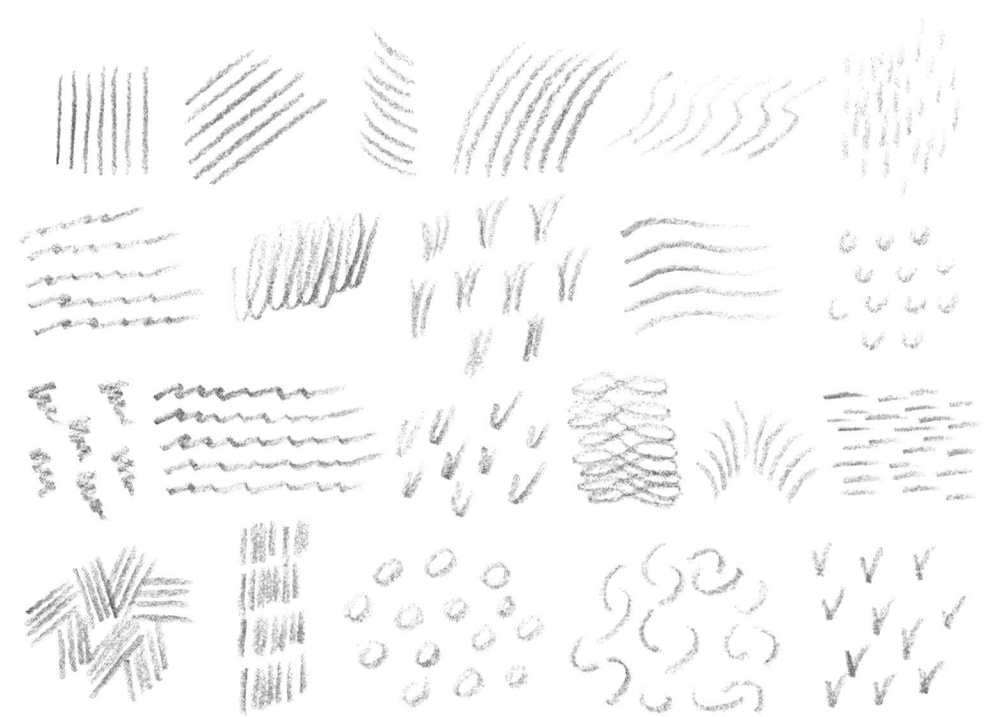

"PAINTING" WITH PENCIL

When you use painterly strokes, your drawing will take on a new dimension. Think of your pencil as a brush and allow yourself to put more of your arm into the stroke. To create this effect, try using the underhand position, holding your pencil between your thumb and forefinger and using the side of the pencil. (See page 8.) If you rotate the pencil in your hand every few strokes, you will not have to sharpen it as frequently. The larger the lead, the wider the stroke will be. The softer the lead, the more painterly an effect you will have. These examples were all made on smooth paper with a 6B pencil, but you can experiment with rough papers for more broken effects.

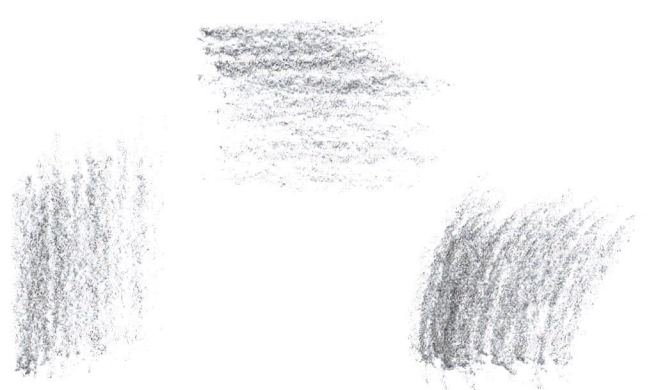

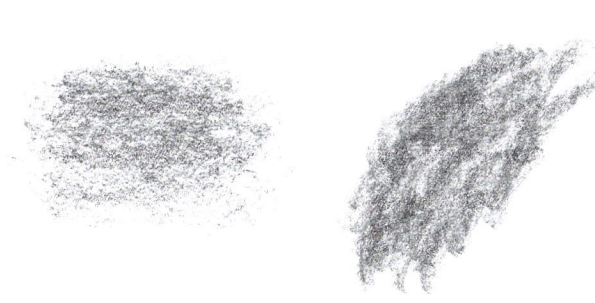

Starting Simply First experiment with vertical, horizontal, and curved strokes. Keep the strokes close together and begin with heavy pressure. Then lighten the pressure with each stroke.

Varying the Pressure Randomly cover the area with tone, varying the pressure at different points. Continue to keep your strokes loose.

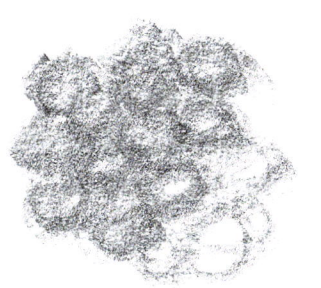

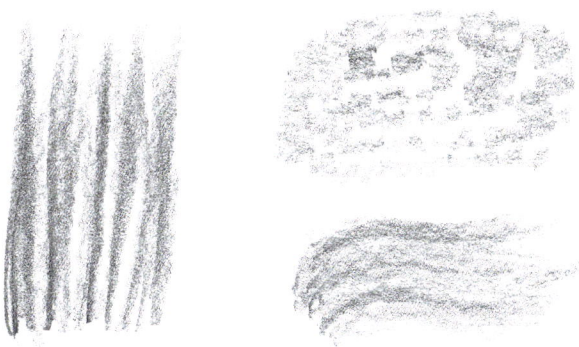

Using Smaller Strokes Make small circles for the first example. This is reminiscent of leathery animal skin. For the second example, use short, alternating strokes of heavy and light pressure to create a pattern that is similar to stone or brick.

Loosening Up Use long vertical strokes, varying the pressure for each stroke until you start to see long grass (above). Then use somewhat looser movements, which could be used for water. First create short spiral movements with your arm (top right). Then use a wavy movement, varying the pressure (bottom right).

TRY OUT DIFFERENT PENCILS

Make a scribble-art design and fill it in using different grades of pencil. Making these marks side by side will help you become familiar with the different pencil grades, as well as the pressure you need to apply to create a specific value. Value is the relative lightness or darkness of the graphite. (See page 12.)

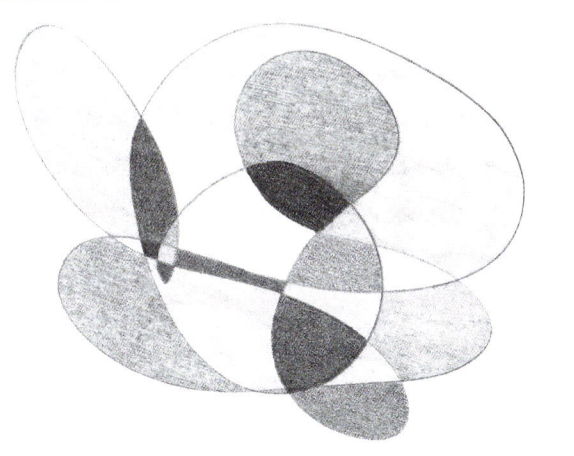

Understanding Value

Now that you have some understanding of how to create solid tones with pencil, experiment with different grades of pencils to learn how to create variations in *value* (the relative lightness or darkness of a color or of black). By shading (adding dark values) and highlighting (adding light values), you produce the value variations that create the illusion of depth and dimension in your drawings, making them appear realistic.

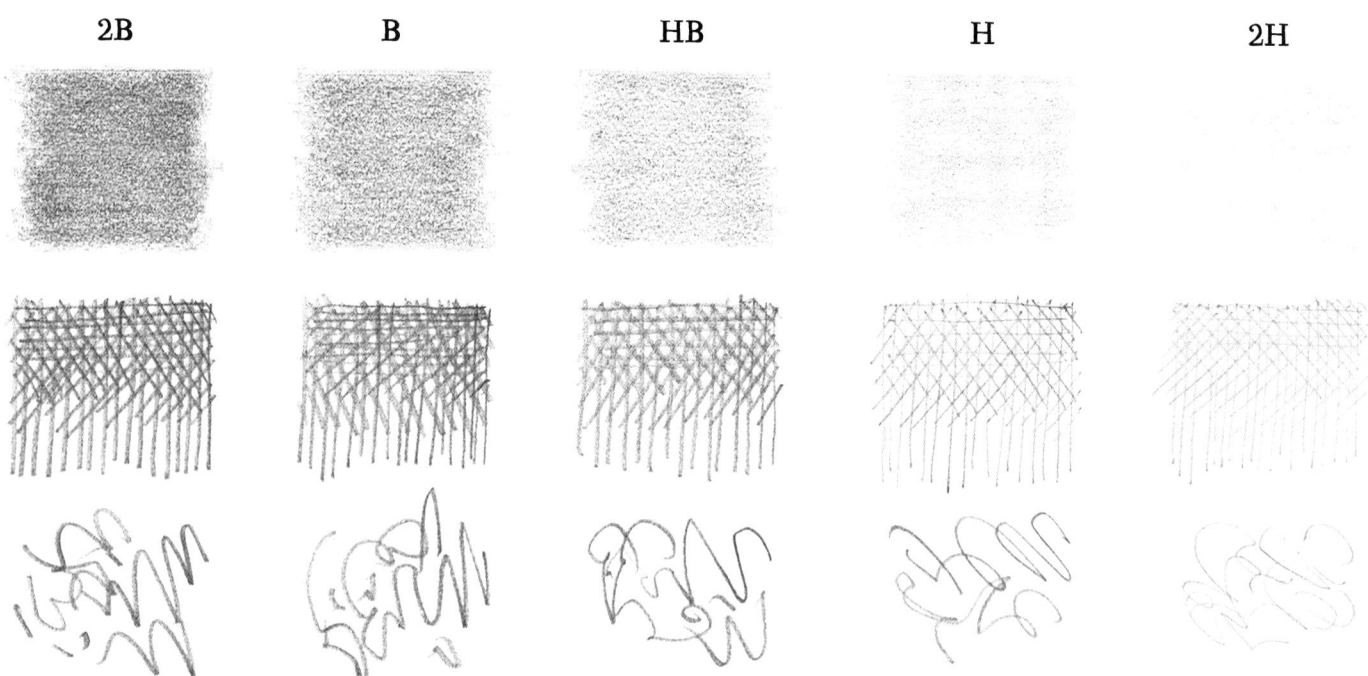

2B	B	HB	H	2H

Value Charts Select a range of pencils from soft to hard. (This chart uses 2B, B, HB, H, and 2H pencils.) Use each pencil to create different techniques, such as linear strokes, crosshatching, and random lines. Use the same amount of pressure with each technique. When your chart is complete, label each different tone with the pencil you used. This chart will help you decide which pencil grades to use for different values and effects.

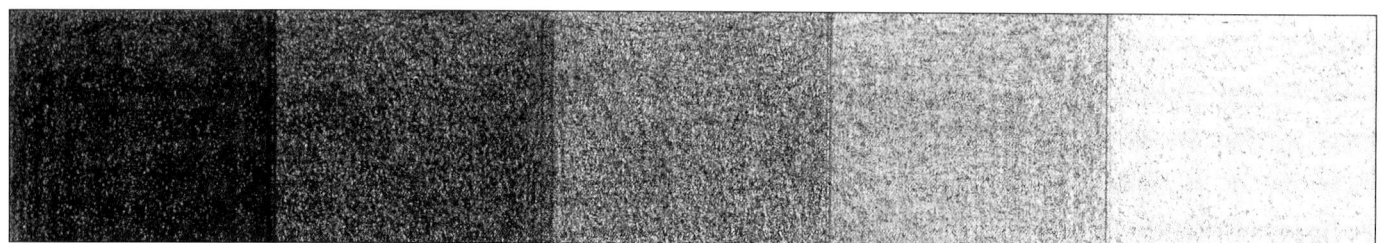

Value Scale Making your own value scale will help familiarize you with the different variations in value. Select a range of pencils. (This scale was made with 2B, B, HB, H, and 2H pencils.) Start with a 2B pencil to fill an area with horizontal, linear strokes. Then fill in the next areas with a B pencil. Continue in this manner until you create the lightest tone with the 2H pencil.

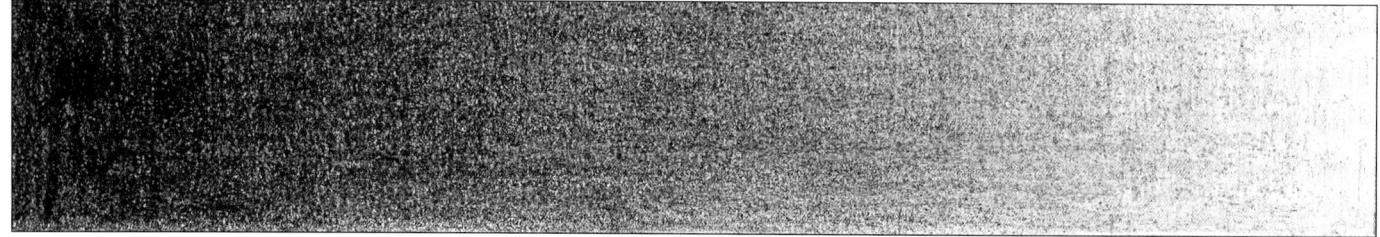

Blended Value Scale Now create a new value scale, this time blending the graphite with a tortillon to make an even, smooth gradation. Start at the far left with your 2B and work your way to the right, blending the graphite evenly to create a smooth texture. When you reach the lightest tones with your 2H, use a very light touch and even pressure to fade the tone off into the white of the paper.

APPLYING SHADING

Artists give a three-dimensional look to a two-dimensional drawing by manipulating values. Value refers to the relative lightness or darkness of a color or of black, and it's the variations in value that help define an object's form. Because value tells us even more about a form than its outline, artists use a variety of techniques to create a full range of shades and highlights, including the ones shown here. The result is more realistic form and dimension.

Flat Shading To shade large areas, create a generalized halftone by using the underhand position.

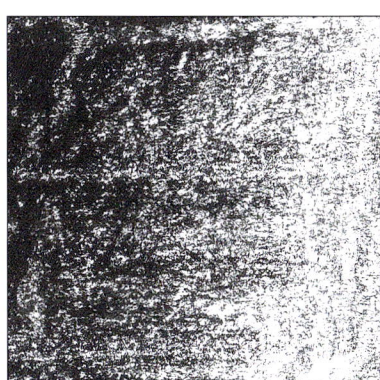

Gradation To produce a gradual shift in value, use the underhand position, varying the pressure from heavy to light.

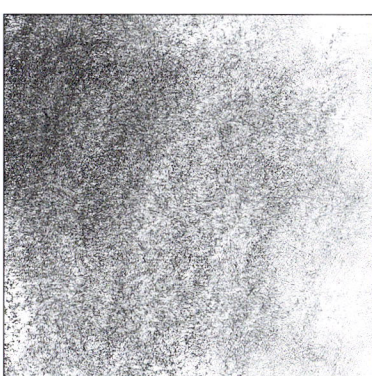

Blending To produce subtle value transitions and soft edges, smudge with your finger or a blending stump.

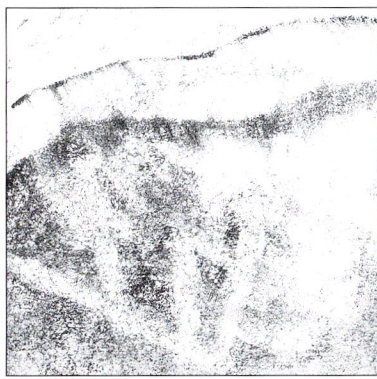

Eraser Strokes To soften edges and vary the line quality, use a small piece of kneaded eraser. (You can also cut off a sharp piece of vinyl eraser.)

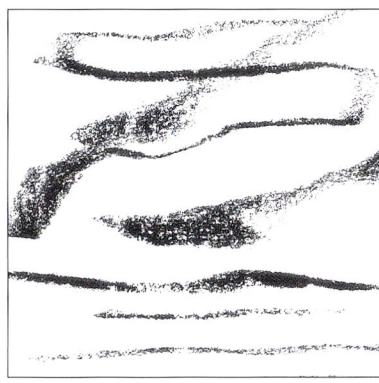

Expressive Lines To draw fluid lines with a dynamic feel, use the underhand position; then push, pull, twist, and vary pencil pressure as you draw.

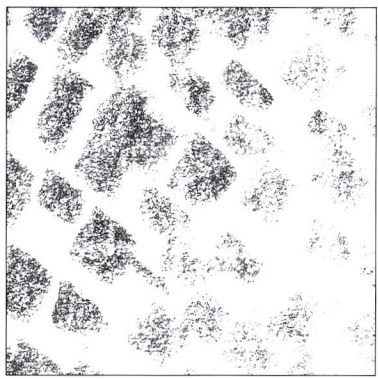

Dotting To create background textures, such as those of a wall or carpet, vary the pressure of your strokes and use your imagination.

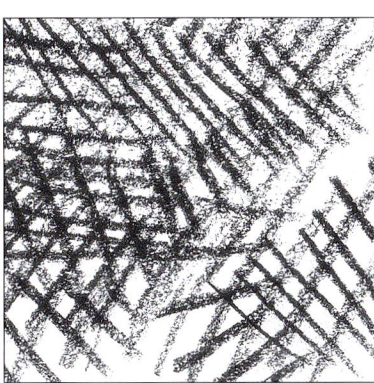

Crosshatching To deepen shadows and enhance form, use crisscrossing strokes. The more strokes that overlap one another, the darker the area becomes.

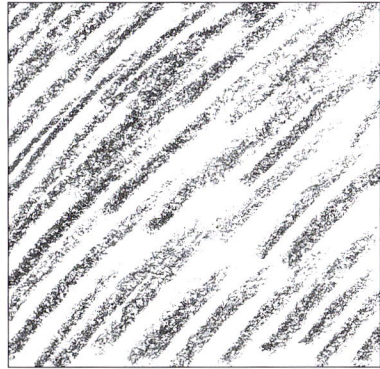

Linear Hatching To create form with shading, make parallel strokes that follow the shape, curve, or direction of the surface. Change the pressure of your strokes to vary the value.

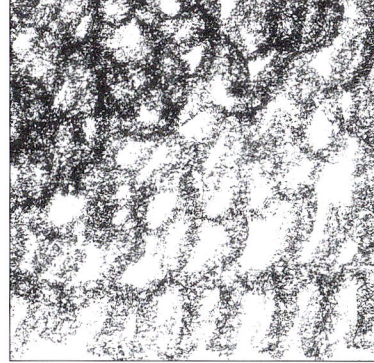

Squiggles For more contrast in your drawings, include loose, circular strokes and squiggles. When used with hatching, these strokes create many interesting textures.

Working with Light & Shadow

Every shape or form we see is created by the reaction of the object's surface to light. To create a realistic image, the subject must be lit in a way that brings out its true form. For example, if you light an object from the front, you won't see the shadows that fall across the form, so it will appear flat. If you light the object from a three-quarter angle, the object will produce shadows; the transition in values will accentuate the object's dimension.

There are two main types of shadows: cast shadows and form shadows. *Cast shadows* are the shadows that the object throws onto other surfaces. *Form shadows* are the shadows that are on the surface of the object itself; these shadows give an object a sense of depth. Form shadows are dependent on the light source; they get darker as they move away from the light.

A drawing with a sharp contrast between light and shadow (very dark darks and very light lights) is considered a "high-contrast" work, whereas a drawing that uses mostly light and mid-range values is called a "low-contrast" work. Adding more contrast to your drawings will make the subject "pop" forward and look more three-dimensional, but you may want to use less contrast for "softer" subjects, such as a lioness nursing her cubs. Explore the difference between high- and low-contrast drawings by studying the examples below.

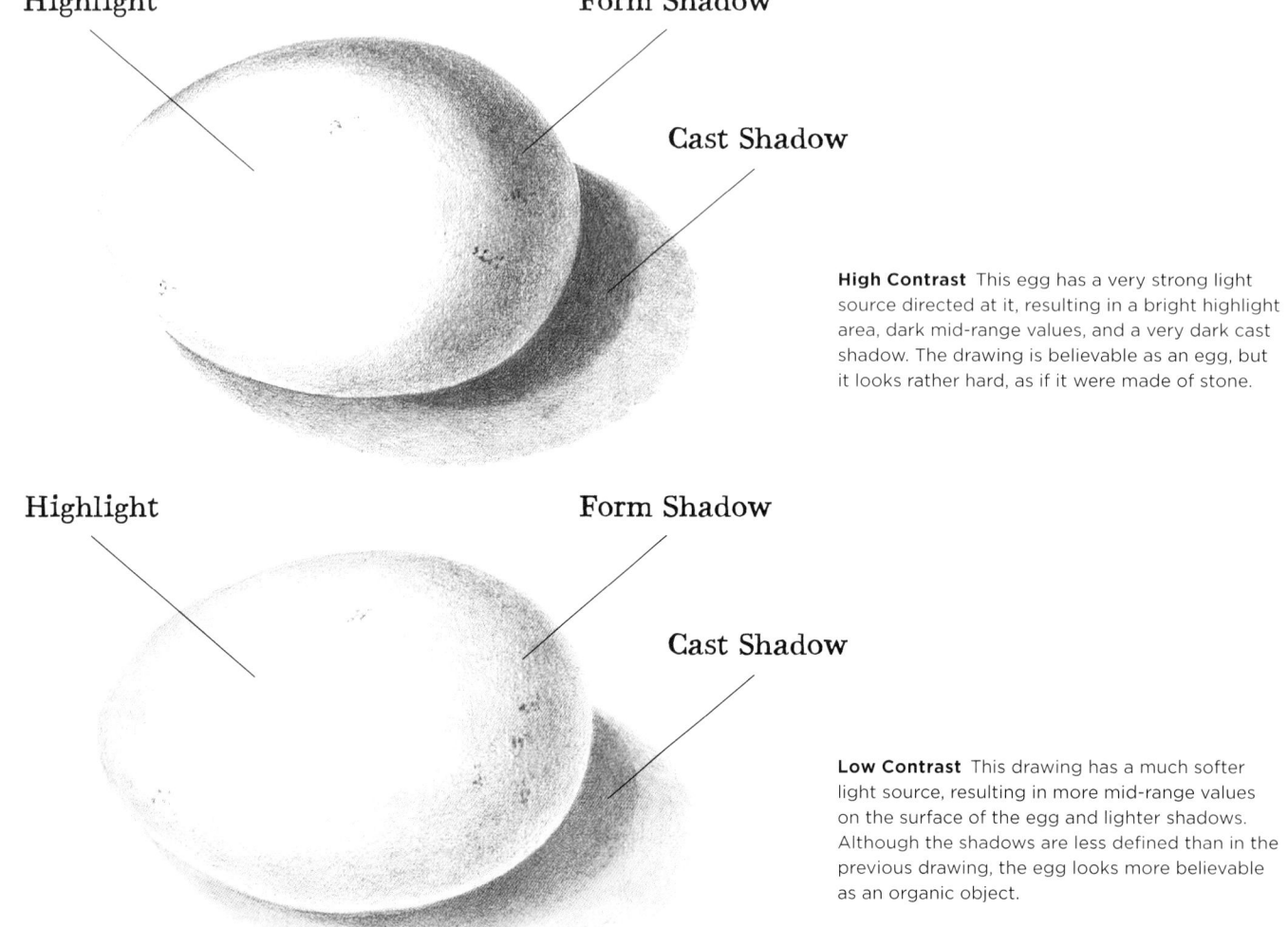

Highlight   Form Shadow

Cast Shadow

High Contrast This egg has a very strong light source directed at it, resulting in a bright highlight area, dark mid-range values, and a very dark cast shadow. The drawing is believable as an egg, but it looks rather hard, as if it were made of stone.

Highlight   Form Shadow

Cast Shadow

Low Contrast This drawing has a much softer light source, resulting in more mid-range values on the surface of the egg and lighter shadows. Although the shadows are less defined than in the previous drawing, the egg looks more believable as an organic object.

Beginning with Basic Shapes

Anyone can draw just about anything by simply breaking down the subject into a few basic shapes: circles, rectangles, squares, and triangles. By drawing an outline around the basic shapes of your subject, you've drawn its shape. But your subject also has depth and dimension, or *form*. As you see in the drawings at right, the corresponding forms of the basic shapes are spheres, cylinders, cubes, and cones. For example, a ball and a grapefruit are spheres, a jar and a tree trunk are cylinders, a box and a building are cubes, and a pine tree and a funnel are cones. That's all there is to the first step of every drawing: sketching the shapes and developing the forms. After that, it's essentially just connecting and refining the lines and adding details.

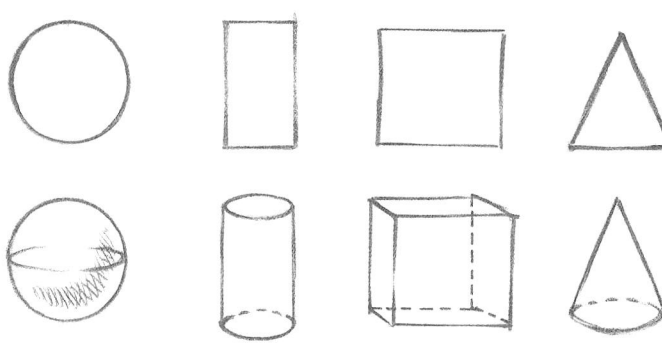

Sphere   **Cylinder**   **Cube**   **Cone**

Combining Shapes Here is an example of beginning a drawing with basic shapes. Start by drawing each line of action (an imaginary line tracing the path of action through a character), then build up the shapes of the dog and the chick with simple ovals, circles, rectangles, and triangles.

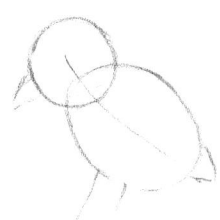
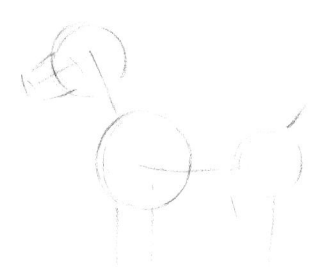

Building Form Once you establish the shapes, it is easy to build up the forms with cylinders, spheres, and cones. Notice that the subjects are now beginning to show some depth and dimension.

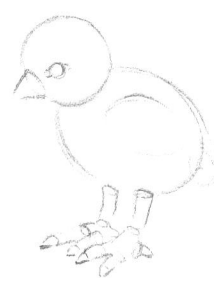
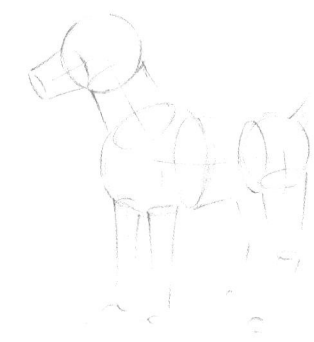

Drawing Through Drawing through means drawing the complete forms, including the lines that will eventually be hidden from sight. Here, when the forms were drawn, the back side of the dog and chick were indicated. Even though you can't see that side in the finished drawing, the subject should appear three-dimensional. To finish the drawing, simply refine the outlines and add a little fluffy texture to the downy chick.

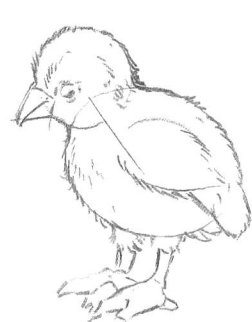
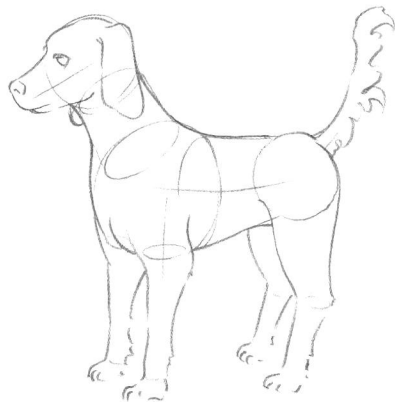

Drawing from Photographs

Photographs are wonderful references for drawings of animals. When you take the photos yourself, try to catch a motion or pose that is characteristic of the animal, such as the position of a cheetah just before it pounces or the stretch of a spider monkey in mid-swing. Take several different shots of the same subject.

When you are ready to draw, look over all your photographs and choose the one you like best, but don't feel restricted to using only one reference source. You may decide you like the facial expression in one photo but the body pose in another; you may even have other references for background elements you'd like to include. Combine your references any way you choose, altering the scene to suit yourself. This is referred to as "taking artistic license," and it's one of the most important "tools" artists have at their disposal.

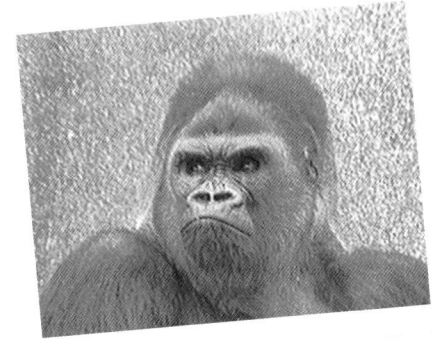

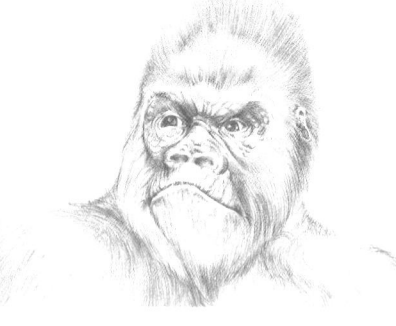

Copying a Portrait This drawing was based on the photo reference shown above. It captured the proud, strong expression and physical characteristics so typical of mature male gorillas. Because the photo was so clear, the drawing follows it faithfully.

Combining References These two photos were used for the drawing at right. The photo of a polar bear walking clearly shows the animal's shape and proportions. But the other photo reference features the face more clearly.

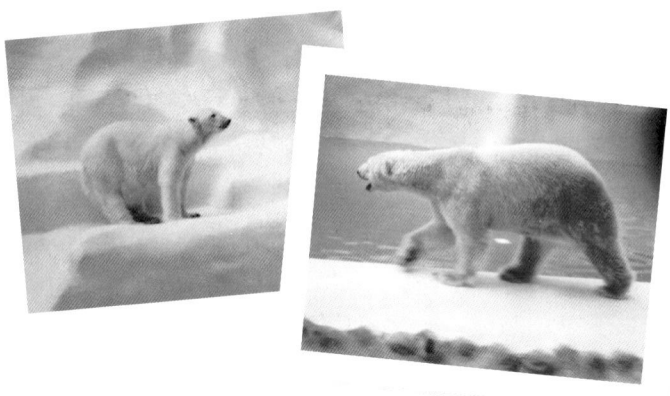

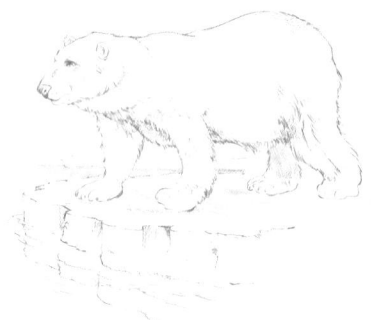

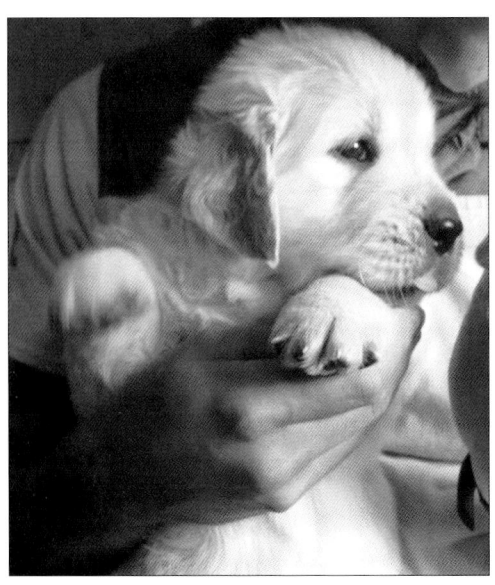

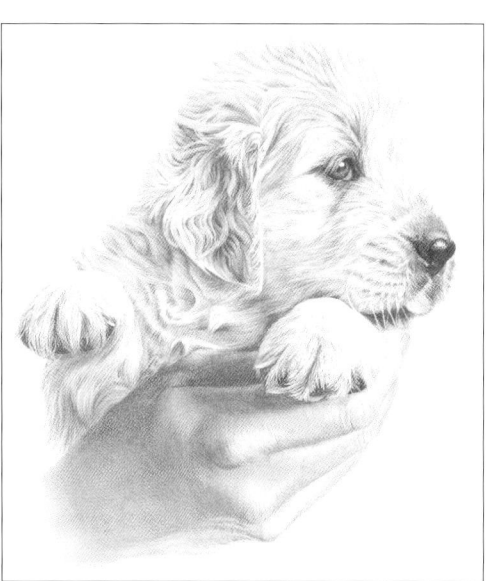

Changing Your Photo In this reference, a hand is holding the puppy, but the rest of the background doesn't work for the composition. The puppy's coat is light, so the darker hand provides an effective contrast. The pup's right paw is blurry in the photo, but it is sharpened in the final drawing.

Tracing & Grid Methods

Although freehand drawing is a good way to get to know the animal's form and represent it accurately, the quickest way to achieve perfect accuracy is to use either the tracing or grid methods. Neither of these methods should be considered "cheating," as both are respected tools that have been used by artists for centuries. Using these methods will give you a perfect outline, but it is up to you to create the composition and final drawing with skill and technique. You also should never become too dependent on these methods; they shouldn't replace freehand drawing. Remember that any distortions in the photo (for example, due to wide-angle lenses) will translate to your drawing, so you'll need to be prepared to correct these distortions later.

Tracing Method Photocopy or print the image you wish to trace. (You may want to enlarge or reduce the image to the desired size.) Then tape a sheet of tracing paper on top of the image, and use a light table to help you carefully trace the outline of the animal, as well as the major facial features. If you don't have a light table, you can create your own transfer paper. Turn over the tracing paper and cover the back with an even layer of graphite. Then place the tracing paper (graphite-side down) on top of your final drawing paper. Use an HB pencil and carefully go over the lines on the tracing paper; the lines will transfer to the drawing paper below.

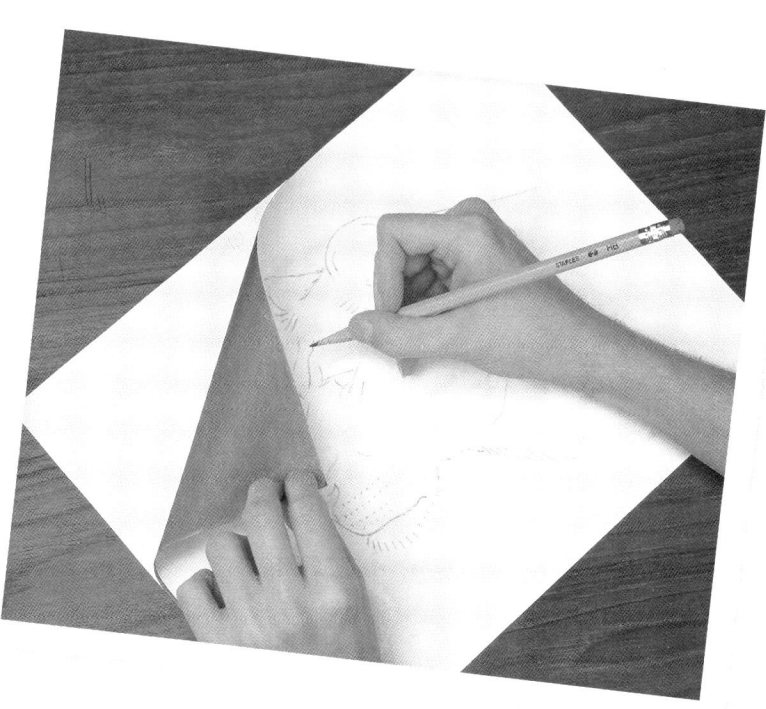

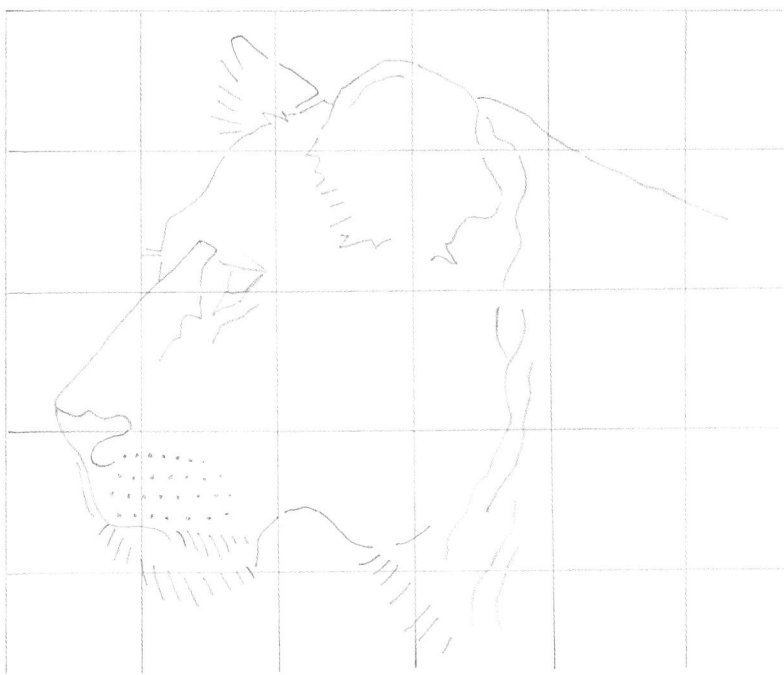

Grid Method Make a photocopy of the reference photo, and then draw a grid of squares (1″ x 1″ is a good size to start with) on the photocopy. Next, draw a corresponding grid on a piece of sketch paper. Make sure both grids have the exact same number of squares, even if the squares are different sizes—this ensures correct proportions. Once you've created the grids, draw what you see in each square of the reference in each square of the second grid. Draw in one square at a time until you have filled in all the squares. Now use the tracing method described above to transfer the drawing to your final paper.

Drawing from Life & Nature

Sketching animals from life gives you a fresh approach to drawing that is spontaneous and original; every pose and composition you discover is unique! Creating a finished drawing on site has its disadvantages. For example, you may not be able to stay on location for the duration of the drawing, and the light shifts as time passes, changing the shadows and highlights. And, of course, most animals are bound to change positions or even walk away as you work, making it difficult for you to capture a good likeness. Instead of trying to produce a final, detailed pencil drawing in the field, use a sketchbook to gather all the information you'll need for a completed piece later. Work quickly and loosely, concentrating on replicating the animal's general shapes, main features, gestures, and expressions. Practice using your whole arm to draw, not just your wrist and hand. Vary the position of your pencil as you stroke, and involve your shoulder in each movement you make. Then jot down notes to complete the information you'll want to retrieve later. When it comes time for the final drawings, you'll be surprised at how often you'll refer to the notes you've recorded in your sketchbook!

USING A VIEWFINDER

If you have a hard time deciding how to arrange the animal or animals on your paper, try looking through a viewfinder. You can form a double "L" with your fingers or use a cardboard frame, as shown below, and look through the opening. Bring the viewfinder closer and hold it out farther; move it around the scene; look at your subject from high and low viewpoints; and make the opening wider and narrower. Choose the view that pleases you most.

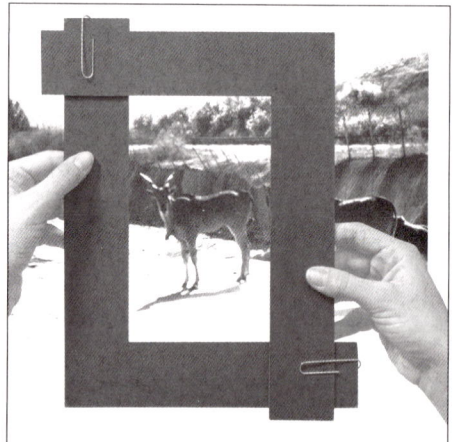

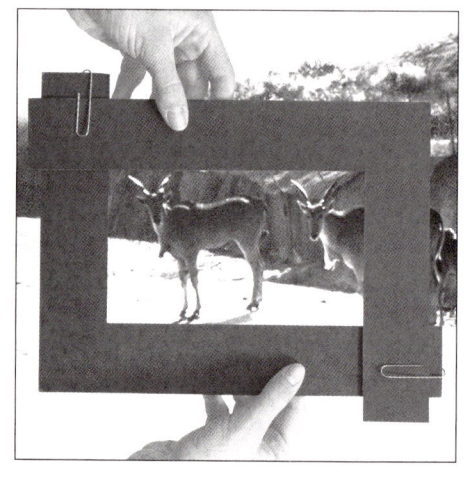

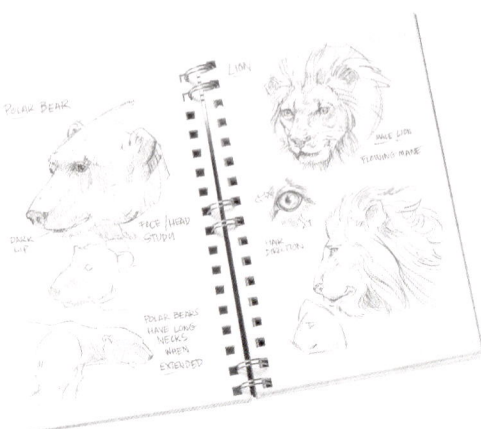

Keeping a Sketchbook When you sketch from life to prepare for a drawing, be careful to take notes about the values, light, and the time of day, as well as any other details you are likely to forget. Sometimes you may want to take the time to more fully render a facial feature, such as an eye, and try sketching each animal from several different angles. Remember that no matter how much time you spend observing a subject, the impression in your mind will surely fade with time, so be as thorough in your notes as you can.

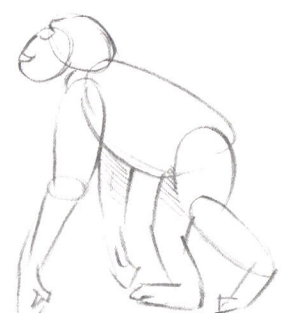

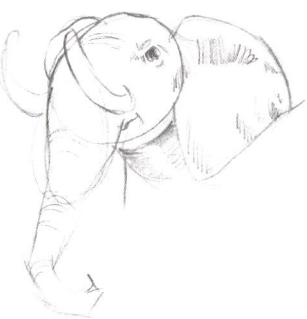

Starting with Basic Shapes Your sketches don't need to be as fully developed as the drawings shown in the sketchbook above. Concentrate on training your eye to see your subject in terms of basic shapes—circles, ovals, rectangles, and triangles—and put them together in a rough drawing. For example, the sketch of the chimpanzee above started with a series of ovals, which were then connected with a few simple lines; the hands, feet, and facial features were merely suggested. The elephant portrait began with a circle, an oval, and rough triangular shapes; from that point, it was easy to sketch out the shape of the trunk and place a few strokes for shading to hint at the elephant's form.

Drawing an animal in the wild is difficult and possibly dangerous, so zoos, wildlife parks, animal sanctuaries, and rescue centers are the preferred source of subjects for drawing on location.

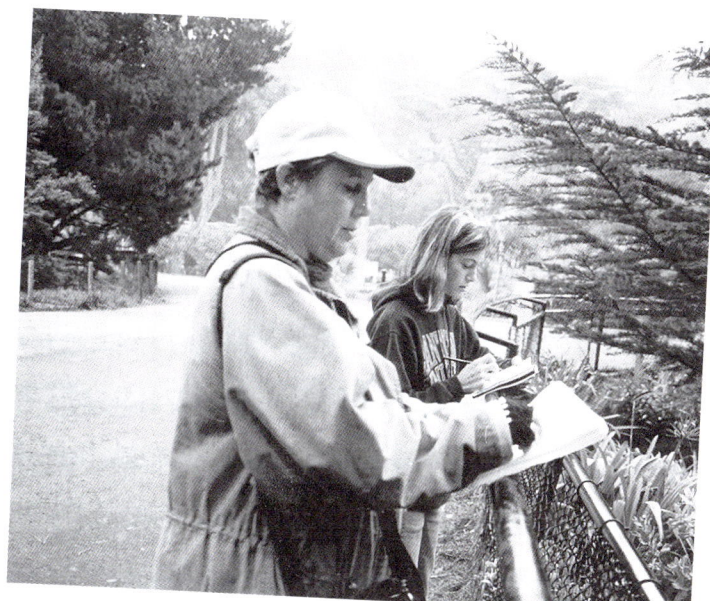

The zoo is an ideal place for sketching a wide range of interesting animals. Before you begin to draw, take some time to observe their general proportions, as well as the way the animals move and how they interact with one another. The more you know about your subject, the more convincing your drawings will be.

WHAT TO TAKE

Your kit can be as simple or as complex as you wish and are capable of carrying. Here's a general list of items to take when drawing on location:

1. A range of pencils (or an HB and a 2B to start) and a pencil sharpener
2. Sketchbook
3. Appropriate clothing and a hat
4. Insect repellent
5. Sunscreen
6. Water bottle
7. Camera (if you're drawing an animal you've never seen before or don't have many references)
8. Something to sit on (if you're going to be in front of one animal for an extended period of time)

WHAT TO DO

1. **Call ahead.** There is nothing more frustrating than turning up on the one day of the year that the animal is getting its annual medical checkup and isn't on view! Make sure to call the facility ahead of time to ensure the subject you want to on display.
2. **Be aware of the animal's habits.** Many animals are most active in the early morning or evening and will sleep out of sight in the afternoon. Is the animal nocturnal? If so, check with the keeper to find out the best time to view it, or arrange a private visit. Find out its feeding times and try to be there then.
3. **Be patient.** If the animal isn't moving or visible when you arrive, wait a while. Animals operate on their own schedules.
4. **Be flexible.** Move on to a different animal if the one you were planning to draw isn't cooperating.
5. **Expect an audience.** People are always curious about what you are doing, especially children. If you are shy or hesitant about being watched, try to find a quiet spot that is out of the way. Some people will show great interest and ask questions about what you are doing. This is a wonderful opportunity for you to tell them about your artwork.
6. **Be polite.** Animals can be sensitive and shy, so don't shout or tap on the glass or wave your arms to attract the animal's attention. Also, don't obscure the best viewing spots. Share these with the public, especially children.

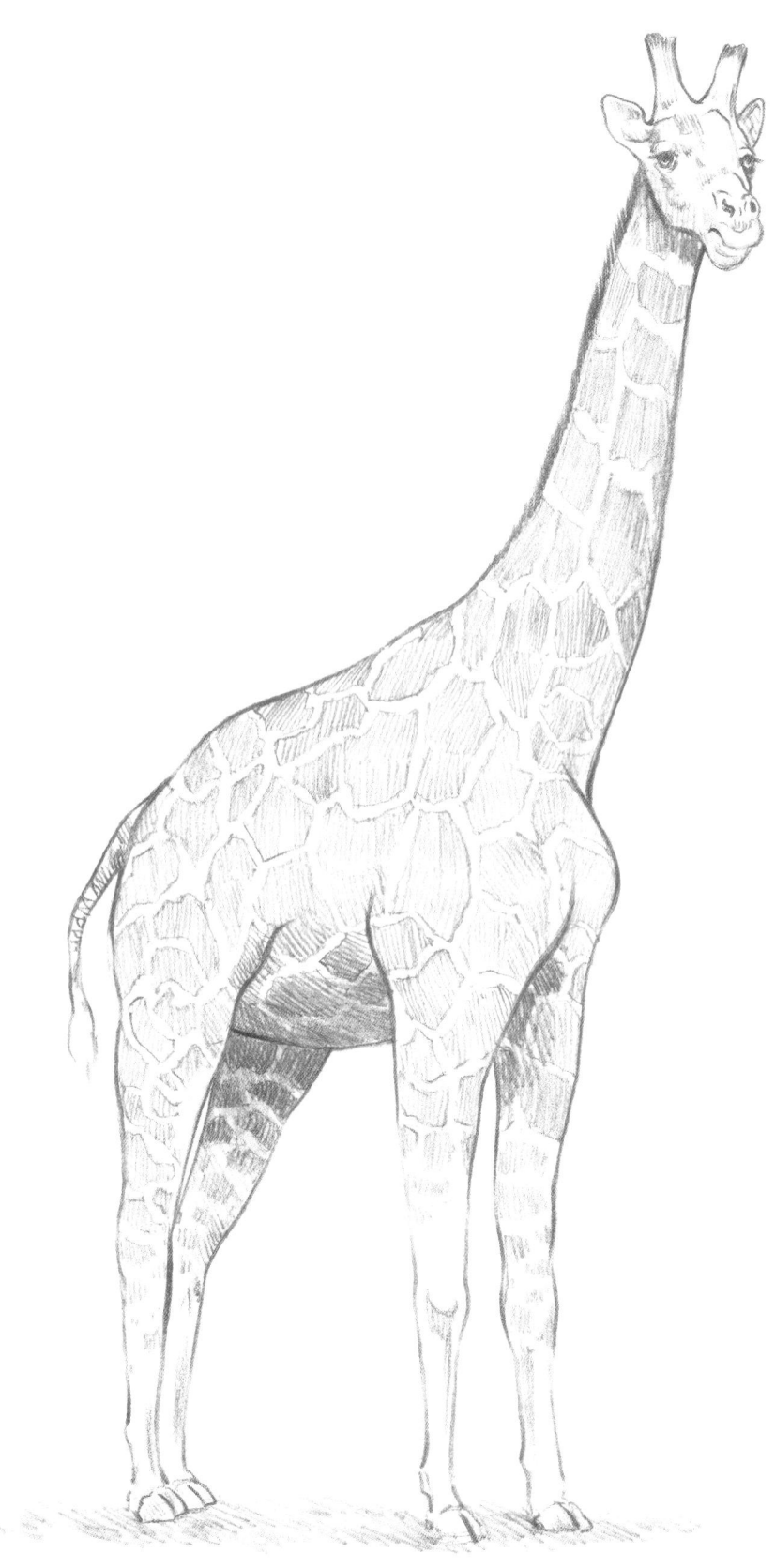

Wild Animals

Drawing wild animals allows artists to polish their observational and technical skills. Intricate details, such as fur, feathers, and scales challenge artists to master shading, texture, and proportion. The dynamic poses and behaviors of wild animals opens a window for artists to further their understanding of anatomy, movement, and form, while rendering the complexities of nature into compelling, lifelike representations.

In this chapter, you'll discover how to draw more than a dozen majestic creatures from across the animal kingdom. From such apex predators as a lion, a polar bear, and a wolf, to a colony of penguins, each project starts with a basic shape and guides you through a seamless step-by-step process to a finished drawing.

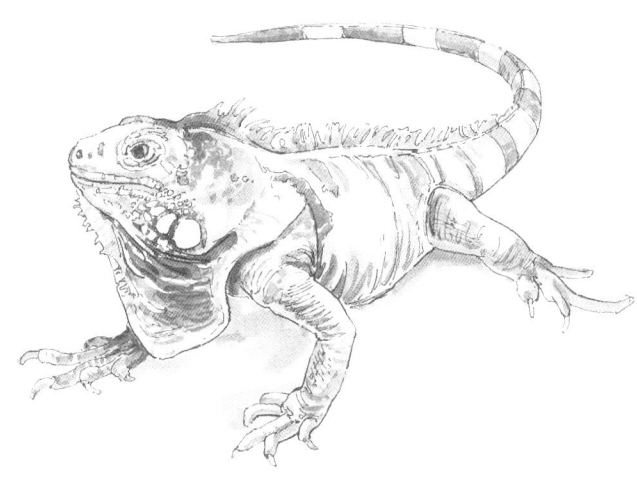

Elephant

Elephants are majestic, awe-inspiring creatures that make for great art. Study them closely before trying to draw them. You'll notice that their back legs bend just like a human's.

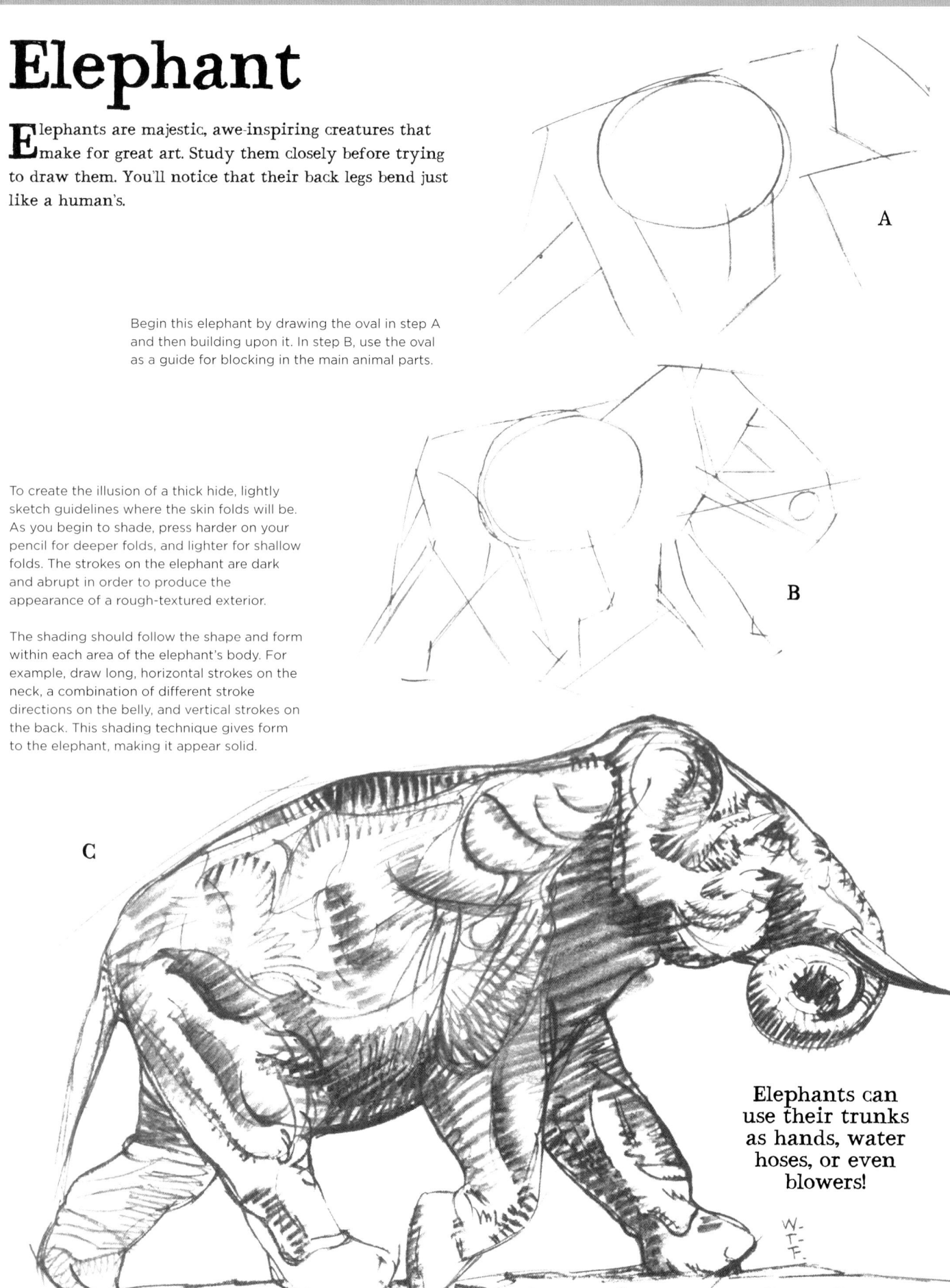

Begin this elephant by drawing the oval in step A and then building upon it. In step B, use the oval as a guide for blocking in the main animal parts.

To create the illusion of a thick hide, lightly sketch guidelines where the skin folds will be. As you begin to shade, press harder on your pencil for deeper folds, and lighter for shallow folds. The strokes on the elephant are dark and abrupt in order to produce the appearance of a rough-textured exterior.

The shading should follow the shape and form within each area of the elephant's body. For example, draw long, horizontal strokes on the neck, a combination of different stroke directions on the belly, and vertical strokes on the back. This shading technique gives form to the elephant, making it appear solid.

A

B

C

Elephants can use their trunks as hands, water hoses, or even blowers!

Gazelle

For the gazelle, attempt to draw both a walking pose (below) and a jumping pose (below right). The steps shown here illustrate how each one begins with completely different block-in lines. When you add the details, try to capture the animal's graceful qualities.

A

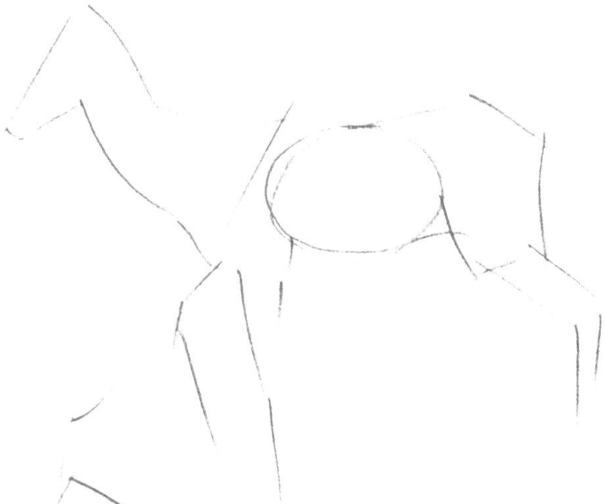

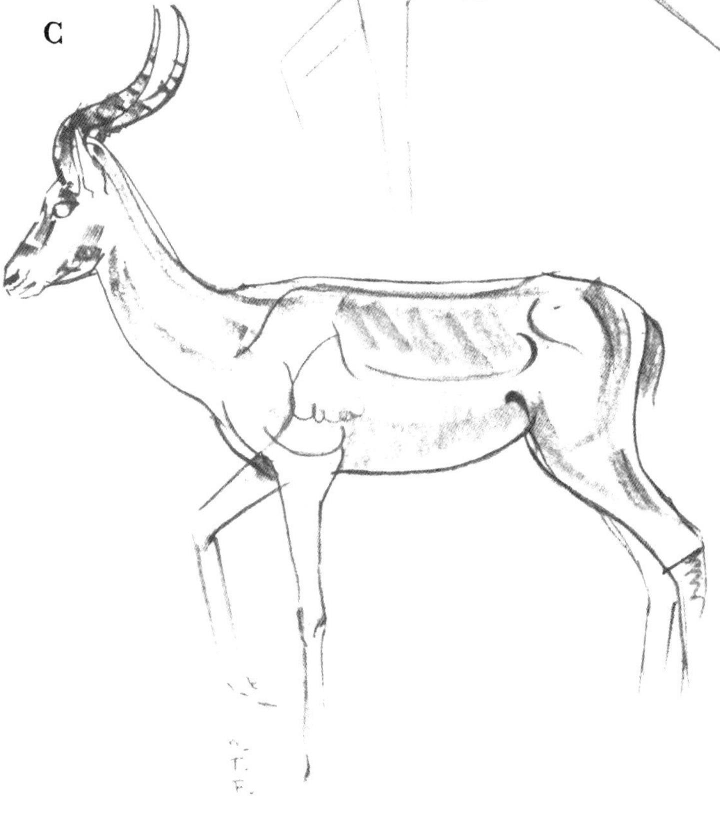

A

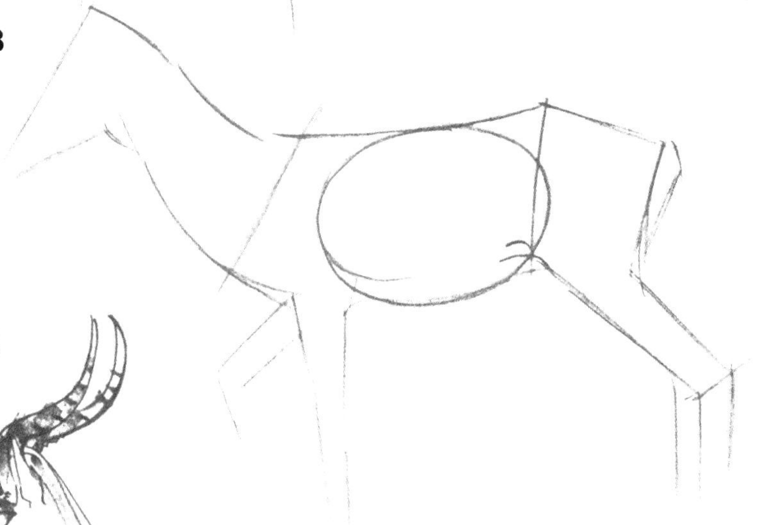

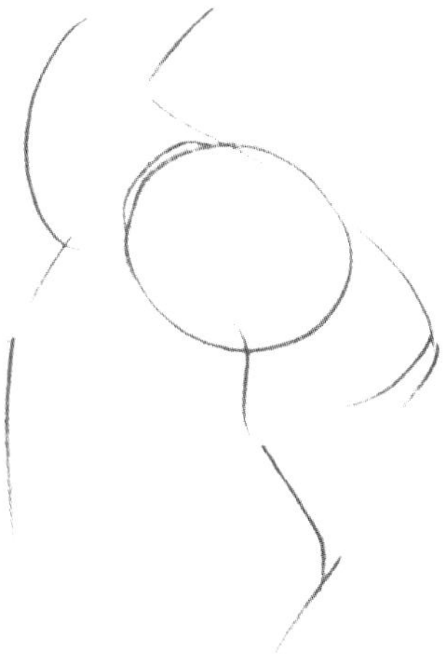

B

B

C

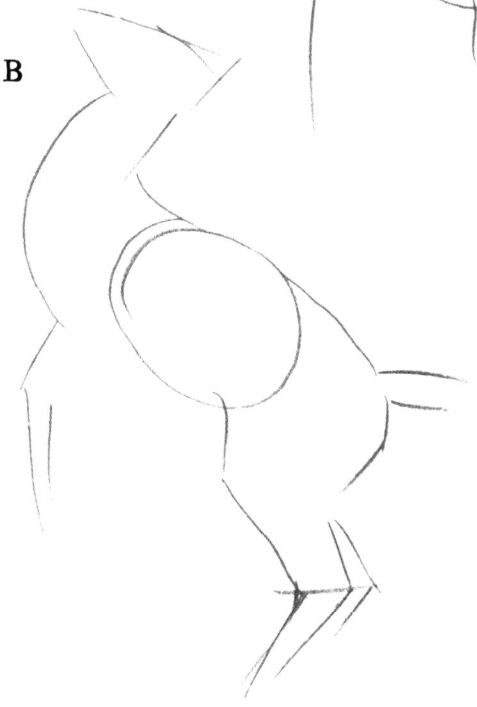

C

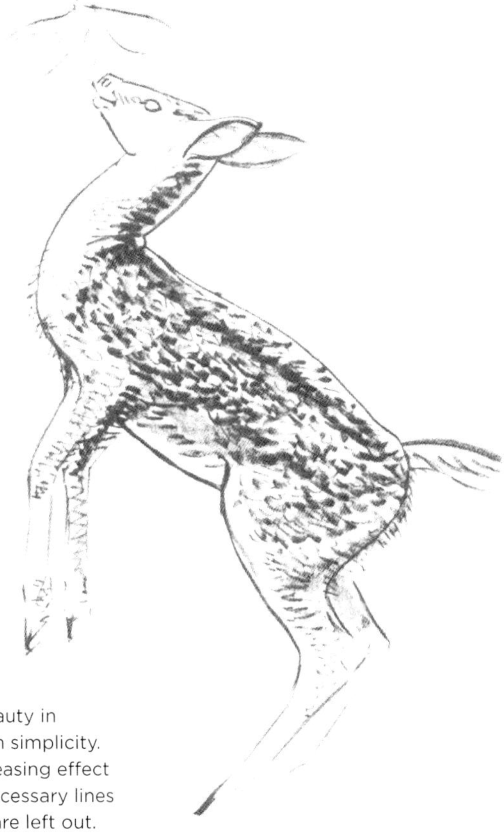

Often, the beauty in drawing lies in simplicity. Notice the pleasing effect when all unnecessary lines and shading are left out.

Giraffe

Accurate proportions are important when drawing the giraffe; when blocking in your drawing, consider how making the legs too short or the neck too thick would alter the animal's appearance.

Step 1 Block in the basic shape of the giraffe, adjusting the lines until you are satisfied with the proportions. Notice that the giraffe's neck is as long as its legs, and its hindquarters slope down sharply.

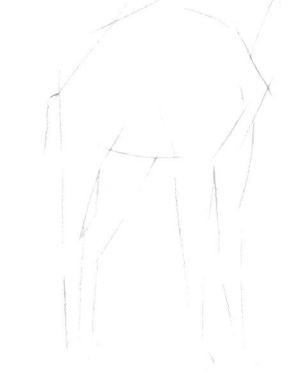

Step 2 Refine the shapes of the legs and rump, smoothing the outline. Then begin placing the features and blocking in the pattern of the coat. Notice how the spots all have slightly different irregular shapes, with small gaps between them.

Step 3 Erase any stray sketch marks and focus your attention on rendering the giraffe's face. (See "Drawing the Head," below.) Then fill in all the dark patches of the coat, adding the mane with a 2B pencil and short, dense diagonal strokes.

Step 4 In this final step, after shading the face, add the shading beneath the giraffe's body and head. To keep the giraffe from appearing to float on the page, draw the ground with tightly spaced diagonal strokes.

DRAWING THE HEAD

Start with a circle for the head and two smaller circles for the muzzle; then add the horns and ears. Draw a curved jaw line, and sketch in the eyes—and eyelashes—and inner ear details. Then refine all the outlines and shade the face, using a soft pencil for the dark areas and changing the direction of the strokes to follow the forms.

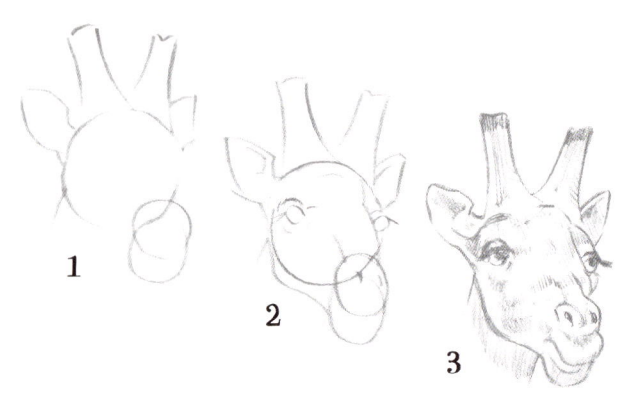

Iguana

This project uses foreshortening, which makes the iguana's head appear larger than its body. Read about foreshortening on pages 75 and 131 before starting this project.

Read about foreshortening on pages 75 and 131 before starting this project.

Step 1 Begin this drawing with a few gesture lines: one for each visible leg and one curving from the top of the head down to the tip of the tail. Block in the head and body, and create the boxy shape of the lizard's mouth and nose.

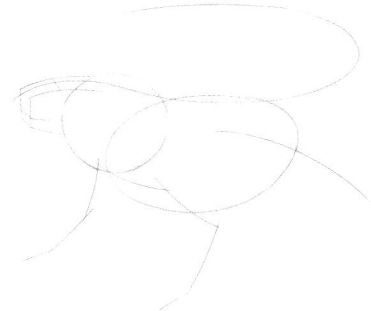

Step 2 Begin to outline the iguana, adding the droop of skin beneath the round chin and defining each toe and claw. Adjust the lines as needed, erasing stray sketch marks as you go.

Step 3 Finish the outline with a waterproof ink pen. Add the striped pattern to the tail and the spikes along the iguana's back. Use a few strokes to show the iguana's rough skin, as well as curving lines that suggest the sag under the skin. After the ink dries, erase any initial pencil marks.

Step 4 Add shading with ink thinned with water. Because the ink used in the previous step is waterproof, don't worry about marring it by applying washes on top. (For extra caution, test each wash on scratch paper before applying it to the drawing; it's difficult to determine the value of an ink wash until it is applied to paper.) Using a pointed soft brush, apply shadows beginning with light washes and slowly building up to darker values, such as those beneath the chin and on the left claw.

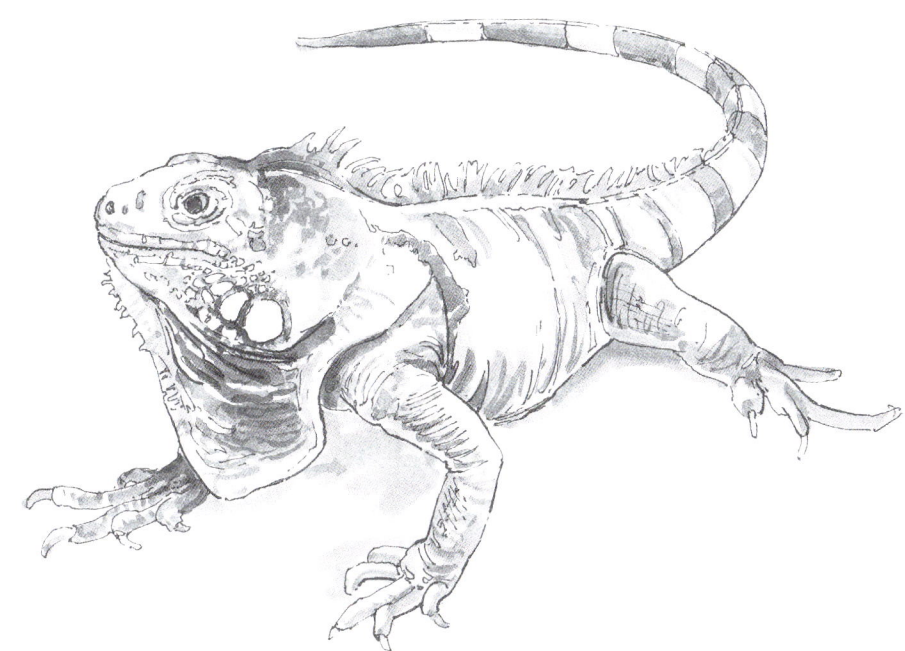

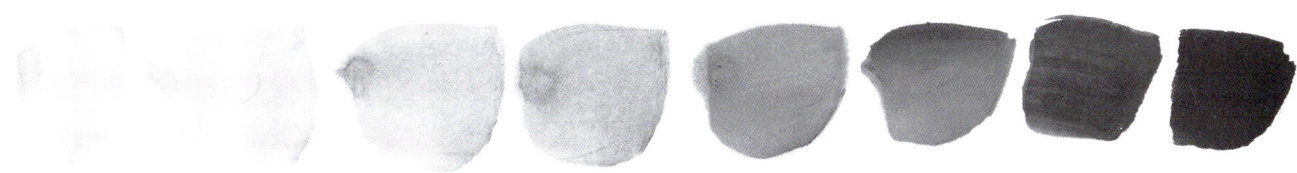

VARYING VALUES WITH INK WASHES

Simply adjusting the amount of water you use in your ink washes can provide a variety of different values. When creating a wash, it is best to start with the lightest value and build up to a darker wash, rather than adding water to a dark wash. To get acquainted with the process of mixing various values, create a value chart like the one above. Start with a very diluted wash at the left, and gradually add more pigment for successively darker values.

Baboon

Baboons are highly intelligent, sensitive, and curious creatures. This straightforward pose has the subject's neutral gaze directed toward the viewer. For an added challenge, introduce a few natural elements into the background to add visual interest.

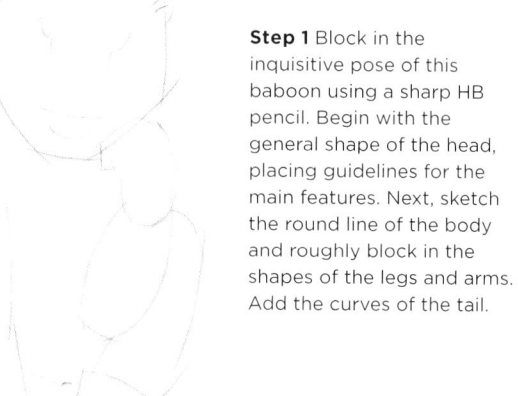

Step 1 Block in the inquisitive pose of this baboon using a sharp HB pencil. Begin with the general shape of the head, placing guidelines for the main features. Next, sketch the round line of the body and roughly block in the shapes of the legs and arms. Add the curves of the tail.

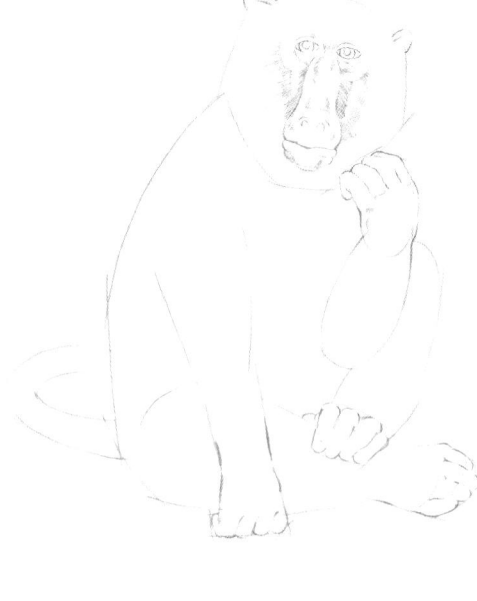

Step 2 Begin adding the facial features. Use a dull HB pencil to shade around the eyes and nose, always stroking in the direction of hair growth. Refine the outlines of the hands and feet, indicating the individual fingers and toes.

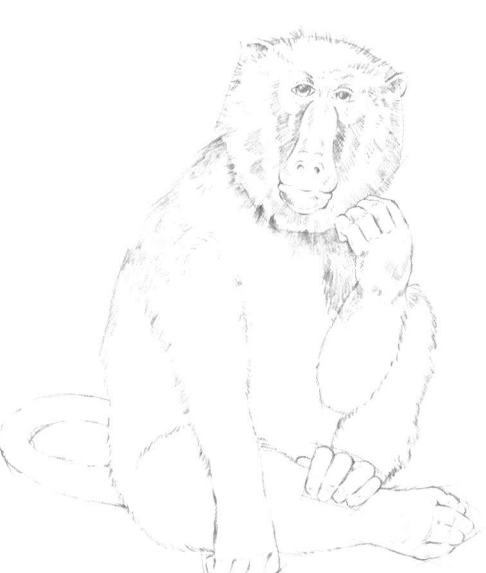

Step 3 Continue to develop the coat texture around the face and on the back. Apply a series of short, parallel strokes that follow the initial outlines from step one.

Step 4 Finish developing the shading on the body, adding strokes to the darkest areas of the baboon but leaving the lightest areas completely white. Add a cast shadow to the ground beneath the baboon with the flattened point of an HB pencil.

Antelope

Antelope are graceful, agile creatures known for their distinctive horns. Start this drawing by sketching the main form using a series of ovals for the body mass.

Step 1 Establish the placement of the antelope's head, muzzle, neck, chest, torso, and rear end.

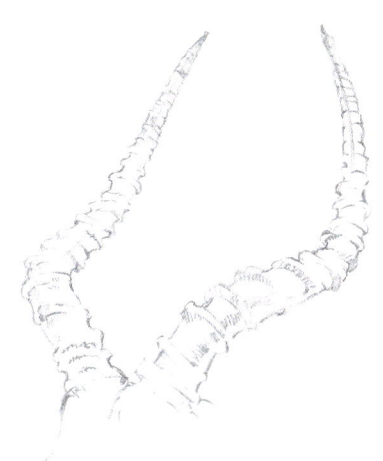

Step 2 Now add the front and back legs, making them the same height as the distance from the top of the head to the bottom of the chest. Use the circles that indicate the chest and rear sections to determine the placement of the legs.

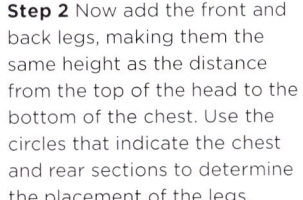

DETAILING THE HORNS

The horns of this antelope have several ridges from the base to the tip that produce a horizontal band pattern. Begin by indicating the bands with marks that wrap around the horns, and then add a small shadow beneath each ridge.

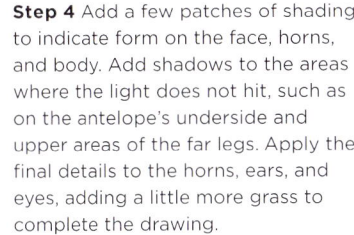

Step 4 Add a few patches of shading to indicate form on the face, horns, and body. Add shadows to the areas where the light does not hit, such as on the antelope's underside and upper areas of the far legs. Apply the final details to the horns, ears, and eyes, adding a little more grass to complete the drawing.

Step 3 Next, refine the outline of the body, connecting the initial shapes with a smooth contour. Lightly sketch in blades of grass and mark the position of the eyes, nose, mouth, and horns, adjusting their placements until satisfied.

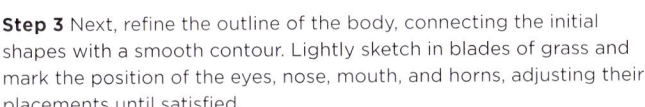

Flamingo

With its long legs and gracefully curved S-shaped neck, the flamingo is an interesting animal to draw. Block out its basic shape before filling in the details. Just a few strokes are enough to indicate its distinctive beak and feathers.

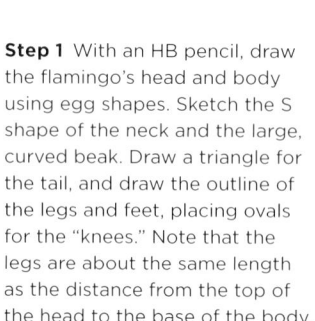

Step 1 With an HB pencil, draw the flamingo's head and body using egg shapes. Sketch the S shape of the neck and the large, curved beak. Draw a triangle for the tail, and draw the outline of the legs and feet, placing ovals for the "knees." Note that the legs are about the same length as the distance from the top of the head to the base of the body.

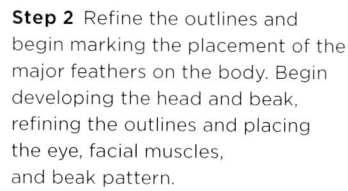

Step 2 Refine the outlines and begin marking the placement of the major feathers on the body. Begin developing the head and beak, refining the outlines and placing the eye, facial muscles, and beak pattern.

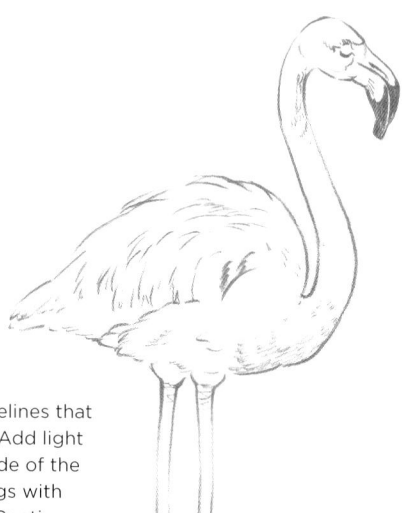

Step 3 Erase any guidelines that are no longer needed. Add light shading to the underside of the body and the upper legs with short, curved strokes. Continue to develop the head with a few feather details and darken the tip of the beak.

Step 4 Finish shading the flamingo's neck and belly using a soft pencil in the underhand position; make short strokes in the direction of feather growth. Shade more intensely on the right and on the underside of the flamingo, since the source of light is coming from the upper left. Add texture to the legs and feet with squiggly lines. To finish, create the final feathers on the flamingo's back with long, curved strokes.

Toucan

Birds come in all shapes, sizes, and textures. This toucan's long, smooth feathers require soft strokes. Soft shading is also used to indicate the smooth texture of this bird's beak.

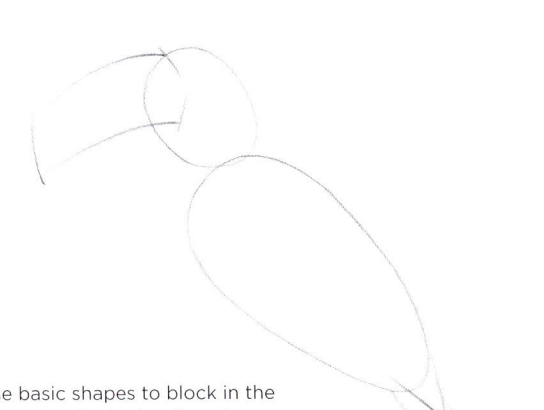

Step 1 Use basic shapes to block in the toucan; establish the body with a long egg shape, the head with an oval, and the tail and beak with rectangular shapes. Make the large beak almost twice as wide as the head, and the tail half as long as the body.

Step 2 Now add the legs and feet, posing the toucan on a branch. Be careful to make your preliminary lines light, as it may take several sketches to make the bird appear balanced over its legs. Mark the opening in the beak and the position of the eye.

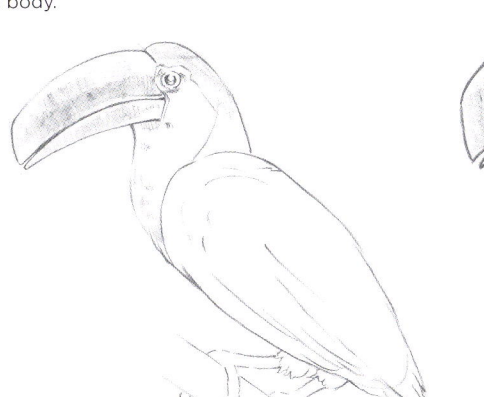

Step 3 Next, refine the outlines and erase any guidelines you no longer need. To suggest the feathers, add a few strokes along the wings and tail. Then begin to shade the beak with long, perpendicular strokes using the side of a sharp HB pencil. Begin shading the top of the head and small areas of the chest.

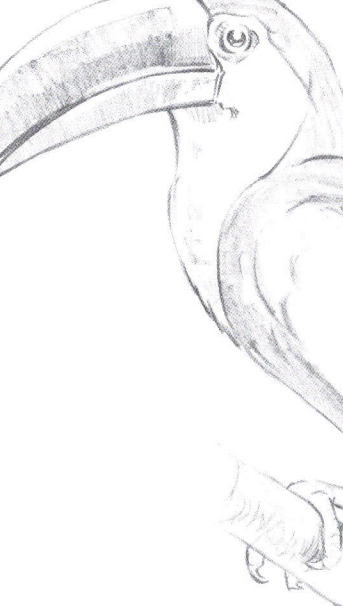

Step 4 Finally, shade the wing and tail using the side of the pencil and stroking in the direction of feather growth, giving the underside the darkest value. Then add the details to the feet and branch, suggesting the cylindrical nature of each with curved strokes.

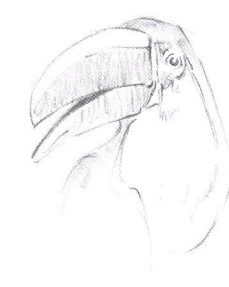

Changing the Viewpoint Once you're comfortable drawing the toucan in profile, try a three-quarter angle. From this viewpoint, the light top of the beak is more visible, and the chest is more prominent than the head. This angle makes a more lively and engaging portrait.

Chimpanzee

Start this drawing by using overlapping ovals for the body. Notice how alternating dark and light shading techniques for the fur helps create dimension.

Step 1 With circular strokes and a sharp HB pencil, build the basic form of the body.

Step 2 Block in the feet and hands with straight lines. Mark the placement of the facial features, sketching in the outlines of the mouth, eyes, brow, and ears.

Step 3 Soften the outlines with uneven, curved strokes and dashes. The outlines should not be solid and smooth; they should suggest the hairy texture of the chimp's coat. Draw the hands and feet inside the guidelines from step two.

Step 4 Erase any initial guidelines and begin shading in the dark coat with a soft pencil. Apply short strokes that follow the direction of the hair growth, adding fewer lines to the highlighted areas and more to the shadows and creases.

Step 5 Shade and add the final details to the face, filling in the eyes and the mouth.

Giant Panda

Pandas are an easy subject to approach when you begin with simple shapes. Start with circles for the head and body; then add ovals for the arms, legs, and paws. Add the details, such as the eyes, nose, and bamboo leaves. Then use soft, short strokes to indicate the texture of the panda's thick black-and-white fur. When rendering hair, always stroke in the direction it grows.

Step 1 First, establish the panda's overall shape and pose. Start with a circle for the head and a larger oval for the body. Then draw a series of ovals for the arms, legs, and feet, dividing the left arm into upper and lower sections. Also, mark the general shape and position of the ears, the eye mask, and the nose.

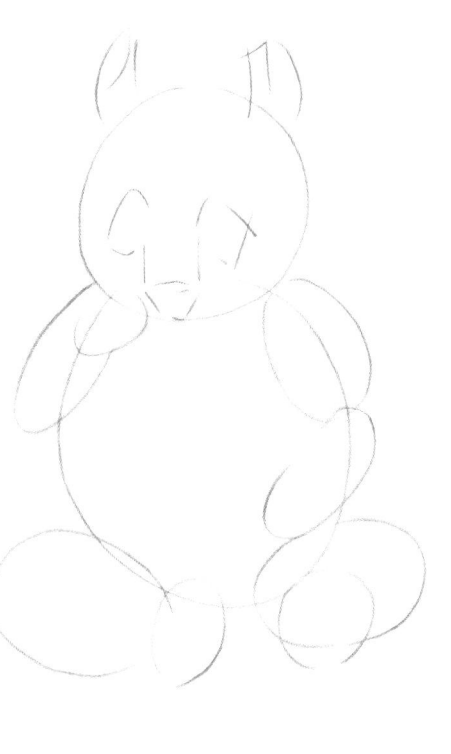

Step 2 Place the eyes, refine the shape of the nose, and sketch in the branch of bamboo. Use the side of a soft pencil and make short, soft marks around the outlines to indicate fur. Then begin shading all the black areas on the coat with an HB pencil, stroking downward in the direction of the hair growth.

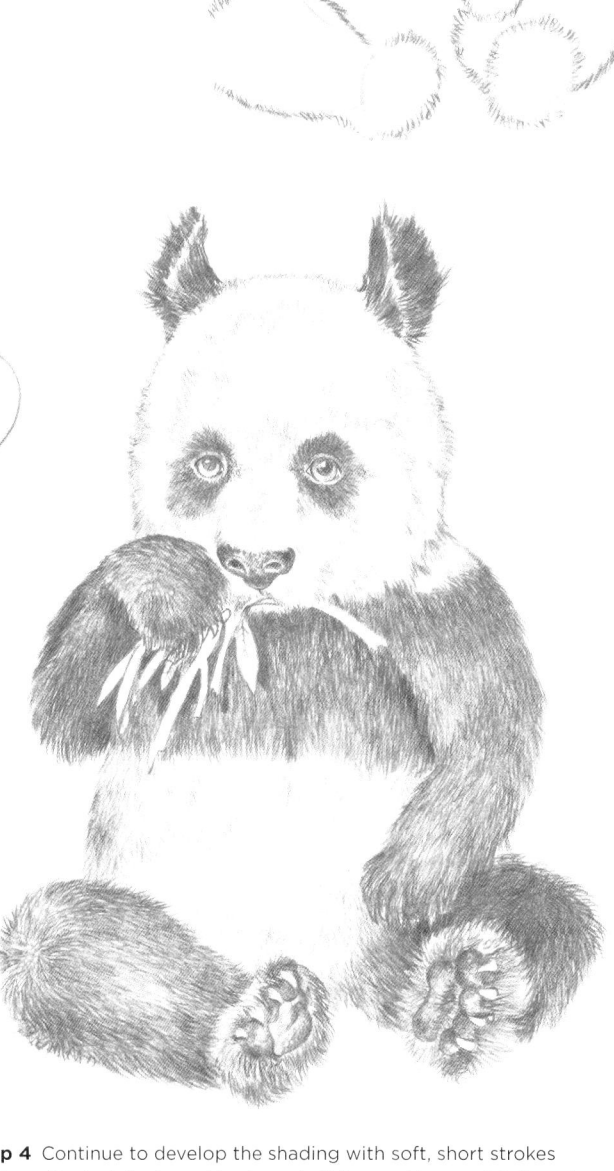

Step 3 Erase any remaining guidelines and continue shading the black areas of fur. Then use a blending stump to smooth the pencil strokes, creating the illusion of soft fur. Add a few closely spaced strokes in the white fur to give it dimension and suggest the underlying muscles. Then draw the footpads and toenails.

Step 4 Continue to develop the shading with soft, short strokes to show the fur's texture. Also keep building up the panda's form by varying the shading of the fur; for example, darken the areas between the arms and the body, as well as the areas on the legs that are closest to the ground. Add the details to finish the feet, claws, nose, and eyes.

Lion

With its muscular frame, massive paws, and huge head, it's no surprise that the lion is at the top of the food chain. This forward-facing subject is at a slight angle. Notice how its right front paw appears larger than the others due to foreshortening. (See pages 75 and 131.)

Step 2 Using the same pencil, sketch the position of the eyes, nose, and mouth. Note that the top of the nose is about halfway down the face, and the eyes are about one-third of the way down. Begin to indicate the lion's form by marking a few lines near the leg joints and on its side; these marks will later serve as guides for shading.

Step 1 Begin by blocking in the basic shape of the lion with a series of short, rough lines. Use an HB pencil so that the markings are light enough to erase thoroughly. Adjust the proportions as much as is needed before moving on.

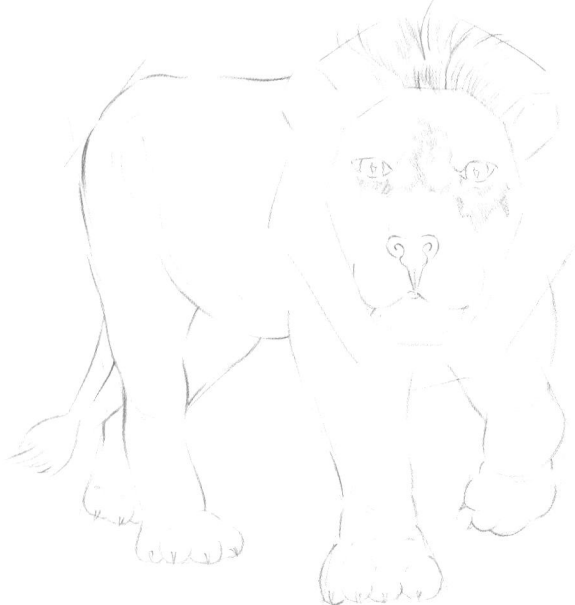

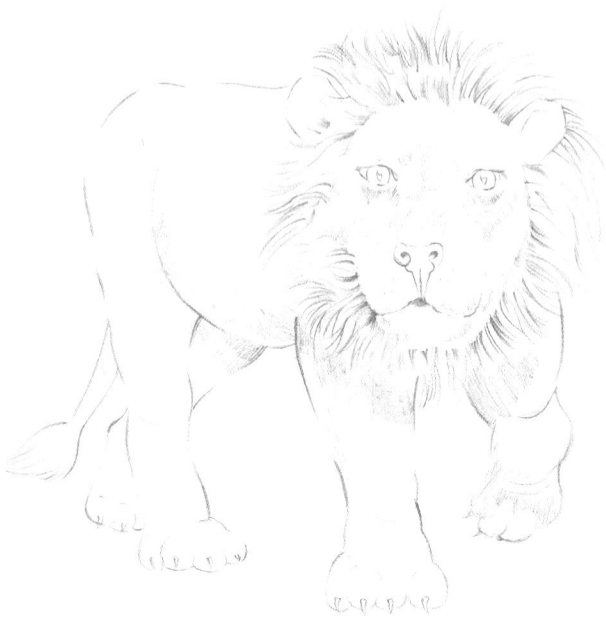

Step 4 Continue to develop the lion's mane, placing the strokes close together and changing the values by altering the pressure on the pencil. This variation in value gives the mane a sense of dimension with a minimum number of strokes. Erase any initial sketch marks and continue to develop the shading on the face. Begin to shade to other areas of the body, including the belly, the upper back, the front legs, and the lifted paw.

Step 3 Start refining the outlines of the lion's body and legs by rounding out the sharp corners. For the mane, begin adding the hair with curved lines, stroking from the edge of the lion's face outward. Next, begin to shade the face, applying small patches of parallel strokes.

Step 5 Continue to build form by shading the dark areas on the face and body. Use short, straight, parallel lines that follow the direction of the hair growth to create a convincing coat. To complete the drawing, use a soft 2B pencil to apply the final details to the lion, such as the dark whiskers, tail, and eyes. Finally, add several strokes near the lion's feet to suggest grass.

COMPARING THE MALE AND FEMALE

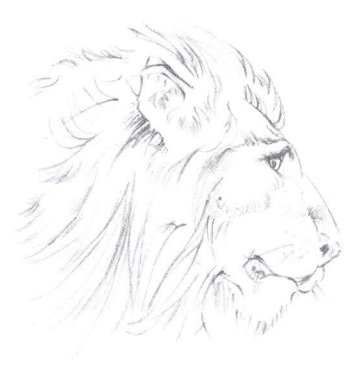

The male lion has a larger head than the female, accentuated by the presence of a shaggy mane. The male also has a broad face and large jaw, making him appear more threatening than the female lion.

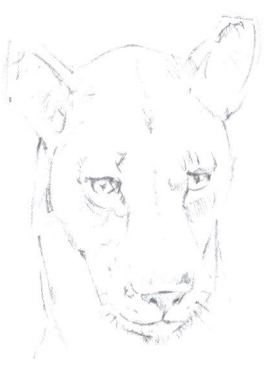

The female lion lacks a mane, making her easy to distinguish from a male. Because of this absence, the head of the lioness appears slimmer with a sleeker look.

Polar Bear

With an oval-shaped body, rounded ears, and angular snout, the polar bear makes for a good beginning drawing project. Start with broad, rounded shapes to block in this bear's massive frame. Then develop the details as you go.

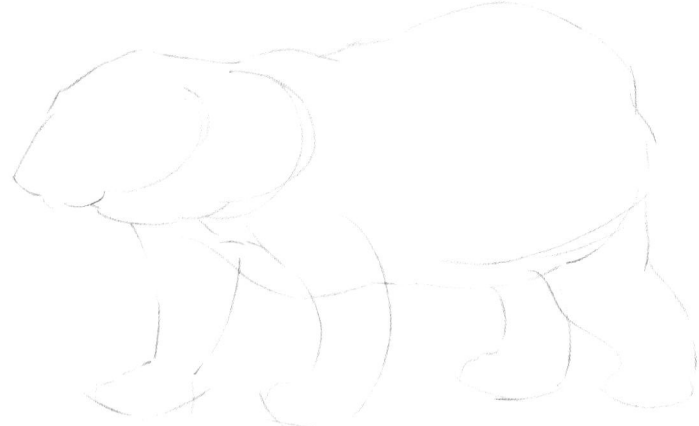

Step 1 Begin by sketching the general outlines of the body, head, and legs, paying careful attention to proportions. Draw a few lines to indicate the length of the neck and two quick strokes for the chest. Notice that the head is slightly lower than the rear, and that the front legs curve slightly inward.

Step 2 Add the ears with two concentric semi-circles and block in the squarish nose. Sketch the thick ice floe beneath the bear's feet. Start with an irregular half-oval and then draw a matching line beneath it, connecting the top and the base with vertical lines.

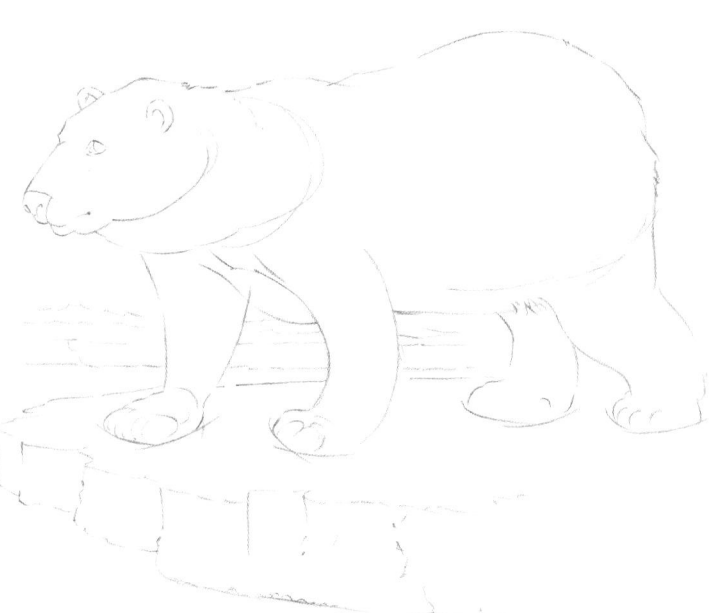

Step 3 Place the eye and begin building the feet with circular strokes. To suggest the mass of ice in the background, add four broken horizontal lines behind the ice floe.

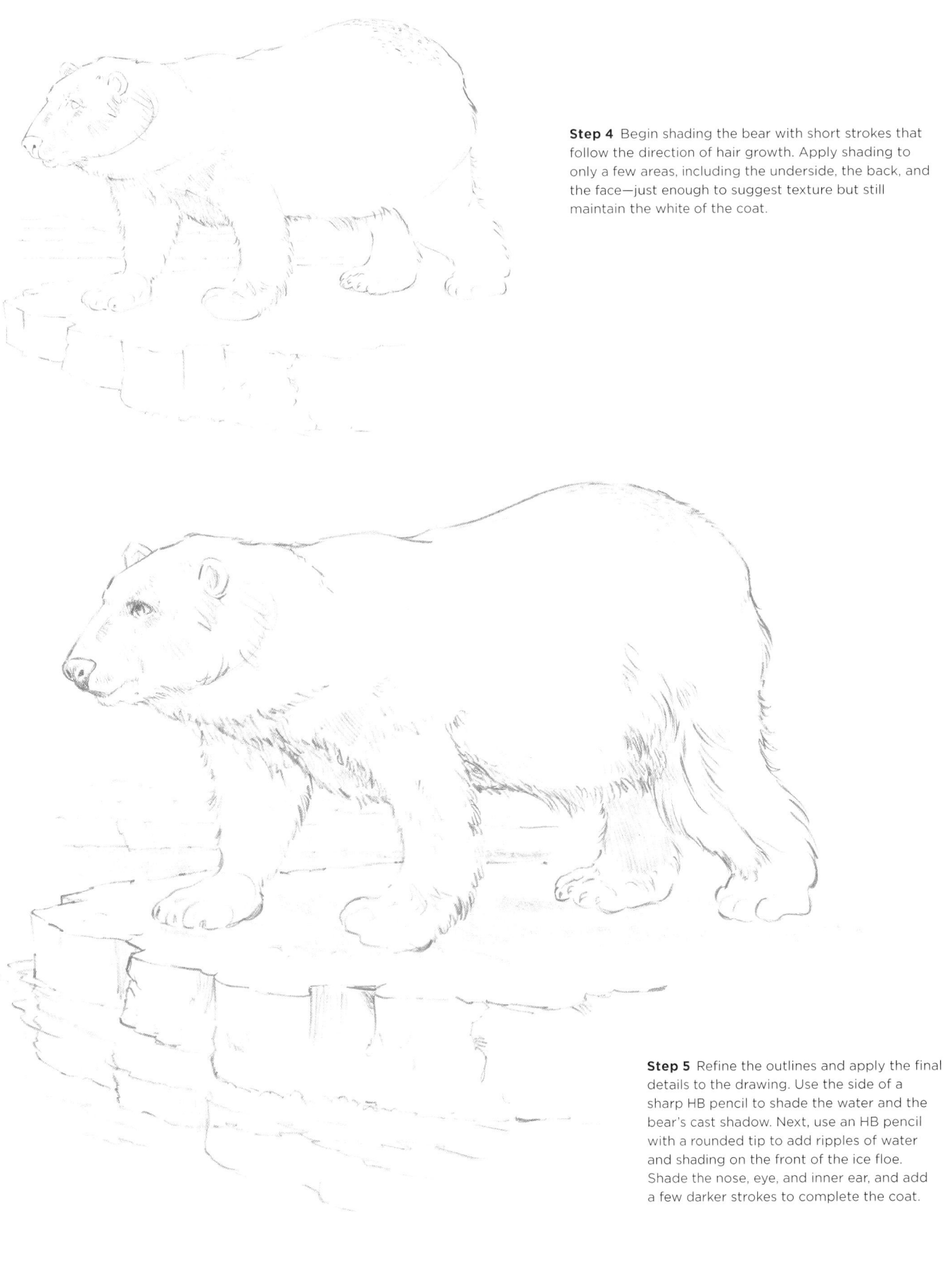

Step 4 Begin shading the bear with short strokes that follow the direction of hair growth. Apply shading to only a few areas, including the underside, the back, and the face—just enough to suggest texture but still maintain the white of the coat.

Step 5 Refine the outlines and apply the final details to the drawing. Use the side of a sharp HB pencil to shade the water and the bear's cast shadow. Next, use an HB pencil with a rounded tip to add ripples of water and shading on the front of the ice floe. Shade the nose, eye, and inner ear, and add a few darker strokes to complete the coat.

Bison

The bison has become a popular subject among artists and photographers in recent years. Perhaps it has to do with the animal's never-changing expression, which strikes a comical note. Use quick, short strokes to indicate its rugged coat. Spend a little additional time on its eyes and muzzle to ensure they appear realistic.

Step 1 Use an HB pencil with a rounded tip to sketch the rough shapes of the bison's face, horns, and mane. Try to make this early composition as symmetrical as possible. Mark off indentations just below the eyes, and square off the face where the "beard" begins.

Step 2 Block in the structure of the face, indicating the different planes of the muzzle and the slope of the forehead.

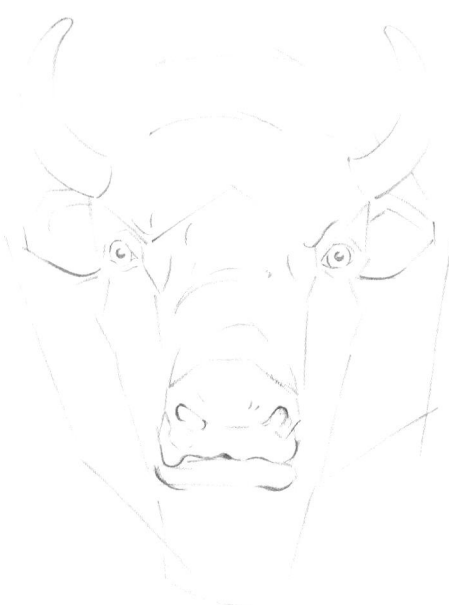

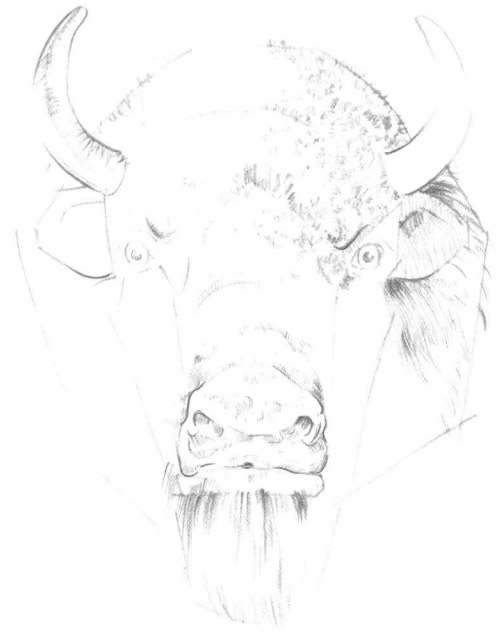

Step 3 Draw the facial features, including the eyes, ears, and nostrils. Place the ears just below the base of the horns, and place the eyes level with the bottom half of the ears. The eyes are extremely far apart; they should be placed slightly wider than the corners of the mouth. Begin refining the outline of the nostrils and mouth.

Step 4 Now begin shading the bison, suggesting various textures. Use long, wavy lines to suggest hair beneath the mouth. To suggest a shorter, curlier coat on the face and the head, use the side of a round-tipped pencil to apply several short strokes and squiggles. Begin shading the horns with curved lines that follow the cylindrical form.

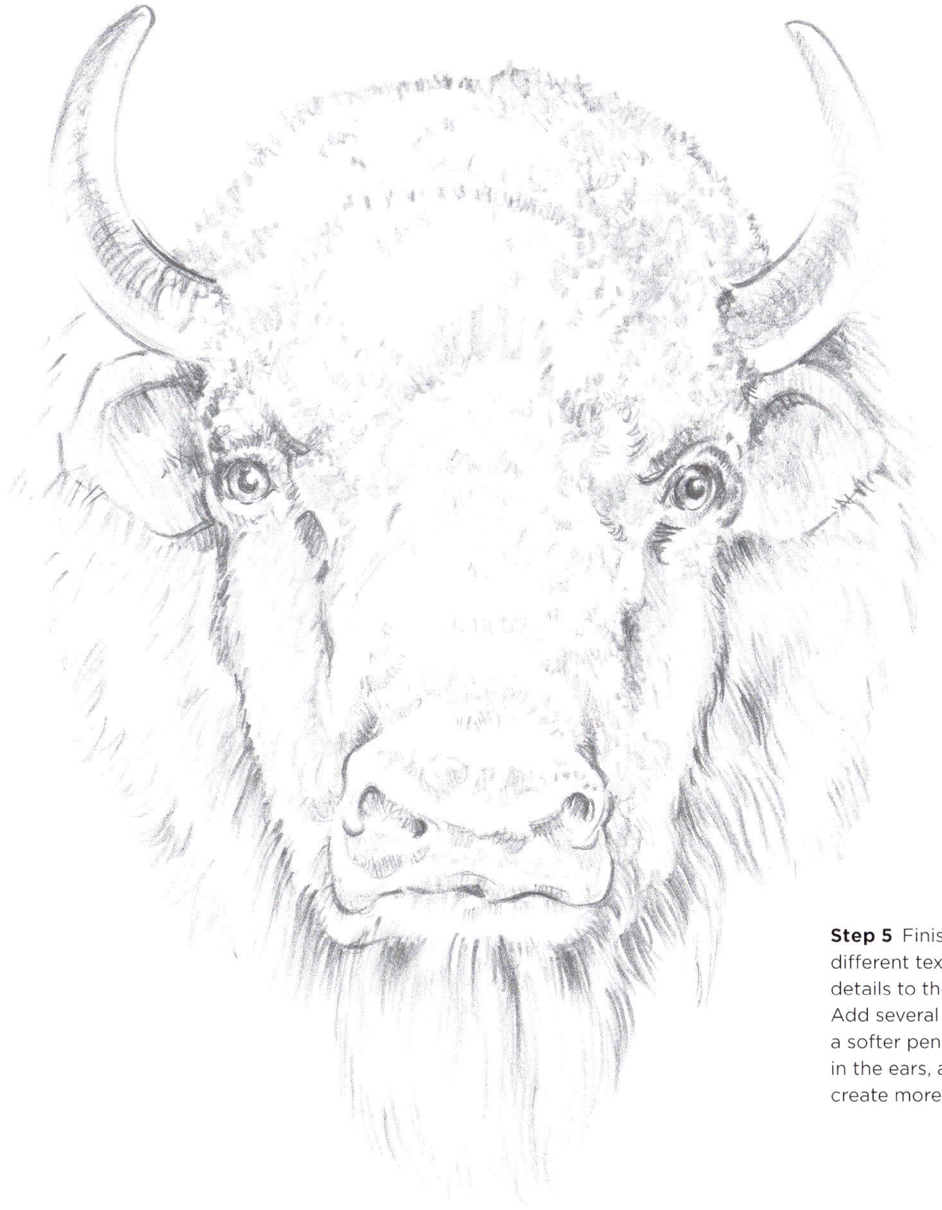

Step 5 Finish shading the different textures, and add the details to the eyes (see below). Add several dark strokes with a softer pencil along the jawline, in the ears, and in the eyes to create more contrast.

EXAMINING THE BODY

From the side, the bison has a flat profile, a low head, short front legs, and high shoulders that give it a rough, almost primitive appearance.

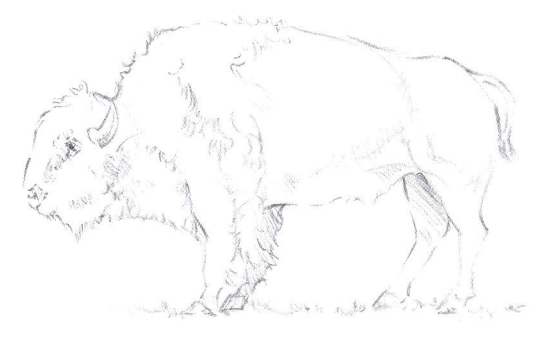

DRAWING THE EYES

Outline the eyelid, iris, pupil, and brow with light, thin lines. Indicate the darkest values by filling in the pupil and part of the iris, leaving a white highlight. Continue to develop the form with shading; then rub a tortillon over areas of the eyeball to soften the highlights and diminish any harsh edges.

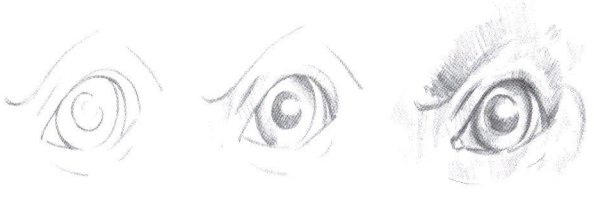

Wolf

This animal is serious and stoic with piercing eyes. You will notice that loose, short strokes are enough to render a realistic-looking coat. Turn back to pages 10 and 11 to review how basic lines can be used to create realistic effects. It might be tempting to rush through these steps, but moving too quickly will impact the quality of your work. Take your time with this one, especially focusing on the eyes, to ensure you capture a realistic likeness.

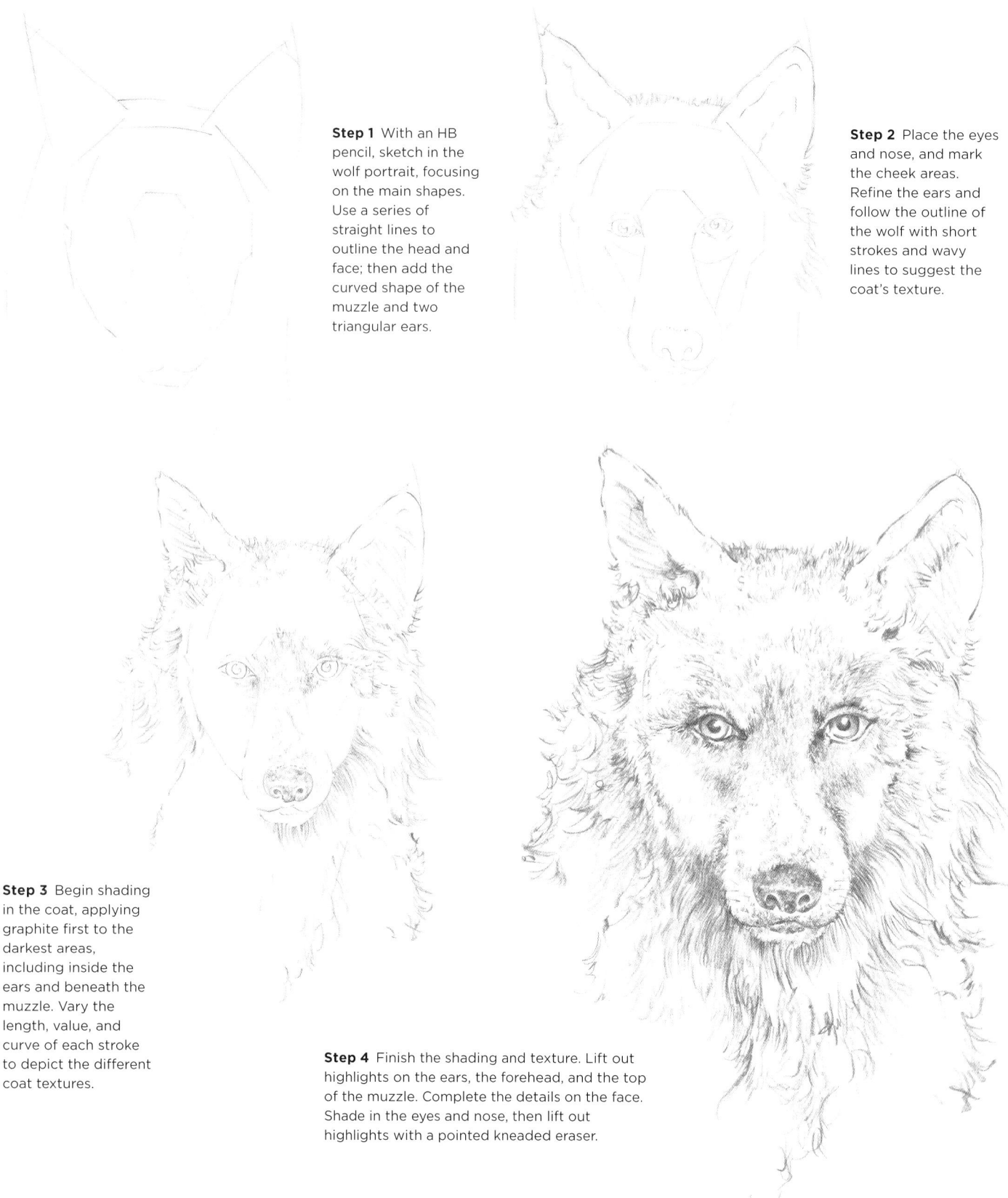

Step 1 With an HB pencil, sketch in the wolf portrait, focusing on the main shapes. Use a series of straight lines to outline the head and face; then add the curved shape of the muzzle and two triangular ears.

Step 2 Place the eyes and nose, and mark the cheek areas. Refine the ears and follow the outline of the wolf with short strokes and wavy lines to suggest the coat's texture.

Step 3 Begin shading in the coat, applying graphite first to the darkest areas, including inside the ears and beneath the muzzle. Vary the length, value, and curve of each stroke to depict the different coat textures.

Step 4 Finish the shading and texture. Lift out highlights on the ears, the forehead, and the top of the muzzle. Complete the details on the face. Shade in the eyes and nose, then lift out highlights with a pointed kneaded eraser.

Penguins

Penguins are curious, if not slightly clumsy, creatures. Their stocky bodies, short flippers, and little legs make them fun to draw. Emperor penguins are highly social, so drawing them in groups is an accurate way to portray them in the wild.

Step 1 Using an HB pencil, sketch the body and head of each penguin with ovals, tilting the positions of the bodies. Arrange them in a U-shaped composition rather than in a straight line to lead the viewer's eye through and around the drawing.

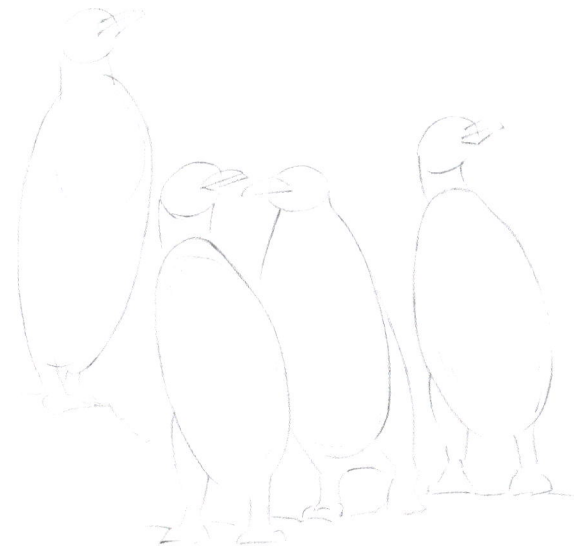

Step 2 Add the beaks with simple curved and straight lines, placing them to the right of the center of each head. Add the short legs and the shapes of the wide, webbed feet. Then draw a few lines to establish the ground.

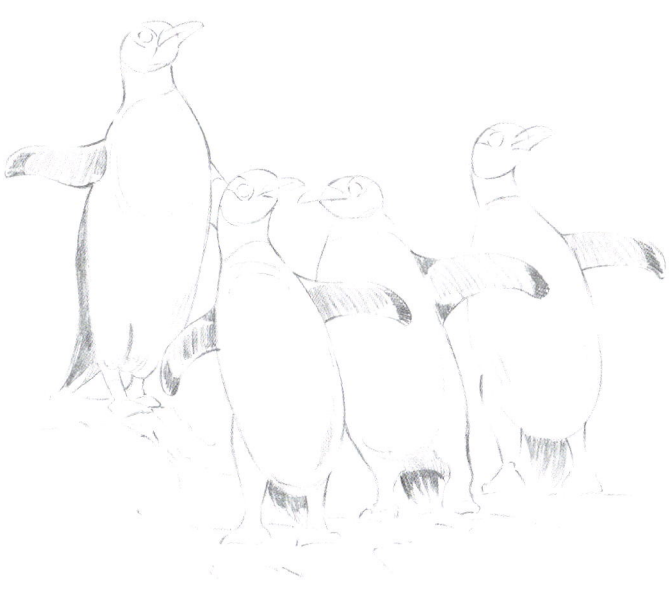

Step 3 Add the eyes and place the wings and tails, shading with parallel strokes and a rounded 2B pencil tip. Add some thin, curving lines beneath their feet to fill in the the ground.

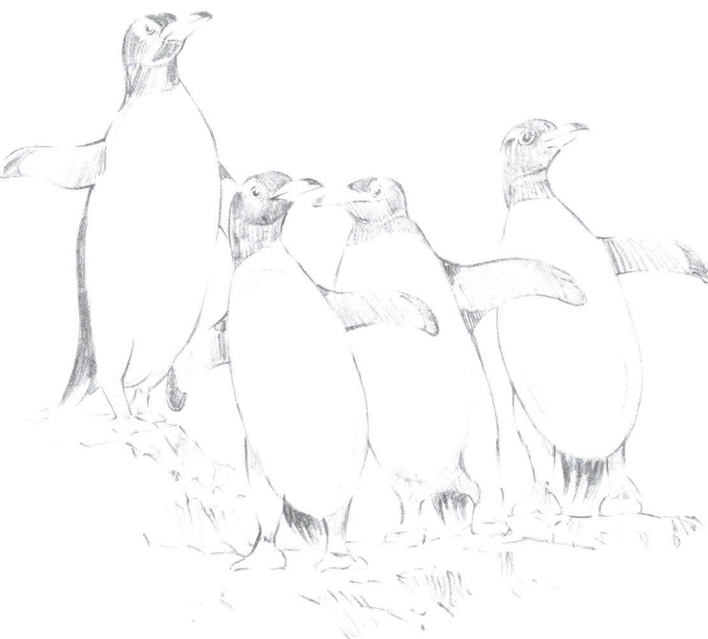

Step 4 Shade the heads and tips of the beaks with parallel strokes with the 2B pencil. Add a bit of shading to the upper legs and place a few strokes to add shadows to the ground.

DEPICTING UNIQUE MARKINGS

The markings on a penguin's head vary according to species. For this Gentoo penguin, leave a white area from the top of the head and under and around each eye. Then circle each eye with short, dark strokes.

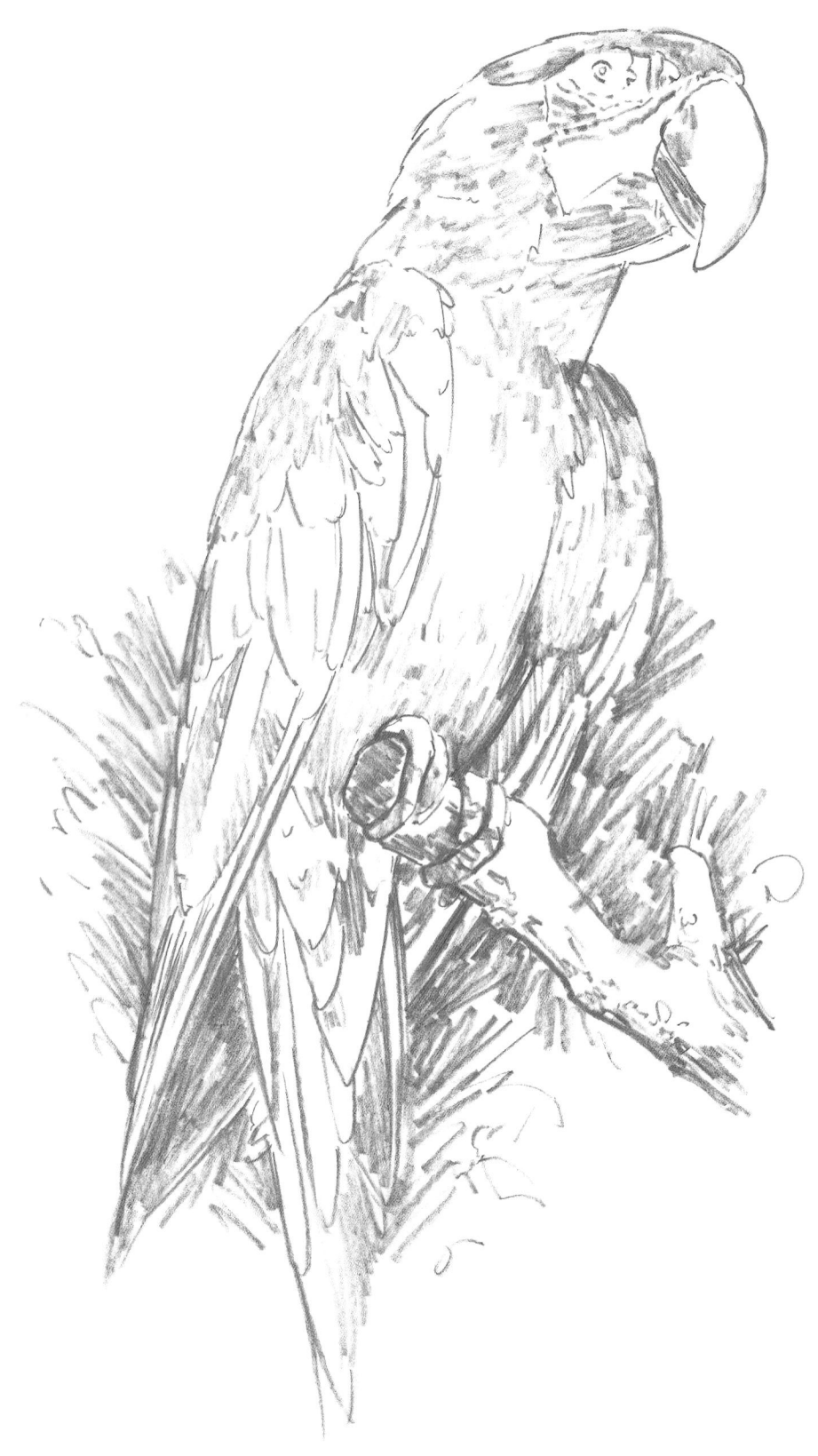

Pets

Whether you love dogs, cats, birds, or hamsters, people who have pets often form deep, emotional connections with their beloved animals. In addition to learning how to realistically render their basic shapes, textures, and signature markings, your pets' habits, expressions, mannerisms, and mischievous behaviors can also spark unlimited artistic inspiration.

In this section, you'll learn how to draw rabbits, a guinea pig, and budgerigars—or parakeets—in addition to a ferret, parrot, and snake. Each of these different tutorials focuses on a unique aspect of that animal to help give you a broad understanding of the process so you can confidently draw your own cherished animal when you are ready to do so.

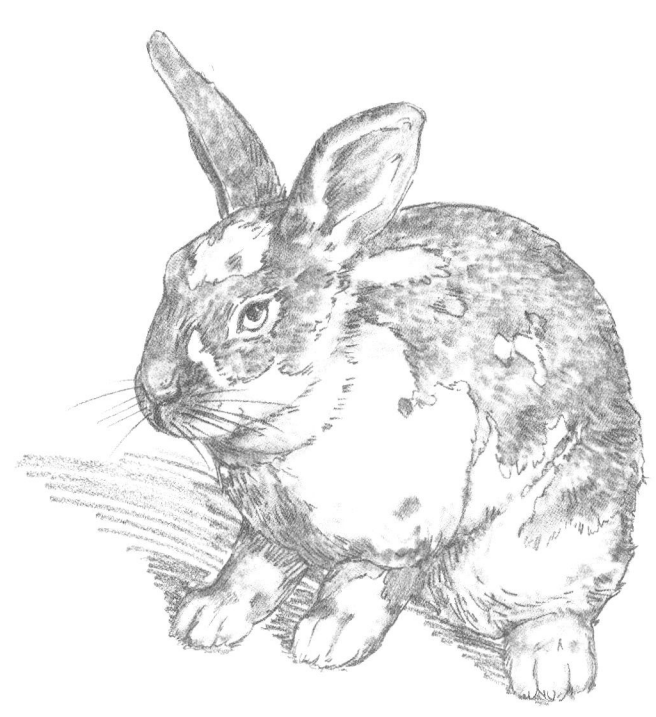

Rabbits

Drawing rabbits requires you to observe them carefully. For example, ear length varies with different breeds. When drawing a particular animal breed, it is always helpful to research that breed so your renderings will be accurate. You will find good references at the library. The poses featured on these two pages are typical positions for rabbits.

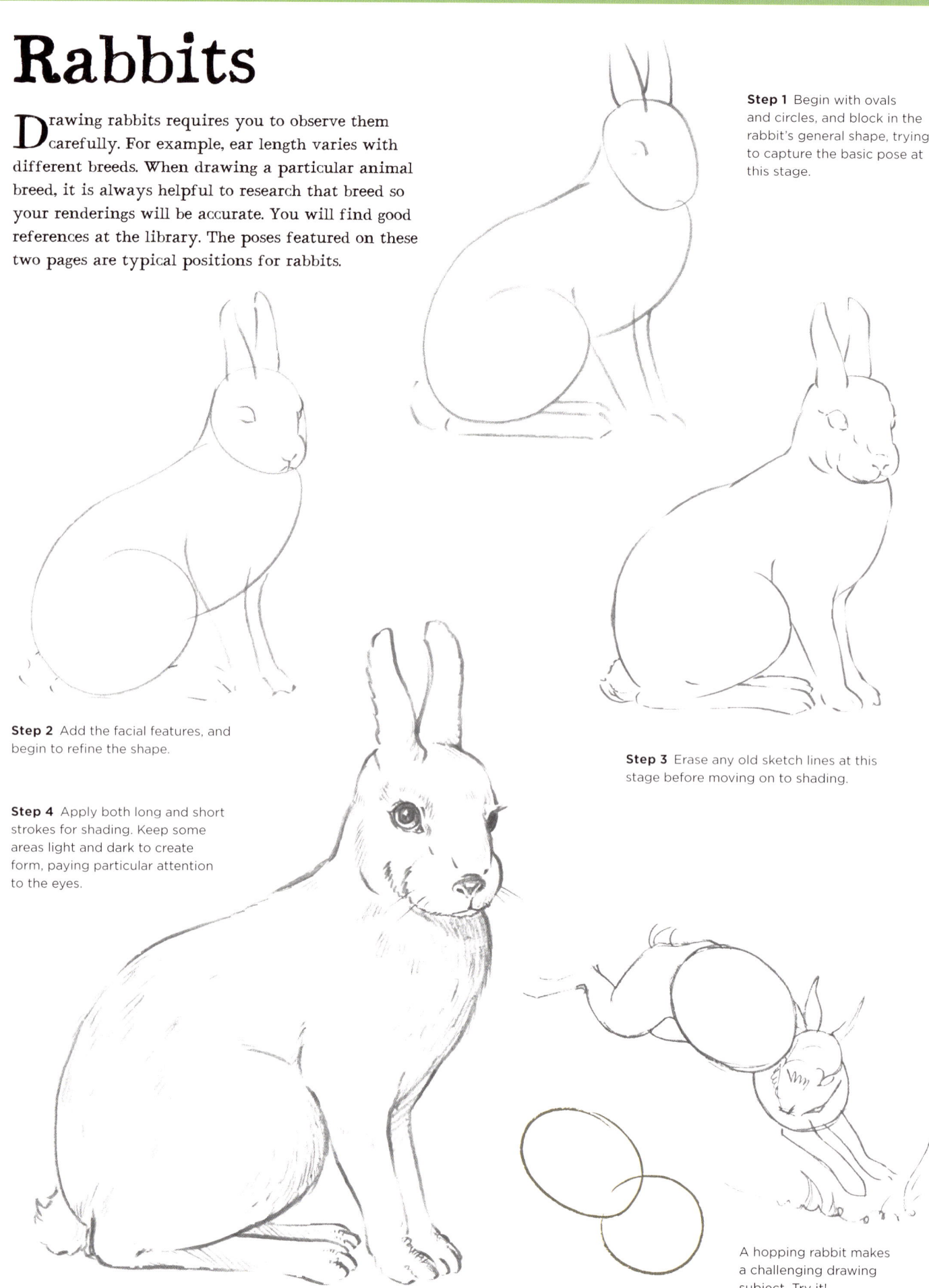

Step 1 Begin with ovals and circles, and block in the rabbit's general shape, trying to capture the basic pose at this stage.

Step 2 Add the facial features, and begin to refine the shape.

Step 3 Erase any old sketch lines at this stage before moving on to shading.

Step 4 Apply both long and short strokes for shading. Keep some areas light and dark to create form, paying particular attention to the eyes.

A hopping rabbit makes a challenging drawing subject. Try it!

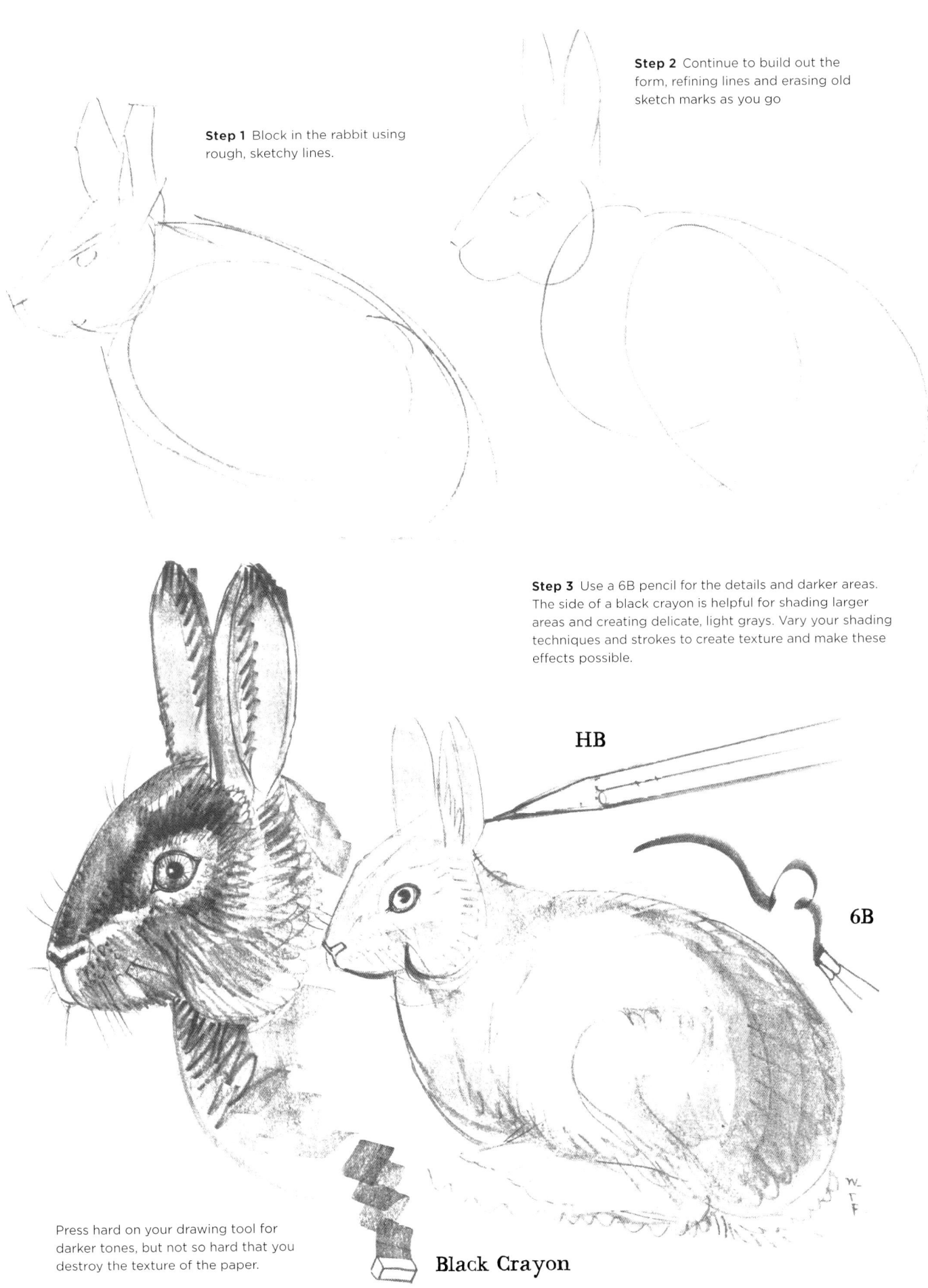

Step 1 Block in the rabbit using rough, sketchy lines.

Step 2 Continue to build out the form, refining lines and erasing old sketch marks as you go

Step 3 Use a 6B pencil for the details and darker areas. The side of a black crayon is helpful for shading larger areas and creating delicate, light grays. Vary your shading techniques and strokes to create texture and make these effects possible.

HB

6B

Press hard on your drawing tool for darker tones, but not so hard that you destroy the texture of the paper.

Black Crayon

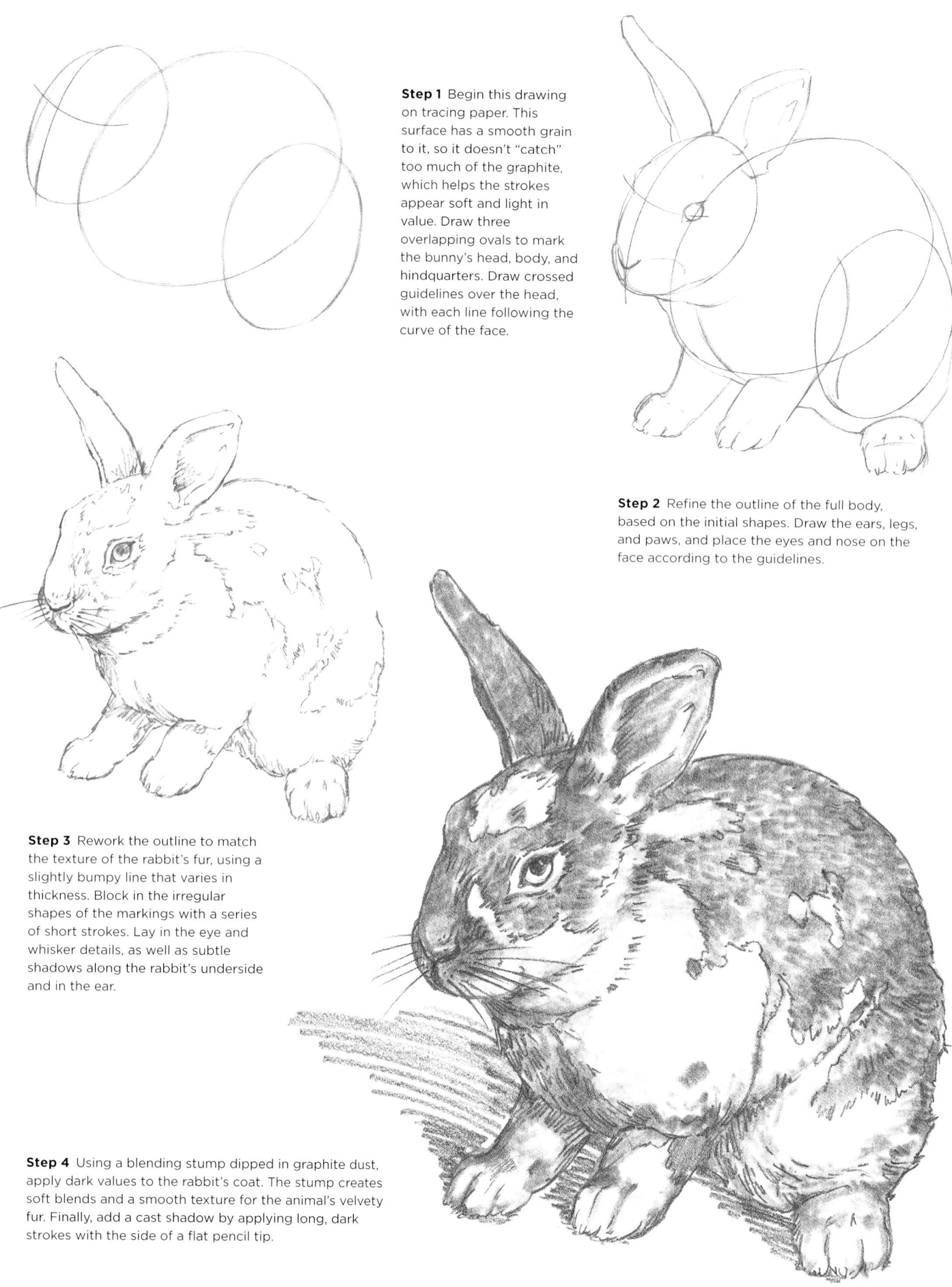

Step 1 Begin this drawing on tracing paper. This surface has a smooth grain to it, so it doesn't "catch" too much of the graphite, which helps the strokes appear soft and light in value. Draw three overlapping ovals to mark the bunny's head, body, and hindquarters. Draw crossed guidelines over the head, with each line following the curve of the face.

Step 2 Refine the outline of the full body, based on the initial shapes. Draw the ears, legs, and paws, and place the eyes and nose on the face according to the guidelines.

Step 3 Rework the outline to match the texture of the rabbit's fur, using a slightly bumpy line that varies in thickness. Block in the irregular shapes of the markings with a series of short strokes. Lay in the eye and whisker details, as well as subtle shadows along the rabbit's underside and in the ear.

Step 4 Using a blending stump dipped in graphite dust, apply dark values to the rabbit's coat. The stump creates soft blends and a smooth texture for the animal's velvety fur. Finally, add a cast shadow by applying long, dark strokes with the side of a flat pencil tip.

Guinea Pig

These balls of fluff have soft, silky coats; tiny little paws and ears; whiskers; and cute, curious eyes. A series of short hatch marks is enough to indicate fur in this project. Leave a tiny speck of white in the eye to show a glimmer of life.

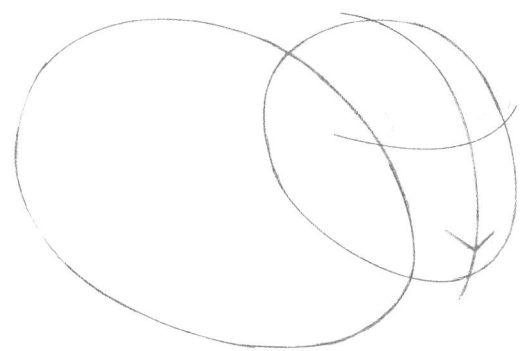

Step 1 Draw the head and body with two overlapping egg shapes. Draw a few guidelines for the features, dividing the face into quadrants and adding a V for the nose.

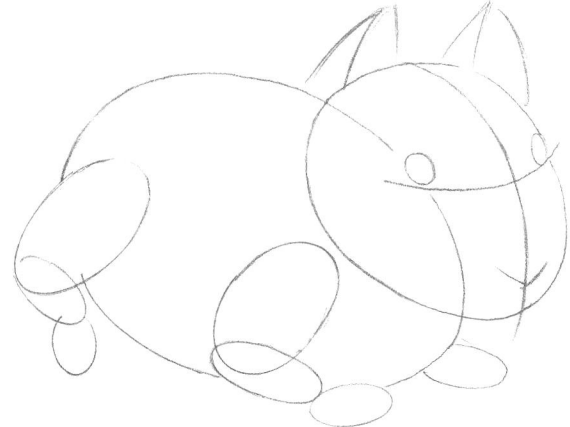

Step 2 Establish the underlying structure, indicating the legs and paws with a series of ovals. Add the position of the ears and place the eyes just above the horizontal guideline.

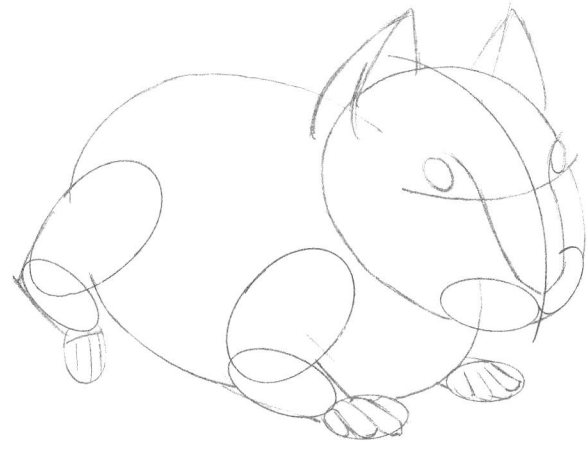

Step 3 Begin to define the toes on the paws. Draw the shape of the nasal area with a U-shaped line. Then use small ovals to define the cheek pouches.

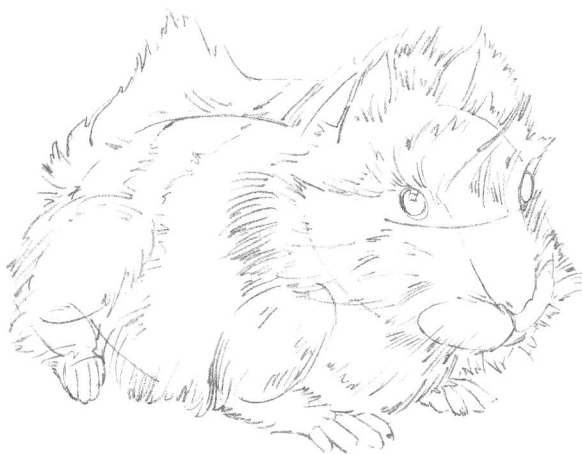

Step 4 Begin to render the thick, furry coat around the basic structure, applying short strokes of varying thicknesses. It's much easier to work out the direction of fur growth and the overall shape of the animal when you know what is underneath.

Step 5 Erase any guidelines and continue to develop the fur. With the broad side of a pencil, stroke light shadows around the edges of the guinea pig to suggest its roundness.

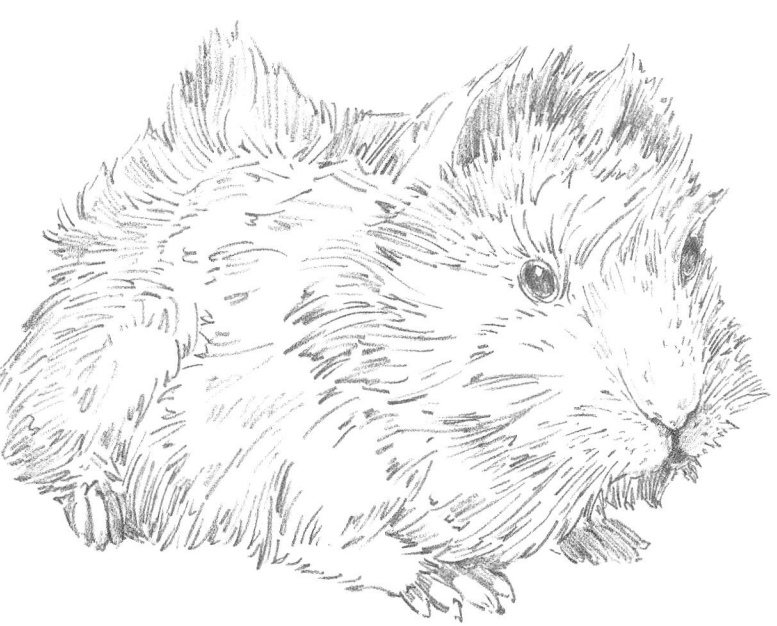

Budgerigars

Budgerigars, also known as "budgies" or parakeets, are a common type of pet bird. They are generally colorful with beautiful markings, and some have spots along the neck. These birds are very animated and will tilt their heads when they are curious about their surroundings.

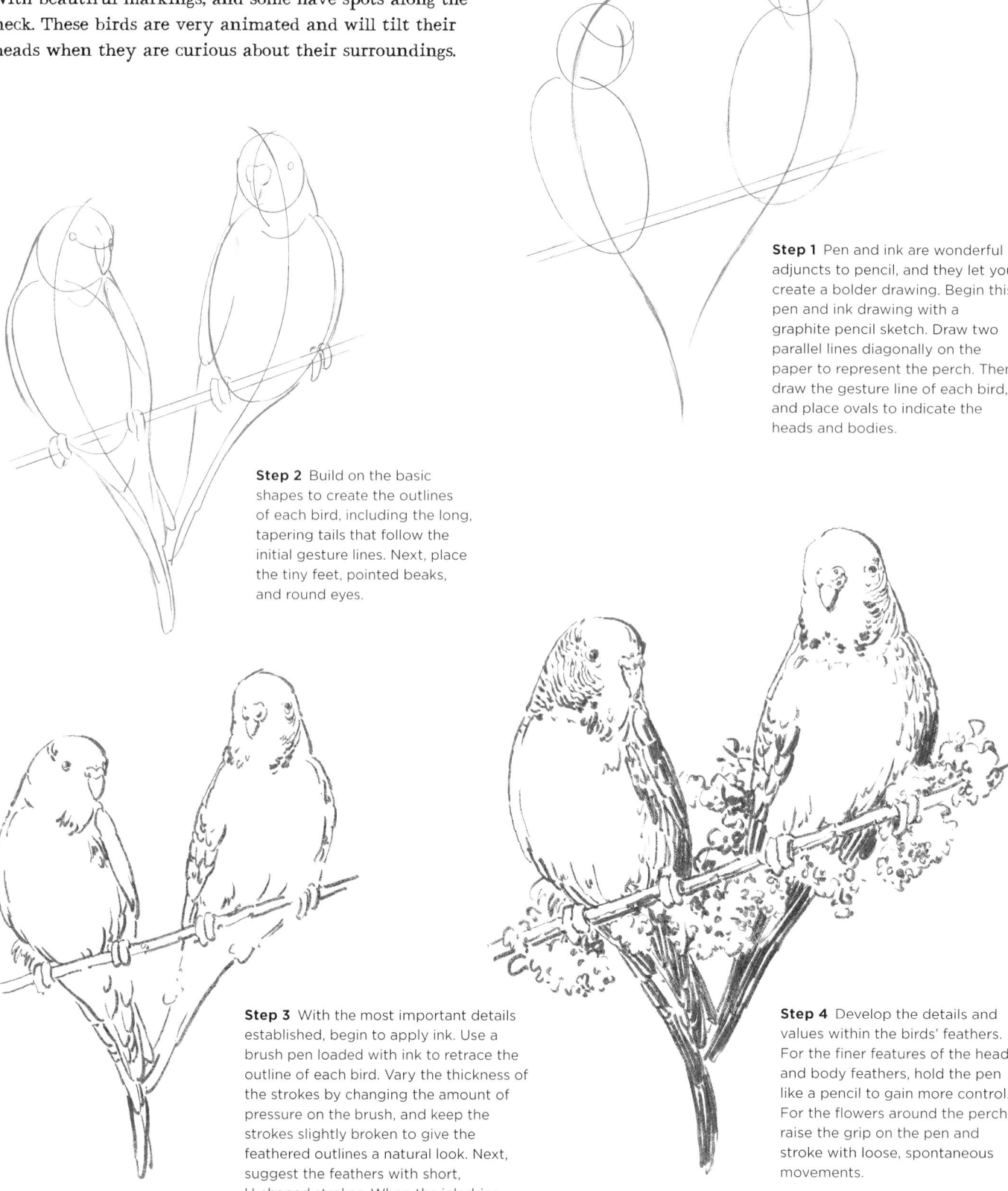

Step 1 Pen and ink are wonderful adjuncts to pencil, and they let you create a bolder drawing. Begin this pen and ink drawing with a graphite pencil sketch. Draw two parallel lines diagonally on the paper to represent the perch. Then draw the gesture line of each bird, and place ovals to indicate the heads and bodies.

Step 2 Build on the basic shapes to create the outlines of each bird, including the long, tapering tails that follow the initial gesture lines. Next, place the tiny feet, pointed beaks, and round eyes.

Step 3 With the most important details established, begin to apply ink. Use a brush pen loaded with ink to retrace the outline of each bird. Vary the thickness of the strokes by changing the amount of pressure on the brush, and keep the strokes slightly broken to give the feathered outlines a natural look. Next, suggest the feathers with short, U-shaped strokes. When the ink dries completely, erase old pencil guidelines.

Step 4 Develop the details and values within the birds' feathers. For the finer features of the head and body feathers, hold the pen like a pencil to gain more control. For the flowers around the perch, raise the grip on the pen and stroke with loose, spontaneous movements.

Ferret

This project begins with a series of connected ovals in a vertically angled line. This standing position is a realistic portrayal of ferret behavior. Ferrets are lean and agile creatures that make for active, playful, and curious pet friends.

Step 1 Build the long, thin body of this ferret around a natural, S-shaped curve. Along this line, place the head, neck, torso, arms, and legs with a series of ovals, making sure the body is properly proportioned and balanced before continuing.

Step 2 Loosely connect the ovals, further defining the ferret's outline. Then add in the curved tail, as well as the front and back paws. Place the cheek and ear.

Step 3 With the basic shape of the animal established, begin working on the coat. Outline the ferret with broken lines to create the illusion of ruffled fur, erasing the previous contoured lines used to establish the ferret's shape. Place the eye and nose at this stage. Refine the paws, indicating a suggestion of separation between the digits.

Step 4 Finish building up the coarse hair of the coat. Use more strokes to define the outer edges of the ferret, following the curvature of its form. To establish variation in value, place the darkest, densest strokes on the far limbs; this also produces the illusion that the limbs are farther back in the picture frame. Add whiskers and refine the eye and ears.

Parrot

Parrots are known for their beautiful color and markings, as well as their distinctive downward-sloping beak. Always make sure to shade feathers in the direction of growth. When drawing a colorful animal in graphite pencil, you can indicate color blocks and variations by adjusting the pressure of your shading.

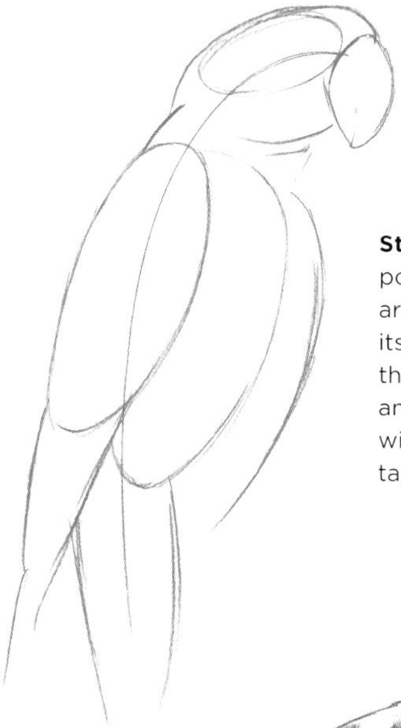

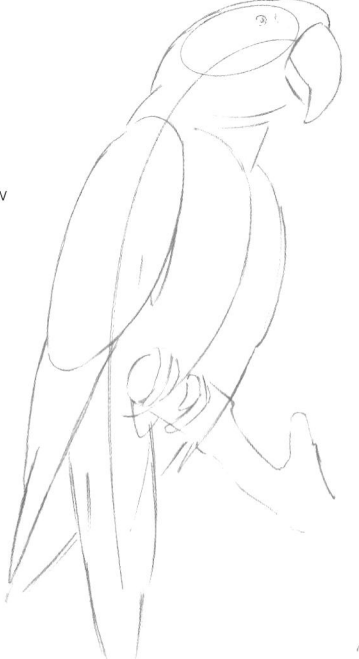

Step 1 Establish the overall pose by drawing a long, curved arc from the parrot's beak to its tail with an HB pencil. On this centerline, place the beak and build the head, chest, wings, and tail with ovals and tapering lines.

Step 2 Place the feet and add a perch to "ground" the parrot. Draw the eye and refine the outline of the beak, defining the upper and bottom parts.

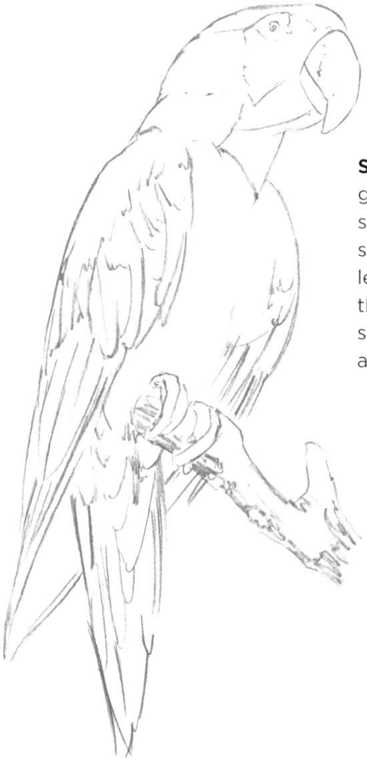

Step 3 Erase any unnecessary guidelines. Give the perch some form by scribbling shadows along the lower and left edges. Continue to refine the outlines, indicating the separations between the wing and tail feathers.

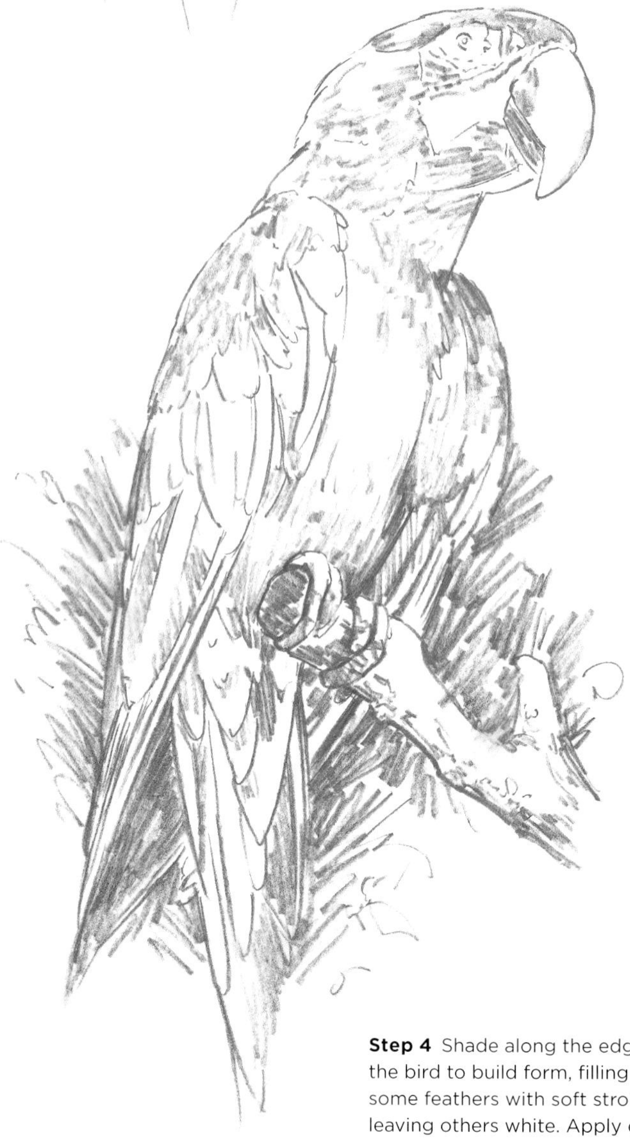

Step 4 Shade along the edges of the bird to build form, filling in some feathers with soft strokes and leaving others white. Apply quick, expressive strokes that radiate from the bird's body to convey spontaneity and dynamism.

Snake

They may not have fur or feathers, but many people keep snakes as pets. To draw this cold-blooded reptile, start with a squiggly line. Use curved lines to help guide you in drawing its thick, tubular shape.

Step 1 Lay in a squiggling gesture line, adding curved marks to define the roundness of the form. These lines will also act as guidelines for the pattern. Finally, rough in the rounded triangle form of the snake's head.

Step 2 Connect the curved strokes to outline the entire body, slightly building up the form of the head as well.

Step 3 Mark the general shapes of the skin pattern. These slightly irregular shapes roughly fall between the curved guidelines established in step 1.

Step 4 Fill in the pattern with a sharp 2B pencil. Keep the values lighter along the top of the snake's body, darkening them toward the ground. Add a few light hatch marks on the light-colored portions of the pattern to give the snake a round appearance. Then, create a ground shadow using short, energetic strokes to suggest a sense of movement.

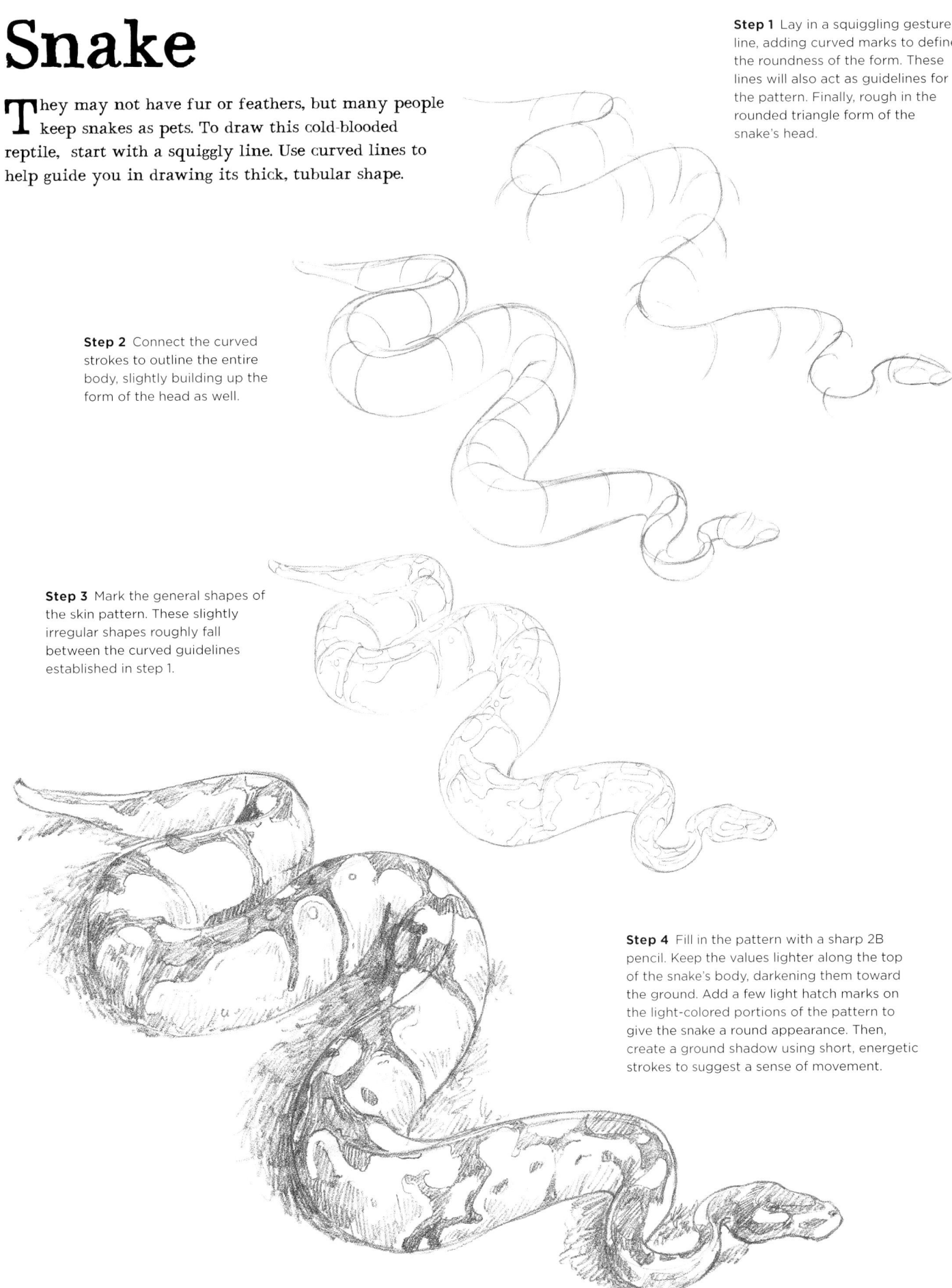

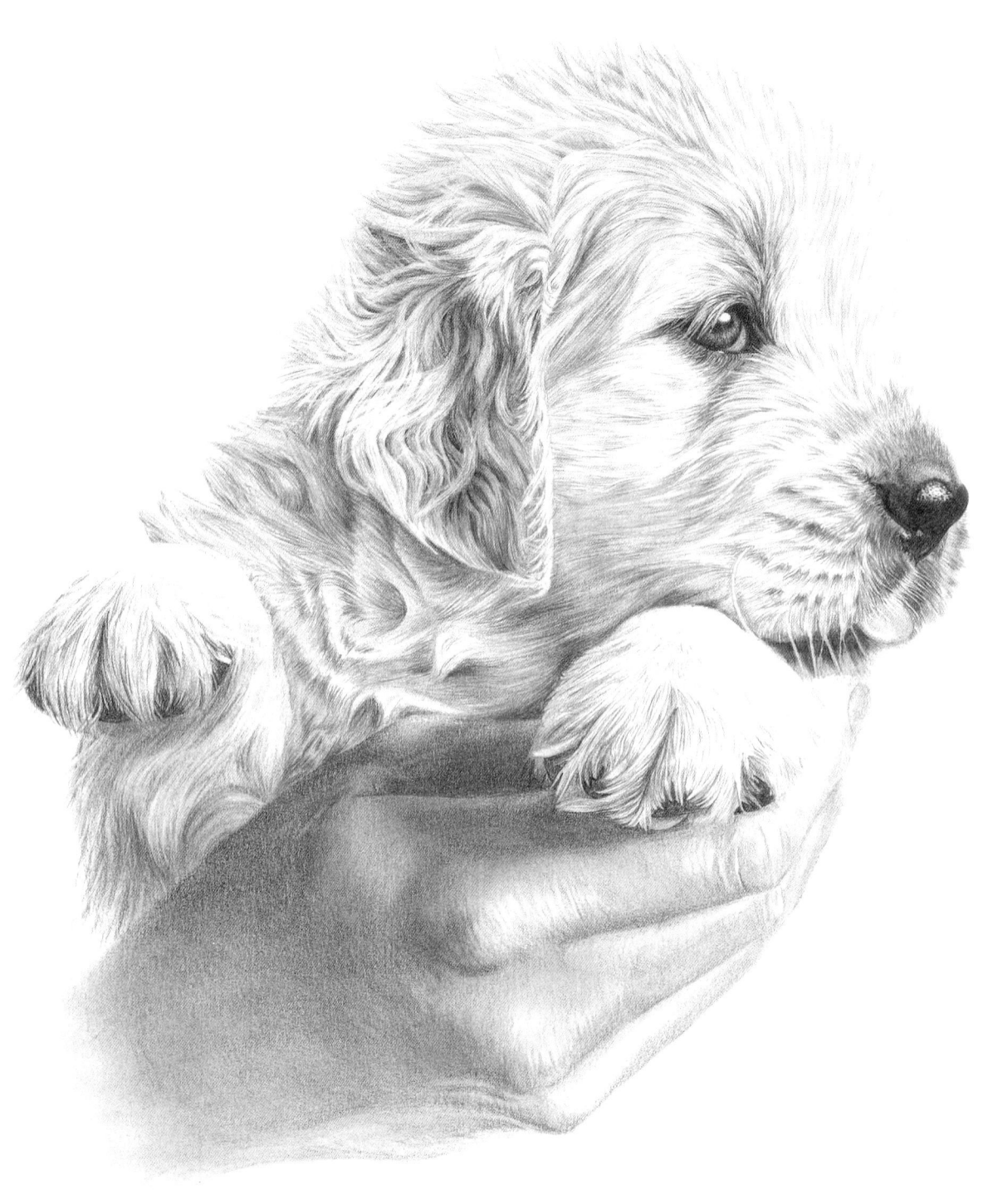

Dogs

Wet noses, floppy ears, fluffy coats, and beseeching eyes are just some of the qualities that make dogs a popular drawing subject. Dogs are known for having a range of expressions that communicate everything from joy, excitement, and curiosity—enough to keep a beginning artist busy, even if they are drawing the same subject over and over again.

This chapter provides a comprehensive overview for learning how to draw dogs of various shapes, sizes, and breeds. In addition to step-by-step tutorials for learning to draw a Great Dane, Irish Setter, English Bulldog, and Golden Retriever, you'll learn basic canine anatomy, fur-shading techniques, and how to capture details with accuracy and precision.

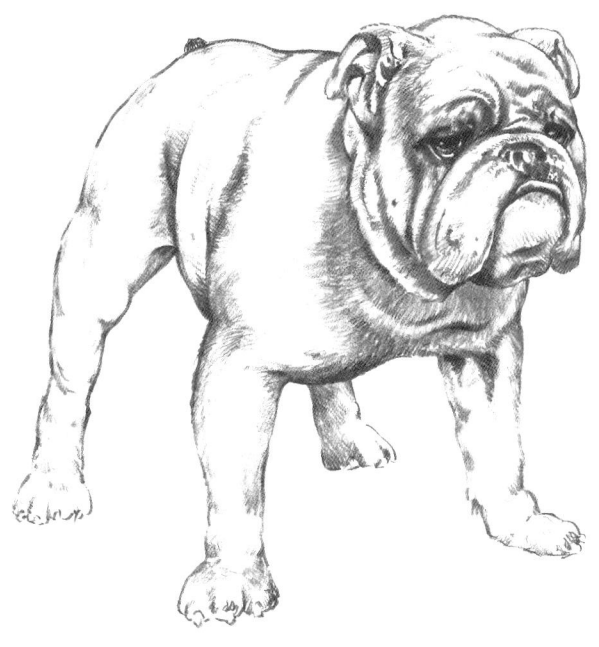

Depicting Dogs

Dogs aren't only a human's best friend, they are also a favorite subject of artists. Even people who don't have a dog of their own find them appealing to draw because they are so accessible and expressive. They also come in so many different shapes and sizes; you can make hundreds of drawings without ever drawing the same dog twice!

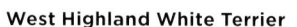

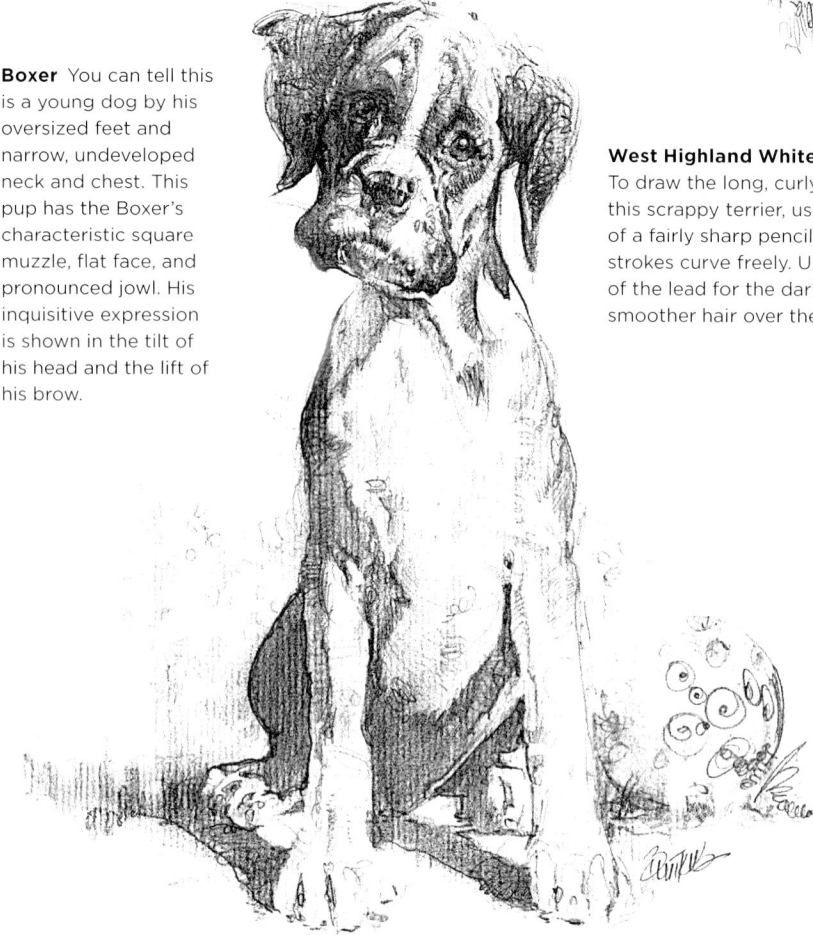

Boxer You can tell this is a young dog by his oversized feet and narrow, undeveloped neck and chest. This pup has the Boxer's characteristic square muzzle, flat face, and pronounced jowl. His inquisitive expression is shown in the tilt of his head and the lift of his brow.

West Highland White Terrier To draw the long, curly hair of this scrappy terrier, use the point of a fairly sharp pencil and let the strokes curve freely. Use the side of the lead for the dark area of smoother hair over the dog's back.

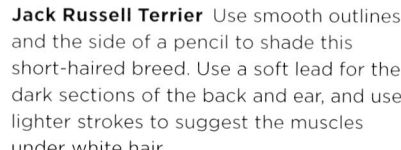

Jack Russell Terrier Use smooth outlines and the side of a pencil to shade this short-haired breed. Use a soft lead for the dark sections of the back and ear, and use lighter strokes to suggest the muscles under white hair.

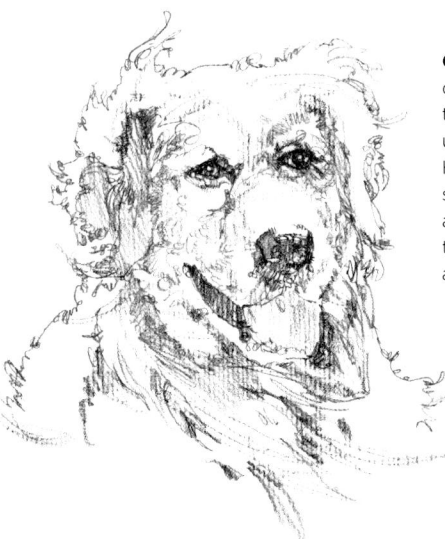

Golden Retriever This dog has a long, silky coat that obscures its underlying shape. Use an HB pencil in long, flowing strokes around the neck and free-form loops around the outline. Shade the eyes and nose darkly with a 2B.

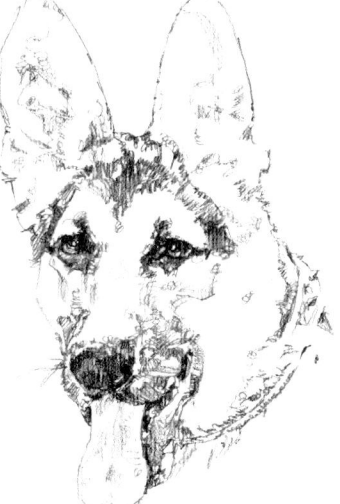

German Shepherd This breed has large pointed ears, a narrow muzzle, and thick fur with a dark "mask" above the eyes. After laying in the middle values with an HB pencil, use a blunt-tipped 2B for the dark areas of fur, making short, vertical strokes in the direction of hair growth.

STUDYING YOUR SUBJECT

Although all dogs have a similar skeletal structure, there are many differences among the various breeds that you'll want to capture in your drawings. Look carefully at your subject—whether a live model or a photograph—and try to duplicate the unique characteristics you see. Is the muzzle pointed or square? Do the ears stick straight up or flop down? Are they sharply angled or round? Is the hair long and straight, short and curly, rough, or smooth? Then when you're ready to start drawing, follow the steps in the box below: blocking, refining, shading, and adding details.

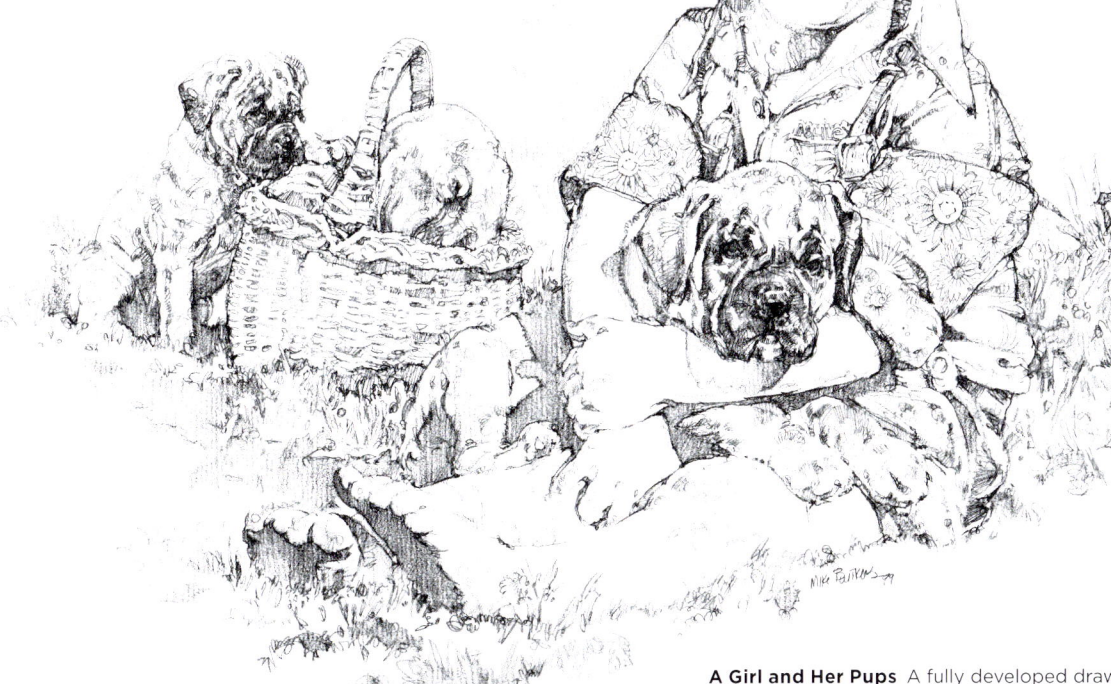

A Girl and Her Pups A fully developed drawing with a background and props tells a story. For complex scenes like this one, it's often easier to work from photographs, since neither puppies nor children tend to stay still for long! Notice the foreshortening on the little girl's legs. (See pages 75 and 131 for more on foreshortening.)

DRAWING STEP BY STEP

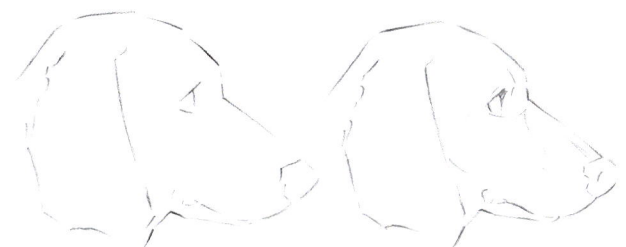

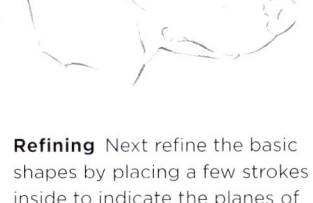

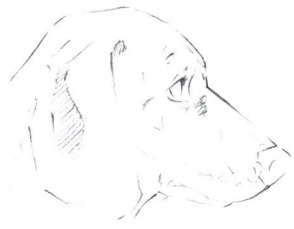

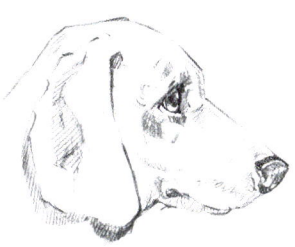

Blocking Begin by blocking in the most simple shapes that make up the overall shape of the head. Use the side of an HB pencil, and make quick strokes to sketch the angles.

Refining Next refine the basic shapes by placing a few strokes inside to indicate the planes of the face and the line of the nostril. Use the same loose pencil technique.

Shading Now refine the lines and develop the form a bit more by blocking in the basic shading. Use the side and point of a rounded HB pencil for this step.

Adding Details Use both the side and tip of a sharp HB pencil to define the hairs and develop shadows further. Use the point of a sharp 2B pencil for deep shadows. Smudge softly.

Proportion & Anatomy

To accurately render the various dog breeds, it's necessary to draw the body parts in the proper proportion. Proportion is the relationship between the different aspects of your drawing. An effective method for establishing proportion is to use one body part as a unit of measurement for determining the size of the other parts. For instance, you can use the dog's head to determine the length and height of the dog's body; the dog to the right is about 4 heads long and 3½ heads high. Make certain the proportions are accurate before working on any details.

Knowledge of basic anatomy will also help you accurately draw your subject. The diagram below illustrates the various parts of the dog. As you study the dogs in this section, notice how these parts differ according to breed.

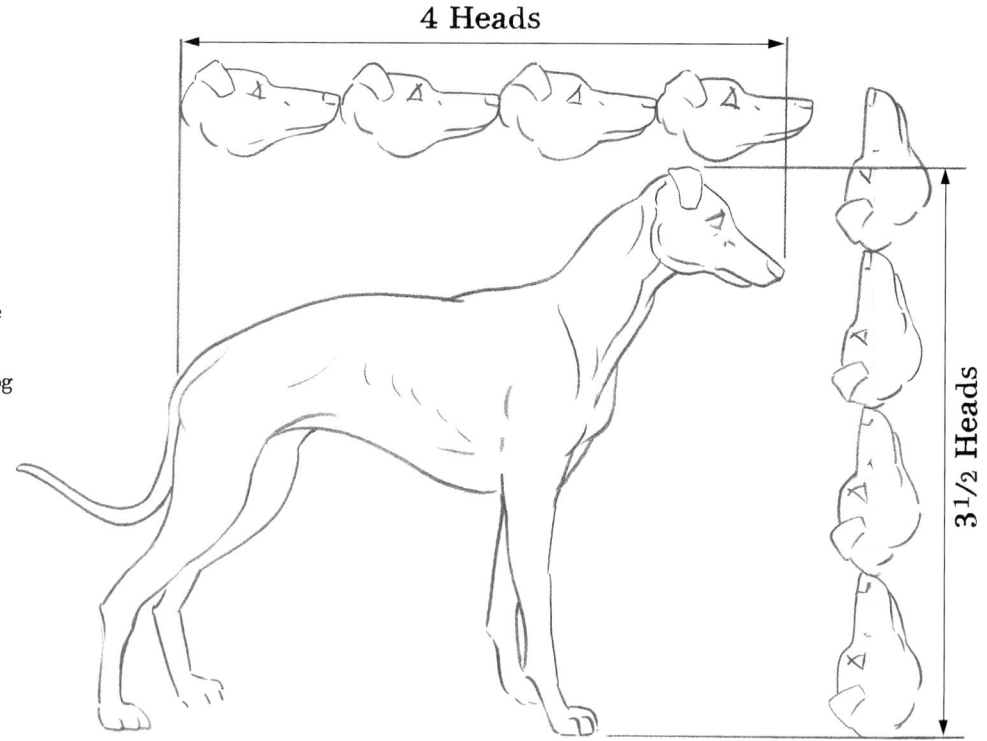

4 Heads

3½ Heads

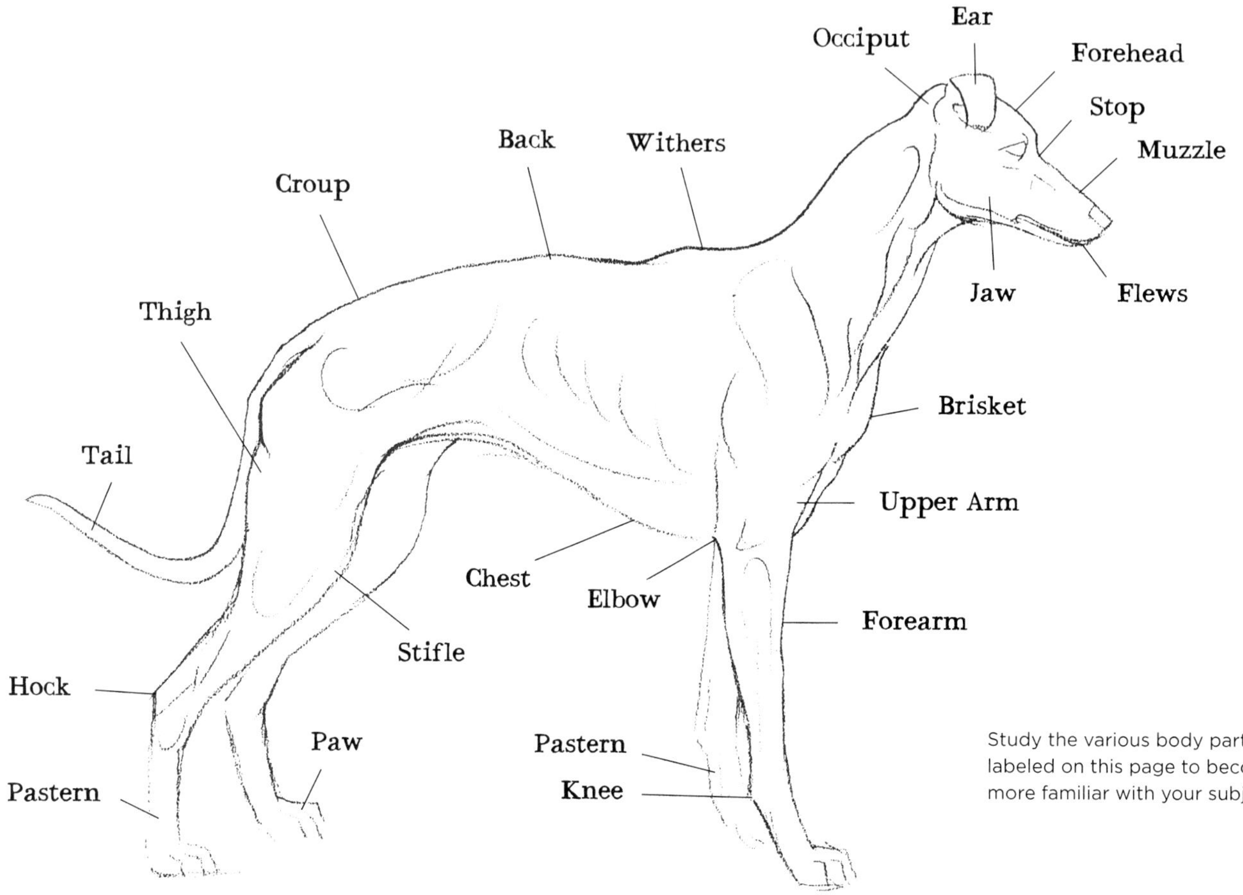

Occiput
Ear
Forehead
Stop
Muzzle

Back
Withers

Croup

Thigh

Jaw
Flews

Tail

Brisket

Upper Arm

Chest
Elbow

Forearm

Stifle

Hock

Paw

Pastern
Knee

Pastern

Study the various body parts labeled on this page to become more familiar with your subject.

Muscular structure also affects an animal's form, determining where the contours of the body bulge and curve. Therefore, knowledge of muscle construction allows you to shade drawing subjects with better insight, and your work will be more convincing.

The diagrams on this page illustrate the dog's basic muscular structure. Study the muscles closely, and keep them in mind as you draw. As you observe your subject or model, consider how the location of the muscles might affect your shading.

Once the basic drawing is correct, you can begin to develop the details. The illustrations below demonstrate in steps how to render a dog's eye and paw. Begin with very simple lines, and slowly refine the shapes. Use a sharp pencil for bringing out the fine details in the eye and for rendering the fur along the paw. Follow the steps closely to achieve a good likeness.

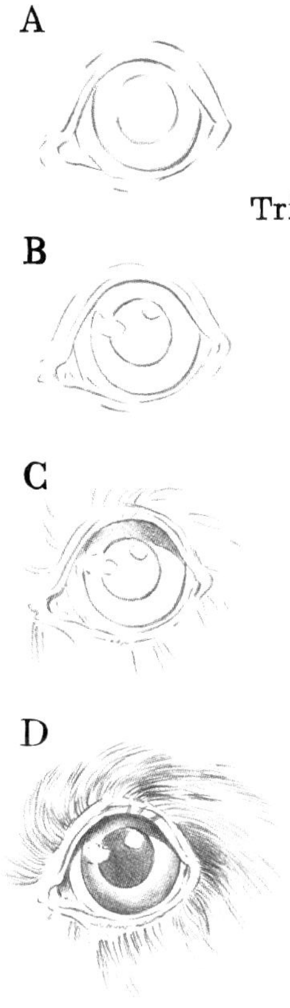

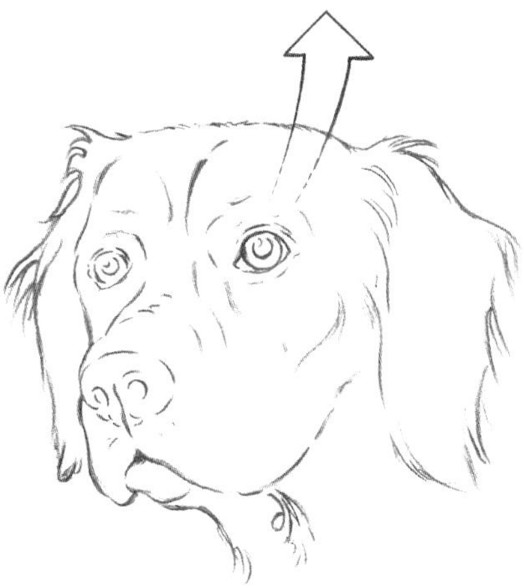

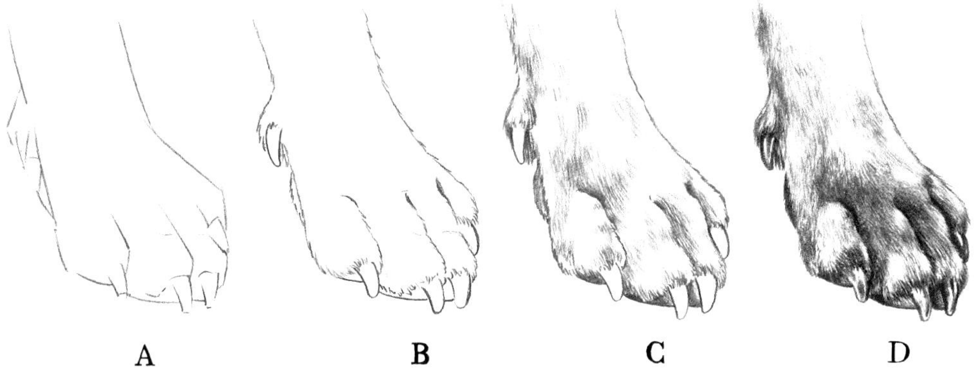

A

B

C

D

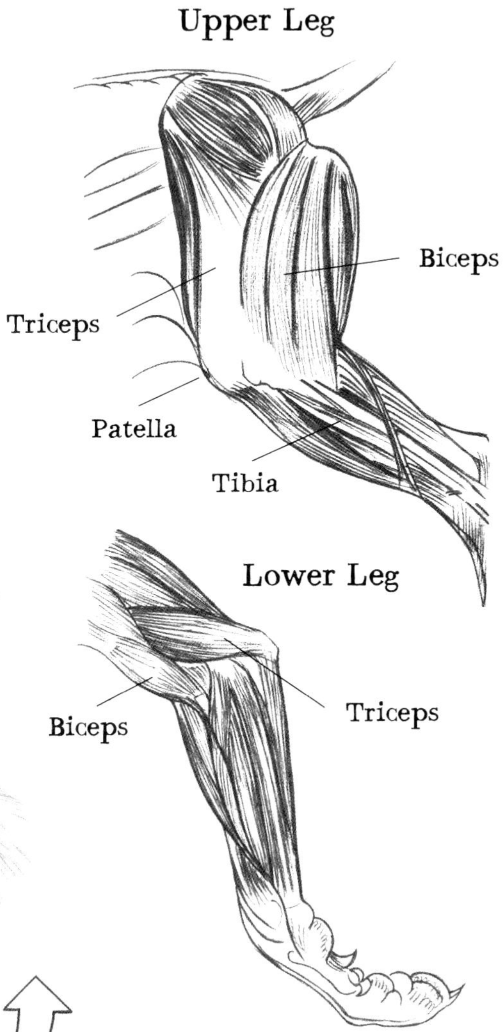

Upper Leg

Biceps

Triceps

Patella

Tibia

Lower Leg

Biceps

Triceps

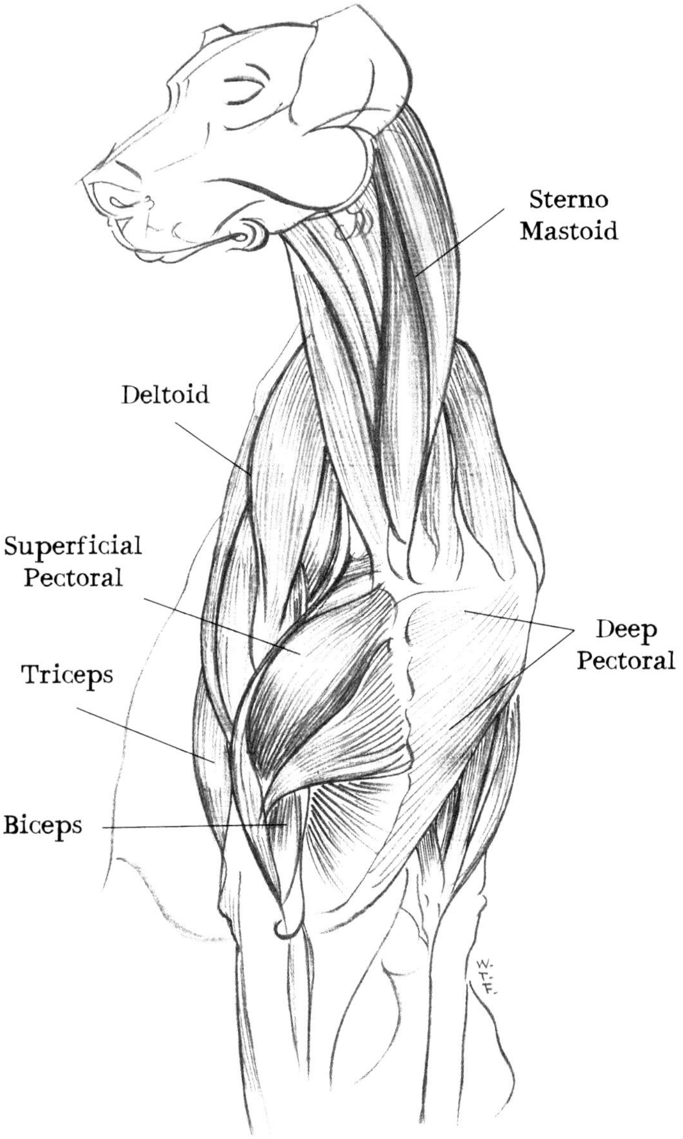

Sterno Mastoid

Deltoid

Superficial Pectoral

Triceps

Biceps

Deep Pectoral

A

B

C

D

Fur Shading Techniques

Mastering shading techniques allows you to transform lines and shapes into three-dimensional objects. By learning how to apply a variety of shading strokes, you will be able to effectively bring out the dog's form and render the texture of the fur. Dogs often exhibit different fur textures. Some areas may be long and wavy, while other areas may be short and smooth.

Note the different kinds of lines each type of drawing tool produces.

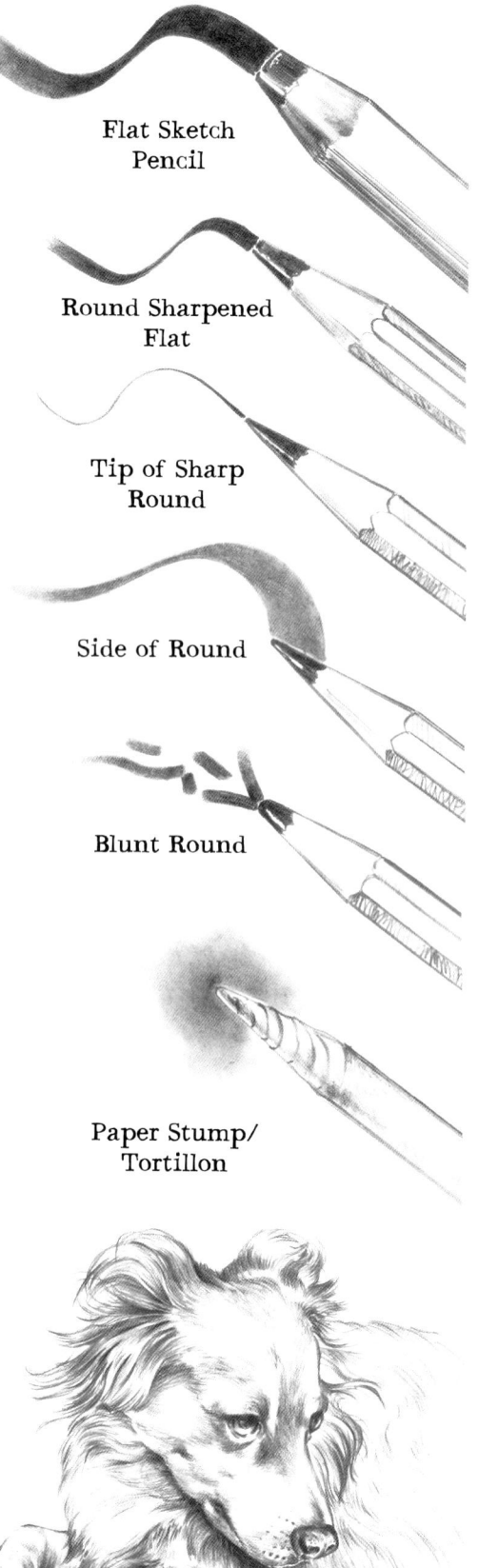

Flat Sketch Pencil

Round Sharpened Flat

Tip of Sharp Round

Side of Round

Blunt Round

Paper Stump/ Tortillon

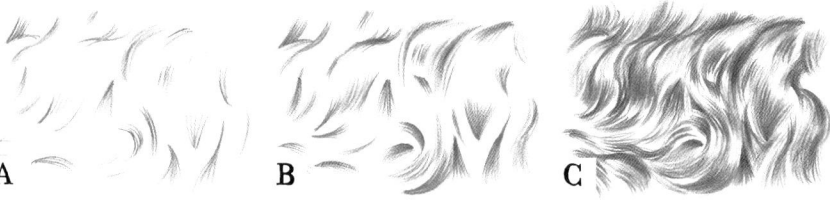

A   B   C

To recreate the thick, wavy fur above (typical of dogs such as Golden Retrievers), lightly sketch a few short curves in various directions. Develop the texture by adding darker strokes, bringing out sections or individual strands within the coat. When drawing a tight rendering, it's important to work slowly and make each stroke deliberate so the fur doesn't appear sloppy.

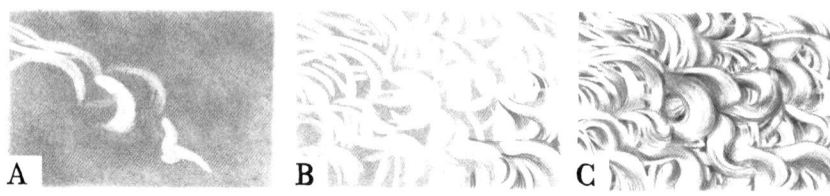

A   B   C

The tight curls above are typical of breeds like the Poodle. To create this texture, use a sharp knife to scrape graphite from a 2B pencil onto the surface. With a soft cloth, gently rub the graphite; then, use the corner of a kneaded eraser to pull out small curls from the gray. Finally, develop the form of the strands by shading with a sharp HB pencil.

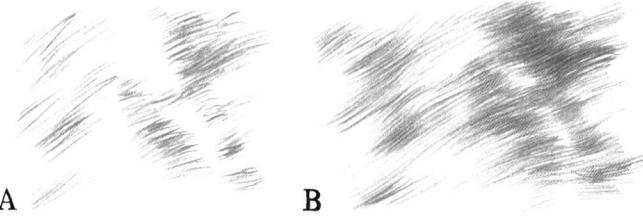

A   B

This fur texture appears shorter and smoother than the fur in the examples above. It can be found on breeds such as Dalmatians, Doberman Pinschers, and Labrador Retrievers. Make sure your strokes follow the direction of the hair growth, creating a sleek coat with mild highlights and shadows.

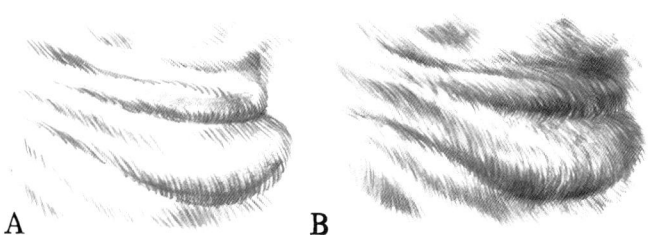

A   B

This type of fur is typical of breeds such as the Shar-Pei, covering loose folds of skin. The shading inside the folds is dark, gradually becoming lighter on top of the folds. By applying strokes in the same general direction, value changes can create unique textures and forms.

Muzzles

Muzzle shape varies depending on the breed. Some are long and narrow, while others are short and wide. These characteristics will affect your drawing, so observe your subjects well. To draw the nose, lightly sketch the basic shapes in step A. Refine the lines, and begin shading inside the nostrils with a sharp pencil in step B. The shading should be darkest near the inside curve of each nostril. In step C, continue shading the nose. Keep in mind that the fur grows outward from the nose, as shown in the final step.

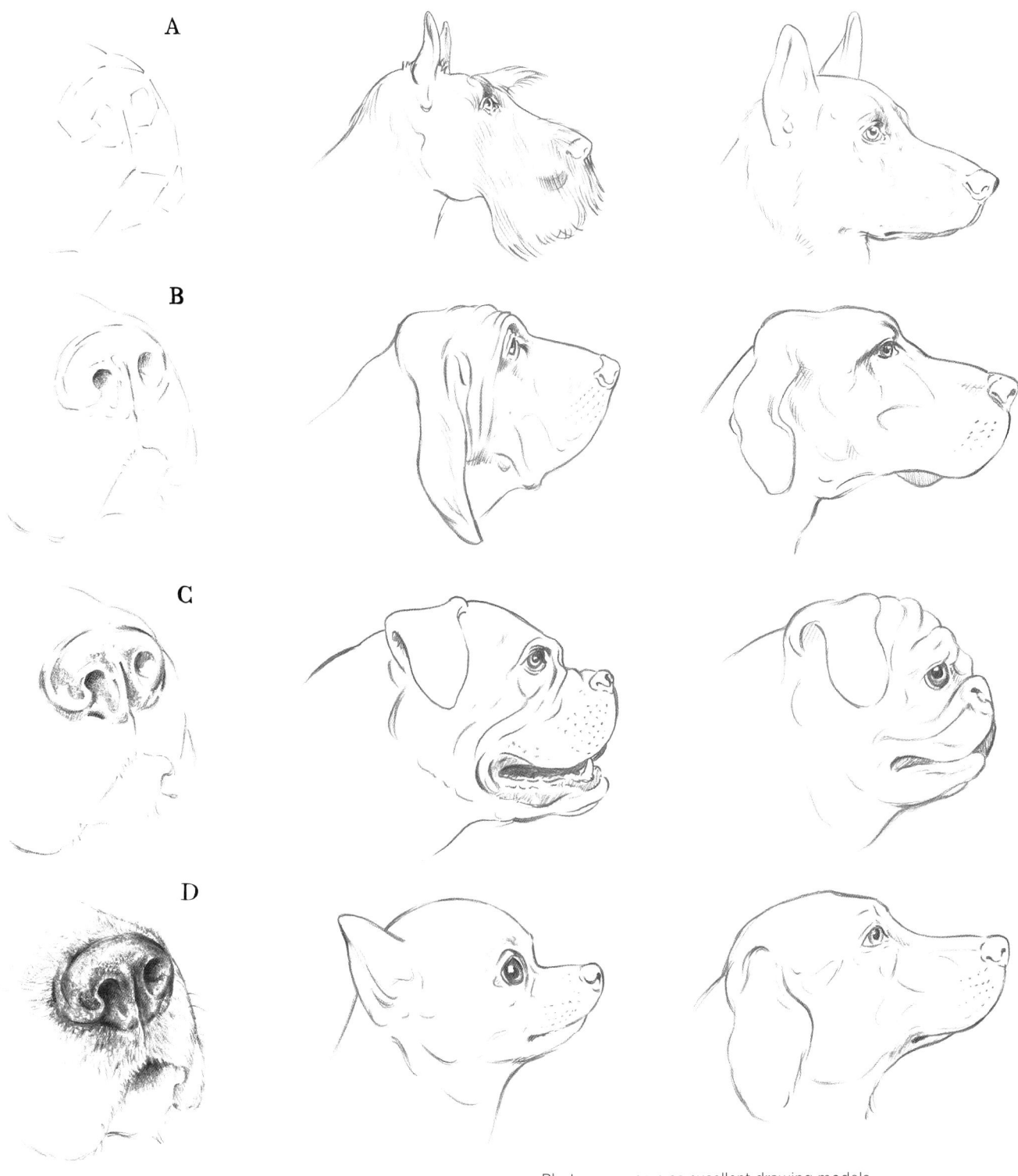

A

B

C

D

Photos can serve as excellent drawing models.
Keep a file of photos for reference while you work.

Puppies

The most important thing to remember when learning to draw is to take it step by step. Focus on learning the drawing process rather than the final product for right now. If you are a beginner, block in with pencil first, and then go over the lines with ink.

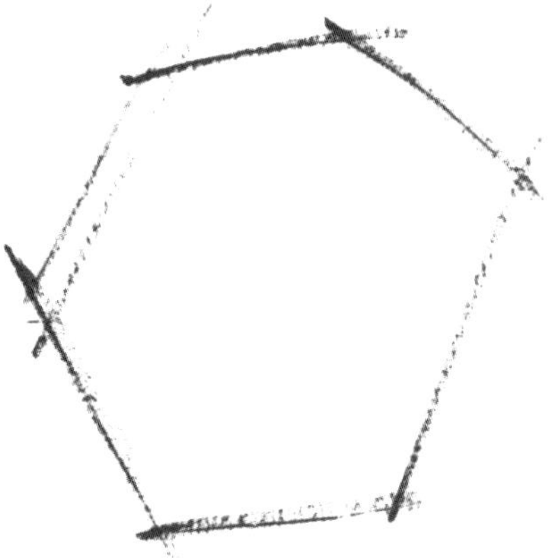

Step 1 Block in the Cocker Spaniel's head with a hexagon shape.

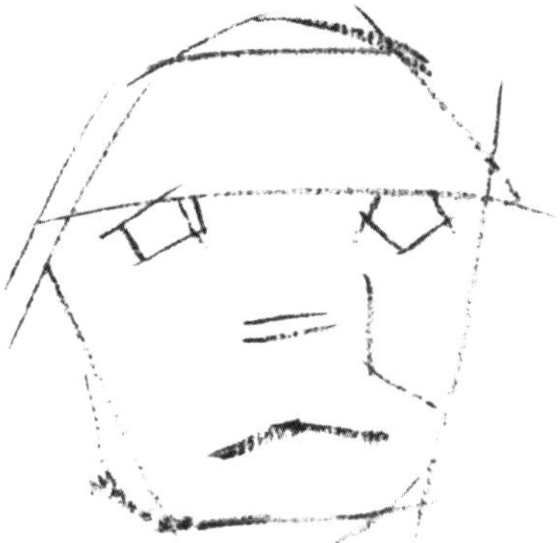

HB

Step 2 Determine placement of the facial features, and block them in with basic lines.

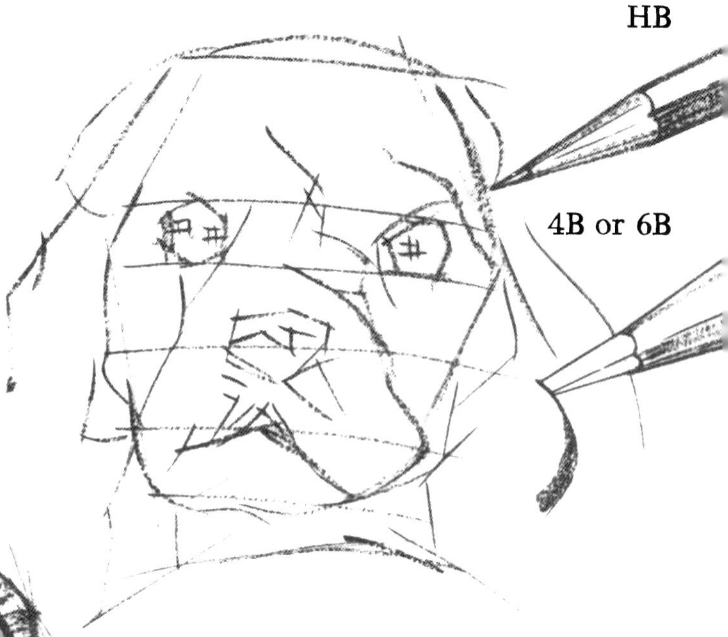

4B or 6B

Step 3 Continue to build out the details, erasing old sketch lines as you go.

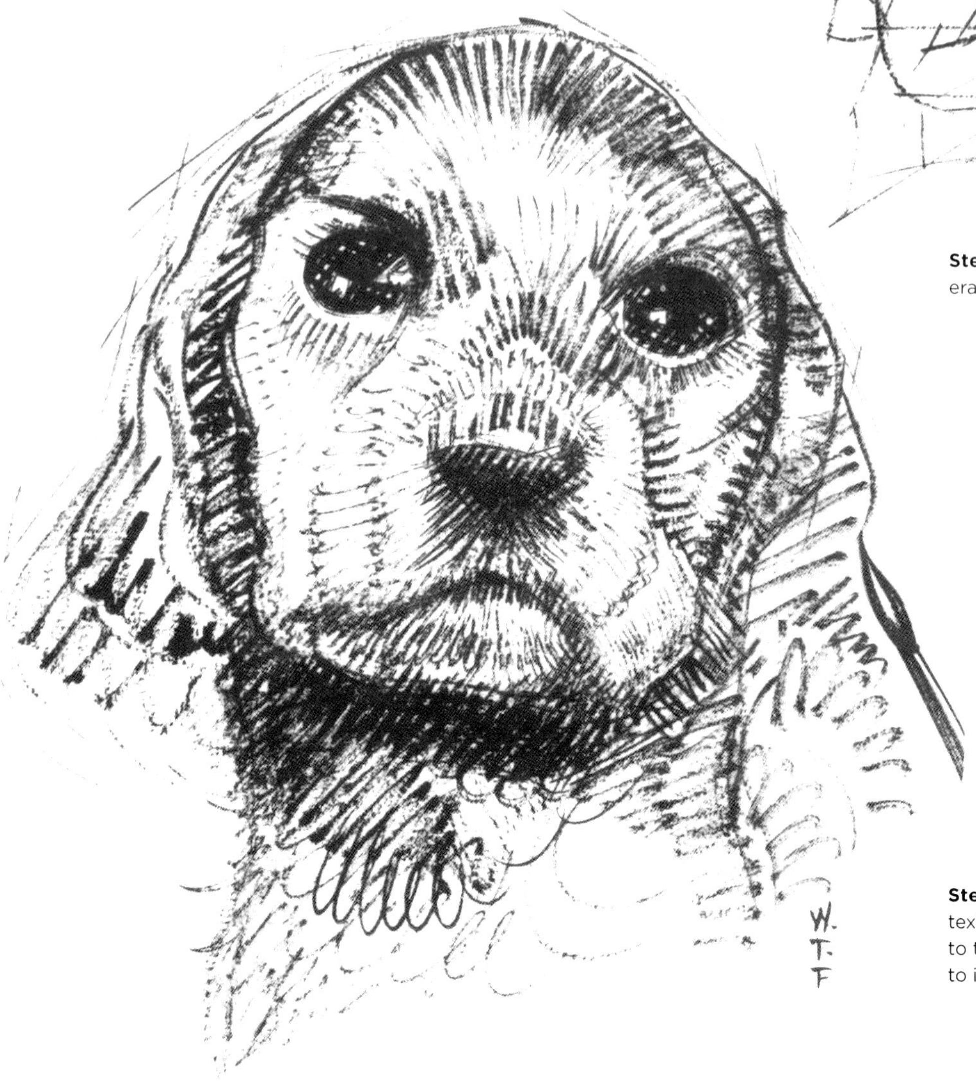

Step 4 Add shading to indicate the texture of the fur. Add dark shading to the eyes, saving a tiny white space to indicate a light source.

W. T. F

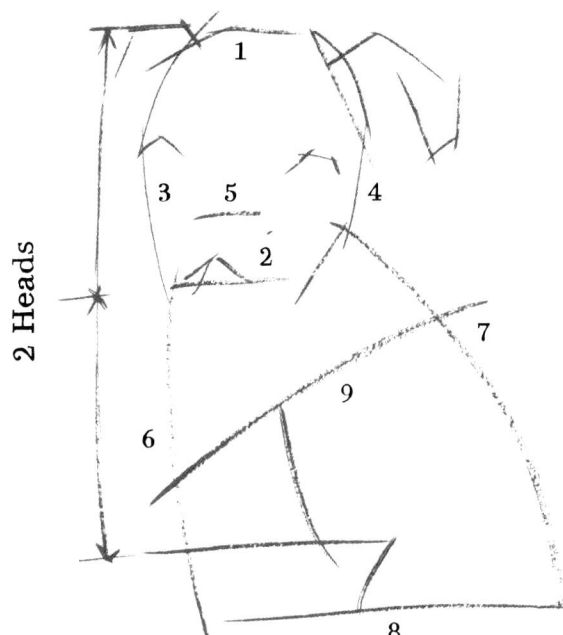

Step 1 Block in the basic shapes using an HB pencil. To help gauge the proportions, notice that the puppy's body is a little more than two times the size of its head. If it helps, draw each line in numbered order, as shown.

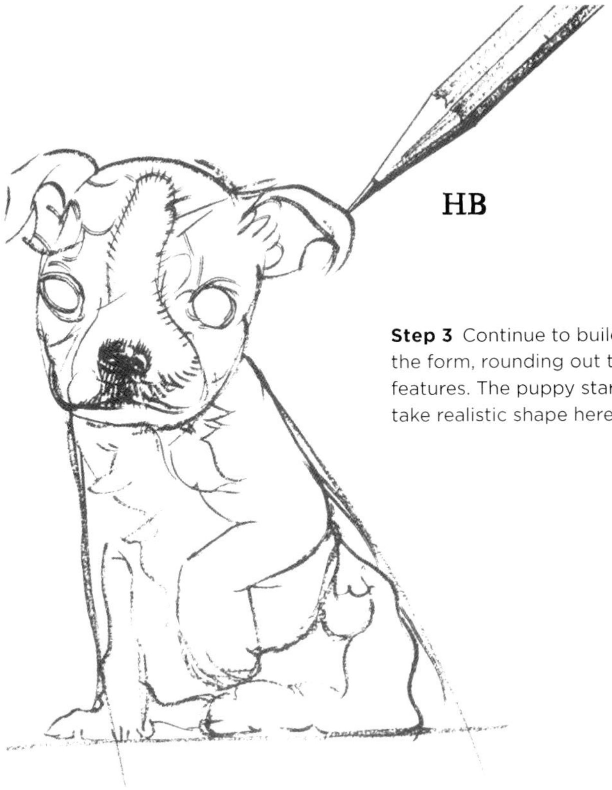

HB

Step 3 Continue to build out the form, rounding out the features. The puppy starts to take realistic shape here.

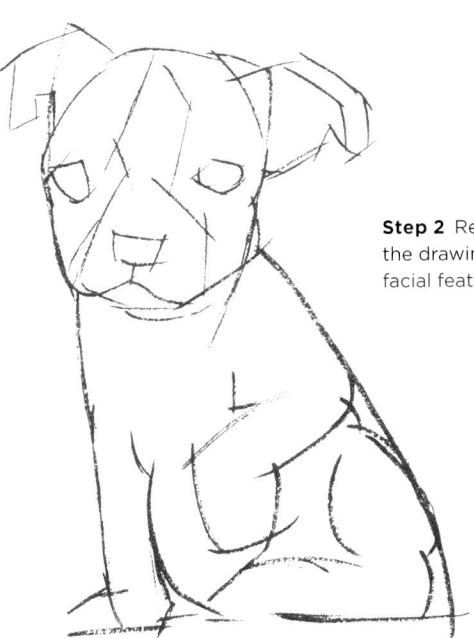

Step 2 Refine the shapes of the drawing, and block in the facial features.

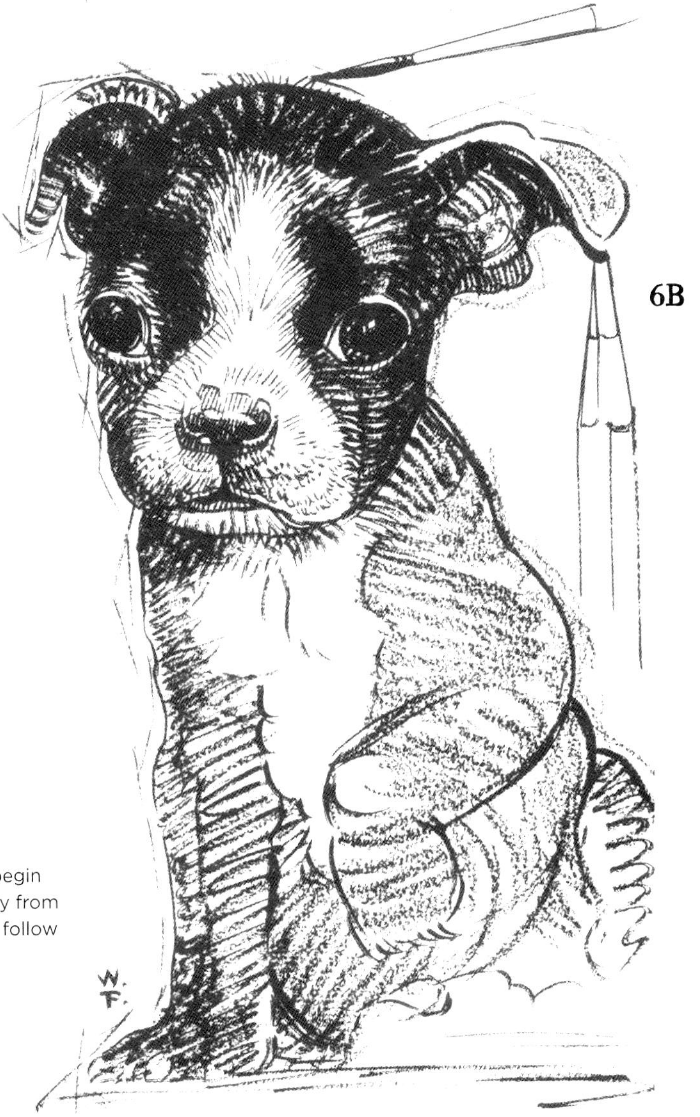

6B

Step 4 Using a 6B pencil, begin shading. Apply strokes away from the nose and spread out to follow the curves of the head.

W. F.

Great Dane

Great Danes have elegant stature and unique faces. While their enormous size may be slightly intimidating (they can reach 30 inches tall at the shoulder), they are actually very gentle and affectionate, especially with children.

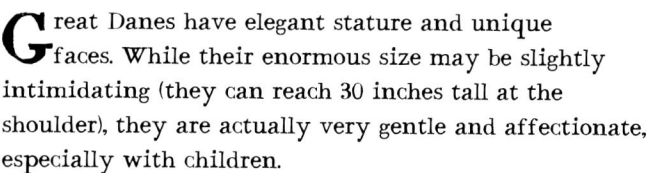

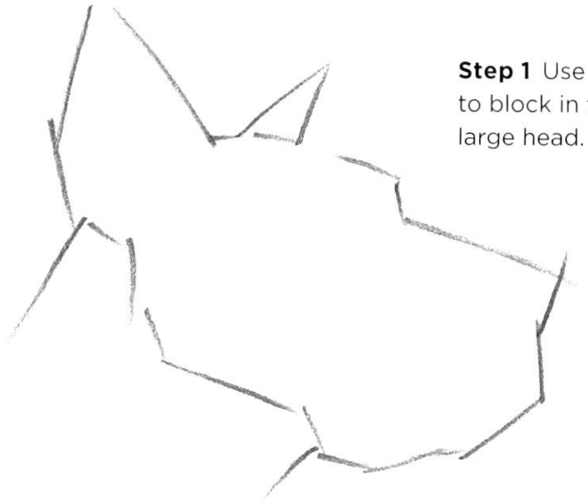

Step 1 Use an HB pencil to block in the dog's large head.

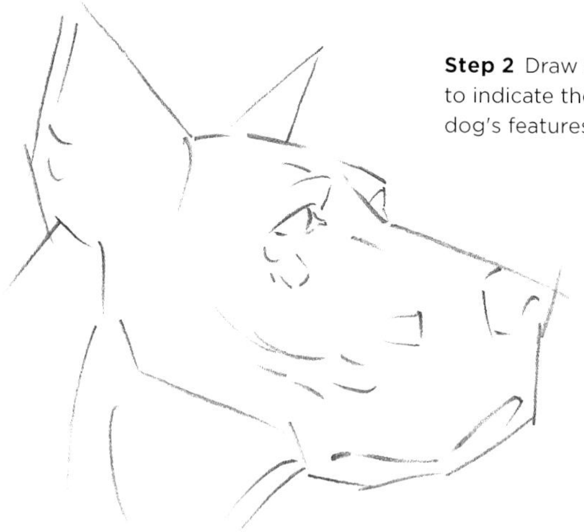

Step 2 Draw rough sketch lines to indicate the placement of the dog's features.

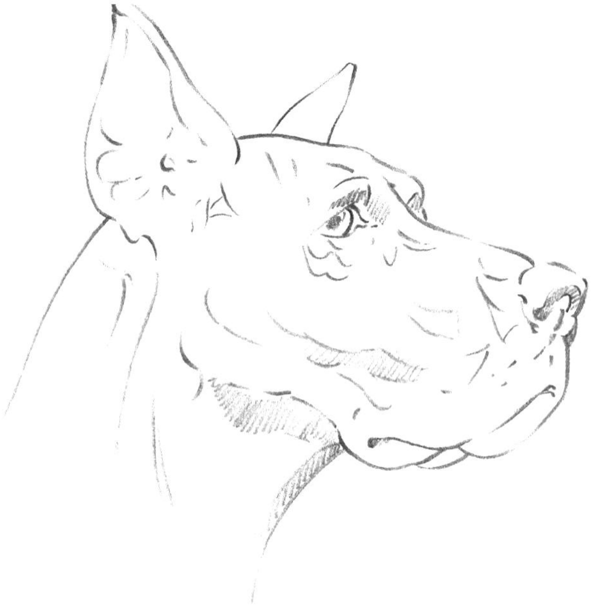

Step 3 Refine the shapes, and lightly shade with a 2B pencil to bring out the form and contours of the head. The minimal shading will give the coat a smooth appearance.

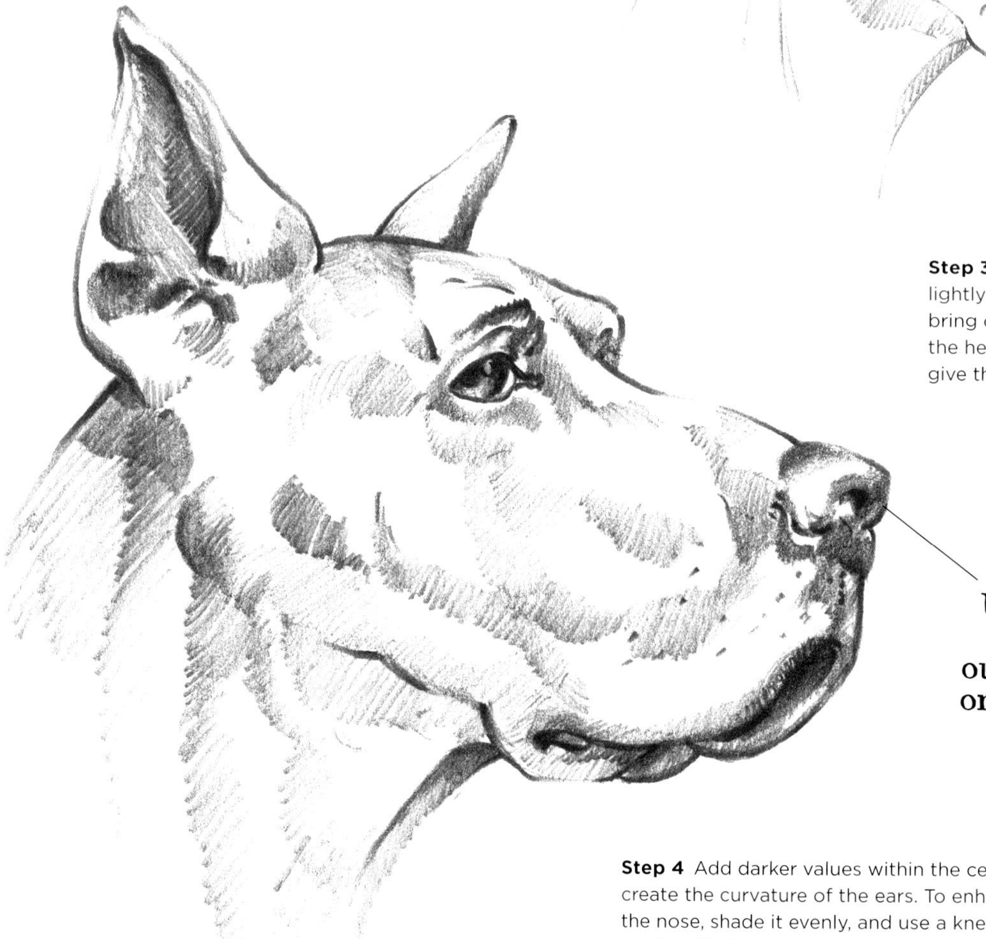

Use a kneaded eraser to pull out the highlight on the dog's nose.

Step 4 Add darker values within the center of the ear to create the curvature of the ears. To enhance the shine of the nose, shade it evenly, and use a kneaded eraser to pull out highlights.

Irish Setter

To capture the active disposition of an Irish Setter puppy, it's best to find a live model to study its mannerisms and expressions. Although the puppies are often shy, if you treat them kindly, they will quickly learn to show affection.

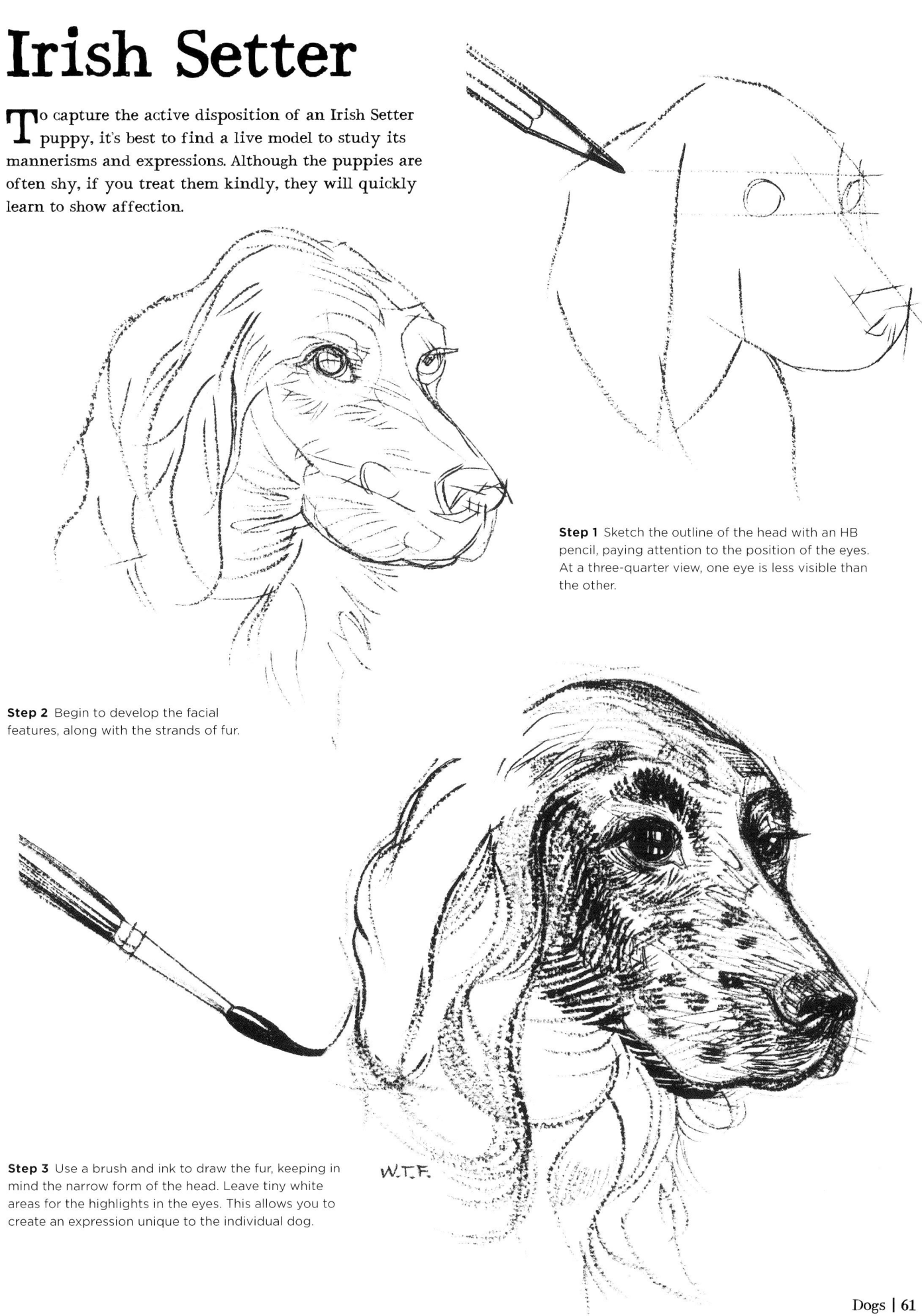

Step 1 Sketch the outline of the head with an HB pencil, paying attention to the position of the eyes. At a three-quarter view, one eye is less visible than the other.

Step 2 Begin to develop the facial features, along with the strands of fur.

Step 3 Use a brush and ink to draw the fur, keeping in mind the narrow form of the head. Leave tiny white areas for the highlights in the eyes. This allows you to create an expression unique to the individual dog.

W.T.F.

English Springer Spaniel

The wavy coat and friendly expression of the English Springer Spaniel seem challenging to draw. Just take your time and follow the steps. You'll see that it's not as difficult as it looks.

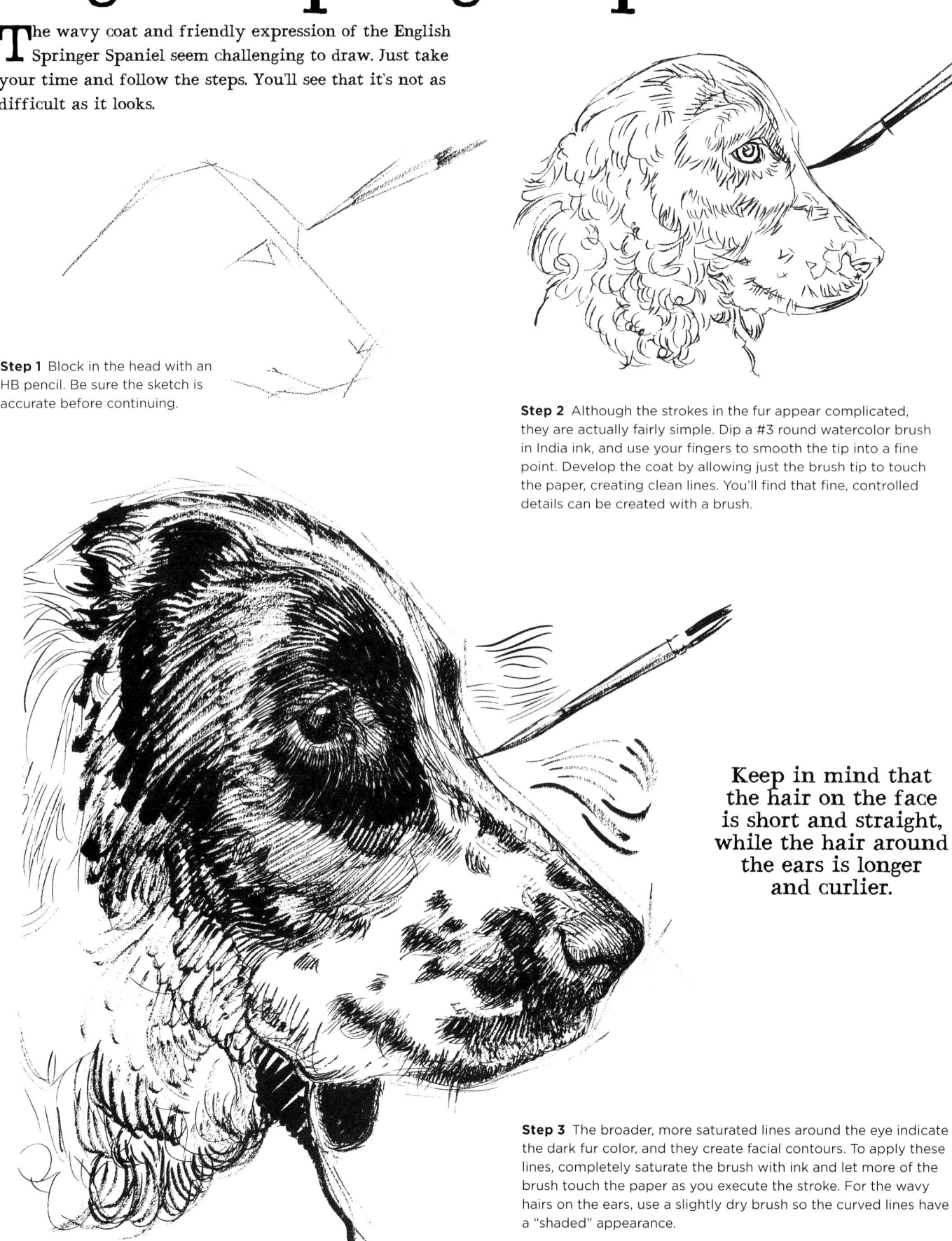

Step 1 Block in the head with an HB pencil. Be sure the sketch is accurate before continuing.

Step 2 Although the strokes in the fur appear complicated, they are actually fairly simple. Dip a #3 round watercolor brush in India ink, and use your fingers to smooth the tip into a fine point. Develop the coat by allowing just the brush tip to touch the paper, creating clean lines. You'll find that fine, controlled details can be created with a brush.

Keep in mind that the hair on the face is short and straight, while the hair around the ears is longer and curlier.

Step 3 The broader, more saturated lines around the eye indicate the dark fur color, and they create facial contours. To apply these lines, completely saturate the brush with ink and let more of the brush touch the paper as you execute the stroke. For the wavy hairs on the ears, use a slightly dry brush so the curved lines have a "shaded" appearance.

Shar-Pei Puppy

The Shar-Pei is probably best known for its loose folds of skin. These wrinkles seem to give this breed a worried expression. The puppy shown here has looser skin than an adult, but eventually, the body will fill out.

Step 1 Use short strokes to create the outline. Indicate the folds with zigzagging lines.

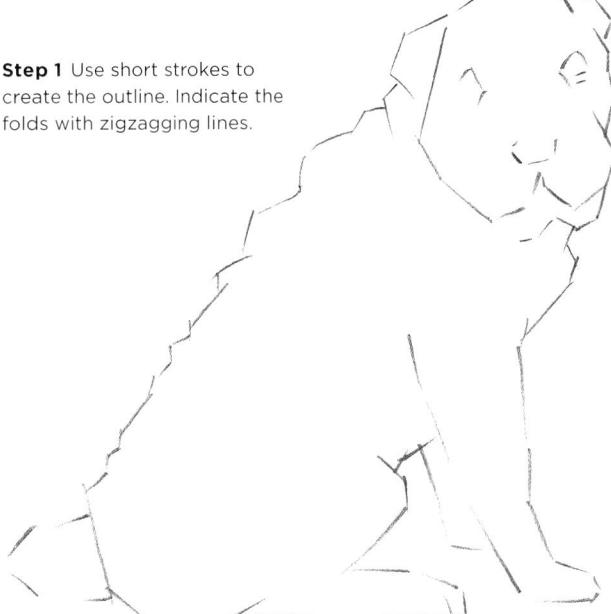

Step 2 To develop the folds, start by lightly shading inside the creases. Give equal attention to each fold so the dog appears realistic.

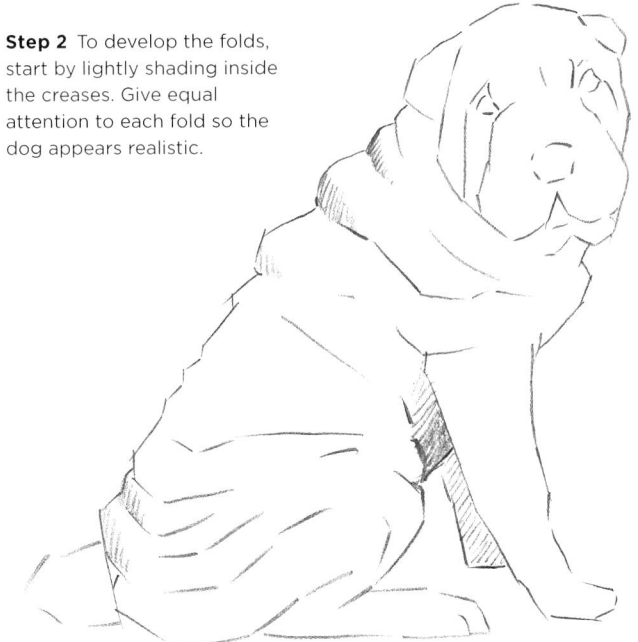

Step 4 Refine your drawing, lifting out highlights with a kneaded eraser and erasing old sketch lines.

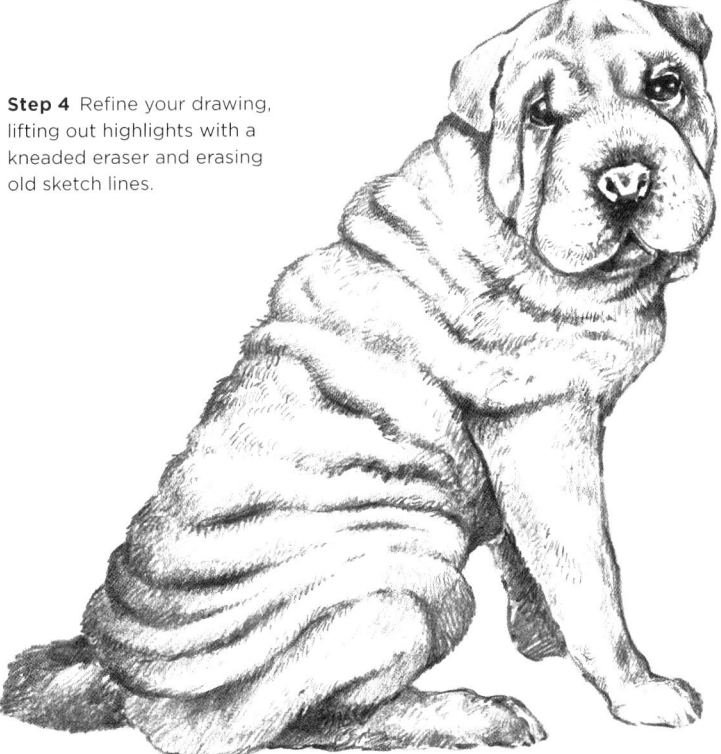

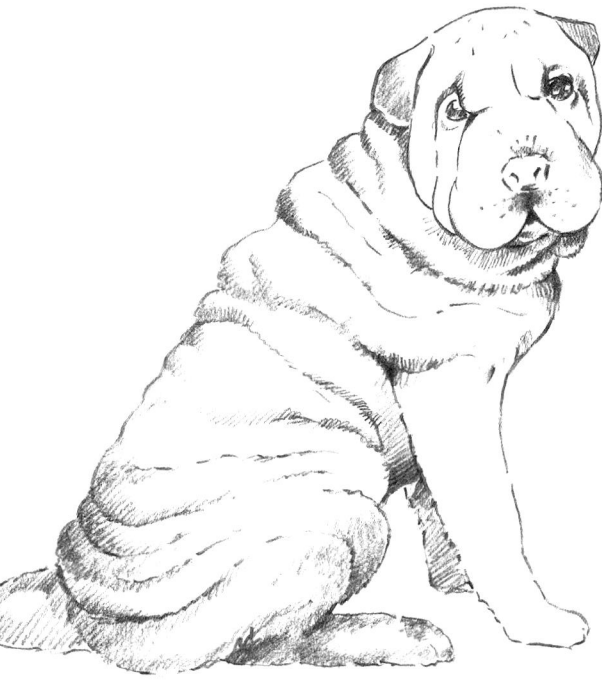

Step 3 Continue to develop the shading with short hatch marks, keeping the values darker between the folds.

English Bulldog

The powerful English Bulldog, with its stocky, muscular body, is a fun, challenging breed to draw. Even though the pronounced underbite of this dog gives it a gruff expression, it is known to be affectionate and docile.

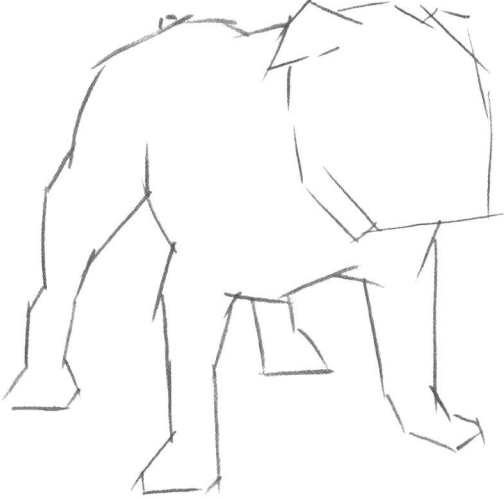

Step 1 Block in the outline with short, straight lines. Keep the legs short and bowed to give the dog its compact, stocky appearance.

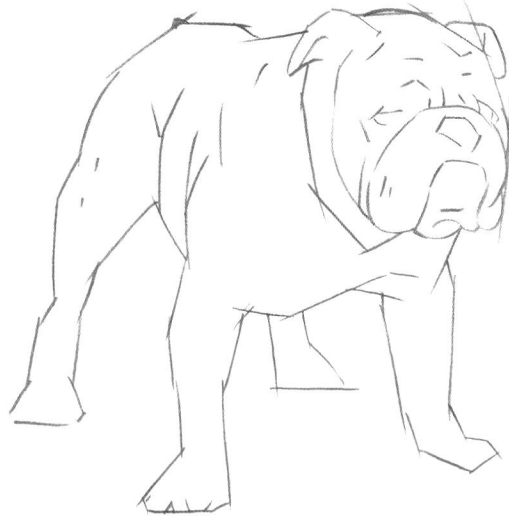

Step 2 As you refine the shape, study the low placement of the eyes. Notice the flat nose that appears to be pushed into the face.

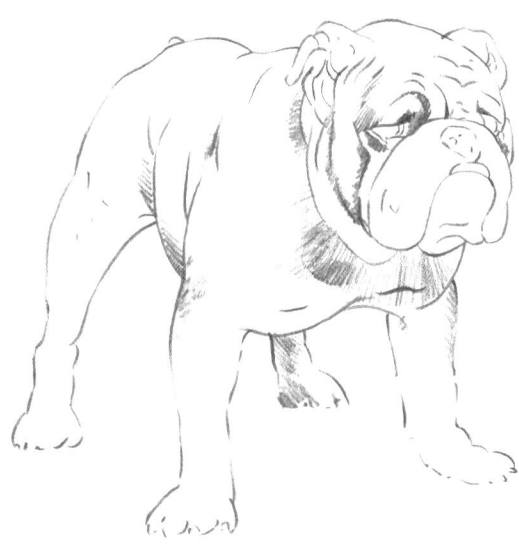

Step 3 Begin shading with a sharp 2B pencil, developing the folds on the face and the contours and shadows along the body. Keep the pencil fairly sharp to make the folds distinct and the fur smooth.

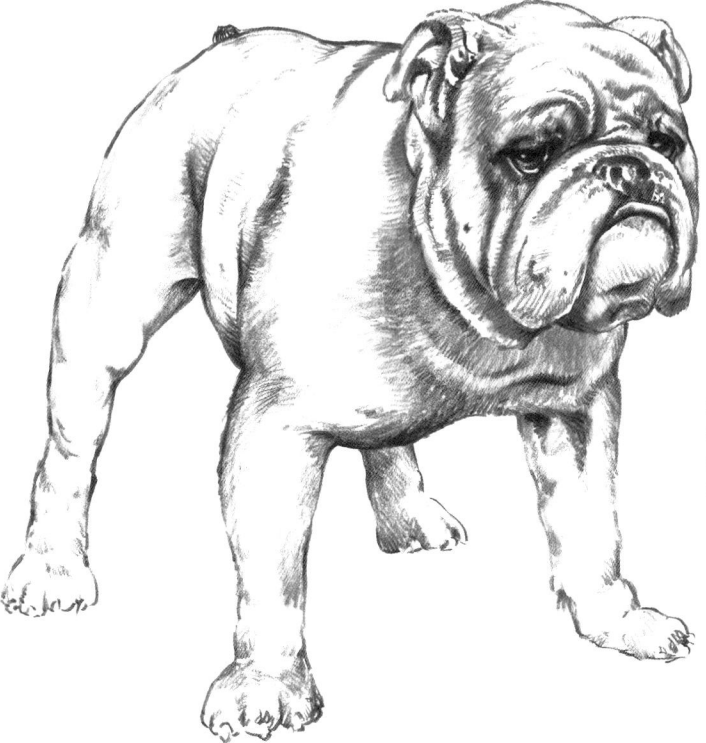

Step 4 Use a sharp pencil to add the details in the eyes. As in all the drawings, work at your own pace, and don't rush when shading the fur. Your attention to detail will be apparent in the final rendering.

Doberman Pinscher

Doberman Pinschers are known for their sleek, dark coats. When drawing the shiny coat, be sure to always sketch in the direction that the hair grows, as this will give your drawing a more realistic appearance.

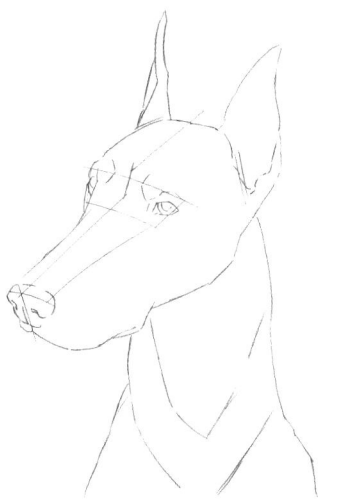

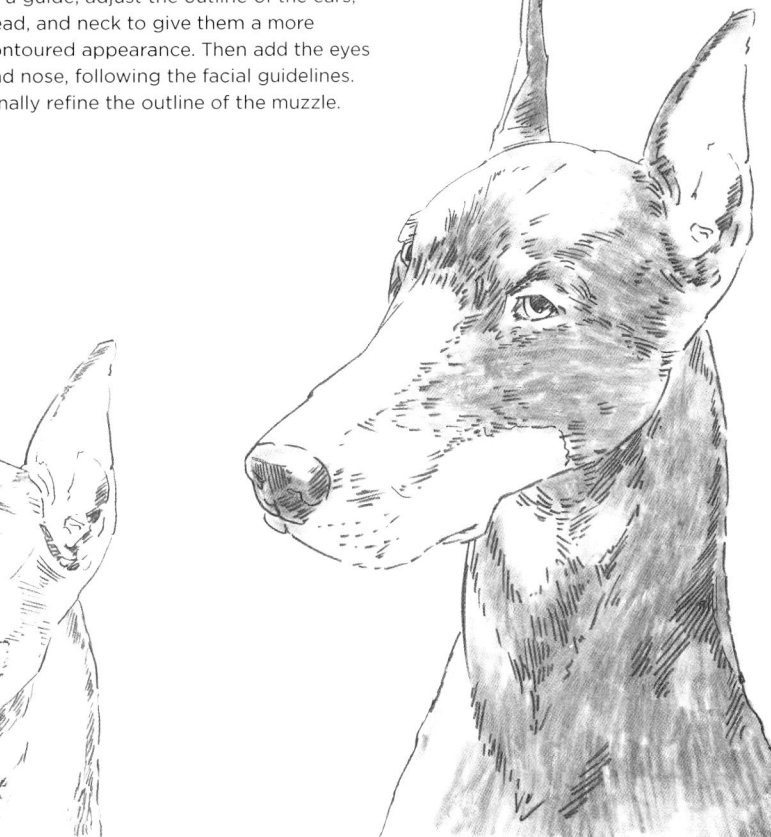

Step 3 Erase any guidelines that are no longer needed. Then begin placing light, broken lines made up of short dashes to indicate where the value changes in the coat are. These initial lines will act as a map for later shading.

Step 2 Using the lines from the previous step as a guide, adjust the outline of the ears, head, and neck to give them a more contoured appearance. Then add the eyes and nose, following the facial guidelines. Finally refine the outline of the muzzle.

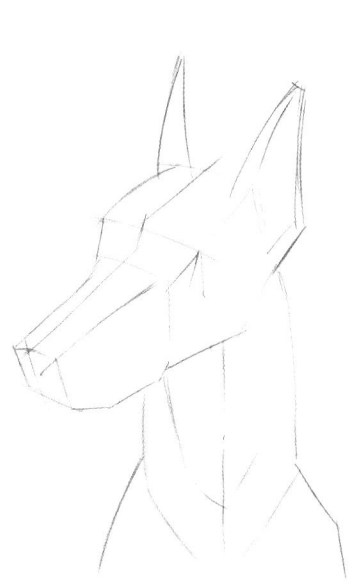

Step 1 With a sharp HB pencil, block in the boxy shape of the Doberman's head and shoulders with quick, straight lines. Even at this early stage, you want to establish a sense of dimension and form, which you'll build upon as the drawing progresses.

Step 4 For the dog's short hair, begin with small, dark hatch marks to establish the bristly, coarse nature of the coat. Then fill in the darks of the eyes and eyebrows, and dot in a few light rows of whiskers at the tip of the muzzle.

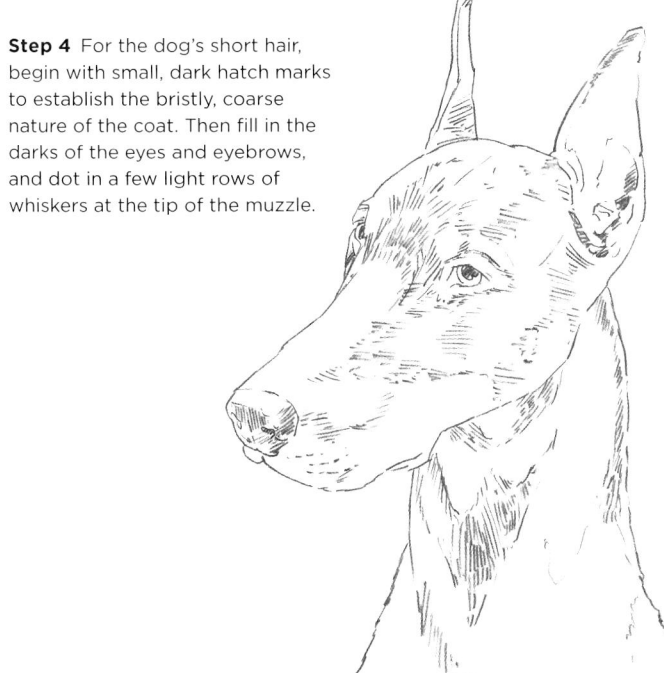

Step 5 Now fill in the remaining darks. First create some graphite dust by rubbing a pencil over a sheet of fine sandpaper. Then pick up the graphite dust with a medium-sized blending stump and shade in the dark areas of the dog's fur and nose. To avoid hard edges, blend to create soft gradations where the two values meet.

Golden Retriever

Golden retrievers are friendly, loyal, and gentle, making them beloved by people around the world. Their warm eyes and highly expressive faces also make them a fun subject to draw.

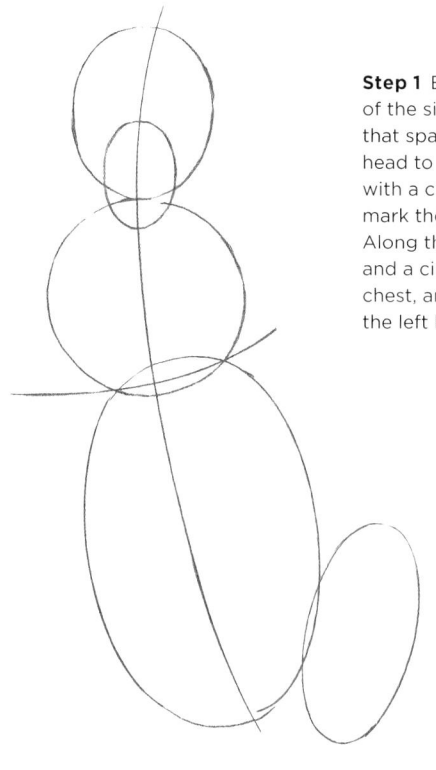

Step 1 Establish the gesture line of the sitting dog with a curve that spans from the top of the head to the ground. Next, cross it with a curved horizontal line to mark the center of the chest. Along the vertical line, add ovals and a circle for the head, muzzle, chest, and body. Place an oval for the left hind leg.

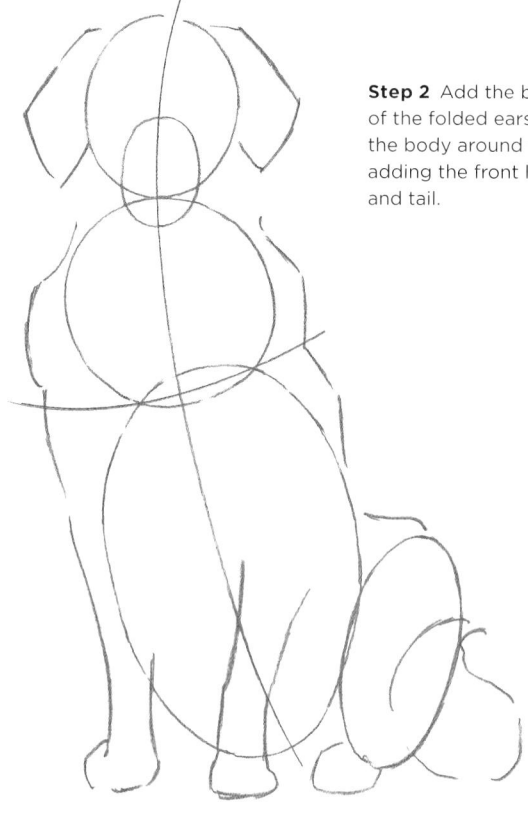

Step 2 Add the basic shapes of the folded ears and outline the body around the ovals, adding the front legs, paws, and tail.

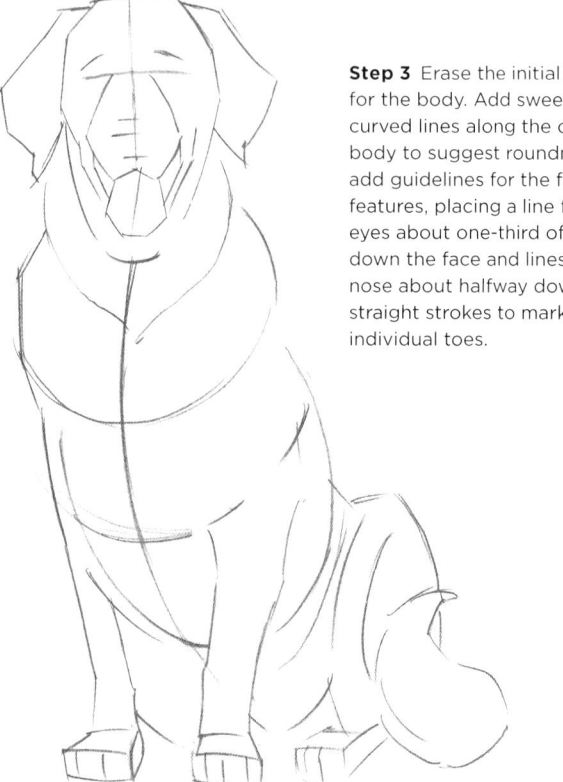

Step 3 Erase the initial guidelines for the body. Add sweeping, curved lines along the chest and body to suggest roundness. Then add guidelines for the facial features, placing a line for the eyes about one-third of the way down the face and lines for the nose about halfway down. Use straight strokes to mark the individual toes.

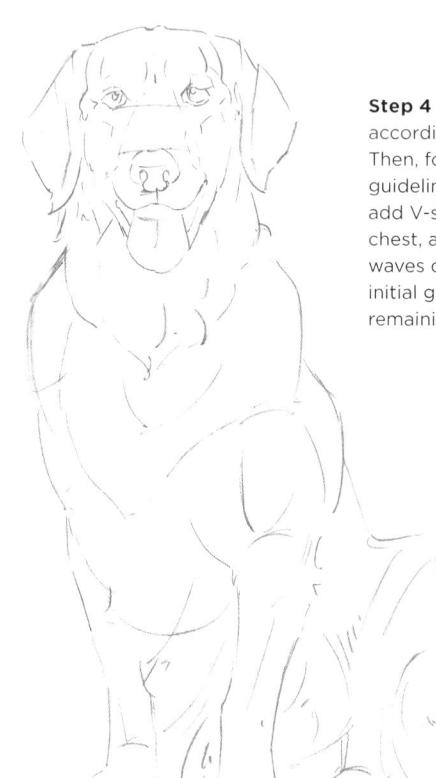

Step 4 Place the facial features according to the guidelines. Then, following the curved guidelines created in step 3, add V-shaped marks over the chest, and sketch in the first waves of the coat. Erase the initial gesture marks and any remaining guidelines.

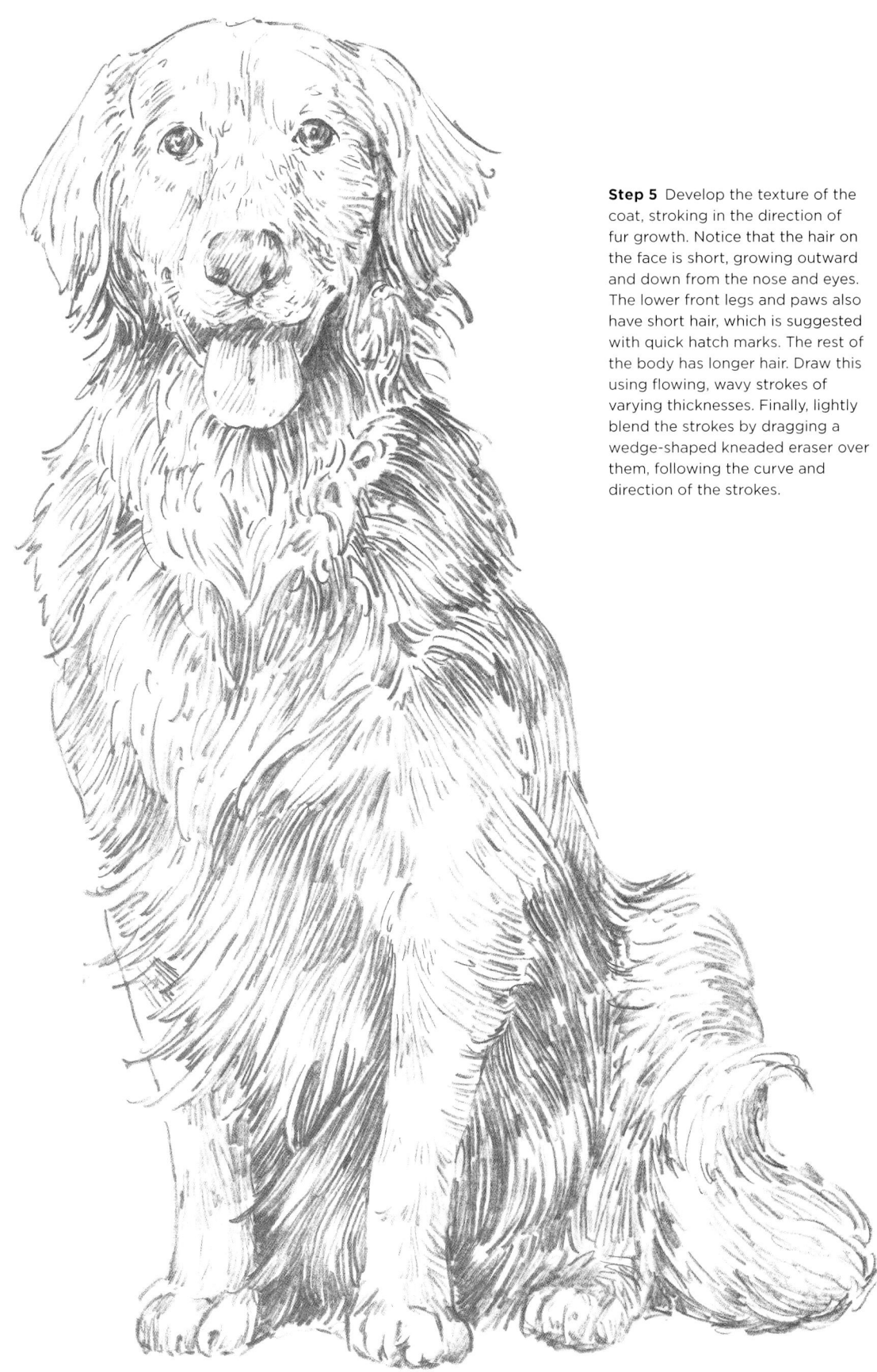

Step 5 Develop the texture of the coat, stroking in the direction of fur growth. Notice that the hair on the face is short, growing outward and down from the nose and eyes. The lower front legs and paws also have short hair, which is suggested with quick hatch marks. The rest of the body has longer hair. Draw this using flowing, wavy strokes of varying thicknesses. Finally, lightly blend the strokes by dragging a wedge-shaped kneaded eraser over them, following the curve and direction of the strokes.

Focusing on Contrast

When working with a light-colored dog, it's particularly important to diminish the level of detail in the background. Light-colored dogs don't have much contrast in their hair, so the background elements can attract the eye. Keep any intricate elements lighter in value and refrain from adding fine details, such as veins in leaves. This will keep the viewer's focus on the dog.

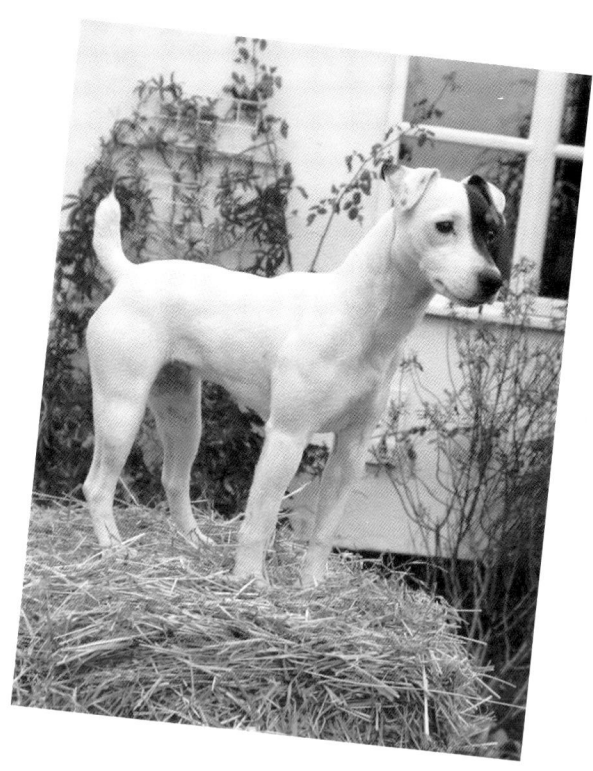

Emphasizing the Subject As is, the photograph has too much detail. Draw the background "out of focus" by lightening the overall values but maintaining enough contrast with the dog's coat. This emphasizes the sleek shape and muscular stature of this mostly white Parson Russell Terrier.

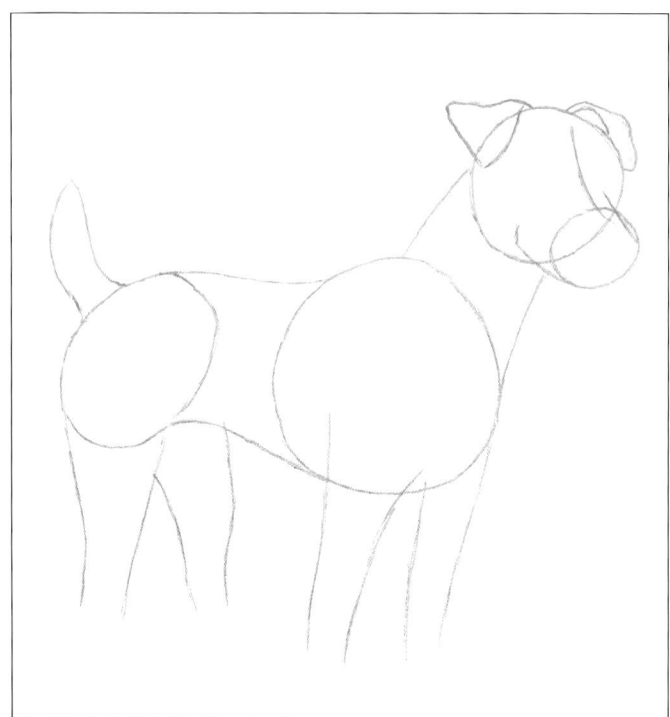

Step 1 Using an HB pencil, sketch circles for the skull, chest, hips, and muzzle. Next, connect the circles to create the outline of the dog's body. Indicate the position of the legs, tail, and ears, and add a guideline up the center of the dog's face to position the features.

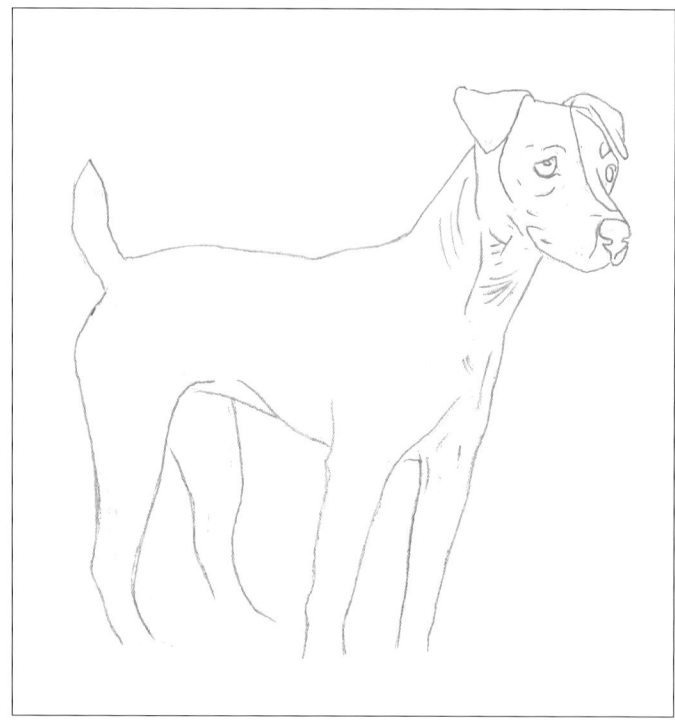

Step 2 Next, focus on refining the outline, following the subtle curves that make up the shapes of the dog. Erase the circular guidelines that are no longer needed. Indicate the shadowed area of the neck and head with a few short strokes, which will speed up the shading process later. Block in the eyes, nose, and brows, but don't indicate the paws because they will be hidden in the hay.

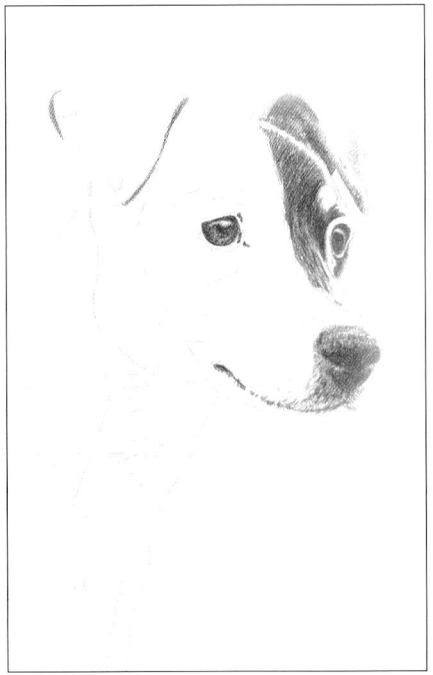

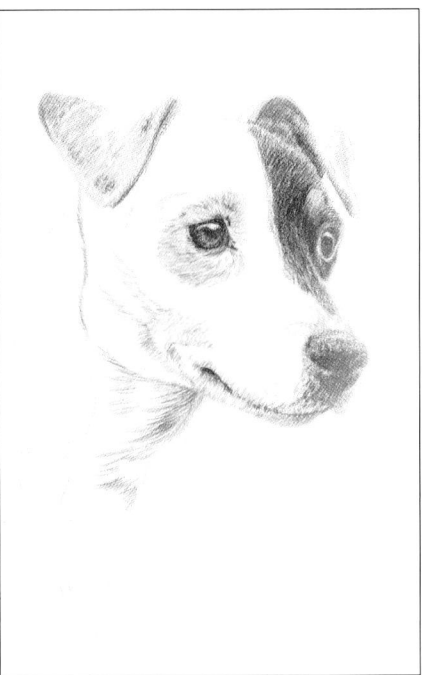

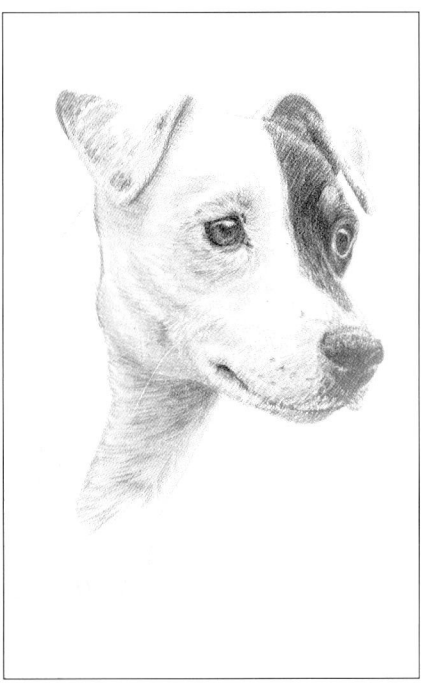

Step 3 Begin the shading by tackling the facial features. Use a 5B pencil and only block in the darkest areas, including the eyes, the shadow on the nose, the mouth, and edges of the ears. The dog has a black patch around its left eye, so darken that, as well.

Step 4 With a sharp H pencil, apply midtones to add hair around the eyes and on the mouth, cheekbone, jawline, and ears, applying short lines that follow the direction of hair growth.

Step 5 Use an H pencil and short strokes to add the lightest areas of hair over the face, gradually fading out the strokes toward the top of the head. Add mid-value dots near the mouth to mark where whiskers grow.

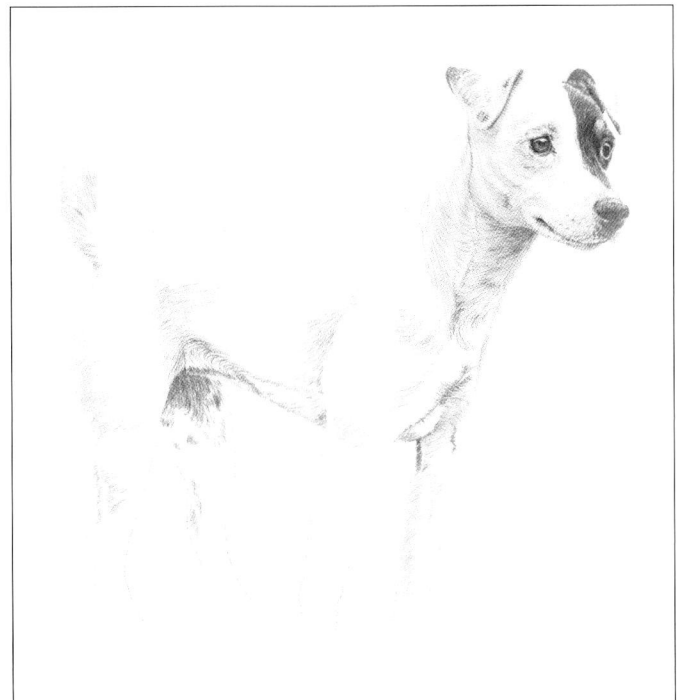

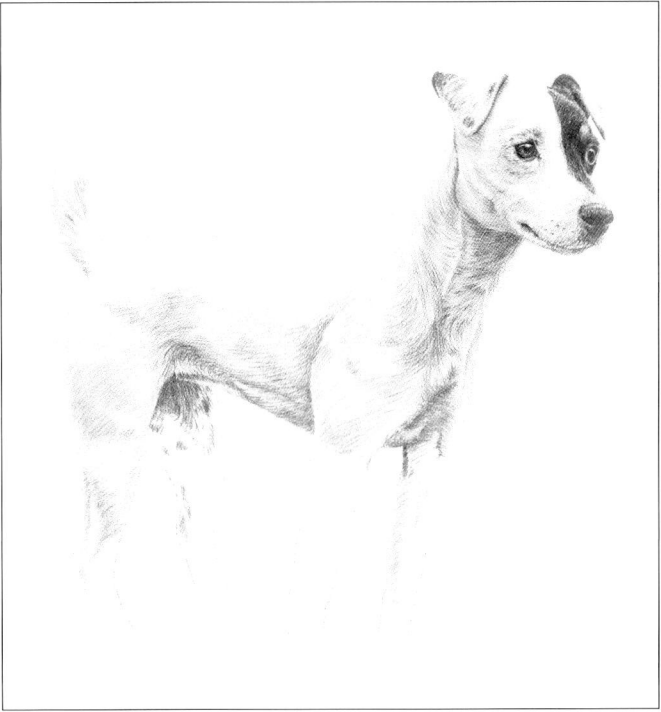

Step 6 Switch to an HB pencil and begin stroking in areas of hair on the torso, first addressing the darkest areas in shadow, such as along the insides of the far legs. Draw short, quick strokes in the direction of the hair growth, accurately communicating the feel of this dog's short, smooth coat.

Step 7 Still using the HB, continue stroking in hair across the entire torso, layering the strokes smoothly and evenly. Develop the shadows of the dog's form that indicate the muscles beneath, such as on the hind and front legs.

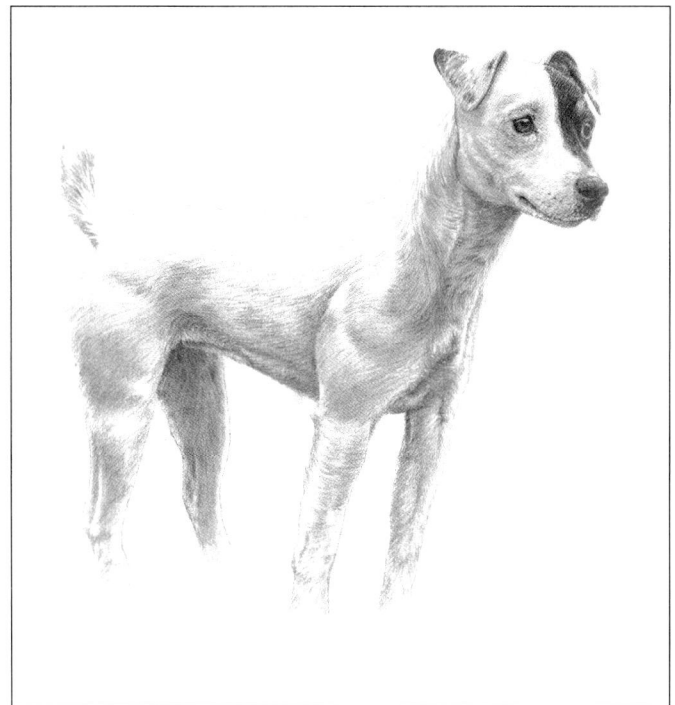

Step 8 Take a second sweep across the body using a 2H pencil, adding the subtle middle and light tones, and reducing the pressure on the pencil for the lightest areas. The muscle definition is an important characteristic of this breed, so pay attention to where the muscles sit, particularly around the shoulder and hind legs. Emphasize them by shading the undersides of the muscles.

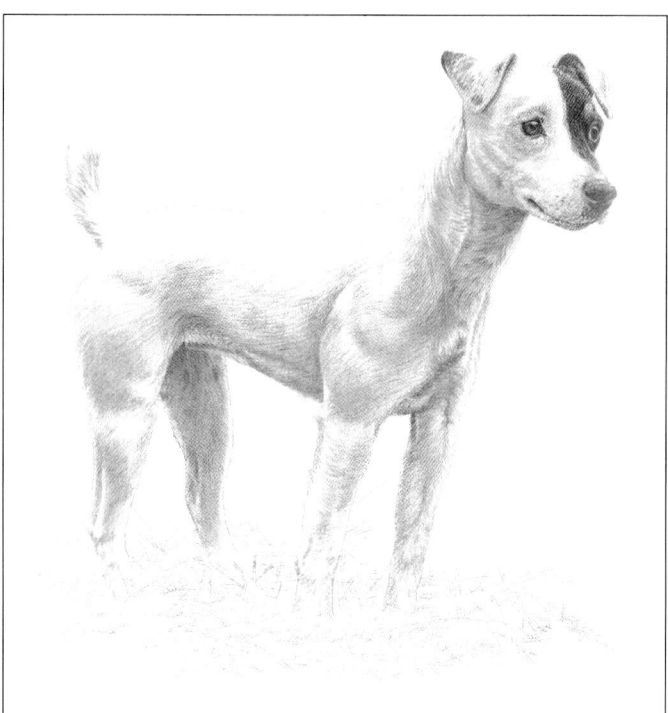

Step 9 Add tone to the hay with an HB pencil. This is the only area that directly touches the subject, so make sure the tone and value complement the dog. Because hay doesn't follow any particular pattern or direction, sketch it in using random pairs of parallel lines that cross each other.

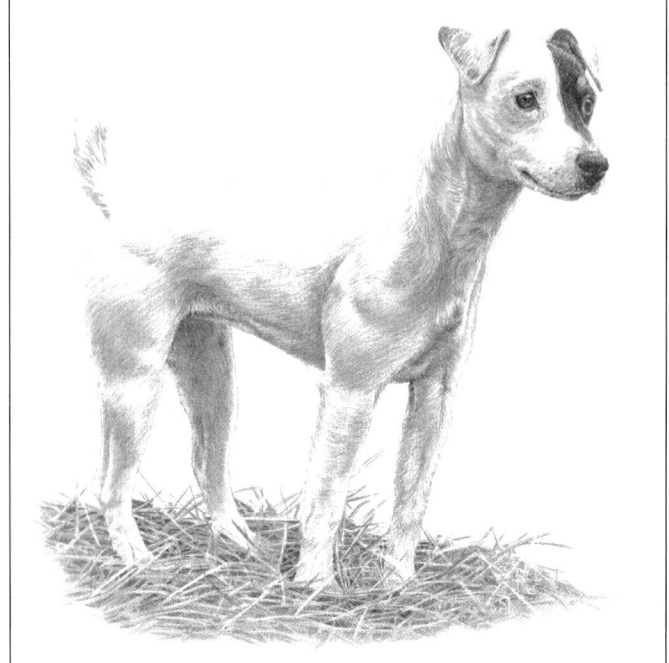

Step 10 With a 2B pencil, fill in the negative areas of the hay with the tone of its darkest shadows. You can see that this simple approach immediately produces the impression of hay. Gradually fade out the edge of the hay along the bottom and sides. If any part of the edge is too harsh, roll tack adhesive over the area to lift out some graphite and lighten the overall tone.

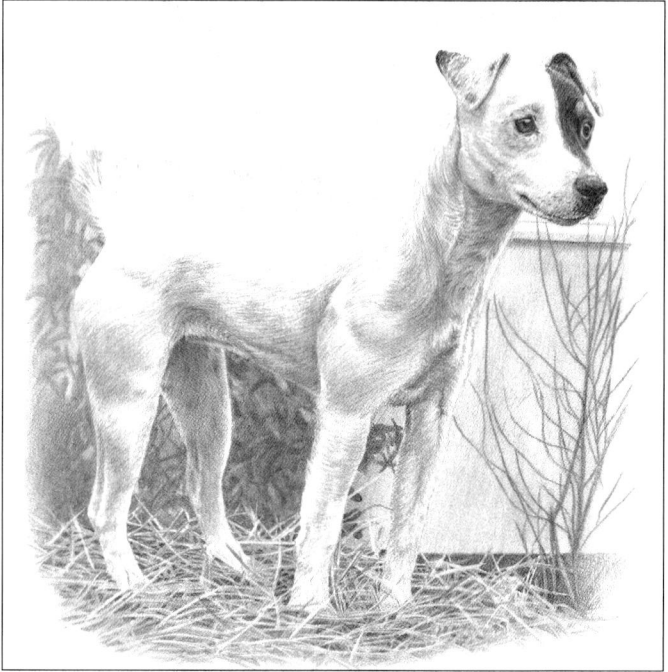

Step 11 Switch to an HB pencil and begin adding the wall and foliage in the background, bringing the dog forward and creating a sense of depth. Add tone to the wall on the right, giving the area interest by adding a cluster of twigs. Next, draw ivy growing up the left two-thirds of the wall. Keep the background elements indistinct by blurring them slightly with a blending stump.

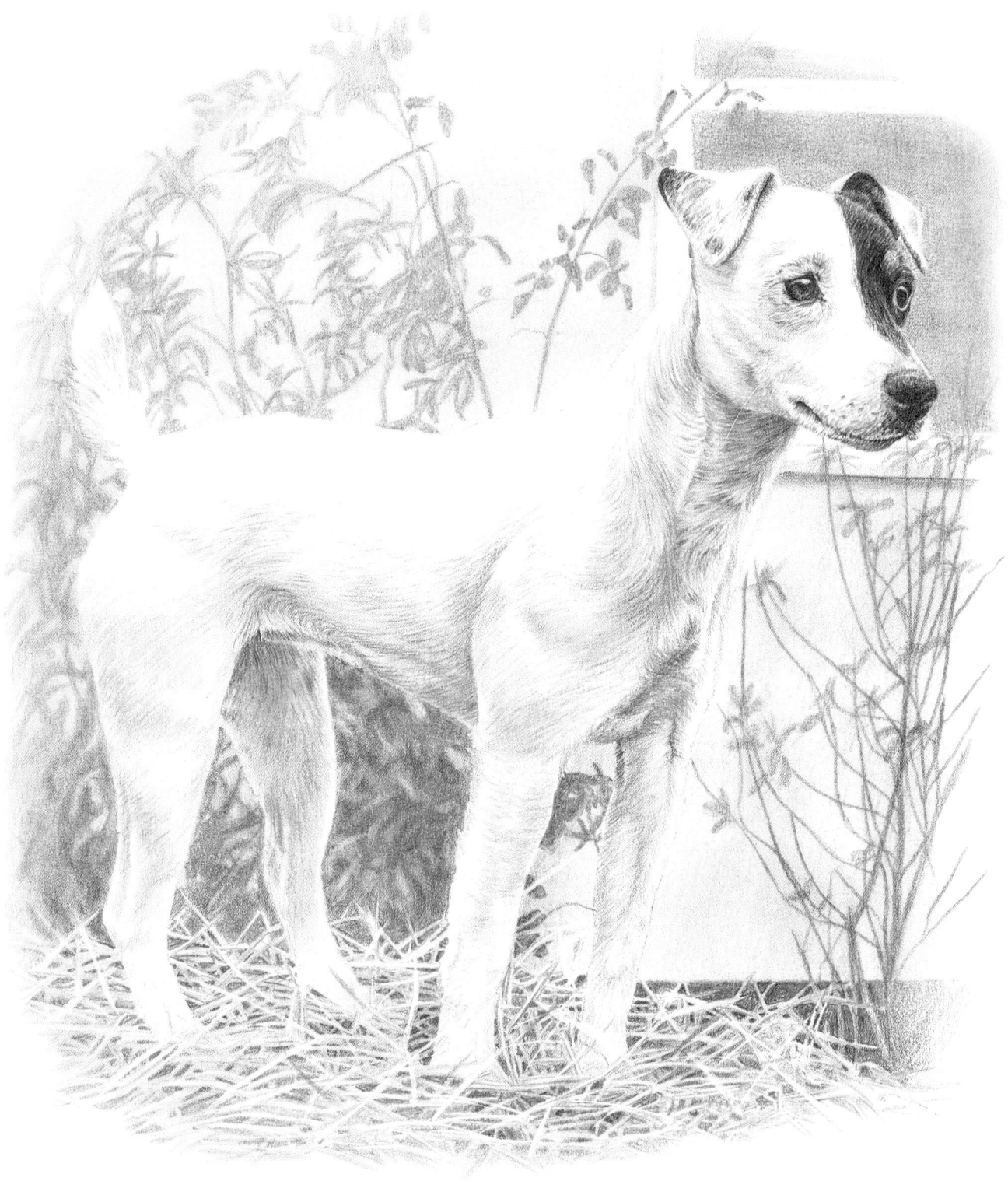

Step 12 Continue working upward with an HB pencil to finish the ivy, ending just above the dog to contrast with the light value of its back. Add a middle value to the window behind the head to contrast with both the light and dark hair. Stand back from the drawing and focus on areas where the dog blends into the background, darkening or lightening where needed. To finish, sharpen details on the dog, and blend any harsh lines within the background.

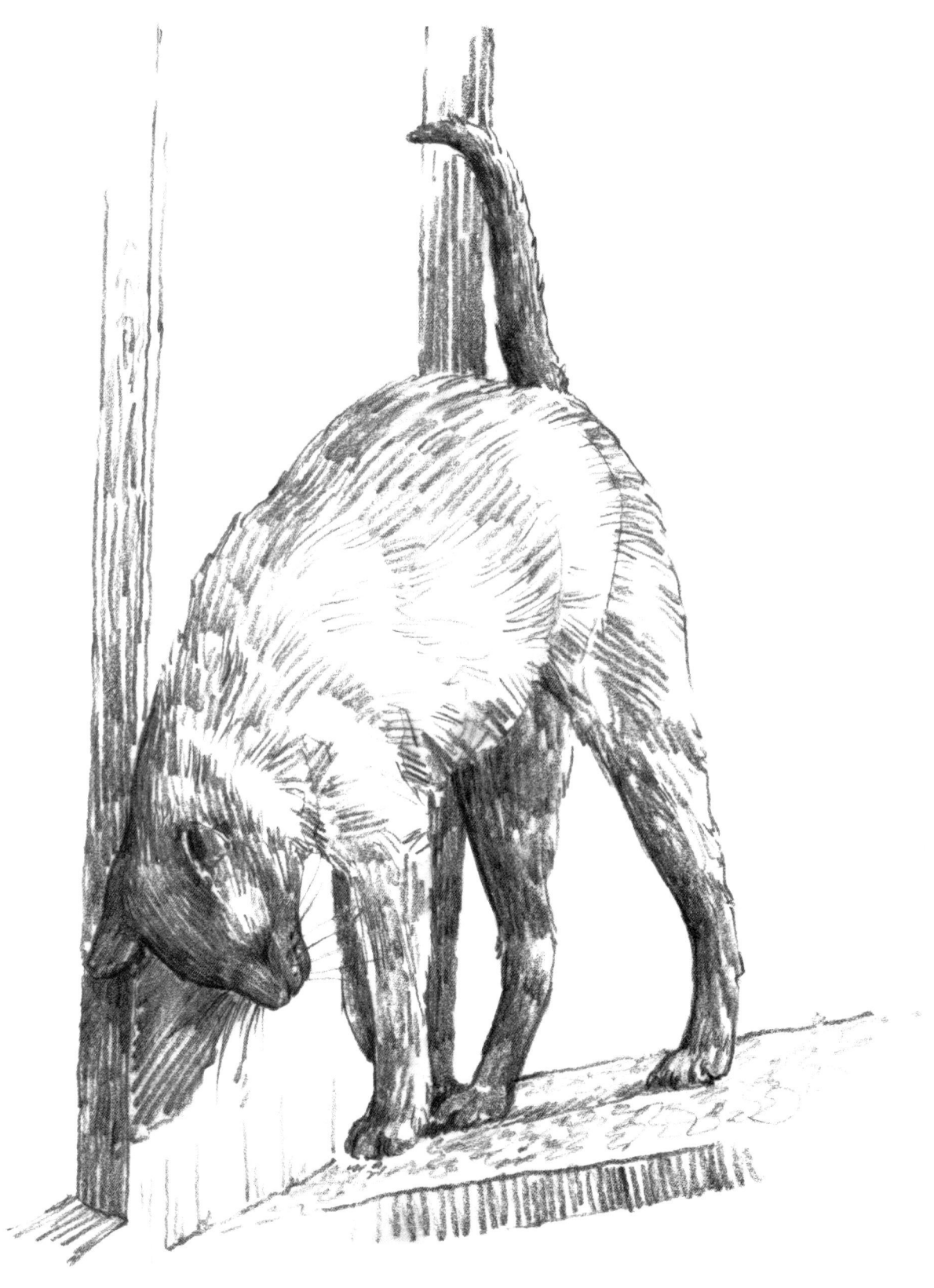

Cats

Cats and kittens are a delightful blend of curiosity, playfulness, and independence, which makes them a wonderful drawing subject. From the boundless energy of a kitten, to an hours-long nap of a cat on a widowsill, the playful antics and quiet moments of cats and kittens make these four-pawed furballs endlessly captivating. Drawing cats in pencil allows artists to capture their graceful forms and intricate details with subtlety and depth. The simplicity of the medium allows for a nuanced portrayal of these beloved creatures, evoking both their mystery and charm.

In this chapter, you'll learn a bit about feline anatomy, as well as how to render and shade ears, eyes, paws, whiskers, and tails with realism. Step-by-step lessons cover cats and kittens in a variety of common poses, giving you the skills you need to draw cats of all shapes and sizes with confidence.

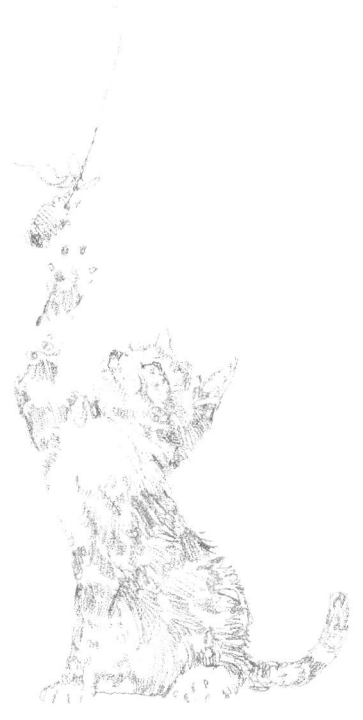

Rendering Cats

Striped cats are great subjects for pencil drawings because their patterned fur makes an impact, even in black and white. And the flexibility of pencil allows you to draw both the fine hairs on your household tabby and the bold markings of a Bengal tiger. Just don't make the mistake of concentrating so much on the pattern of the fur that you lose sight of the animal's form. Study the techniques below, and keep them in mind when drawing your portraits.

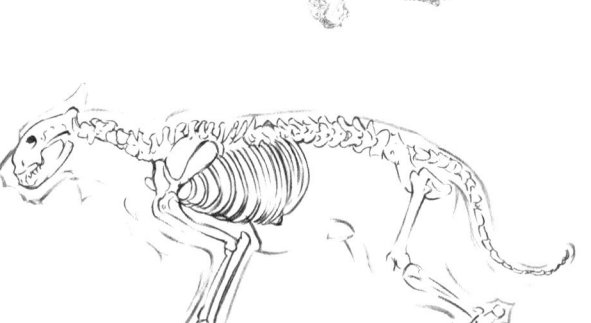

Shading to Establish Form Use the side of an HB pencil to shade some of the stripes, curving the lines to follow the forms of the legs and body. Then draw short strokes over the shading with the pencil tip, following the direction of hair growth.

Building on a Framework A little knowledge of a cat's anatomy will help you draw one accurately. (See page 76.) Look at the size relationships between the head and the body and how long the legs are in proportion to the depth of the rib cage. Knowing where the leg joints are will help you draw the correct angles of the legs, paws, and shoulders.

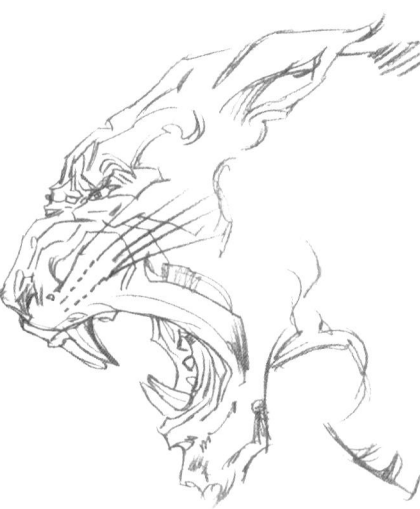

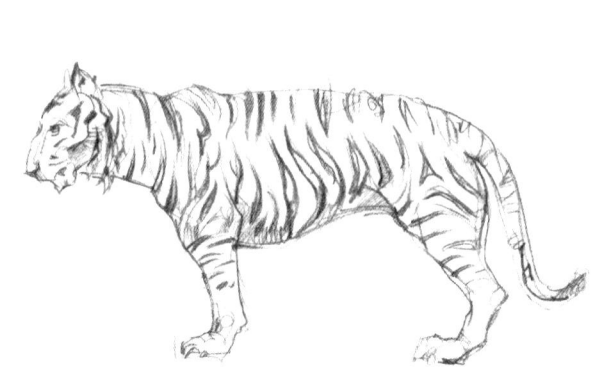

Studying the Profile To draw this tiger so it doesn't look like a large-sized tabby cat, emphasize its longer nose, wider muzzle, and rounder ears. Use a flat-tipped pencil to lay in the pattern of stripes, curving them to follow the tiger's form.

Expressing Character Cat expressions are a lot of fun to draw, especially the exaggerated snarl of a big-toothed tiger. use the round tip of an HB pencil, and focus on developing the lines of the muscles around the eyes and muzzle.

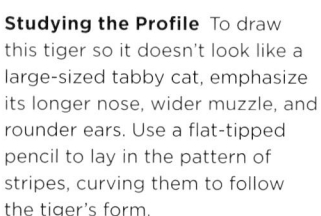

Drawing Kittens Kittens at play are appealing subjects, but they are difficult to draw from life; try drawing from photos instead. Using an HB pencil, break down the forms into a few simple shapes and then refine the outlines. Use the side of the pencil to suggest the fur pattern, rather than rendering each stripe perfectly.

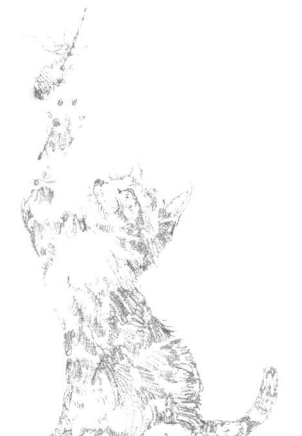

Foreshortening Unless you are viewing your subject in profile, there will always be a part that is closer to you. The drawing technique, called "foreshortening," allows you to create the illusion of depth by shortening the part of an object that is coming toward you. In this drawing of a tiger, notice the cat's foreshortened front legs and body. If he were standing, there would be much more distance between his paws and his chest, and his head would not be positioned in the middle of his body! By distorting the proportions this way, you will be able to convey a sense of depth and perspective.

DEPICTING CAT FUR PATTERNS

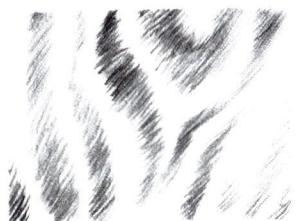

Tabby Cat Tabbies have distinctive striped fur. Shade in the undercoat with the side of an HB. Draw the coat pattern using a 2B with a rounded point, and smudge to soften.

Ocelot Ocelots have variegated spots. Lightly place the overall pattern with the side of an HB. Use a sharp, pointed 2B to add the darker outlines. Vary the pressure for value changes.

Cheetah This cat's spots are smaller than an ocelot's and look more solidly black. Use a sharp, pointed HB, and vary the pressure as you stroke and then lift the pencil, creating soft edges.

Leopard Leopard spots have a definite rosette pattern. Apply short strokes using the sharpened point of an HB. Darken here and there with pressure variation and the point of a 2B.

Proportion & Anatomy

A basic understanding of a cat's anatomy will help you draw it accurately. You don't need to memorize the names of the parts or learn to draw the bones and muscles. Just familiarize yourself with the structures so that your drawings are in correct proportion. Proportion is the harmonious relation of parts to each other or to the whole, particularly in terms of size and shape.

Head length is a common measuring unit for determining the size of other parts of a subject (or of the whole). Notice that the height of the cat's body (to the top of the shoulder) is approximately three head lengths. Keep the cat's proportions in mind as you block in your drawings.

Familiarity with the cat's musculature will also help improve your drawing skills, especially your shading technique. Generally, areas with large, smooth muscles need light, simple shading, whereas the areas of smaller, overlapping muscles require more complex shading. Study the illustrations below to see how the muscles and tendons wrap around the cat's skeletal structure.

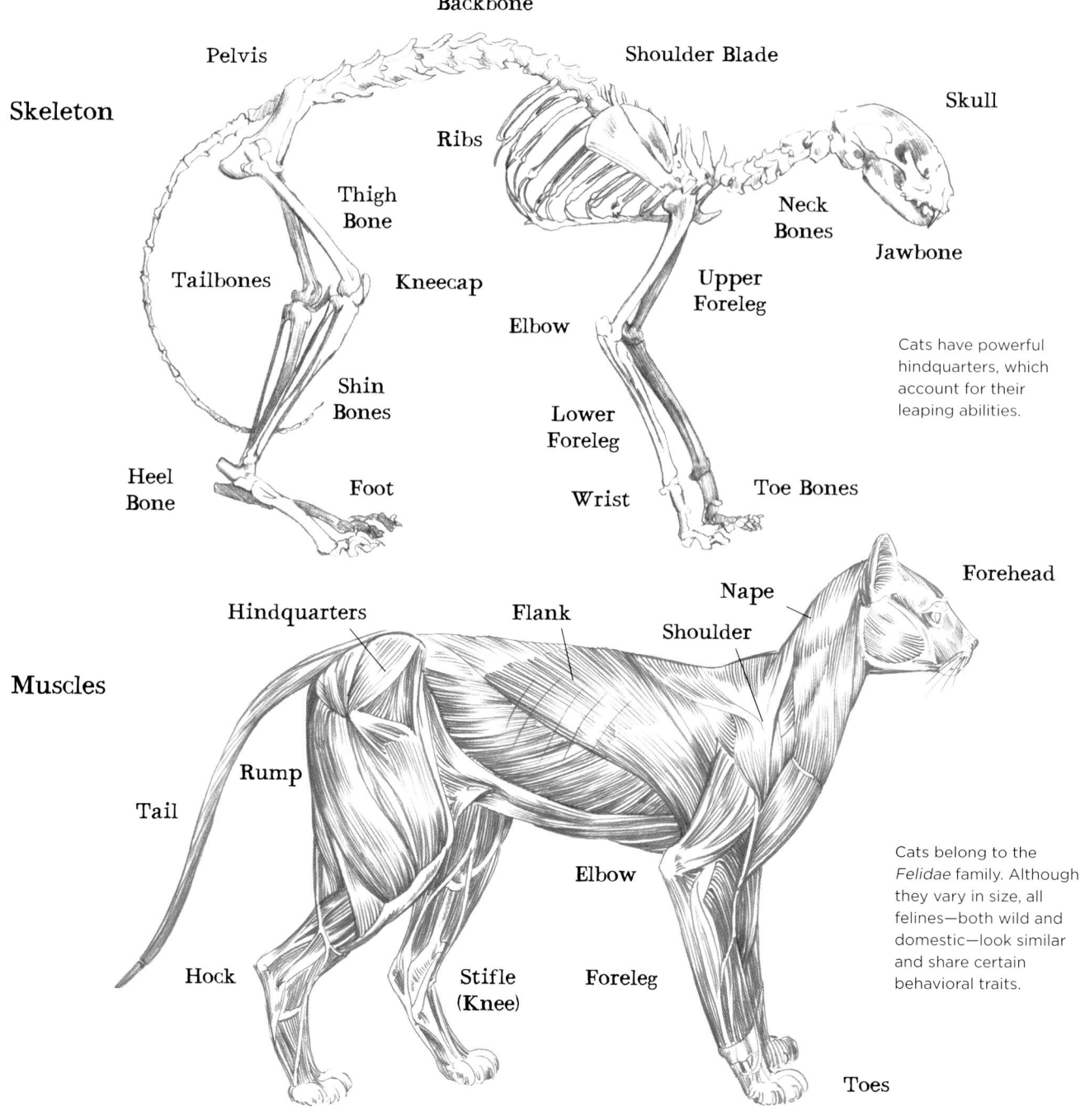

Skeleton

Backbone · Pelvis · Shoulder Blade · Skull · Ribs · Thigh Bone · Neck Bones · Jawbone · Tailbones · Kneecap · Upper Foreleg · Elbow · Shin Bones · Lower Foreleg · Heel Bone · Foot · Wrist · Toe Bones

Cats have powerful hindquarters, which account for their leaping abilities.

Muscles

Hindquarters · Flank · Nape · Forehead · Shoulder · Rump · Tail · Elbow · Hock · Stifle (Knee) · Foreleg · Toes

Cats belong to the *Felidae* family. Although they vary in size, all felines—both wild and domestic—look similar and share certain behavioral traits.

The Cat's Head

The cat has a rounded head with a short face marked by protruding cheekbones and a short muzzle. The skull has large, round eye sockets and thirty sharp teeth.

Skull

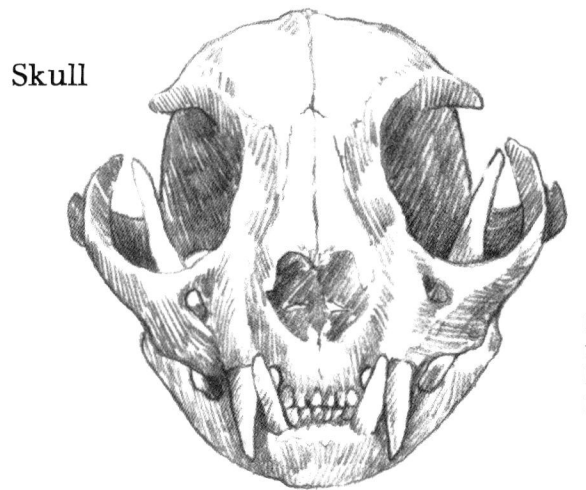

Remember the underlying form of the skull to help you keep the facial features in proper proportion.

Although all cats' heads are basically the same shape, profiles do vary among breeds. Be sure to study the shape of your subject's head before drawing it. Notice whether the cat's face is flat, pointed, or square. Look at the position of the nose compared with the eyes, and the eyes with the top of the head. Check the proportions of all the features before getting started. Begin by lightly roughing out the basic shape. Then refine the shape until you achieve a likeness to the subject. Do many sketches from different angles. If you do, your skills will quickly improve!

This cat has the angular profile, wedge-shaped nose, and large, pointed ears typical of short-haired breeds.

Skull

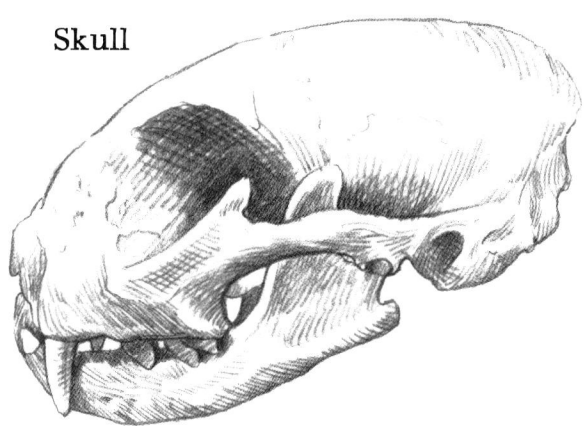

Jawbone

When rendering cats (or any subject), it is best to work from live models or photographs. Trying to draw from memory or imagination is much more difficult. Collect photos of cats and kittens from catalogs, magazines, and books, and keep them in a file for future reference.

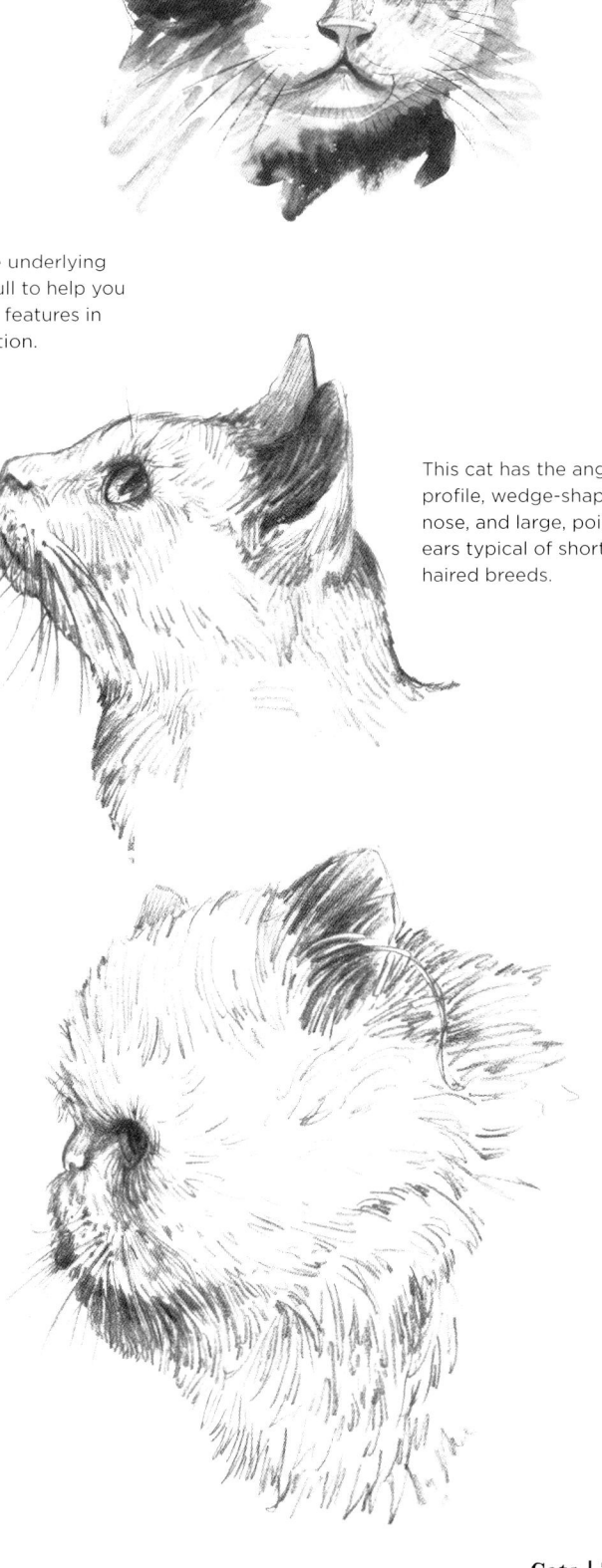

Shading Techniques

Solid Fur

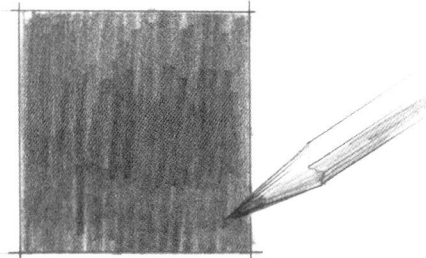

Step 1 Use the side of an HB lead to cover the surface with even, vertical strokes. Apply layer upon layer to build depth.

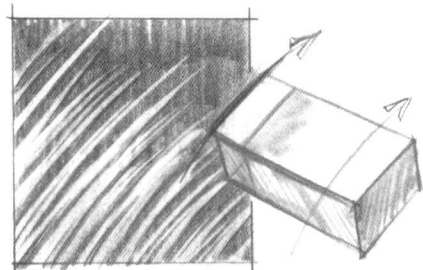

Step 2 Use the corner of a firm block eraser to pull out thick, light hairs in the direction of growth. Practice lifting the eraser at the end of the stroke to make a tapered point.

Striped Fur

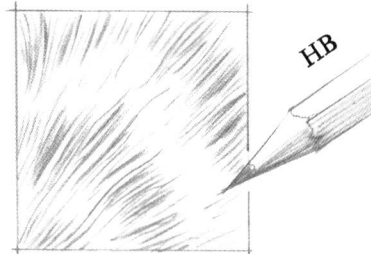

Step 1 For striped fur, begin to suggest the dark areas with the side and point of an HB pencil.

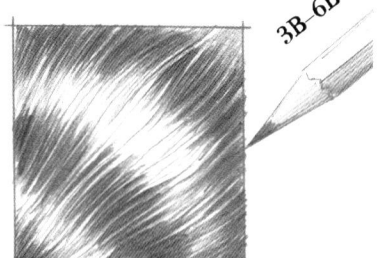

Step 2 Refine the texture, and add details and darkest values with pencils ranging from 3B to 6B. Use a blending stump to soften the darkest areas.

Thick Fur

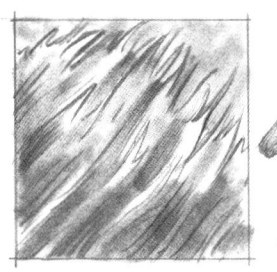

Step 1 Create thin, dark lines with an HB pencil; then rub a blending stump over some of the lines to soften and smudge them.

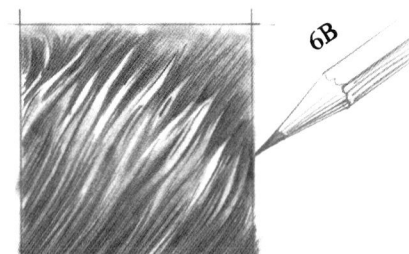

Step 2 Use a sharp 6B pencil to refine the texture, stroking in the direction of fur growth. Enhance the white areas with an eraser.

Whiskers

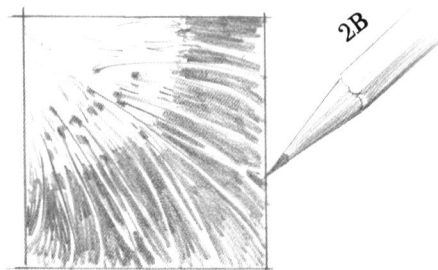

Step One With the side and point of a 2B pencil, indicate the fur and whiskers.

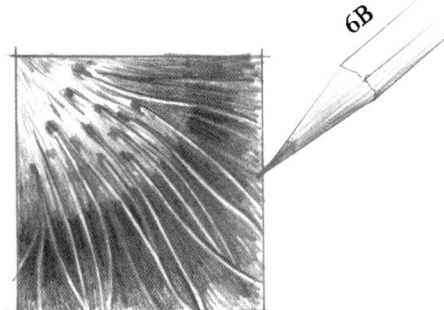

Step Two Use a 6B pencil to refine the whiskers and shade the darkest areas.

Using Brush and Ink
You can create different effects with a round watercolor brush and India ink. Try diluting the ink for lighter values. Use a wet brush for smooth lines or a dry brush for more texture.

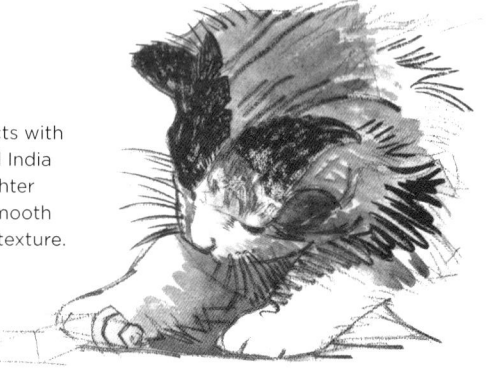

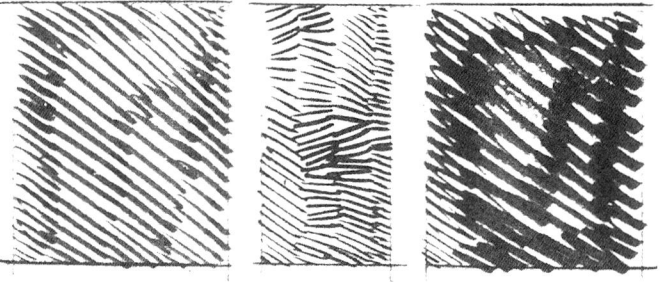

For short, fine lines (middle), hold the brush vertically to the paper and stroke lightly with just the tip of the brush. For long, broad lines (left and right), increase the pressure on the brush and apply more ink.

Feline Features

Cats have very distinctive features, and the features vary between individuals and among breeds. Look carefully at your subject. Notice the general shape, proportion, and position of each feature and how each one relates to the others. These details make each cat unique. You may want to practice drawing the features separately before attempting a complete rendering.

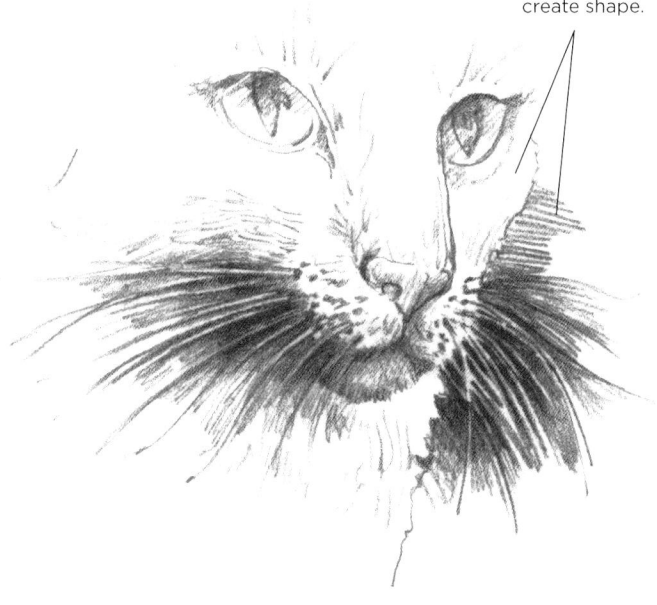

Use dark against light and light against dark to create shape.

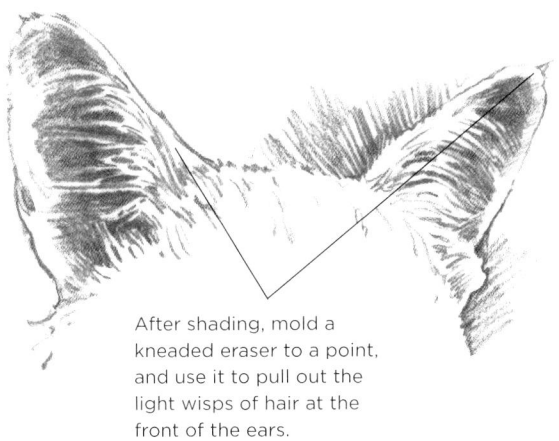

After shading, mold a kneaded eraser to a point, and use it to pull out the light wisps of hair at the front of the ears.

To draw the ear, first block in the general triangular shape with an HB pencil. Then observe your subject, and refine the shape. Compare the shape of the outer edge to that of the inner edge; note the angles and where each side meets the head. Once satisfied with the outline, use a soft lead pencil to create the three-dimensional form of the ear.

Draw whiskers in the direction of growth with long, sweeping strokes. Use a sharp pencil to draw the whiskers on a light background, or use an eraser to lift them out of a dark background. Don't forget to add the dark hair follicles around the cat's muzzle.

Sketch the eye as a circle, tilted up at the outer corner. After roughing in the general shape, concentrate on rendering the eyeball and the hair surrounding the eye. Add layers of shading with a soft lead pencil to create depth. Remember to always leave a white highlight in or near the pupil to indicate reflected light.

The cat's ears can rotate independently of one another.

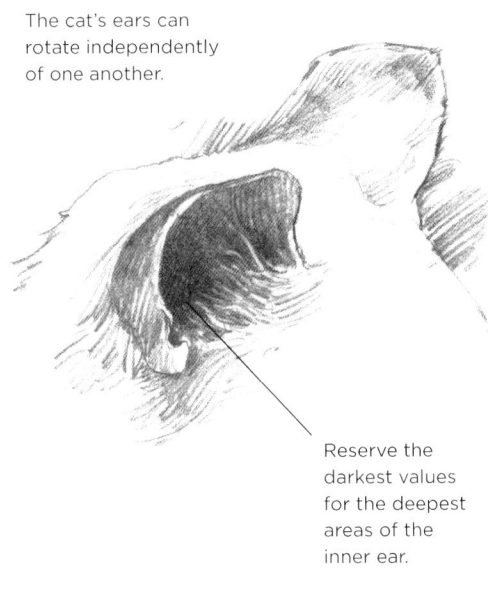

Reserve the darkest values for the deepest areas of the inner ear.

The nose is a triangle shape, and the mouth area is an inverted Y shape. Remember that the nose is three-dimensional, and it should fit on the cat's face naturally—it shouldn't look as if it has been pasted on the face as an afterthought. Notice how the varying values suggest depth and form in the example.

Hair should always be drawn in the direction of growth.

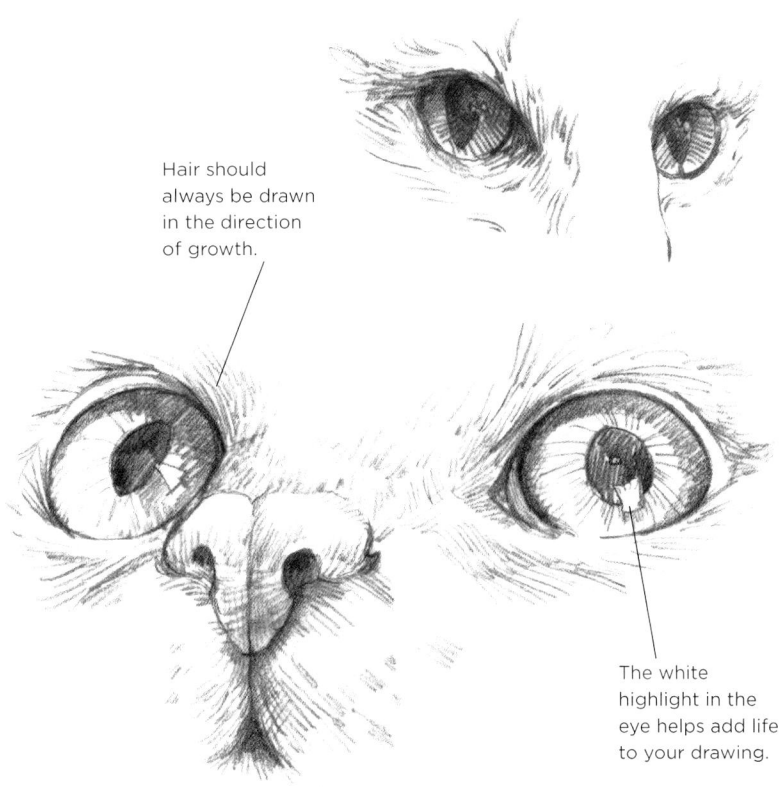

The white highlight in the eye helps add life to your drawing.

Front View A sharp-pointed pencil is best for blocking in the basic shapes, as shown in steps A and B. Step C illustrates how to sketch the eyes, ears, and nose. In step D, finalize the placement of the facial features, and apply shading in step E.
Side View This head is created with straight lines, as opposed to round shapes. Draw the lines in the numbered order shown in A. Follow the remaining steps to complete the drawing. Use a 2B pencil to apply shading in step D.

Front View

Side View

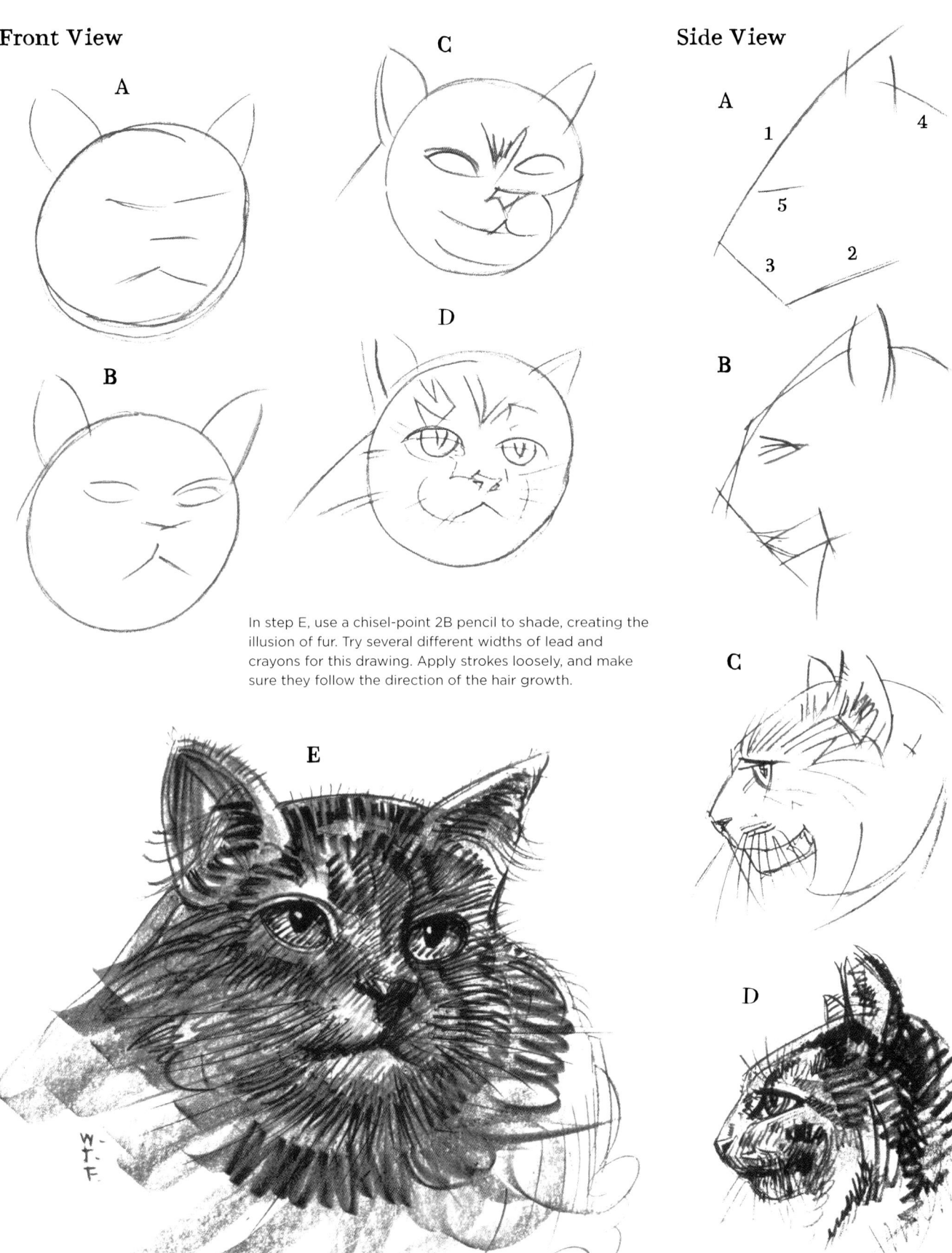

In step E, use a chisel-point 2B pencil to shade, creating the illusion of fur. Try several different widths of lead and crayons for this drawing. Apply strokes loosely, and make sure they follow the direction of the hair growth.

Paws & Tails

Cats explore their surroundings with stealth, essentially walking on their toes. They have strongly developed footpads, which help their balance and allow them to move silently. They also have sharp, curved claws that can be extended as weapons or used for traction to help them climb. When you draw, be sure to include details such as claws and footpads to make your subject look convincing. Begin drawing the paws with a simple outline, and then sketch in the individual toes and pads. For the fur, make certain your pencil strokes follow the direction of the fur growth; use denser strokes in the shaded areas. Longer strokes on the footpad will illustrate the difference in texture between the pad and the fur, and short, curved lines around the edges of the feet will help distinguish the toes.

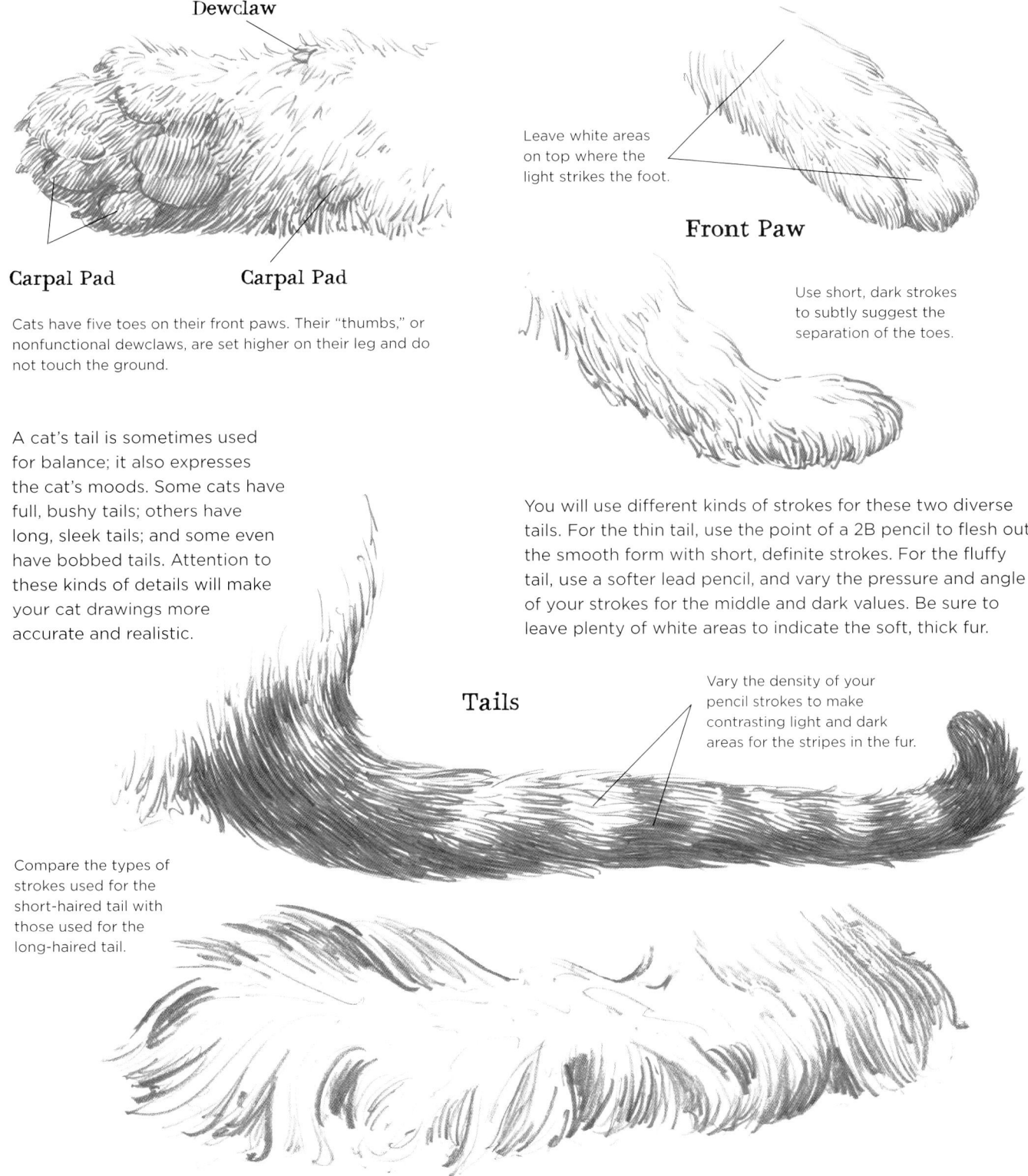

Dewclaw

Carpal Pad

Carpal Pad

Cats have five toes on their front paws. Their "thumbs," or nonfunctional dewclaws, are set higher on their leg and do not touch the ground.

Leave white areas on top where the light strikes the foot.

Front Paw

Use short, dark strokes to subtly suggest the separation of the toes.

A cat's tail is sometimes used for balance; it also expresses the cat's moods. Some cats have full, bushy tails; others have long, sleek tails; and some even have bobbed tails. Attention to these kinds of details will make your cat drawings more accurate and realistic.

You will use different kinds of strokes for these two diverse tails. For the thin tail, use the point of a 2B pencil to flesh out the smooth form with short, definite strokes. For the fluffy tail, use a softer lead pencil, and vary the pressure and angle of your strokes for the middle and dark values. Be sure to leave plenty of white areas to indicate the soft, thick fur.

Tails

Vary the density of your pencil strokes to make contrasting light and dark areas for the stripes in the fur.

Compare the types of strokes used for the short-haired tail with those used for the long-haired tail.

Persian Cat

The Persian is a stocky cat with long, silky hair. It has a large, round face with short, broad features and small ears. To depict the quality of this Persian's fur, keep your pencil strokes uniform and deliberate. Notice that this example has been developed much further than the previous examples were.

Step 1 When you block in this cat, notice that the eyes are two different shapes. This is because the head is viewed at a three-quarter angle. Block in the basic shape of the cat, making curved lines to suggest its roundness and to show changes in the form.

Flowing, curved lines are used to indicate the cat's form beneath the fur.

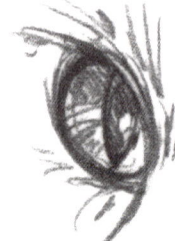

EYE DETAIL
At this view, the angle of the cat's right eye is important; the pupil remains perpendicular and is partially covered by the bridge of the nose.

Step 2 Use uniform pencil strokes to indicate the layers of fur around the head, chest, and back. Notice the way the pencil strokes are used to refine the features. Use a sharp HB pencil to shade the eye and to draw the fine lines of the nose and whiskers. Next use 2B and 4B pencils to bring out the thick texture of the fur. Remember that the lines should always be drawn in the direction that the hair grows.

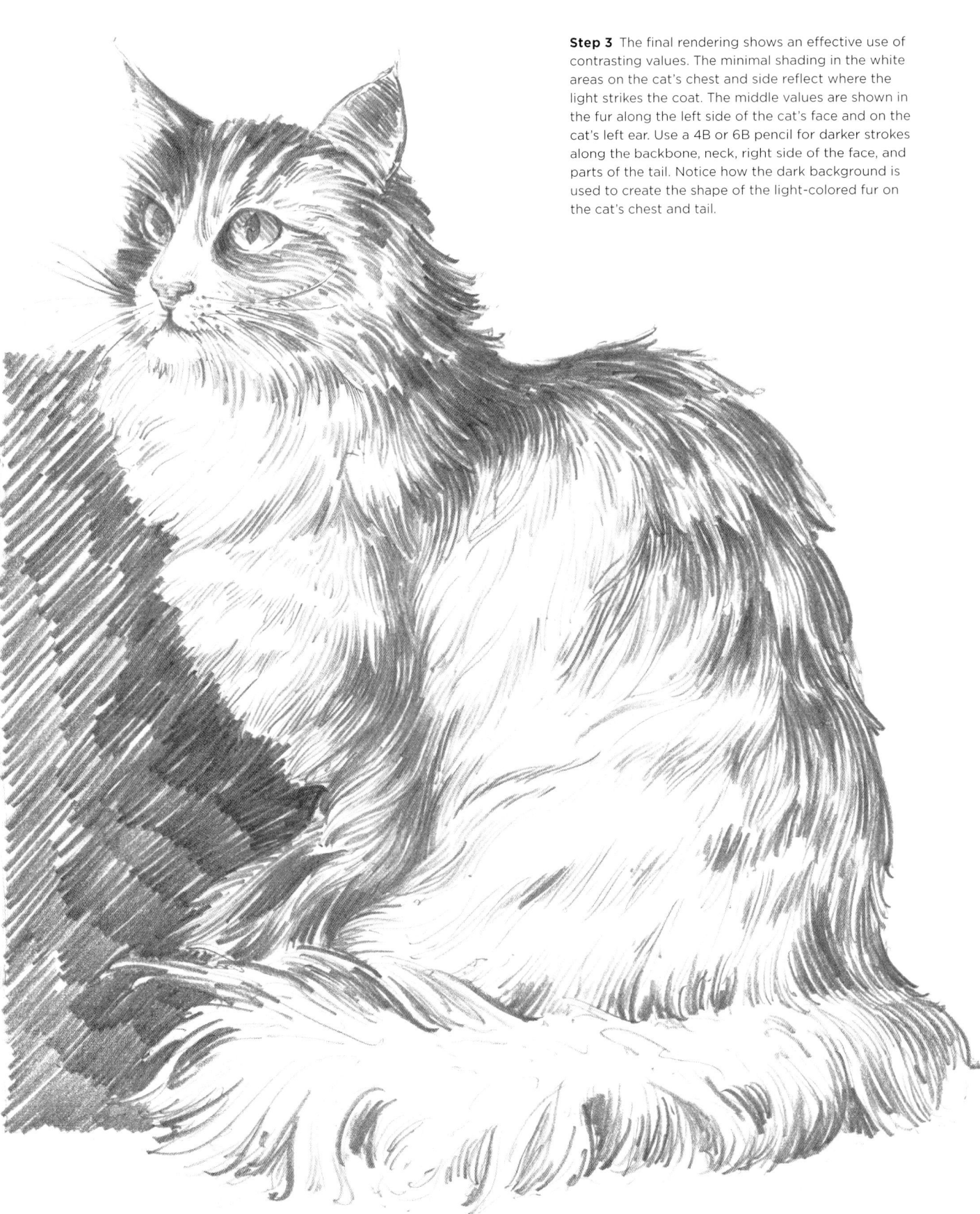

Step 3 The final rendering shows an effective use of contrasting values. The minimal shading in the white areas on the cat's chest and side reflect where the light strikes the coat. The middle values are shown in the fur along the left side of the cat's face and on the cat's left ear. Use a 4B or 6B pencil for darker strokes along the backbone, neck, right side of the face, and parts of the tail. Notice how the dark background is used to create the shape of the light-colored fur on the cat's chest and tail.

Tabby Cat

Patterns and textures can add interest to an otherwise ordinary subject. For this sketch, the pairing of a ridged carpet and striped cat produces an eye-catching study in contrasts.

Step 1 Begin with a sideways S to establish the cat's gesture line, using a tighter curl for the tail. Then establish the basic shapes using a circle for the head and ovals for the chest, body, and haunches. To create guidelines for the cat's features, center a cross over the face and add two dashes to indicate the position of the mouth and nose.

Step 2 Now draw a smaller oval over the cat's stomach, blocking in the bulging fur of its underbelly. Then create the full outline of the cat's body, adding its four legs. Next draw the triangular ears and place the eyes, nose, and mouth.

Step 3 Next go over the outline with short, broken strokes that better depict the fur. In addition, define the toes and paw pads, and add a few lines to suggest the crease at the cat's shoulder. Also add more detail to the face, marking the stripes and filling in the crescent shapes of the pupils.

Step 4 Erase any guidelines you no longer need, and map out the basic tabby pattern of the cat's coat. Use curving lines to suggest the cat's rounded form. Then scribble in the contrasting parallel lines of the carpet, and place the first lines of the ottoman behind the cat.

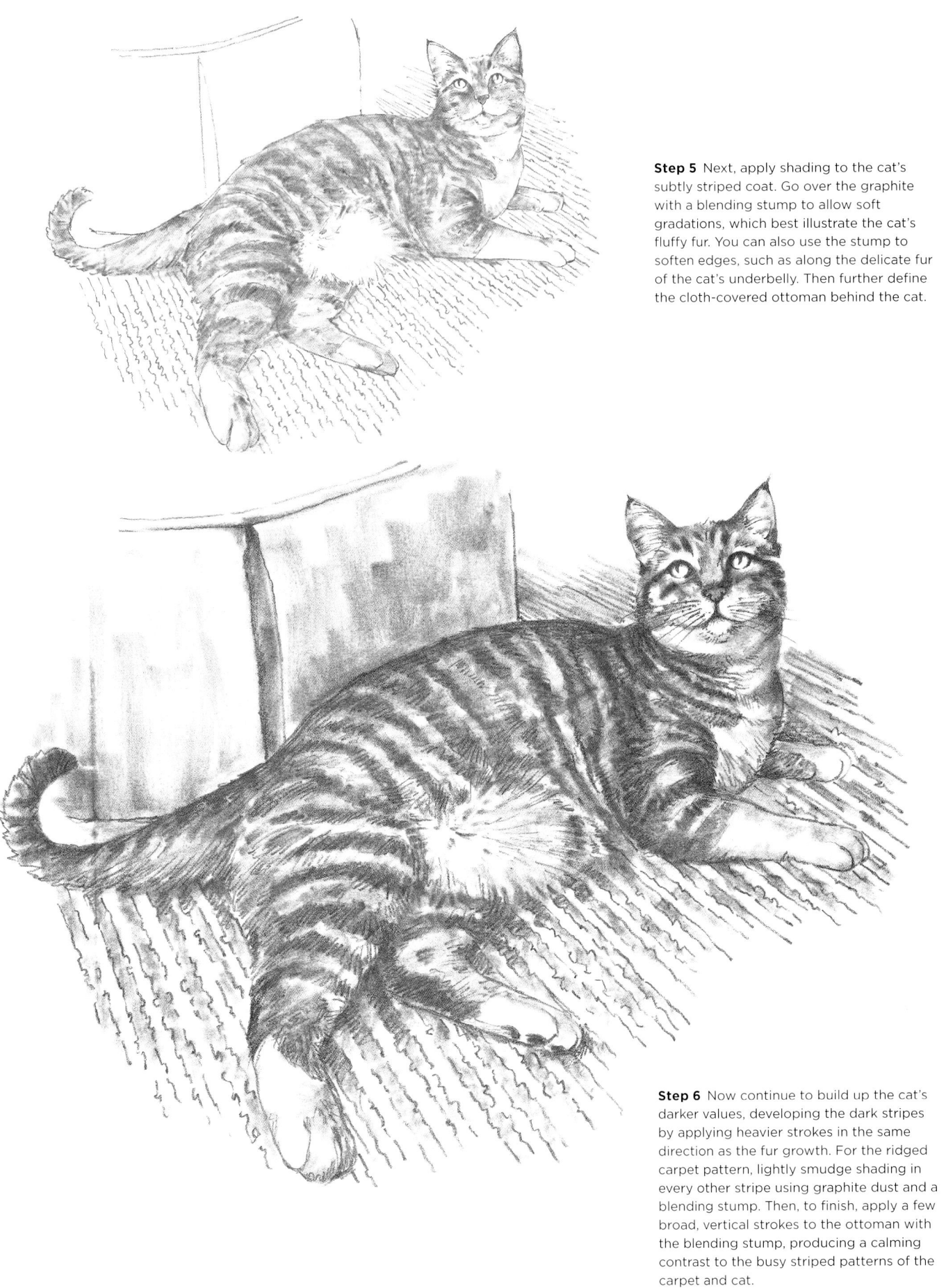

Step 5 Next, apply shading to the cat's subtly striped coat. Go over the graphite with a blending stump to allow soft gradations, which best illustrate the cat's fluffy fur. You can also use the stump to soften edges, such as along the delicate fur of the cat's underbelly. Then further define the cloth-covered ottoman behind the cat.

Step 6 Now continue to build up the cat's darker values, developing the dark stripes by applying heavier strokes in the same direction as the fur growth. For the ridged carpet pattern, lightly smudge shading in every other stripe using graphite dust and a blending stump. Then, to finish, apply a few broad, vertical strokes to the ottoman with the blending stump, producing a calming contrast to the busy striped patterns of the carpet and cat.

Short-Haired Cats

The cat is an agile animal, athletic and alert. Its fine sense of balance allows it to prowl easily along narrow ledges or fences. This subject is slim and muscular with a narrow, wedge-shaped head, large ears, and long, thin tail. Because this cat is facing front, its body must be foreshortened. (See page 75.)

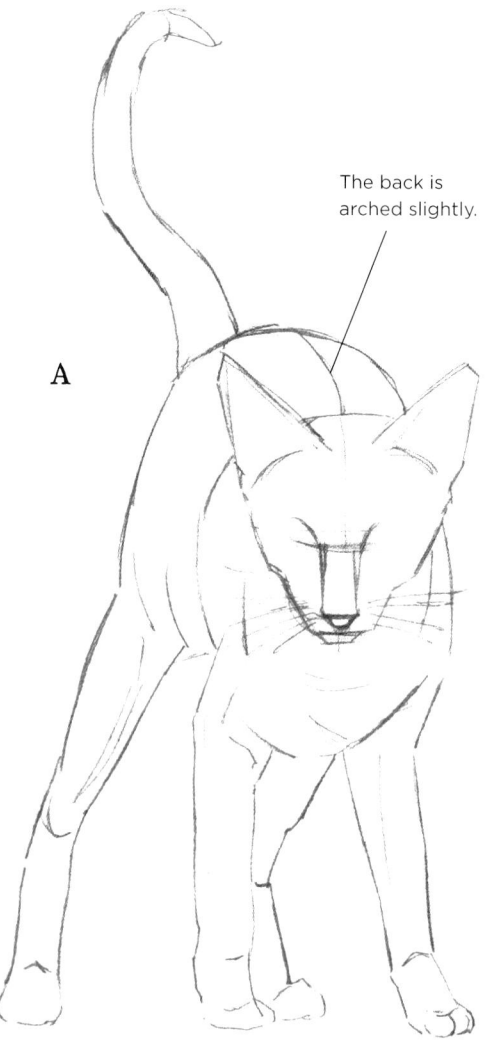

The back is arched slightly.

A

Block in this pose carefully, using ovals for the chest and haunches. When you're comfortable with the body proportions, block in the legs and tail, as shown in step A.

Use a tortillon to blend the pencil strokes, creating variations in value.

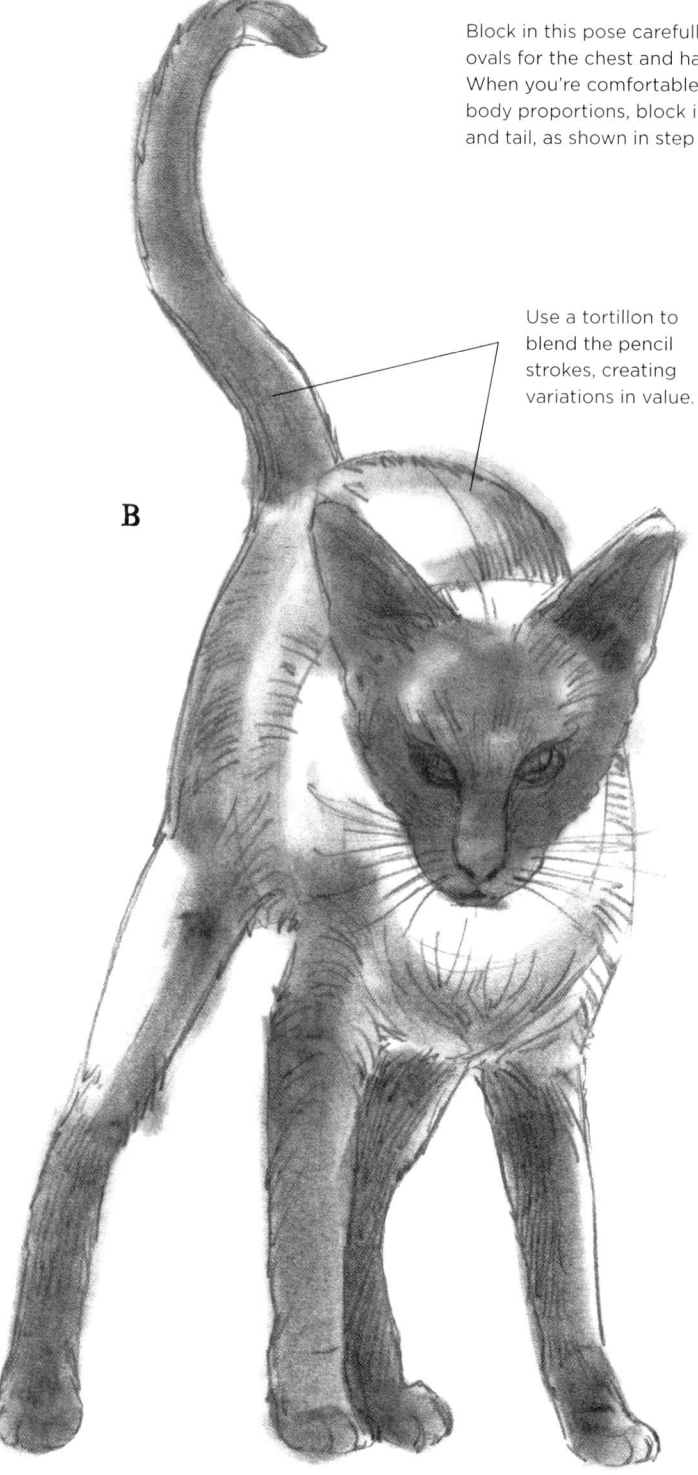

B

Add the facial features in step B, and then develop the shading. Use a 6B pencil for the dark areas of the face, legs, tail, and body. Then use a paper stump to blend the lead, creating soft, smudgy areas. Finish the drawing with a sharp 4B pencil to bring out the hairs on the face and body.

Be sure to emphasize this cat's distinct almond-shaped eyes and relatively large ears.

This grooming cat presents another challenging pose, so it's important that you take your time blocking it in. In step A, use ovals to establish the placement of the major body parts, and draw guidelines along the skull and backbone to help you place the curves of the cat's body. Remember that the cat's front left leg is supporting the weight of its upper body, so it needs to be placed correctly. If it isn't, the cat will look as if it is about to fall over.

For a difficult pose like this one, it is important to observe your subject closely.

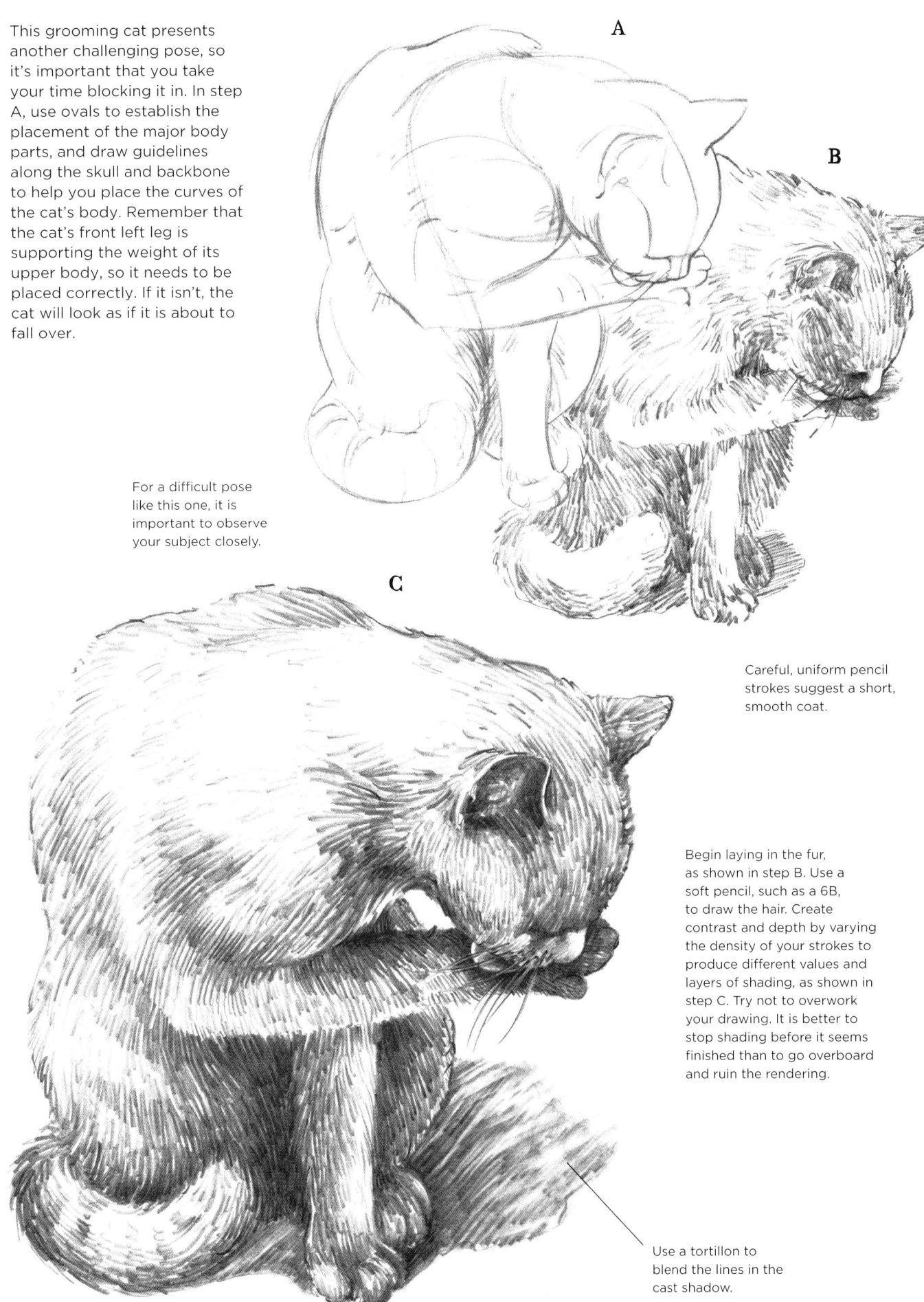

Careful, uniform pencil strokes suggest a short, smooth coat.

Begin laying in the fur, as shown in step B. Use a soft pencil, such as a 6B, to draw the hair. Create contrast and depth by varying the density of your strokes to produce different values and layers of shading, as shown in step C. Try not to overwork your drawing. It is better to stop shading before it seems finished than to go overboard and ruin the rendering.

Use a tortillon to blend the lines in the cast shadow.

Common Behaviors

Cats have fastidious habits. They crouch down low to eat or drink. Capturing this pose requires careful planning, but it's just a matter of applying foreshortening techniques. Remember, a key to mastering foreshortening is to draw what you really see, not what you think you should see.

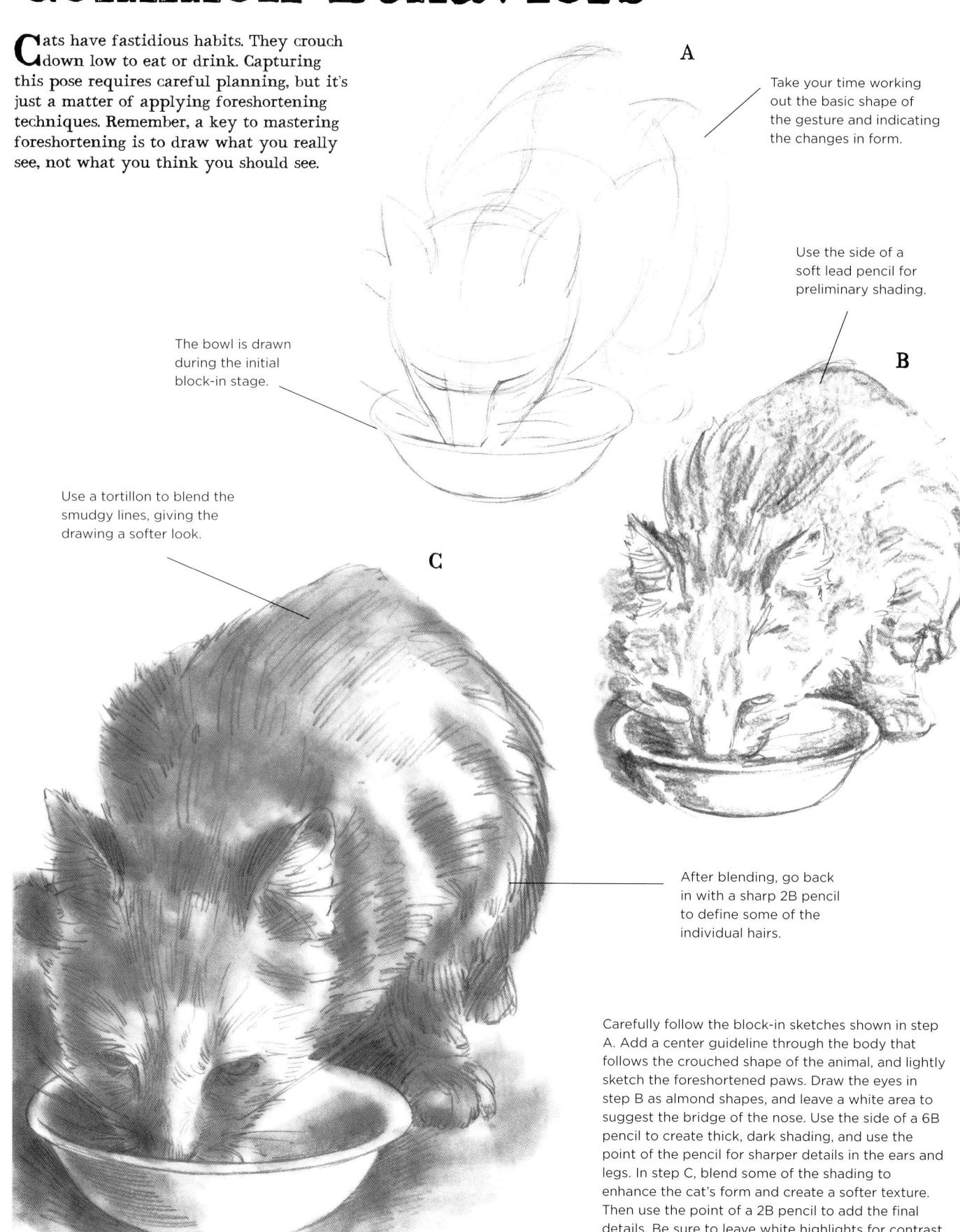

A

Take your time working out the basic shape of the gesture and indicating the changes in form.

Use the side of a soft lead pencil for preliminary shading.

B

The bowl is drawn during the initial block-in stage.

Use a tortillon to blend the smudgy lines, giving the drawing a softer look.

C

After blending, go back in with a sharp 2B pencil to define some of the individual hairs.

Carefully follow the block-in sketches shown in step A. Add a center guideline through the body that follows the crouched shape of the animal, and lightly sketch the foreshortened paws. Draw the eyes in step B as almond shapes, and leave a white area to suggest the bridge of the nose. Use the side of a 6B pencil to create thick, dark shading, and use the point of the pencil for sharper details in the ears and legs. In step C, blend some of the shading to enhance the cat's form and create a softer texture. Then use the point of a 2B pencil to add the final details. Be sure to leave white highlights for contrast.

Cats use body language to express themselves. A cat will mark its territory by rubbing its body against something to transfer its personal scent to the object. Sometimes a cat will rub against people's legs to show affection and send a greeting. The contrast between the rounded, diagonal body of this cat and the vertical lines of the wall makes an effective composition.

Change the angles of the strokes for the shadow and the wall, and vary the length of the strokes for the cat's fur.

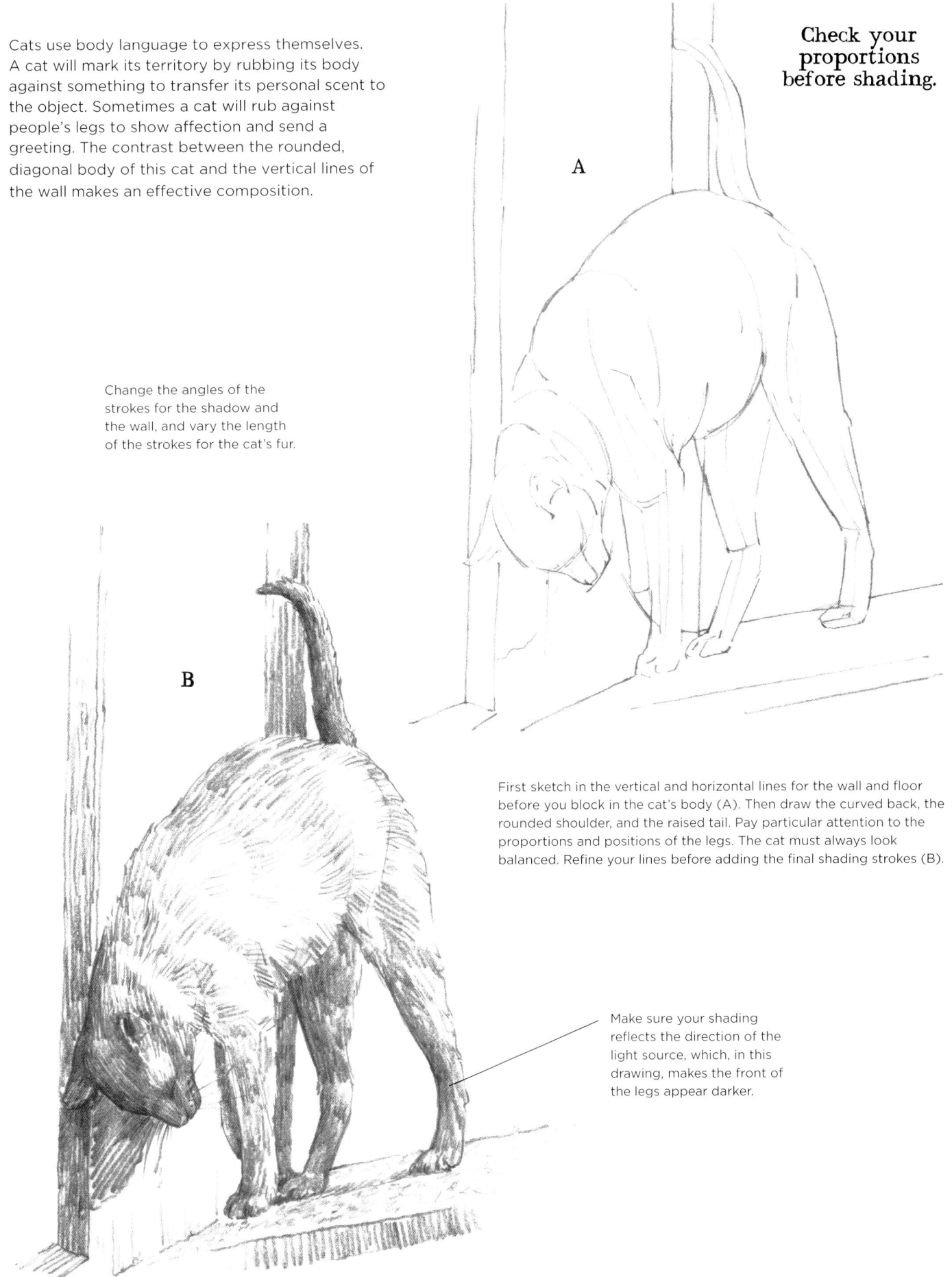

A

B

First sketch in the vertical and horizontal lines for the wall and floor before you block in the cat's body (A). Then draw the curved back, the rounded shoulder, and the raised tail. Pay particular attention to the proportions and positions of the legs. The cat must always look balanced. Refine your lines before adding the final shading strokes (B).

Make sure your shading reflects the direction of the light source, which, in this drawing, makes the front of the legs appear darker.

Cats | 89

Kittens in Action

This kitten is particularly challenging to draw because its head is tilted away from the viewer. The sides of its face must be foreshortened so the top of the head appears larger and closer, and the chin appears smaller.

A

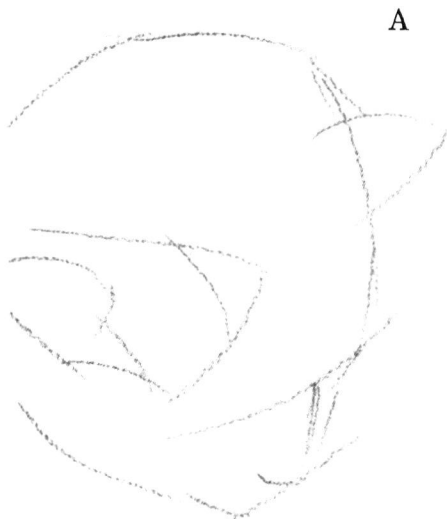

B

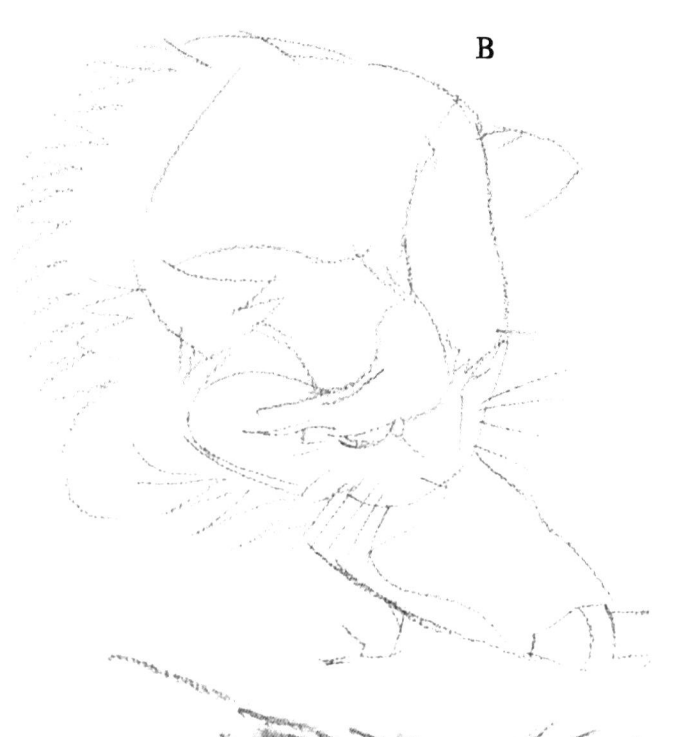

Block in the head (A). Take care when drawing the kitten's right ear. Because this ear is pointed toward the viewer, it also needs to be foreshortened. That is, the sides of the ears must be drawn shorter than they actually are to create the illusion that the tip of the ear is closest to the viewer. Notice, also, that this ear appears much larger than the kitten's left ear. This is another technique that is used to create depth in a drawing. In general, larger objects appear closer to the viewer, and smaller objects appear farther away.

C

Develop the shapes further (B). Observe your subject and make certain the proportions are correct. Then use a brush and varying values of India ink to suggest the kitten's fur in step C. Notice how the loose, sketchy strokes give a sense of playfulness to the drawing.

Kittens' wrestling sessions and stalking games are a means of developing and honing their hunting skills.

Cats can be amused for hours with toys or movable objects. They are also adept at manipulating inert objects to make them move, just so they can chase and catch them. Try to catch this sense of playfulness in your composition. In this drawing, the interest area is the mass of yarn entangling the kitten's paws. Notice how many different techniques are used to direct attention to this spot. Here, the yarn is created using negative shapes against a dark background. The use of negative space is an effective way not only to create interest but also to delineate form.

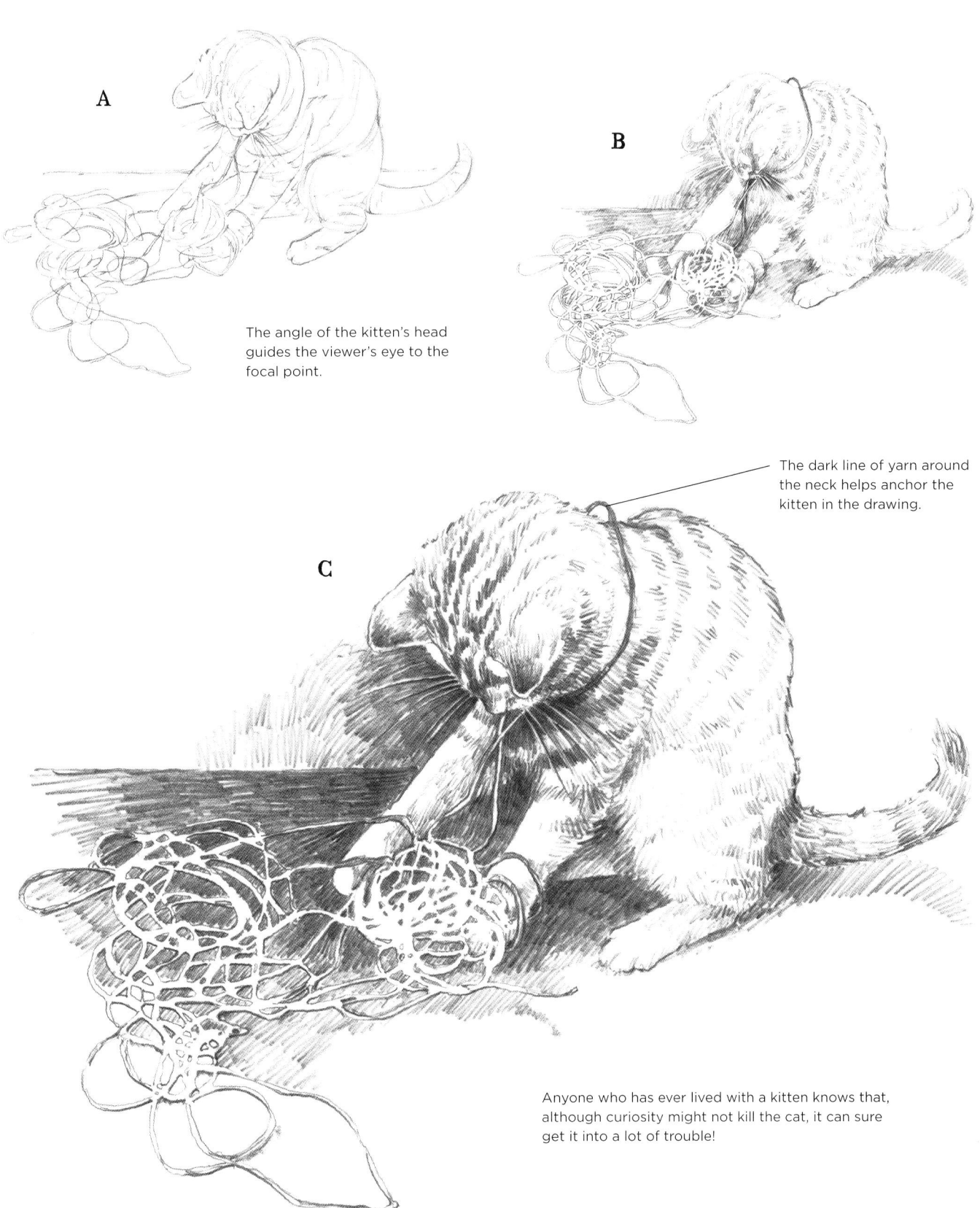

A

The angle of the kitten's head guides the viewer's eye to the focal point.

B

The dark line of yarn around the neck helps anchor the kitten in the drawing.

C

Anyone who has ever lived with a kitten knows that, although curiosity might not kill the cat, it can sure get it into a lot of trouble!

Climbing Kitten

Cats love to climb, although this kitten has found itself in a precarious situation. Note that kittens have round, barrel-shaped bodies, whereas adult cats have long, lanky bodies.

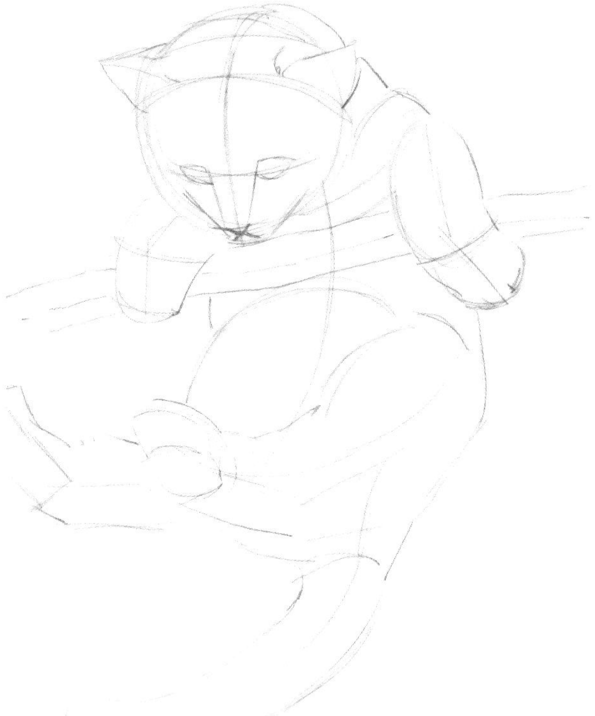

Step 1 Sketch in the branch so that it is at a slight angle. Then block in the kitten's body around the branch. Be careful not to make the body too elongated; show it curving around and under the branch. Use a sharp HB pencil to lightly indicate the face, belly, legs, and tail.

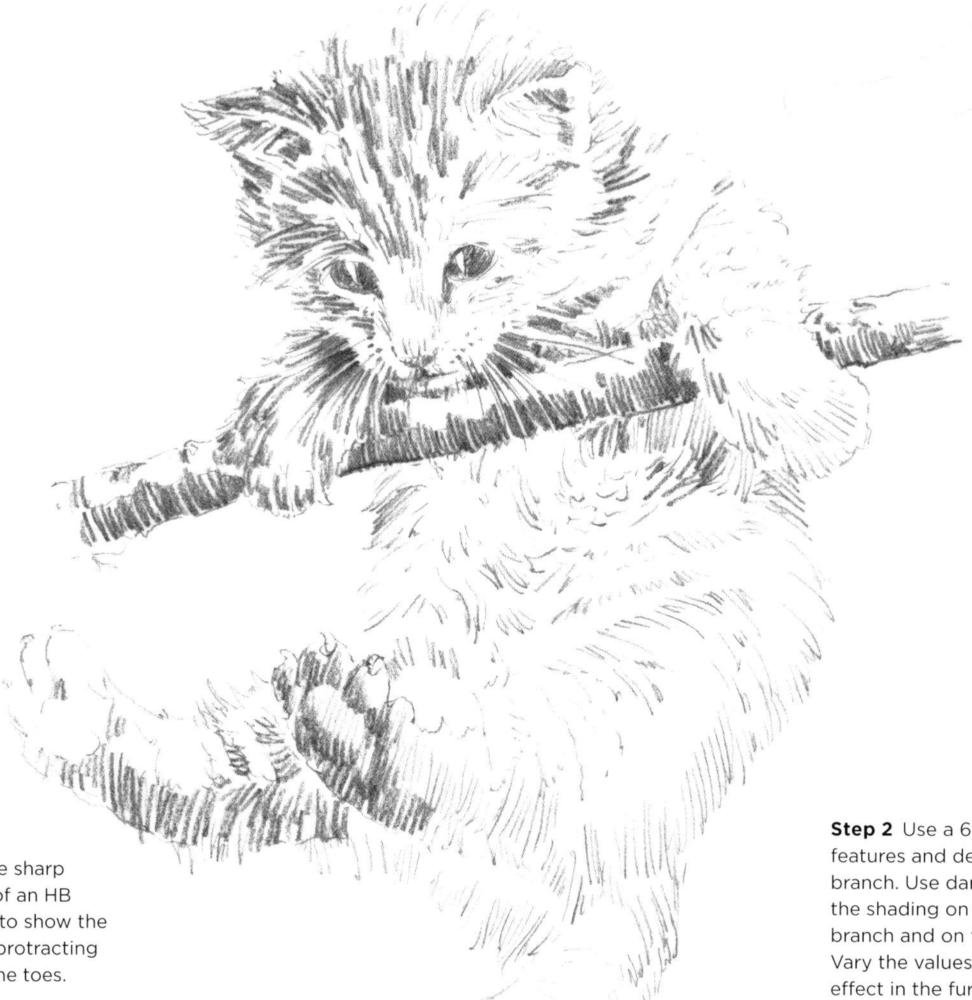

Use the sharp point of an HB pencil to show the claws protracting from the toes.

Step 2 Use a 6B pencil to flesh out the features and develop the fur and the branch. Use dark, uniform strokes for the shading on the underside of the branch and on the kitten's footpads. Vary the values to create a striped effect in the fur.

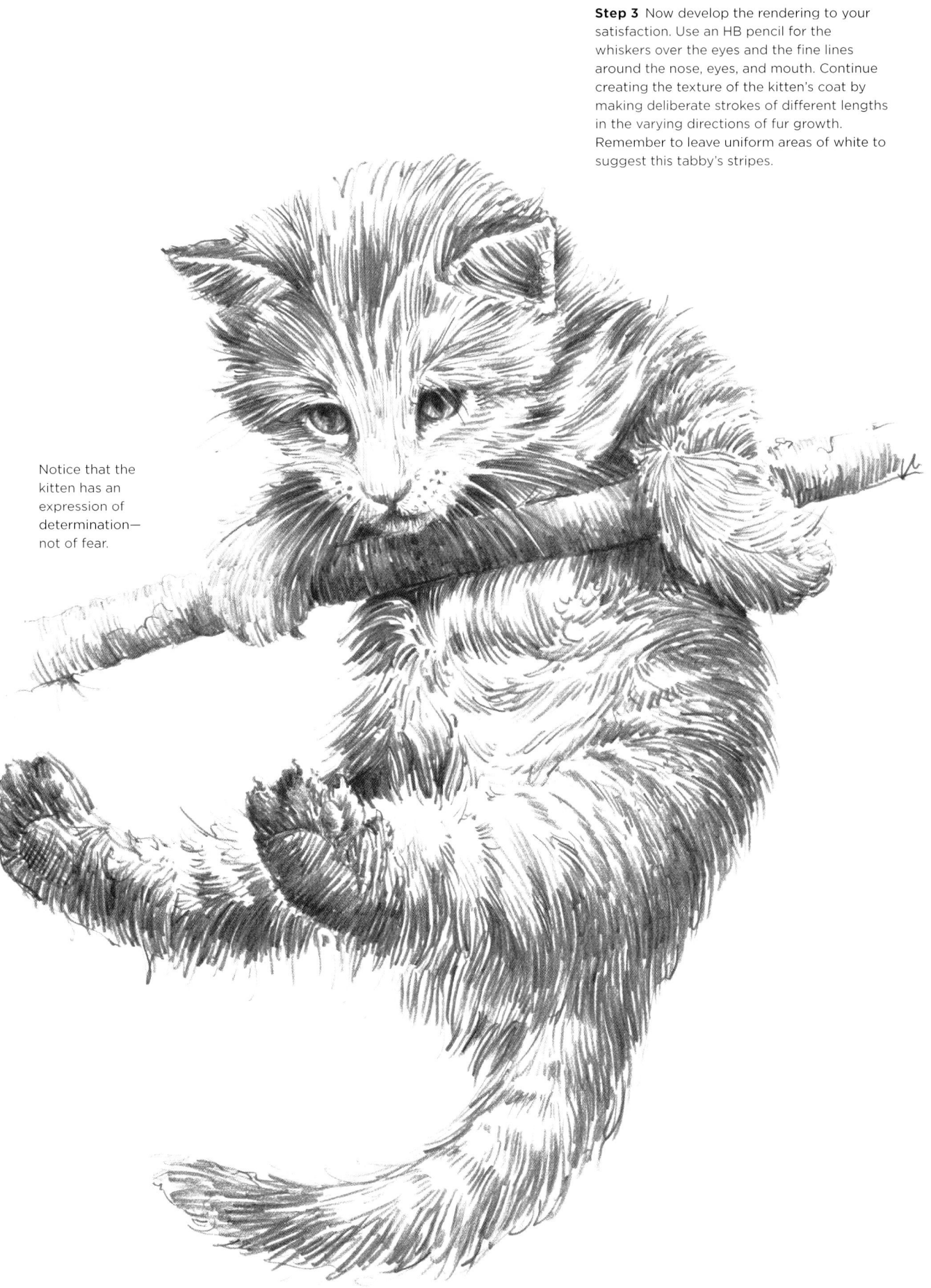

Step 3 Now develop the rendering to your satisfaction. Use an HB pencil for the whiskers over the eyes and the fine lines around the nose, eyes, and mouth. Continue creating the texture of the kitten's coat by making deliberate strokes of different lengths in the varying directions of fur growth. Remember to leave uniform areas of white to suggest this tabby's stripes.

Notice that the kitten has an expression of determination— not of fear.

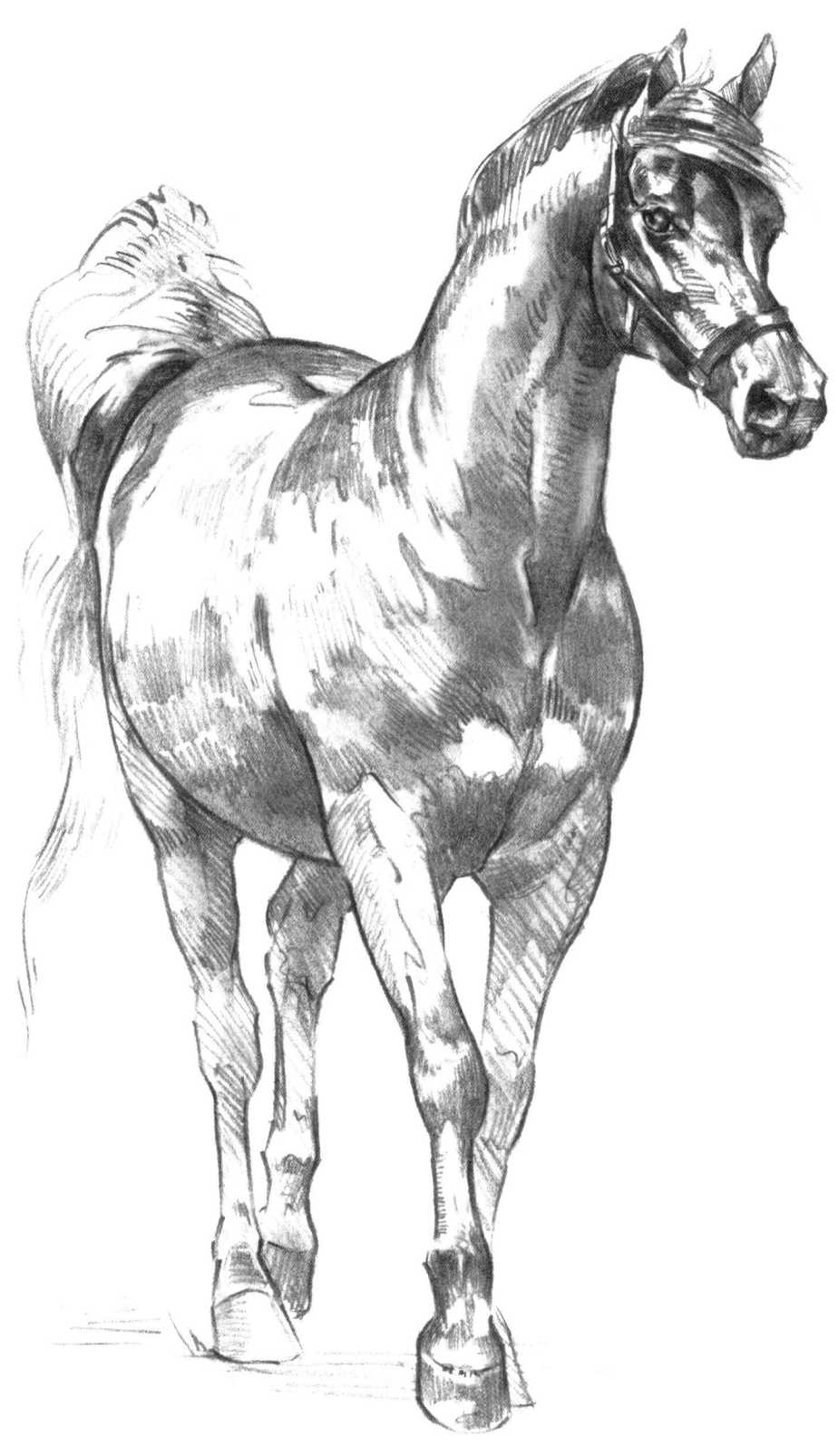

Horses

Horses have long been a favorite subject among pencil artists. Their muscular bodies, flowing manes, and graceful postures offer no shortage of challenges. Artists rendering these magnificent creatures in pencil need to be precise to properly capture their beauty and elegance. Whether depicting a horse and rider or a foal simply grazing, artists must learn how to capture scenes of energy and serenity. The natural beauty and spirit of these animals make them a rewarding subject to sketch, whether in fine detail or bold, expressive strokes.

The lessons and tutorials in this chapter will set you on a path to drawing horses and ponies with confidence. Study the tips, techniques, and lessons in this chapter. With time and practice, you will master the art of drawing horses.

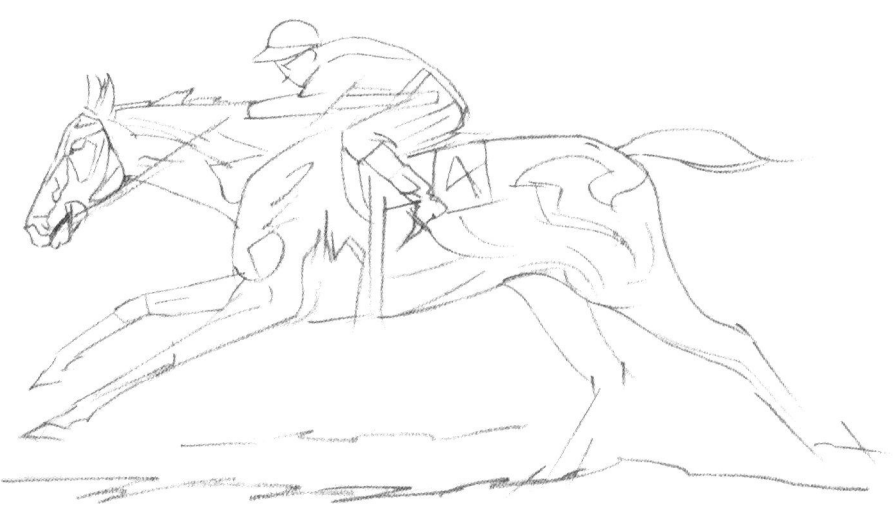

Proportion & Anatomy

Some knowledge of the horse's anatomy and proportion is important for correctly blocking in the basic shape of the subject at the beginning of each drawing.

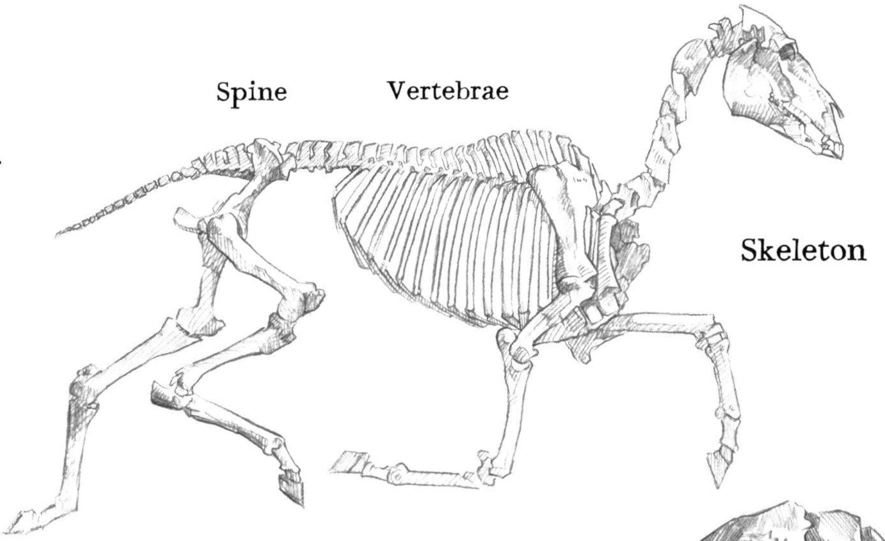

Spine   Vertebrae

Skeleton

The horse's large eye is set high on its elongated head. Notice the width of the skull from the forehead to the lower jaw and the long, tapered nose.

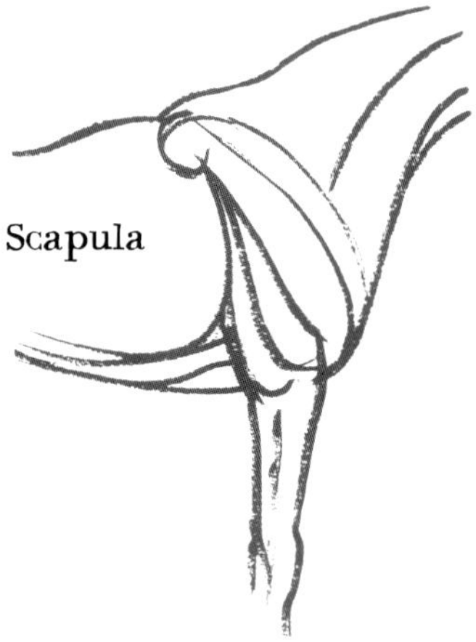

Scapula

To make realistic drawings, keep in mind that the horse's structure is determined by its skeleton. You don't need to learn the names of all the parts of the horse's anatomy, or even how to draw them; just keep the basic sizes and shapes in mind as you draw. For example, note the triangular shape of the skull, the depth of the rib cage, and the joints in the legs. The vertebrae are slightly higher in the area over the rib cage, forming the base of the horse's withers.

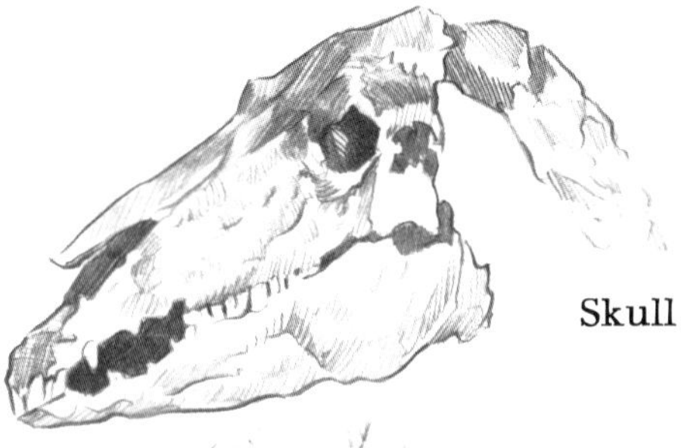

Skull

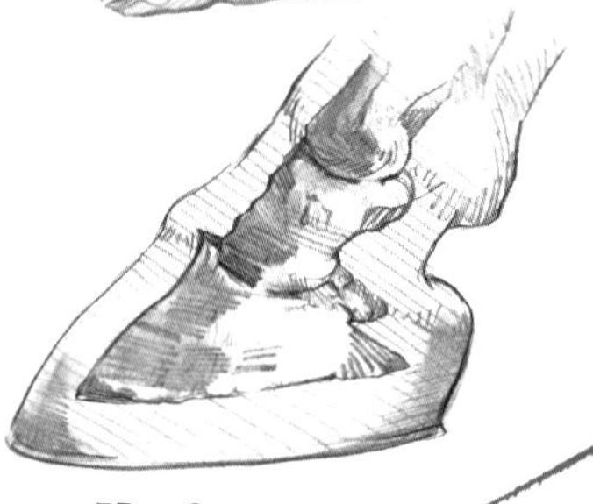

The hoof is a hard protective covering for the single toe of each foot.

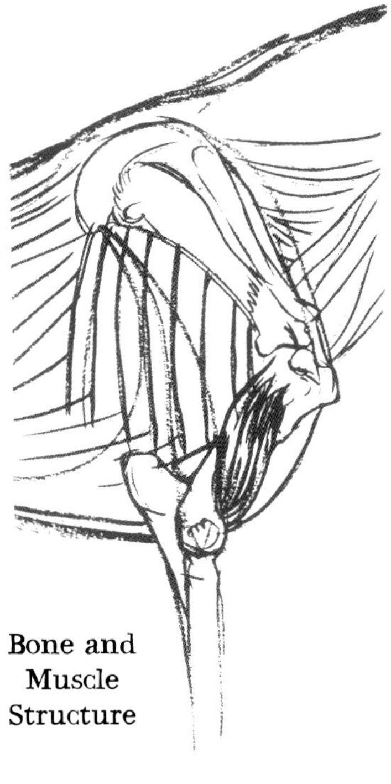

Hoof

Head

Head

Head

Head

Head

1/2 Head

Head

4 Heads Long

1/2 Head

Head

Head

Bone and Muscle Structure

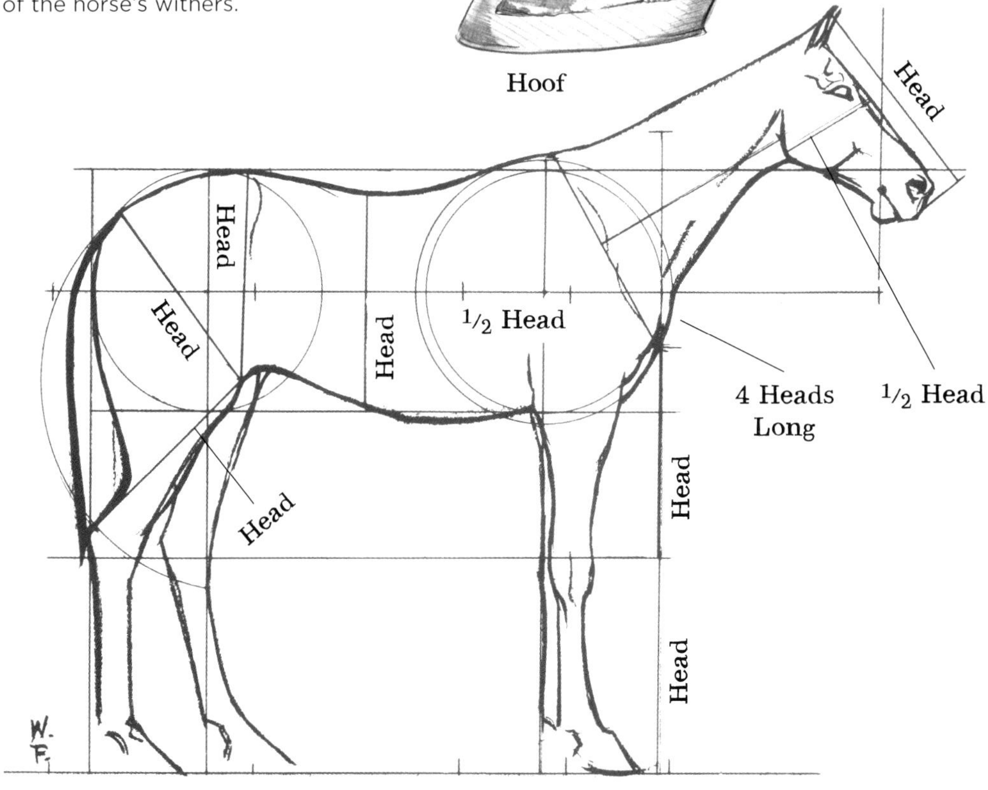

W. F.

Familiarity with the horse's anatomy and musculature will help you make your drawings look realistic. Generally, areas with large, smooth muscles will be shaded lightly, whereas the areas of smaller overlapping muscles will require more complex shading. Study the illustrations to see how the muscles and tendons wrap around the horse's skeletal structure.

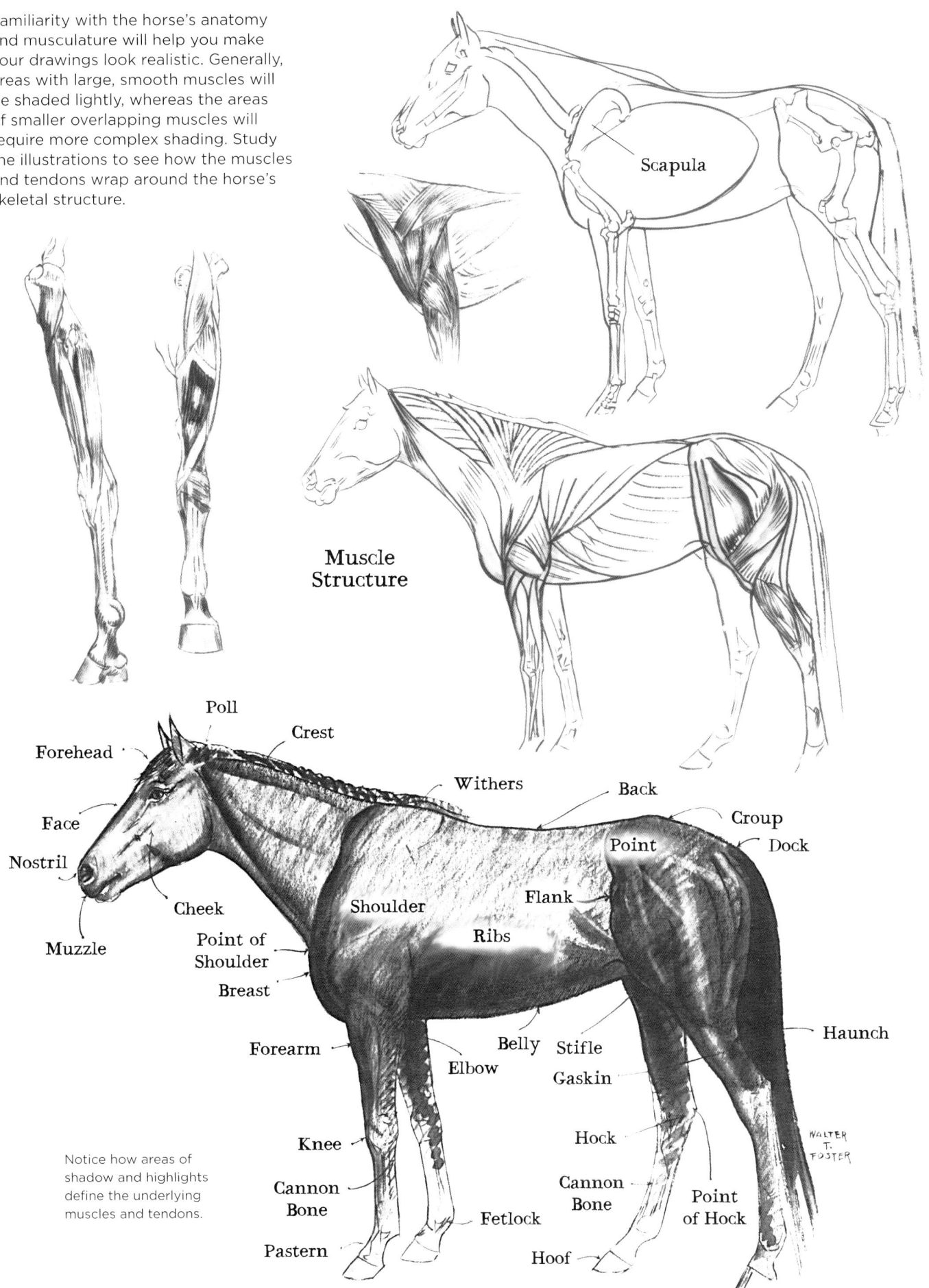

Scapula

Muscle Structure

Poll

Crest

Forehead

Withers

Back

Face

Croup

Point

Dock

Nostril

Flank

Shoulder

Cheek

Ribs

Muzzle

Point of Shoulder

Breast

Belly

Stifle

Haunch

Forearm

Elbow

Gaskin

Knee

Hock

WALTER T. FOSTER

Cannon Bone

Cannon Bone

Point of Hock

Notice how areas of shadow and highlights define the underlying muscles and tendons.

Fetlock

Pastern

Hoof

Shading Techniques

Techniques for graphite and charcoal are similar to those for watercolor paint. (See page 99.) There are many more shading techniques than the ones covered here, but these are typically used for drawing animals in general. One of the most important rules is to shade in the direction of hair growth, as it makes your drawings look more realistic. Note that graphite is easier to blend than charcoal. Graphite is also easier to erase or lift from the paper. The graphite techniques on pages 98–99 are shown in the left column; the charcoal techniques are shown in the right column.

Graphite   Charcoal

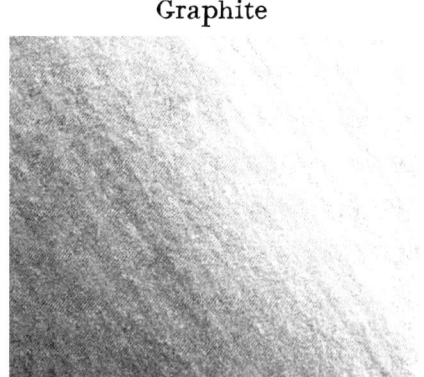 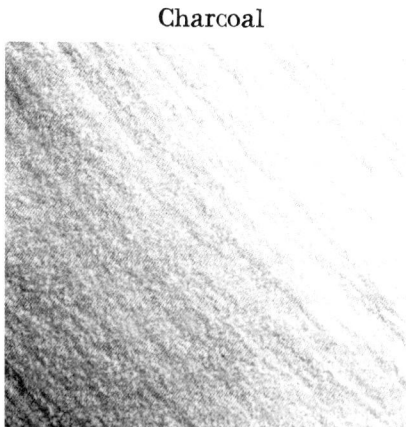

Gradation Start with a soft pencil, such as a 6B, and turn the pencil on its side. With a good amount of pressure, lay in the darkest value, gradually lessening the pressure as you move down. You may switch to a harder pencil as you move to the lighter values. You can also blend strokes by layering them on top of one another.

Hair Using a sharp graphite or charcoal pencil and a sweeping stroke, quickly move your hand in an arc, lifting the pencil from the paper at the end of the stroke. It's best to lift the pencil at the end of the hair (from the darkest to lightest), but experiment to find out what works for you. With a little practice, you will master the art of drawing hair.

Blended Gradation These examples show gradated values that were blended and softened with a tortillon. This technique works well for moving tones into a lighter area.

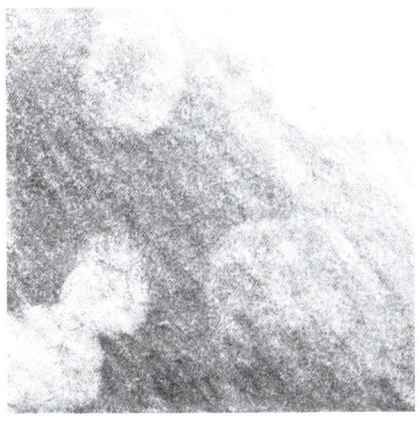

Erasing These examples show how tone can be lifted from the page using a kneaded eraser (such as for creating highlights). A kneaded eraser is the most effective tool for this, as it can be molded to fit small areas or flattened out for larger areas. Remember that charcoal is harder to lift out than graphite.

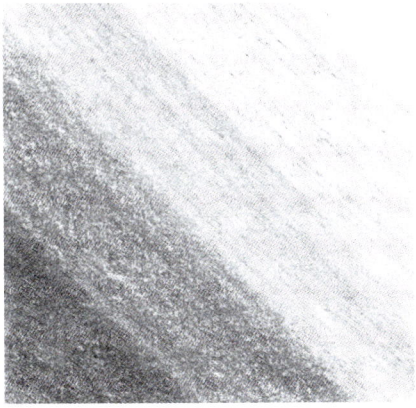

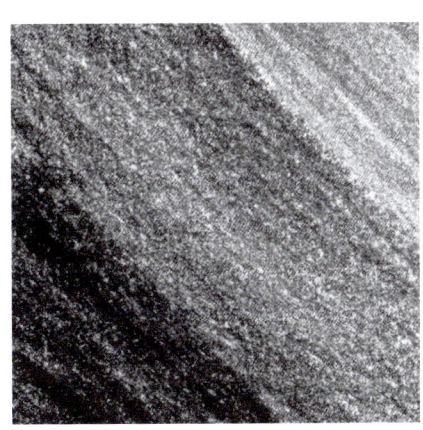

Pencil Hardness Here are examples of how pencil hardness affects value. The banding indicates where a harder pencil was used to shade. By varying the amount of pressure, you can achieve a wide range of values in your drawings.

Crosshatching These samples illustrate the way that layering in different directions creates texture and adds interest. If you use this technique, it should be used throughout the drawing for consistency. Crosshatching works especially well for preliminary drawings.

WATERCOLOR TECHNIQUES

Drybrushing Load a brush with a wash of paint and dab the bristles on a paper towel, eliminating most of the moisture. Pull the brush lightly across the paper's surface for a texture that suggests mane and tail hair.

Gradation Pull a horizontal band of a wash across the top of the paper. Add more water to your brush as you stroke down, creating a transition from dark to light that can suggest form.

Wet-on-Dry Paint wet color onto dry paper or paint wet over a dry layer of color. This gives you a good amount of control over the paint's spread, which is great for painting details.

Eyes & Muzzle

Facial features, such as eyes and muzzles, are a good place to start learning to draw horses. If you're a beginner, you might want to practice drawing the parts separately before attempting a complete rendering. Study the drawings on this page, and look at the way the shapes and forms change as the viewing angle changes.

Practice by making many sketches of these features from several different angles. Copy the examples here, or use your own models. Often, details, such as the expression in the eye or the shading around the nostril, are what separate an average drawing from a remarkable one. Start by sketching the general shape with an HB pencil, and then refine the lines until you are satisfied.

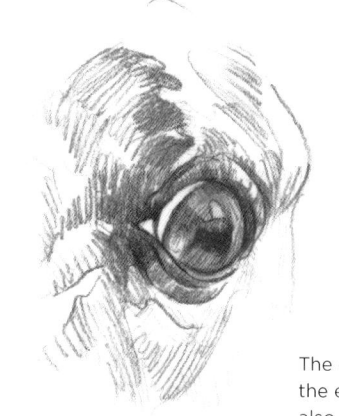

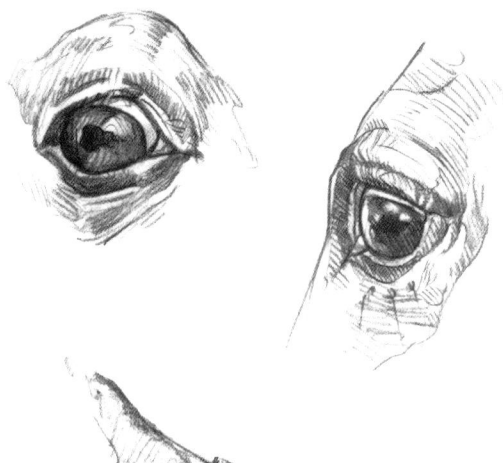

The eyeball is a sphere, so the eyelid covering it will also be spherical in shape.

As is true for all mammals, horses' eyes reveal their emotions and personality.

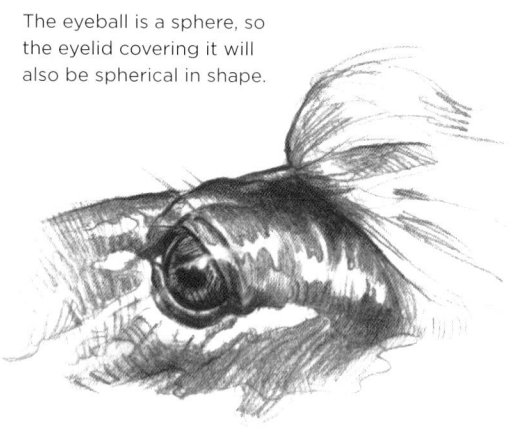

Horse muzzles are not very fleshy, so the planes of the face are quite distinct, revealing the underlying structure of the skull.

When drawing horses—or any subject—it is best to work from live models or photographs. Trying to draw from memory or imagination is much more difficult. Collect photographs of horses and foals from catalogs, magazines, and books, and keep them in a file for reference.

The forms of the muscles, veins, and tendons are also easily discernible under the surface of the horse's skin and sleek coat.

Changes in values and in pencil stroke direction help make your drawings look three-dimensional.

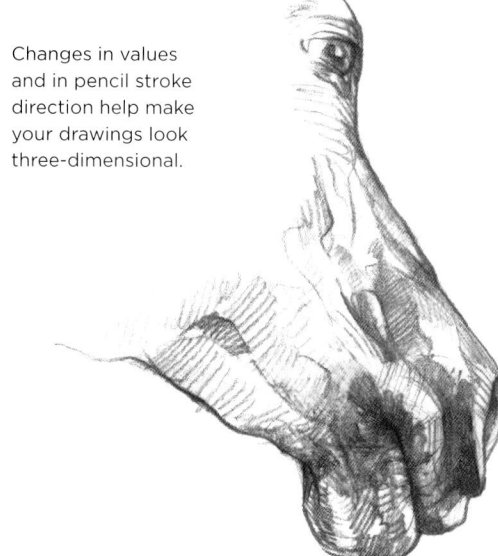

Horses have a few large teeth in the front of their mouth, with a gap on either side between the front incisors and the rear molars.

Ears & Hooves

The position of the horse's ears reveals its mood. For example, ears pricked forward usually indicate alert interest, whereas ears laid back are a sign of anger, discomfort, or fear. As you practice drawing the ears in different positions, note how shading is used to define the form of the ears.

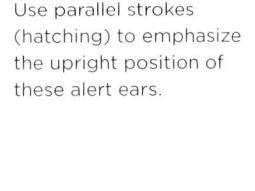

Use parallel strokes (hatching) to emphasize the upright position of these alert ears.

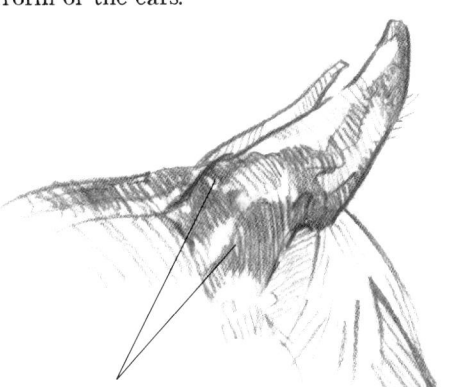

Vary the direction of your pencil strokes to delineate the round form of the ear.

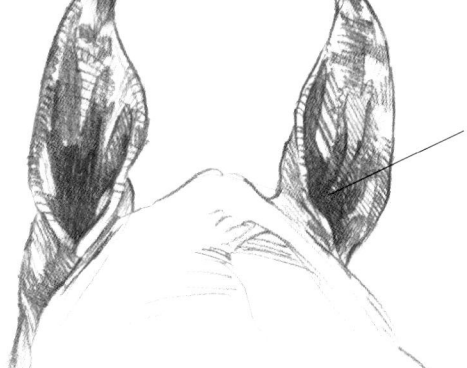

Reserve the darkest values for the inner ear.

The hoof is a hard covering that encloses the underlying toe bone. The frog is the softer, more tender area in the bottom of the hoof. Notice that the hoof is longer in front and shorter in back; make sure your drawings reflect the proper angle of the hoof.

Horseshoes are nailed into the outer hoof wall, but the horse feels no pain because the wall has no nerve endings—just as it doesn't hurt when you trim your fingernails.

Shoe

Frog

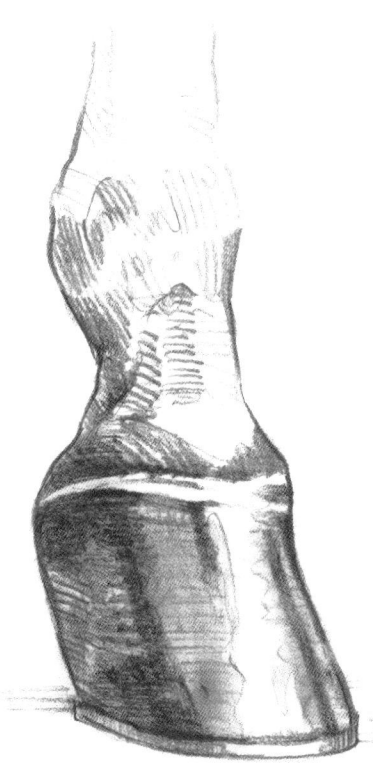

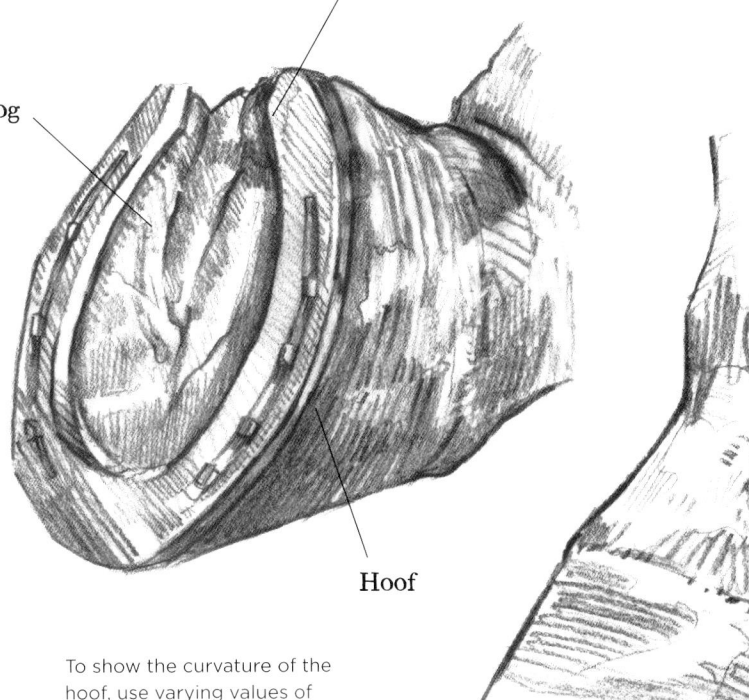

Hoof

To show the curvature of the hoof, use varying values of light and dark. Be sure to leave a highlight where the light strikes the hoof.

Examining Profiles

The following five profile drawings are a small sampling of the differences in some common breeds. Note the slight variations in each. Oftentimes, the profile of the head is characteristic of a particular breed.

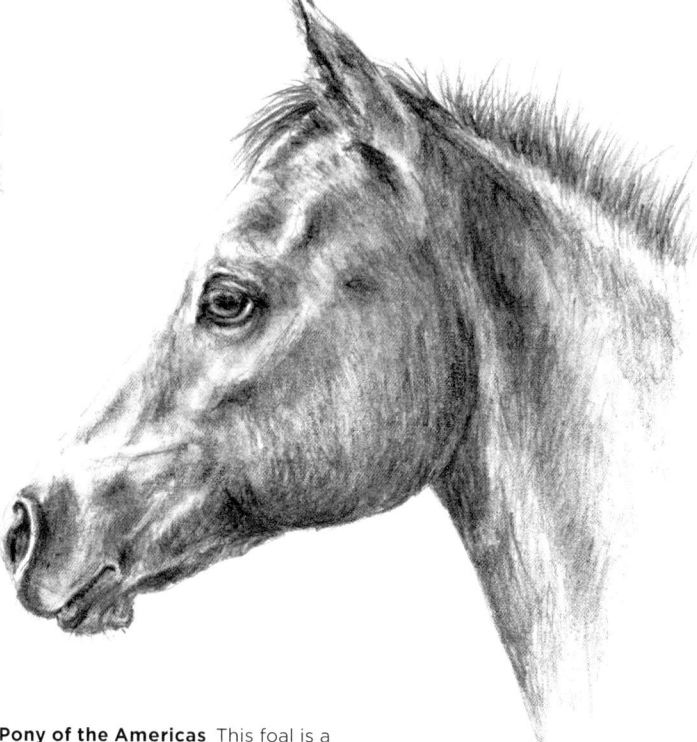

Arabian This refined, fine-boned horse originated in the deserts of the Arabian Peninsula. Known for its speed and stamina in extreme conditions, the Arabian's beauty and grace are unparalleled.

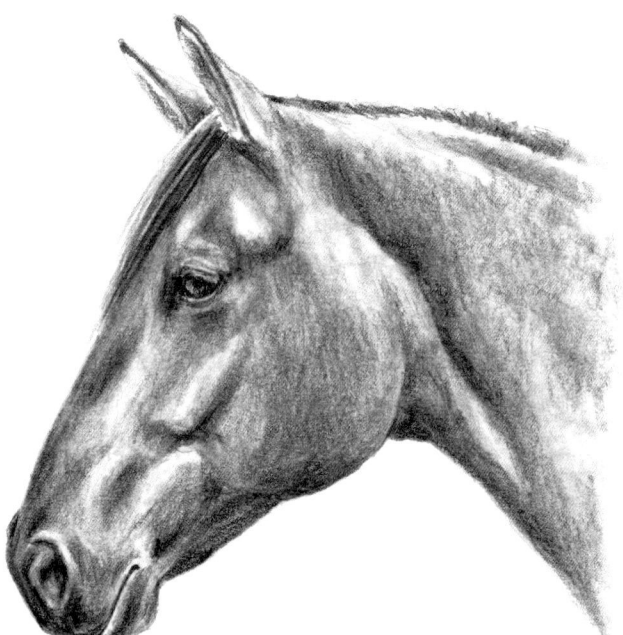

American Quarter Horse A compact breed originating in North America, the American Quarter Horse is known for its speed and durability at a quarter-mile sprint. Primarily bred as a work horse and often used in ranch work, today's Quarter Horse is found across the globe.

Pony of the Americas This foal is a miniature version of the larger Appaloosa horse. The pony possesses the same characteristics as its larger cousin, including spots, but the pony measures between 46 and 56 inches, making it the perfect size for children to mount.

Haflinger Native to Austria, the Haflinger evolved in the Tyrolean area of the Alps. The breed takes its name from the village of Hafling, which is now part of Italy. Believed to be a horse with Arabian influence, the Halflinger is small in stature but mighty in heart. Always chestnut in color, varying in shade from blonde to dark chocolate, its mane and tail are long, thick, and vary from flaxen to white in color.

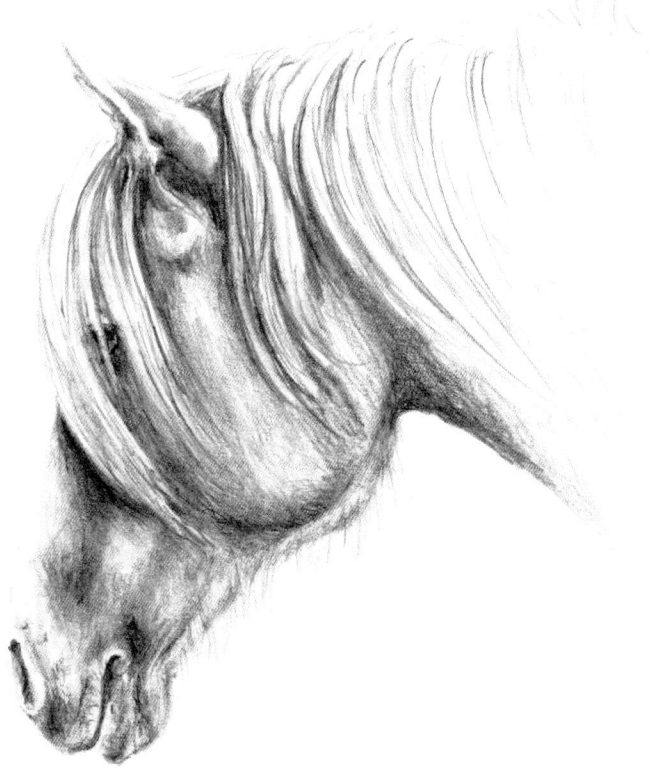

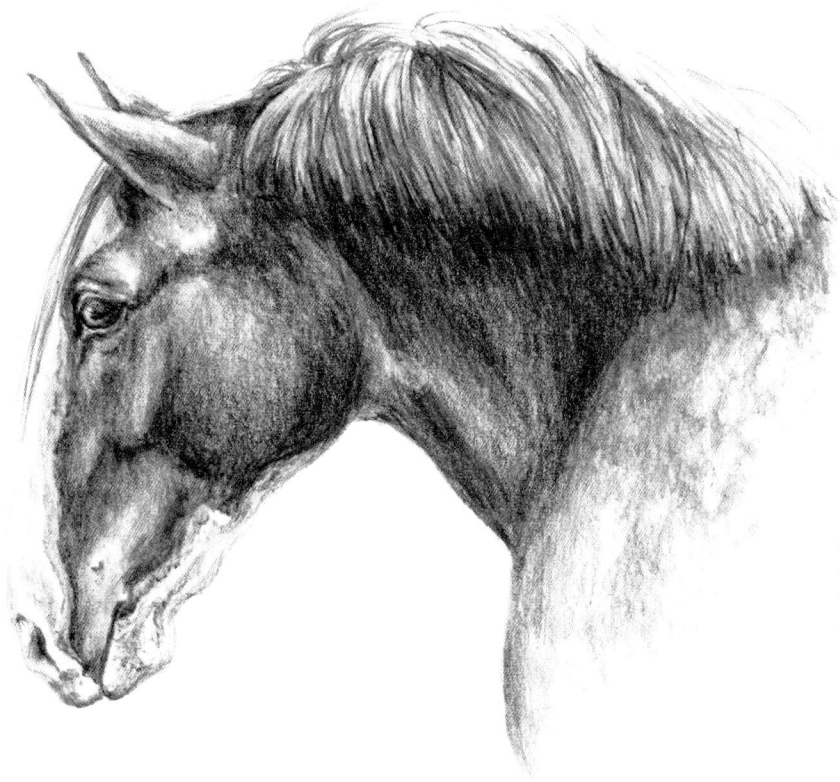

Shire A large, big-boned draft breed specifically bred for heavy work, this horse originated in the Shires of England and is one of the world's largest breeds. It can be black, brown, or gray in color. Today's Shires make beautiful parade horses, pulling large, decorative wagons, and can still be seen in their traditional roles in England.

Basic Profile

In the early stages of your drawing, it's important to establish accurate proportions; you don't want to make major adjustments after you've started adding tone and detail. To get the proportions as precise as possible, use plenty of guidelines to block in the basic shapes. Constantly adjust the lines as you compare sizes, shapes, and angles with your references. Learning this process of creating and working within guidelines will help you work successfully from your own references.

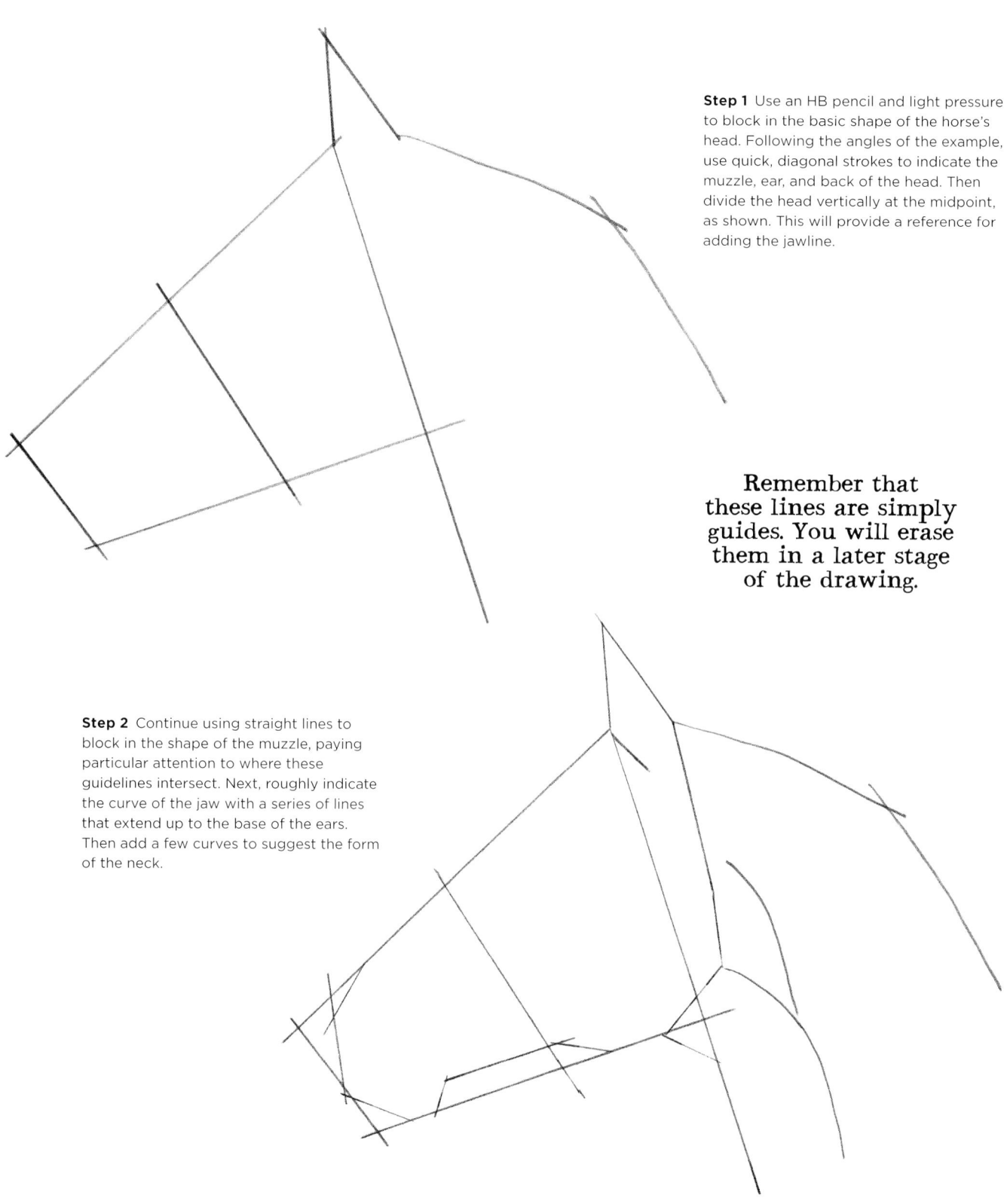

Step 1 Use an HB pencil and light pressure to block in the basic shape of the horse's head. Following the angles of the example, use quick, diagonal strokes to indicate the muzzle, ear, and back of the head. Then divide the head vertically at the midpoint, as shown. This will provide a reference for adding the jawline.

Remember that these lines are simply guides. You will erase them in a later stage of the drawing.

Step 2 Continue using straight lines to block in the shape of the muzzle, paying particular attention to where these guidelines intersect. Next, roughly indicate the curve of the jaw with a series of lines that extend up to the base of the ears. Then add a few curves to suggest the form of the neck.

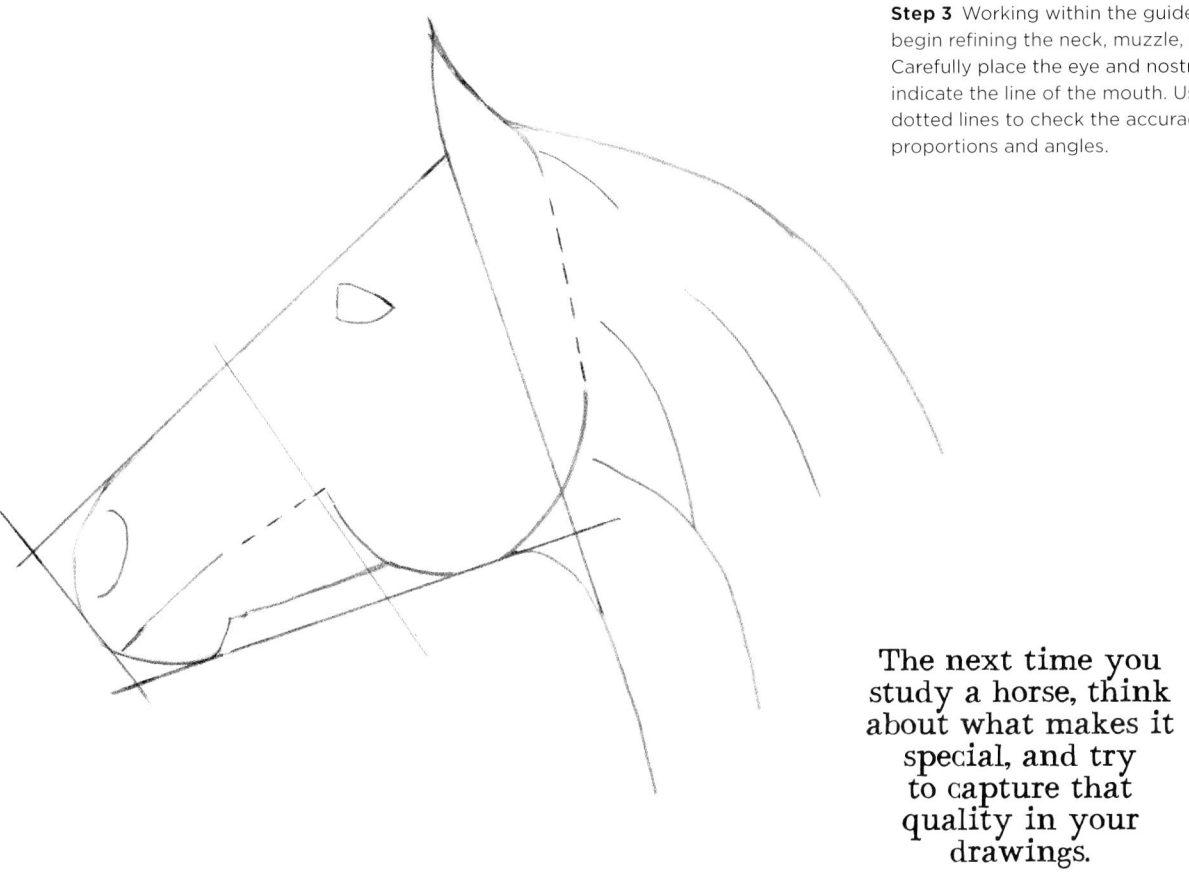

Step 3 Working within the guidelines, begin refining the neck, muzzle, and jaw. Carefully place the eye and nostril; then indicate the line of the mouth. Use the dotted lines to check the accuracy of your proportions and angles.

The next time you study a horse, think about what makes it special, and try to capture that quality in your drawings.

Step 4 Develop the facial features and further refine the outlines, following the subtle curves of flesh around the mouth. Then block in the mane and forelock with strokes that follow the direction of hair growth. Keep your strokes light in these initial stages.

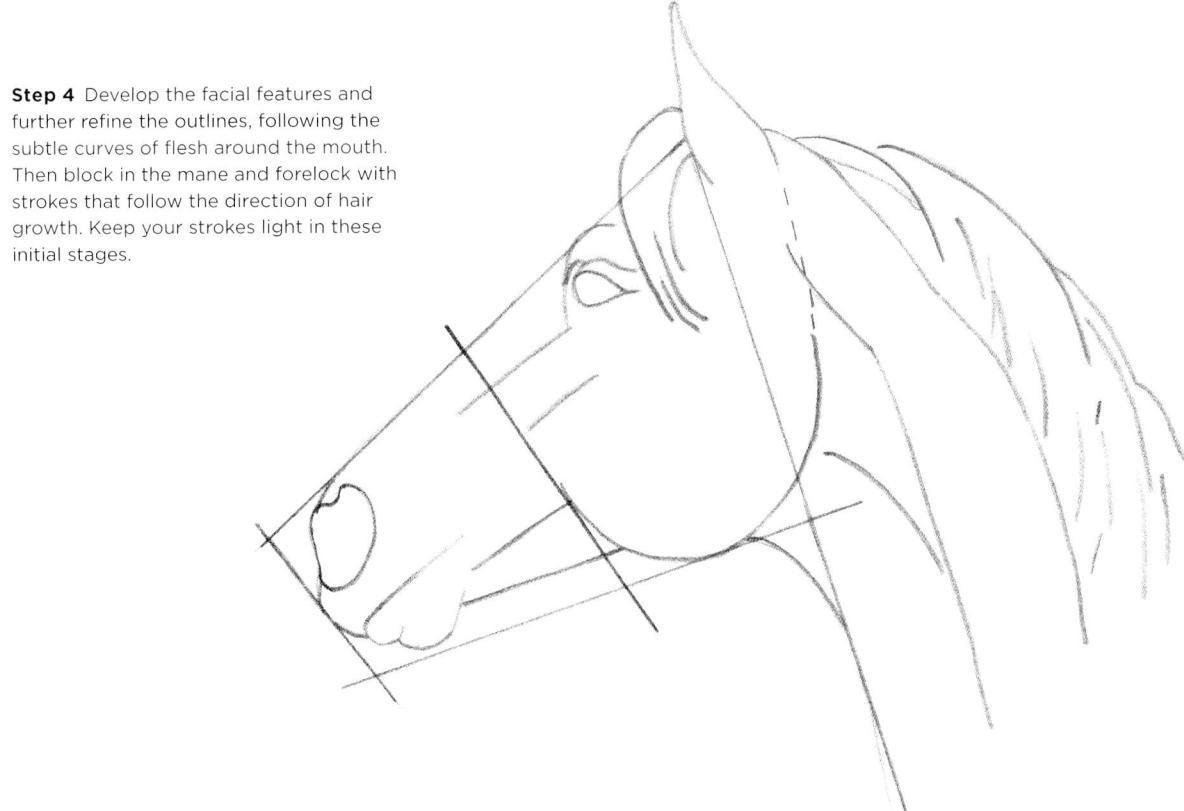

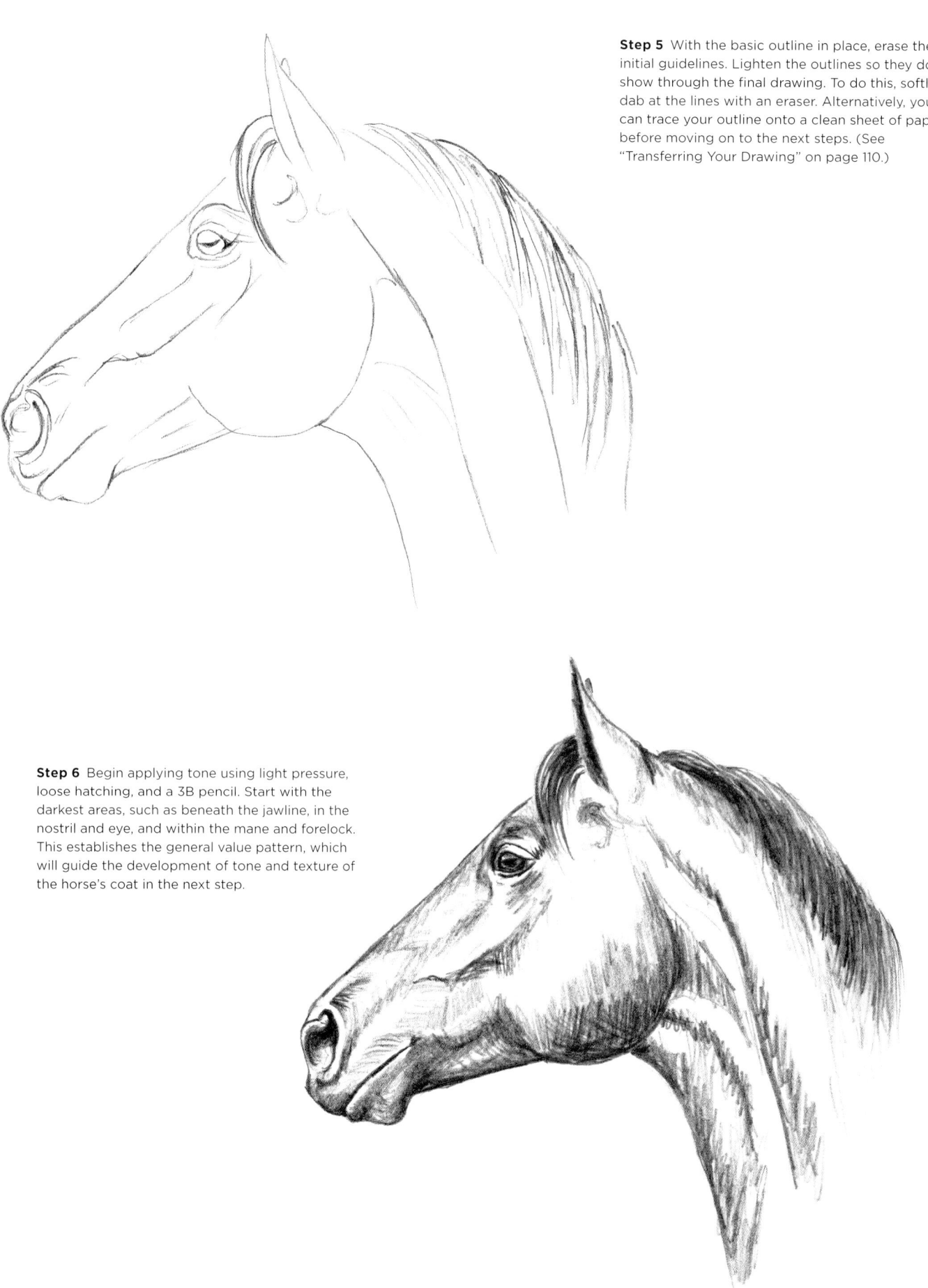

Step 5 With the basic outline in place, erase the initial guidelines. Lighten the outlines so they don't show through the final drawing. To do this, softly dab at the lines with an eraser. Alternatively, you can trace your outline onto a clean sheet of paper before moving on to the next steps. (See "Transferring Your Drawing" on page 110.)

Step 6 Begin applying tone using light pressure, loose hatching, and a 3B pencil. Start with the darkest areas, such as beneath the jawline, in the nostril and eye, and within the mane and forelock. This establishes the general value pattern, which will guide the development of tone and texture of the horse's coat in the next step.

The Thoroughbred line of
horses dates back to the 17th century
when English mares were crossed with
Arabian stallions. Bred primarily for
racing, this speedy horse is known for
its natural speed and athleticism.

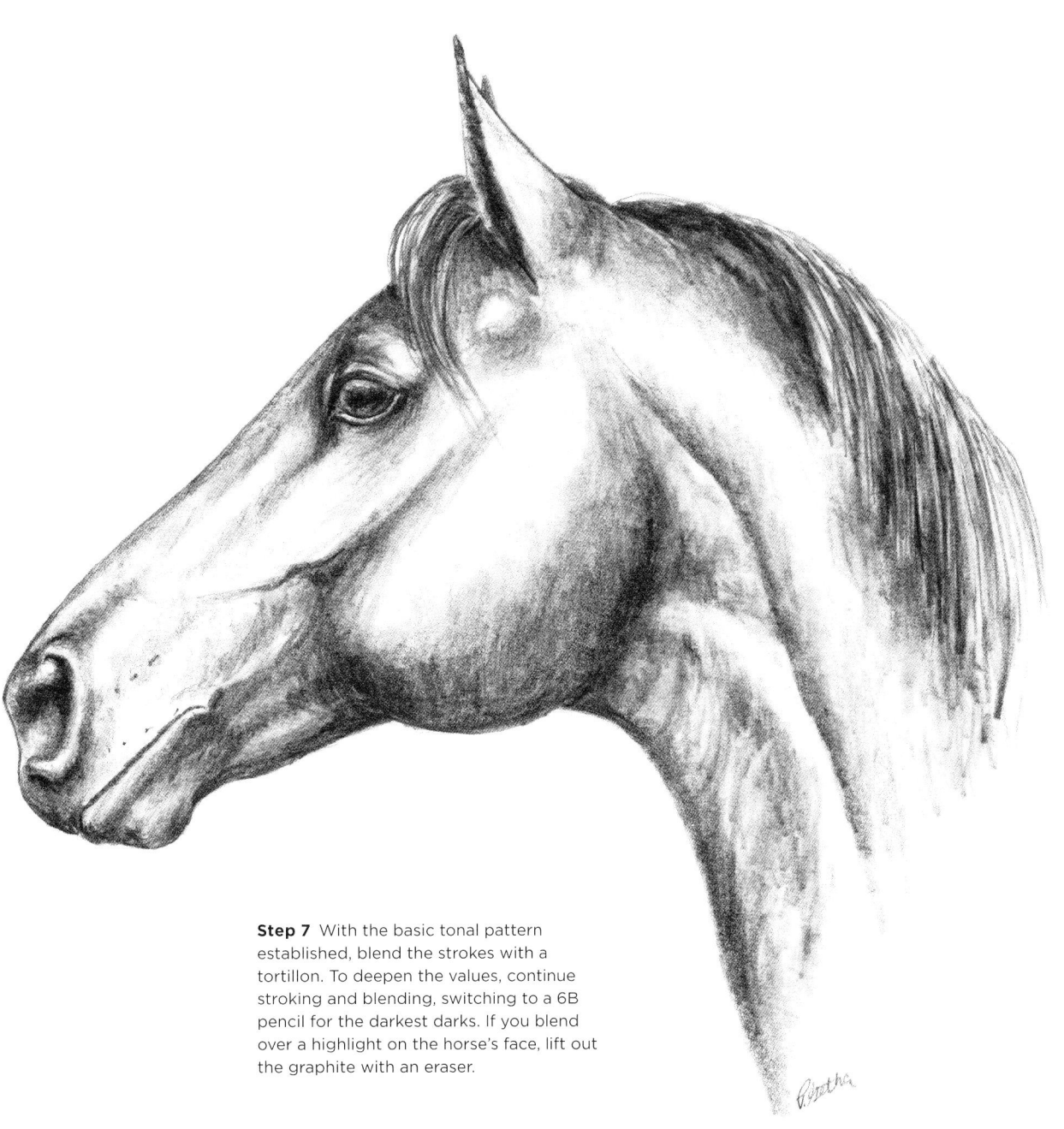

Step 7 With the basic tonal pattern
established, blend the strokes with a
tortillon. To deepen the values, continue
stroking and blending, switching to a 6B
pencil for the darkest darks. If you blend
over a highlight on the horse's face, lift out
the graphite with an eraser.

Arabian Portrait

When searching for a reference, remember that you aren't limited to just one photo, and that using multiple sources is an effective option. You can use artistic license (the artist's prerogative to change a subject or scene) to combine aspects of different photos. For example, if you find one reference with a pleasing composition but can't make out the details, you can use other shots that are better suited to provide this information.

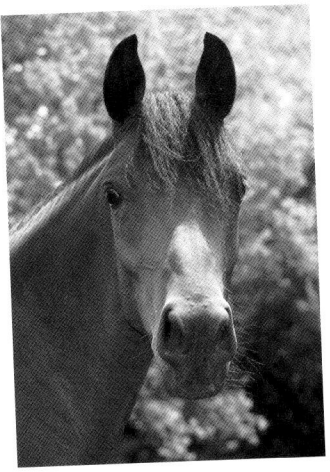 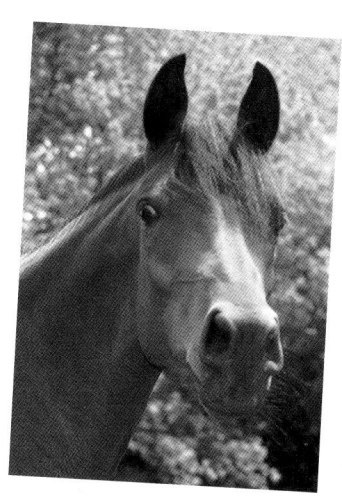

Combining References Two photo references were used for this drawing. The angle of the head and composition in the left photo is strong, but the horse is out of focus. The right photo compensates for this, as the details appear much sharper.

Step 1 Begin with ovals for the head and muzzle; then add several guidelines, as shown, to create reference points for adding the facial features. For example, the uppermost horizontal curve indicates the position of the top of the eyes. Add two lines indicating the neck and a curved line for the jaw. Then carefully place the basic shapes of the ears.

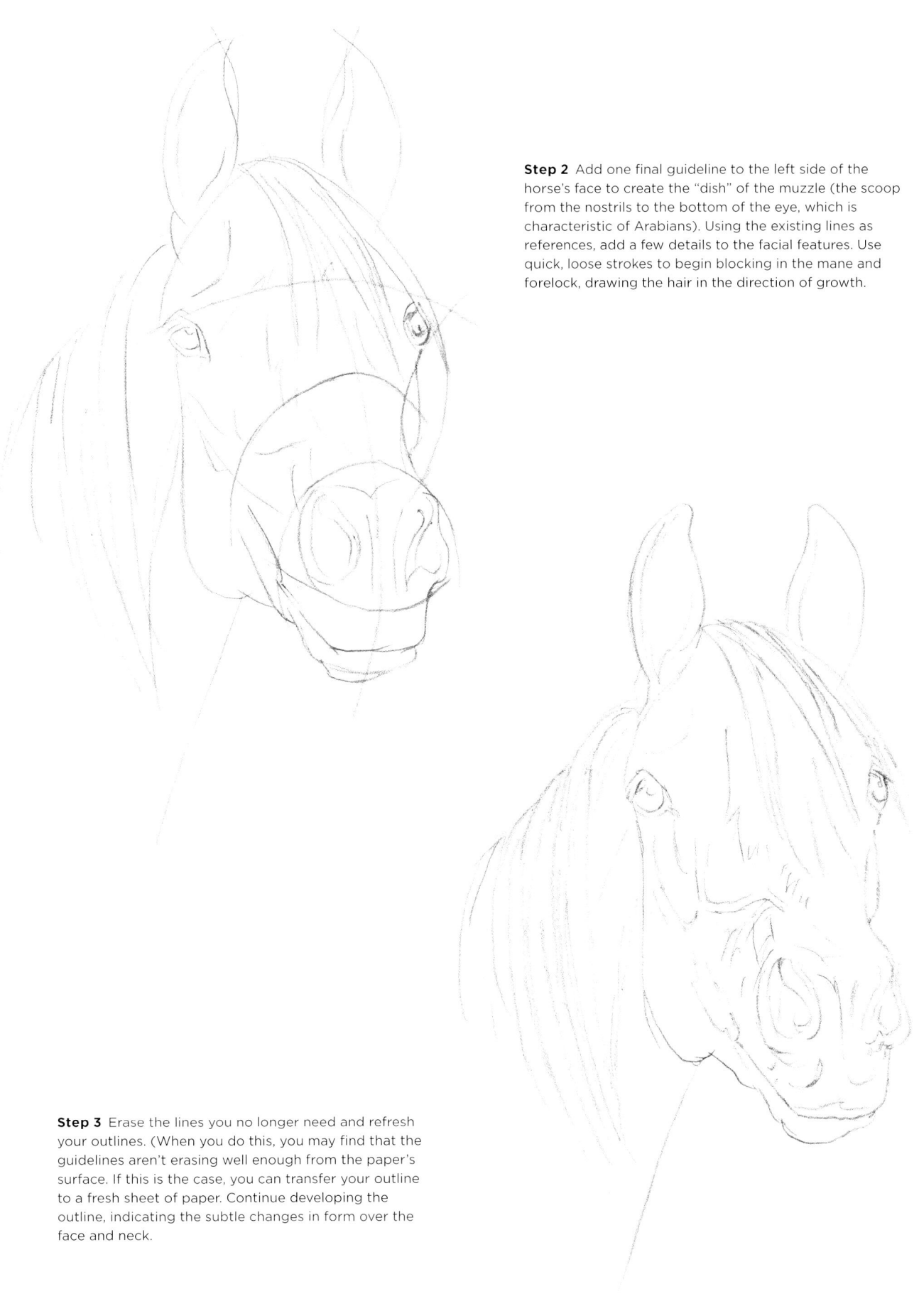

Step 2 Add one final guideline to the left side of the horse's face to create the "dish" of the muzzle (the scoop from the nostrils to the bottom of the eye, which is characteristic of Arabians). Using the existing lines as references, add a few details to the facial features. Use quick, loose strokes to begin blocking in the mane and forelock, drawing the hair in the direction of growth.

Step 3 Erase the lines you no longer need and refresh your outlines. (When you do this, you may find that the guidelines aren't erasing well enough from the paper's surface. If this is the case, you can transfer your outline to a fresh sheet of paper. Continue developing the outline, indicating the subtle changes in form over the face and neck.

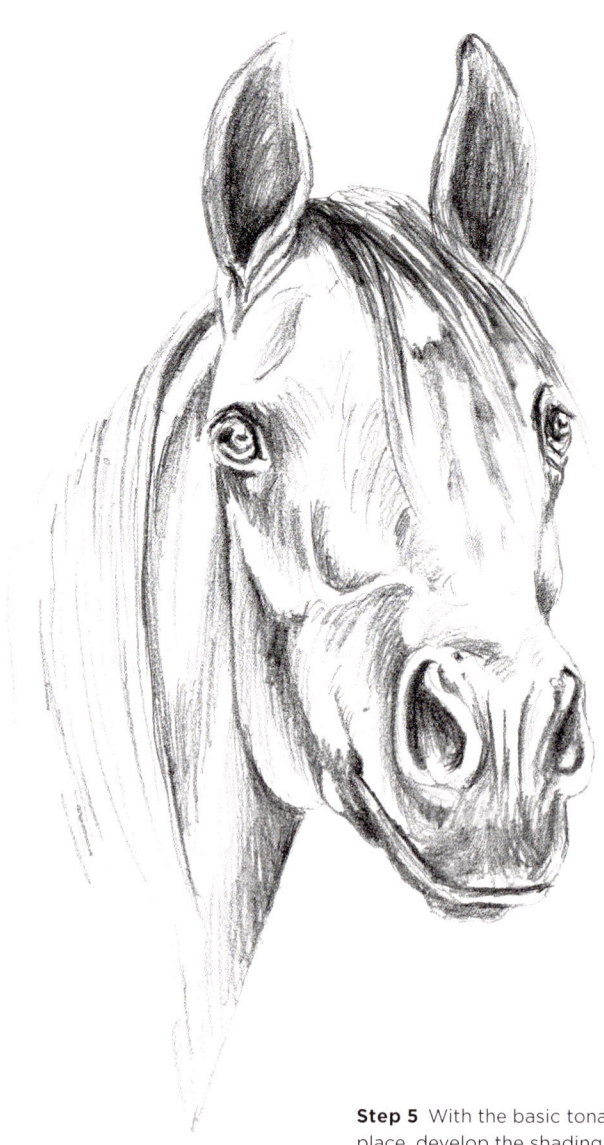

Step 4 Switch to a 3B pencil and begin applying tone to the horse. Hatch in the shadows of the ears, face, and neck, stroking along the curves to suggest form. Use loose, light strokes so they will be easier to blend later. Gradually build up the value of the forelock with long, light pencil strokes, leaving gaps for areas of highlight.

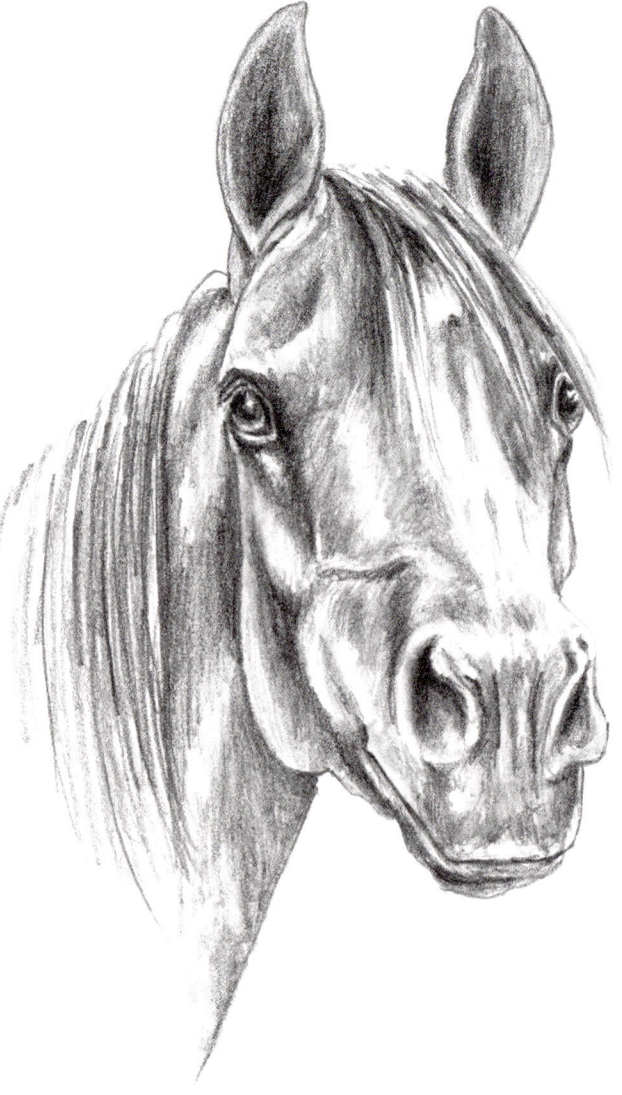

Step 5 With the basic tonal pattern in place, develop the shading to darken the overall value of the horse. Use a tortillon to soften and blend the layers of strokes for a more even, unified tone. Build up the mane with strokes of varying values to give it a realistic hair texture.

TRANSFERRING YOUR DRAWING

Once you've established an outline on your paper, you may find that your initial guidelines and sketch marks are difficult to erase. If this is the case, you can transfer your outline to a fresh sheet of paper. Simply coat the back of your sketch with a layer of graphite, pressing down firmly to create an even layer of coverage. Now turn your paper right-side up and place it over the new sheet of paper. Tape or hold the papers together and lightly trace your outline. The lines will transfer onto the new sheet of drawing paper. You can also buy graphite transfer paper for this purpose.

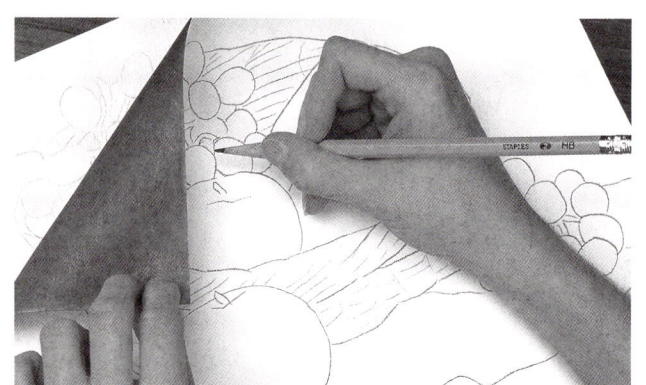

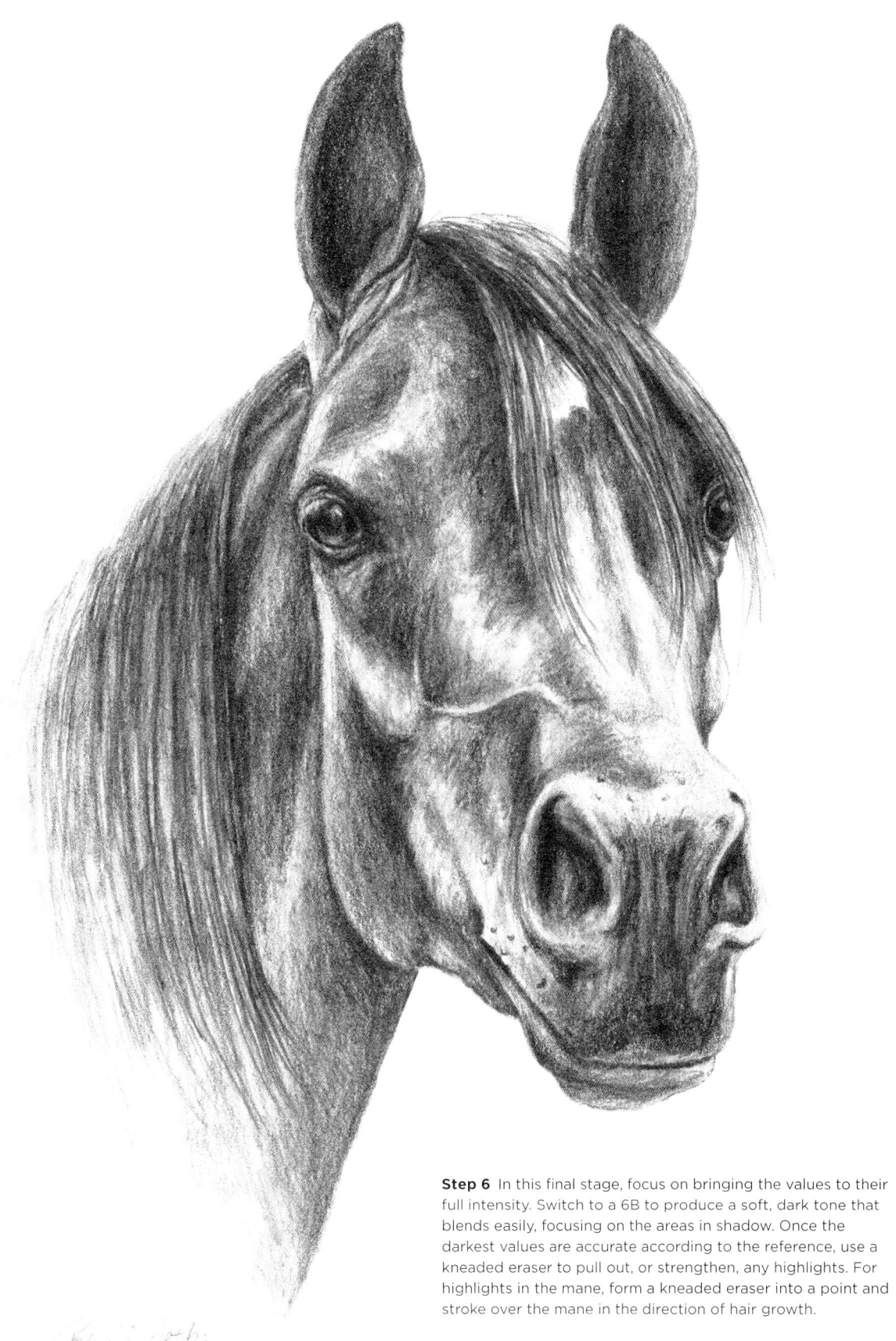

Step 6 In this final stage, focus on bringing the values to their full intensity. Switch to a 6B to produce a soft, dark tone that blends easily, focusing on the areas in shadow. Once the darkest values are accurate according to the reference, use a kneaded eraser to pull out, or strengthen, any highlights. For highlights in the mane, form a kneaded eraser into a point and stroke over the mane in the direction of hair growth.

Pony

Ponies are not just small horses; they are a distinct species. They are more sure-footed and have a stronger sense of self-preservation.

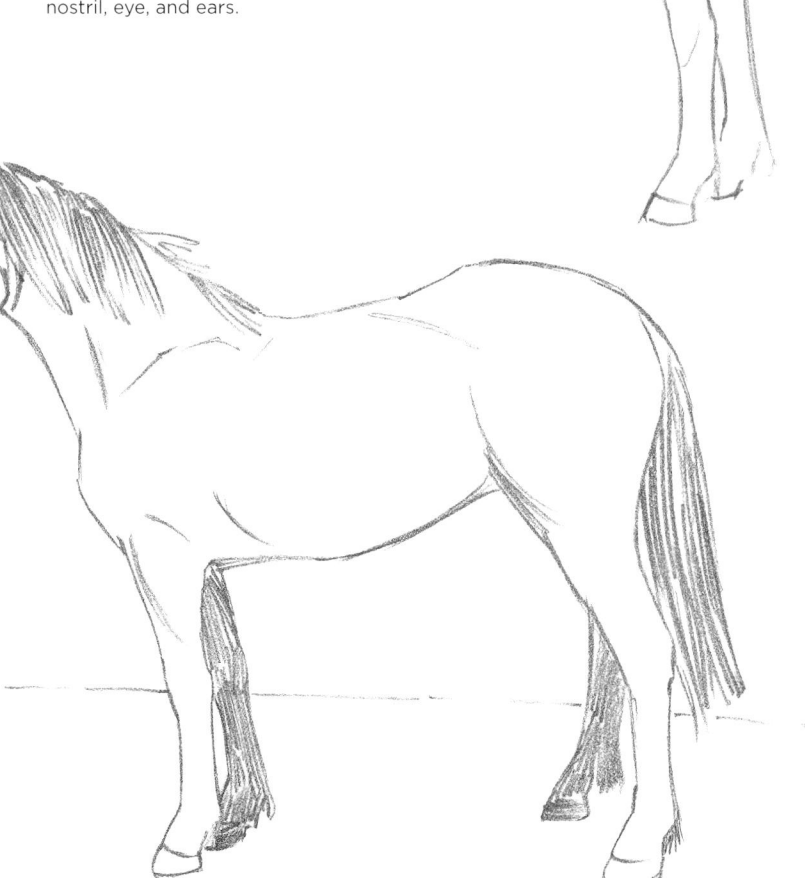

Step 1 With an HB pencil, sketch the bulk of the pony onto your paper. Use overlapping ovals for the chest, body, and haunches. Then place the gentle curves of the neck, blocking in the head with short, angular strokes. Add ovals to block in the curvature of the jaw and muzzle.

Step 2 Building on the lines from step 1, outline the entire pony. Block in the legs, carefully sketching the hooves and joints. Quickly suggest the mane and tail with a few long strokes, and place the mouth, nostril, eye, and ears.

Step 3 Now erase the initial oval guides and shade the outside legs with long, vertical strokes. Then create the texture of the mane and tail with long, straight strokes to represent strands of hair. To give the body form, add a few marks to suggest the major muscles. You can give the face form with a few areas of light, solid shading. Then outline the halter.

BLOCKING OUT WITH BASIC SHAPES

Drawing the horse's body is easier if you break down the animal into basic shapes. Start with circles, cylinders, and trapezoids—as shown on the horse at right—to develop a sense of the size and proportion of the parts of the horse, such as the head, neck, belly, and legs. Then simply connect these shapes, refine the lines, and add a few details to produce a realistic outline of your equine subject.

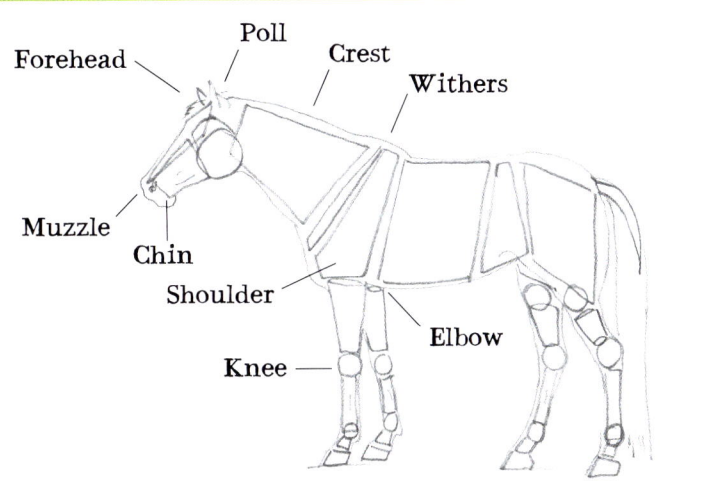

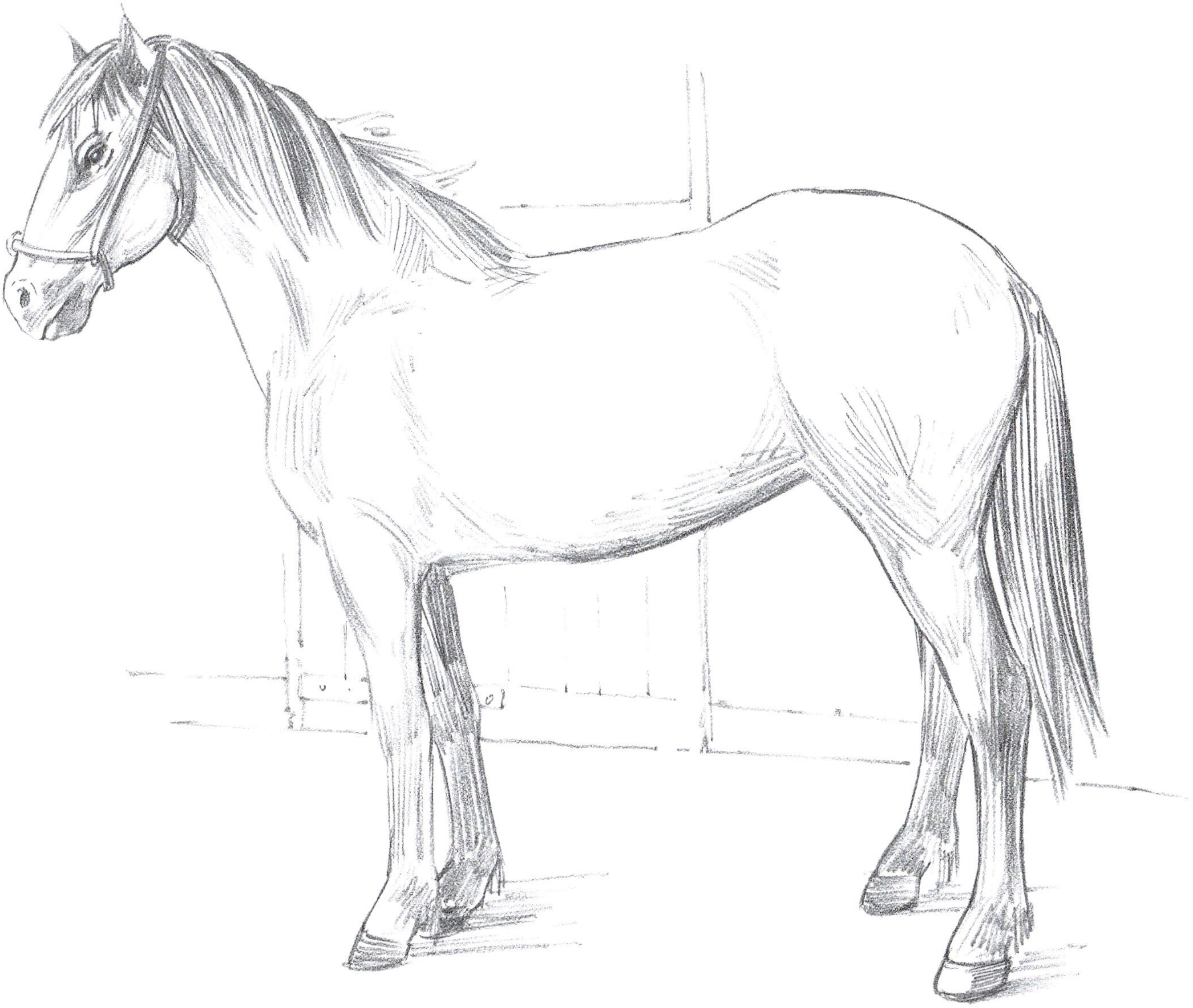

Step 4 Ground the pony by adding a few cast shadows and faint lines for the stable in the background. Keep these lines thin and light so that they don't compete with the pony. Now finish the body of the pony by shading with parallel strokes that follow the muscle structure. This hatching technique creates a slightly stylized effect. Finish by touching up the facial details with additional shading.

Foal's Body

Foals have a great zest for living and a sense of fun. They love to run and kick, and they are fond of showing off. Try to capture this playfulness in your drawings.

B

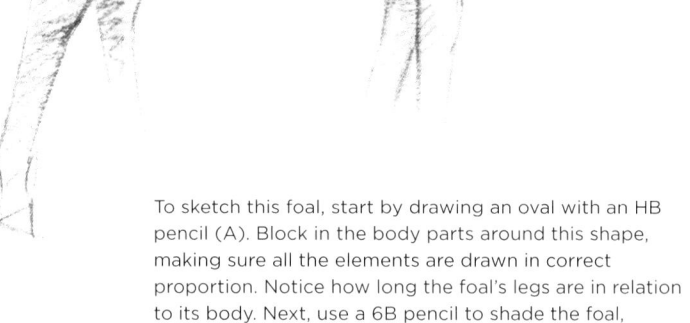

A

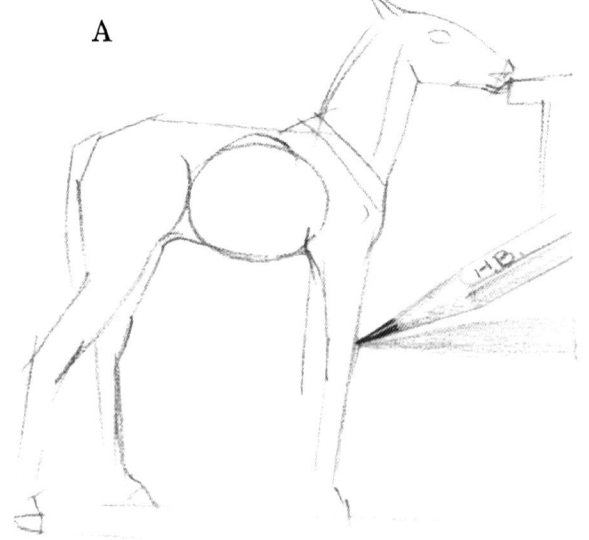

To sketch this foal, start by drawing an oval with an HB pencil (A). Block in the body parts around this shape, making sure all the elements are drawn in correct proportion. Notice how long the foal's legs are in relation to its body. Next, use a 6B pencil to shade the foal, blending out some areas with a tortillon for a soft, rounded effect (B).

B

A

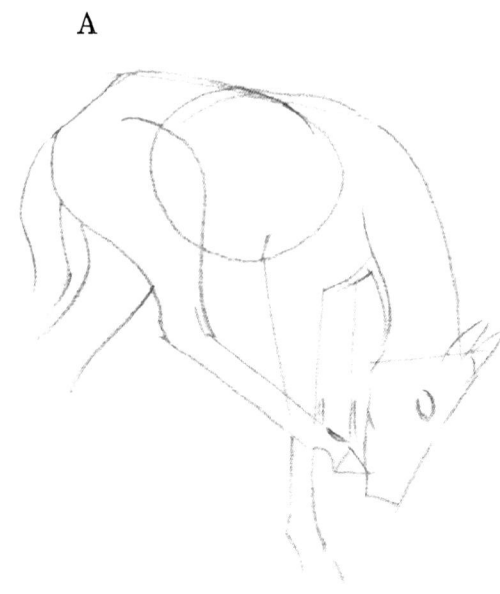

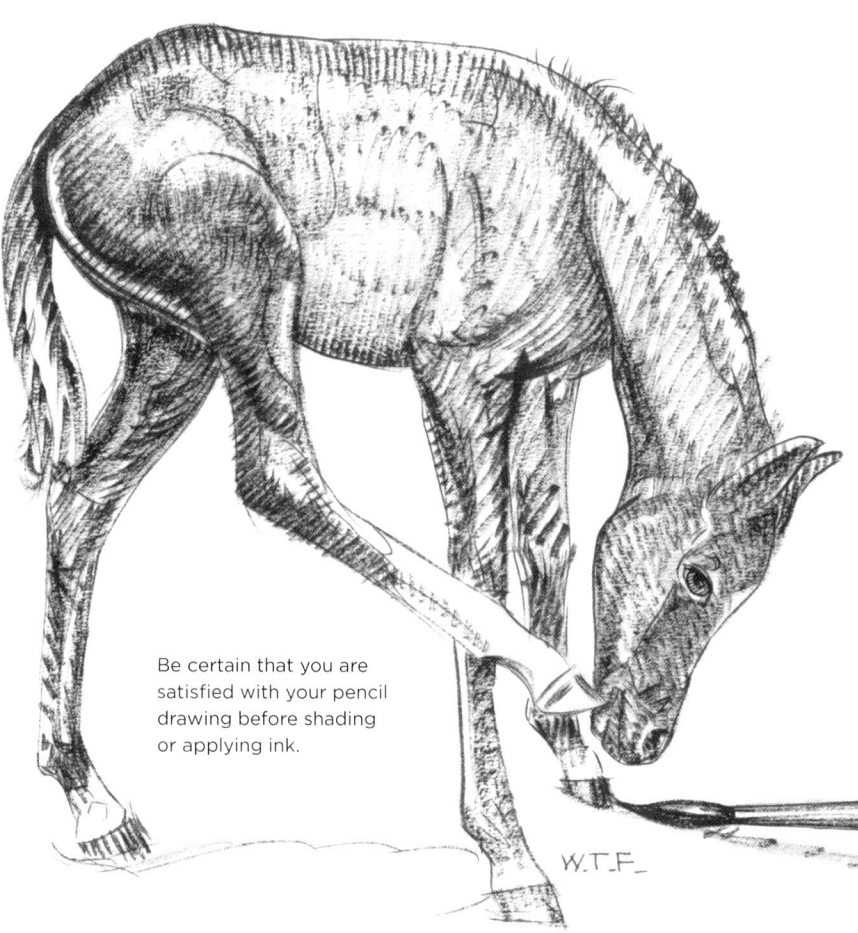

This drawing was made on rough-textured paper and finished using a drybrush technique. After working out the outline of the foal in pencil (A), apply the light and middle values with washes of India ink or black watercolor paint. Then use a dry brush and undiluted ink to lay in the darkest shadows and details (B). The drybrush technique produces rough, broken lines with feathered edges and is an easy way to create texture.

Be certain that you are satisfied with your pencil drawing before shading or applying ink.

Here again, layers of ink washes are used to achieve a more solid rendering. After blocking in the basic shape of the body with an HB pencil (A), refine the lines until you are satisfied with the proportions and outline. Use a clean brush to apply plain water over the foal's body, being careful to stay within the outlines. Next, load the brush with diluted ink, and wash it over the body in smooth, even layers (B). This technique is called wet-on-wet, and it produces soft, loose blends. Note, however, that the washes are more difficult to control with this method than when painting wet-on-dry or with the drybrush technique.

Experiment with either painting wet-on-wet or allowing the paper to dry between washes. As you apply your washes, leave some areas lighter for highlights, and brush on extra layers of ink for the dark areas on the neck and belly. Use the tip of a dry brush to draw the fine outlines and details.

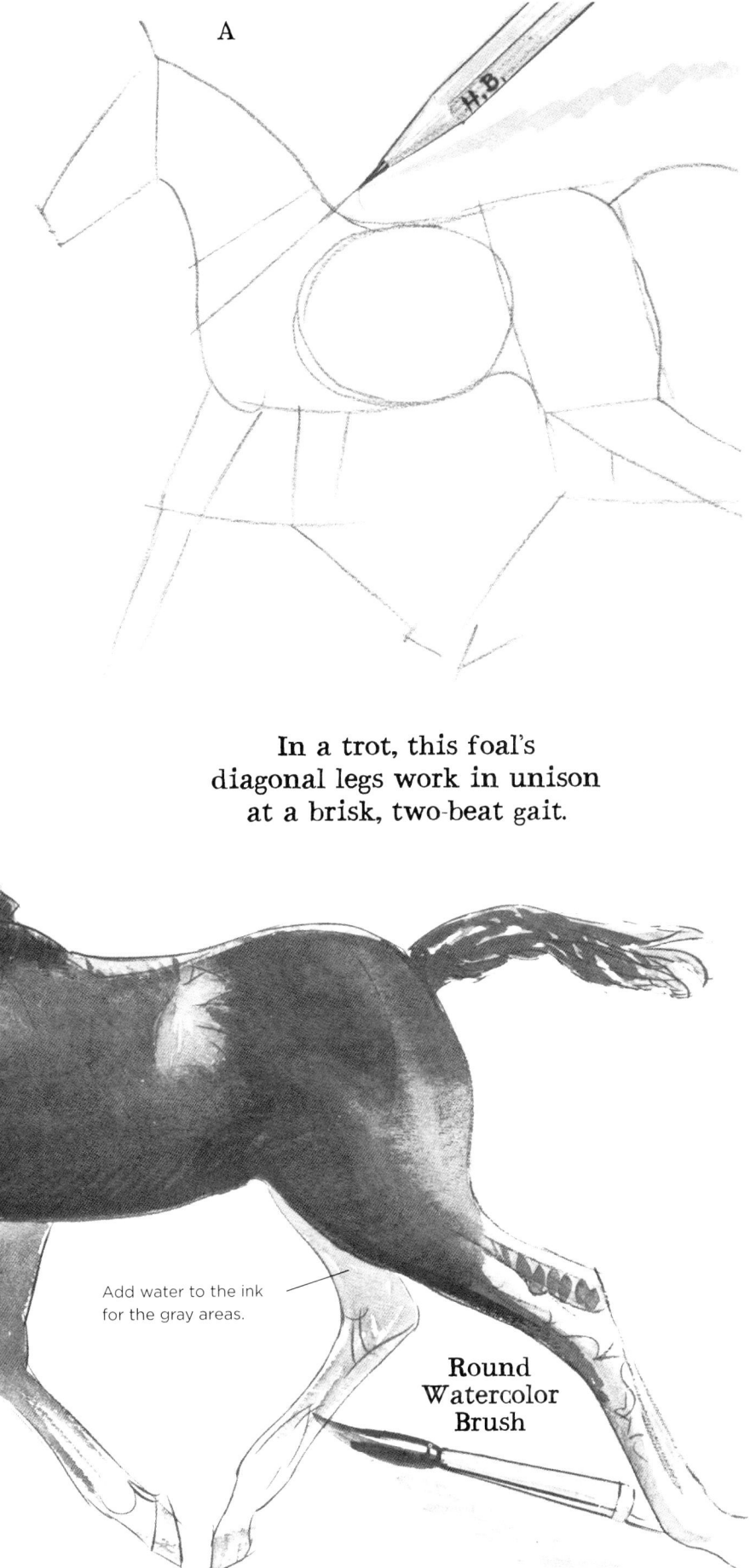

A

In a trot, this foal's diagonal legs work in unison at a brisk, two-beat gait.

B

Apply multiple layers of diluted ink for the darkest areas.

Add water to the ink for the gray areas.

Leave some areas white for contrast.

Round Watercolor Brush

W.T.F.

Arabian

The Arabian is a high-spirited horse with a flamboyant tail carriage and distinctive dished profile. Though relatively small in stature, this breed is known for its stamina, graceful build, intelligence, and energy. Try to capture the Arabian's slender physique and high spirit in your drawing.

Block in the body with an HB pencil, placing the oval for the body at a slight angle to indicate that the body will be foreshortened (A). When blocking in the head, take care to stress the concave nose, large nostrils, and small muzzle. As you start shading (A and B), keep the lines for the tail and mane loose and free, and accent the graceful arch of the neck.

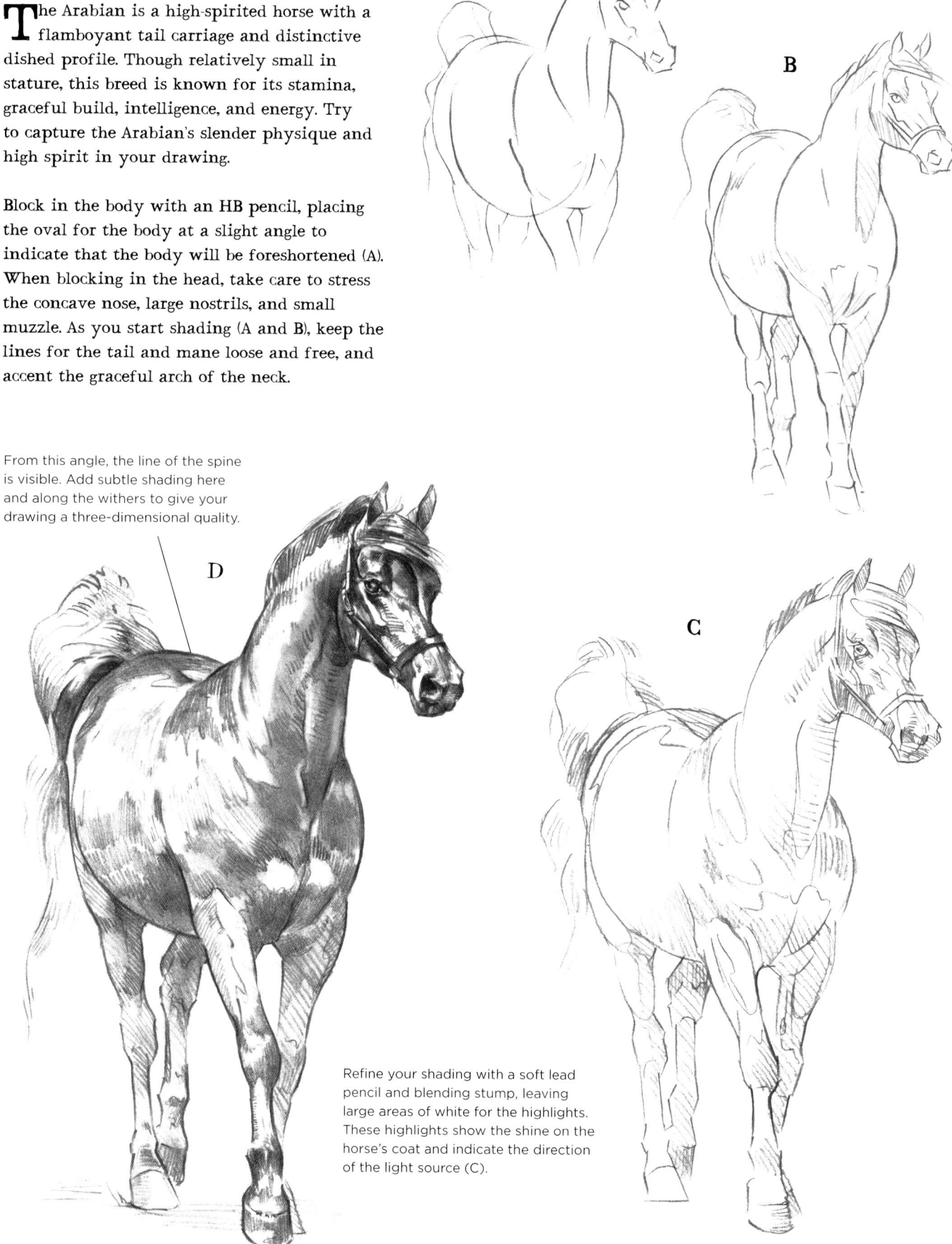

A

B

From this angle, the line of the spine is visible. Add subtle shading here and along the withers to give your drawing a three-dimensional quality.

D

C

Refine your shading with a soft lead pencil and blending stump, leaving large areas of white for the highlights. These highlights show the shine on the horse's coat and indicate the direction of the light source (C).

Shetland Pony

One of the smallest of the pony breeds, the Shetland is a hardy animal originally from the Shetland Islands off of northern Britain. This pony exhibits the characteristic small head, thick neck, and stocky build of the breed.

As you block in the pony's body, carefully observe its proportions. The length of its body is about two and a half times the length of its head. Start with large circles and ovals to capture the pony's solid build (A). Use hatching strokes to start indicating the middle values as shown (B). Use a blending stump for the darkest areas (C). Use the side of the lead and a blending stump for light, wispy strokes to finish off this light-colored pony (D).

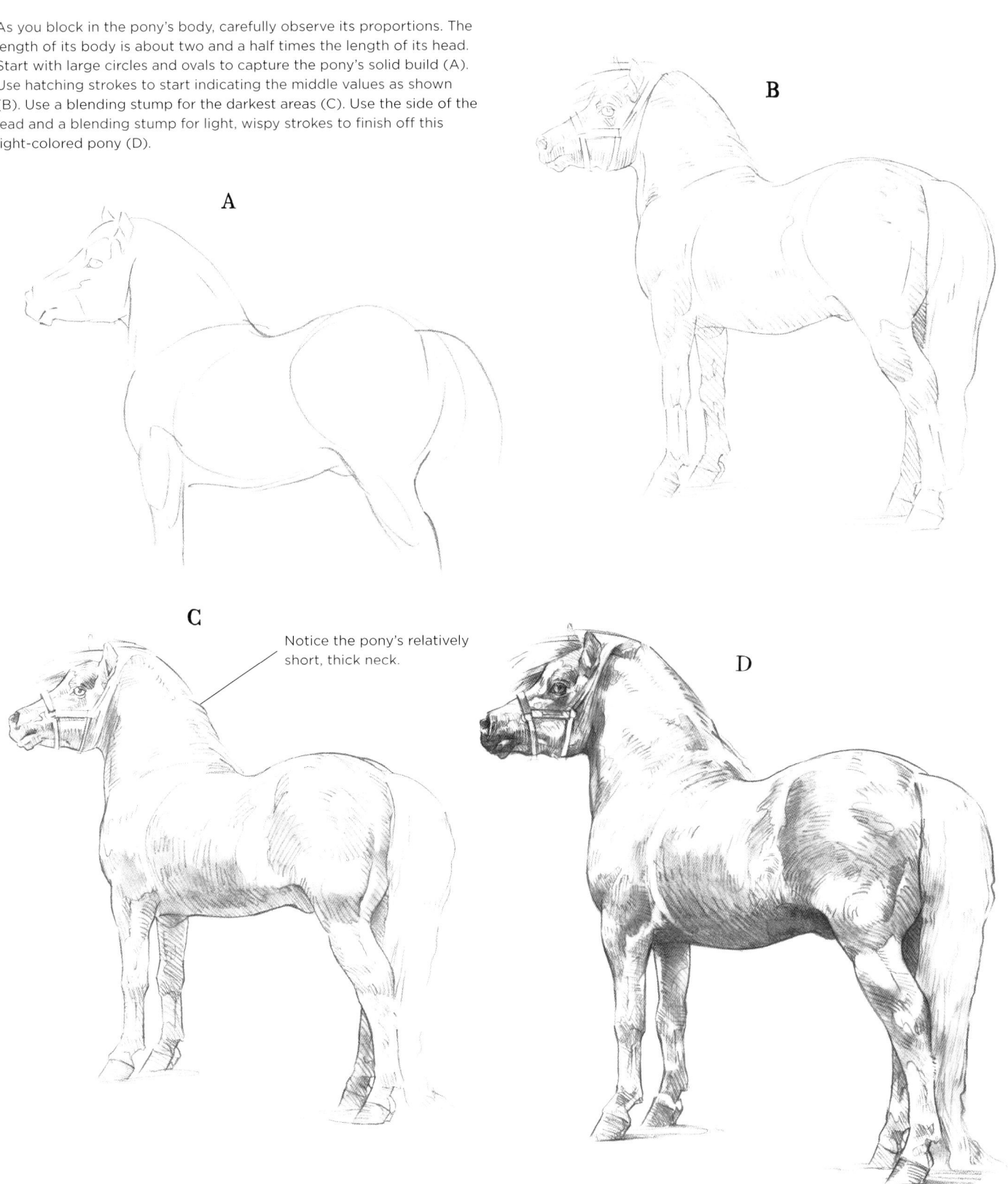

A

B

C

Notice the pony's relatively short, thick neck.

D

American Quarter Horse

The American Quarter Horse is a powerfully built, muscular breed, known for its agility and superior cattle-cutting abilities. The name quarter horse is derived from the breed's capacity to run at high speed for distances up to a quarter of a mile. Emphasize the strong hindquarters and muscular neck when you draw this horse.

This horse is viewed from the rear and at an angle, so you will need to use foreshortening techniques in your drawing. (See pages 75 and 131.) Foreshortening means to reduce or distort parts of a drawing in order to convey the illusion of depth as perceived by the human eye. In this case, the horse's side is shortened to show that the front of the horse is farthest from the viewer. As a consequence, the rump and hindquarters appear larger in relation to the horse's front end.

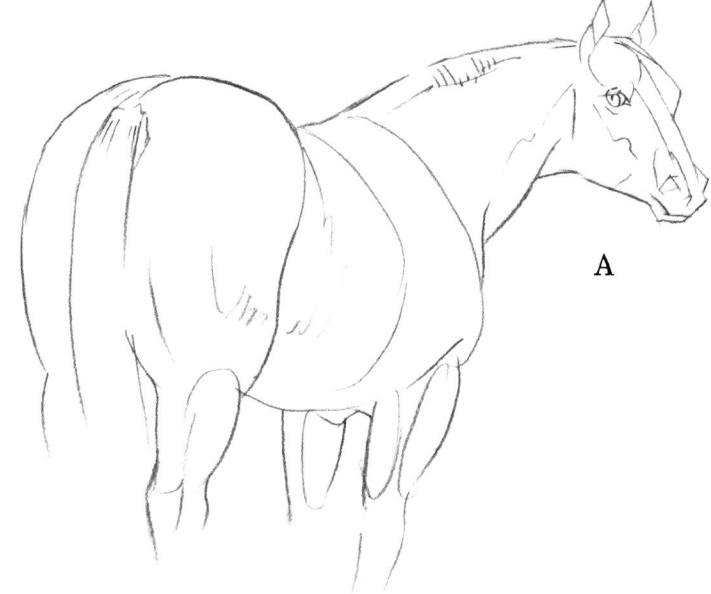

A

For this complex pose, you'll need to take your time and block it in carefully. Look closely at the distances between the parts of the horse and their sizes in relation to one another. Also pay attention to the form of the legs; this is a new viewpoint that allows you to define the back of the legs, knees, and hooves (A). Check your proportions carefully, and then begin suggesting the shadows and muscle areas (B).

This area has been foreshortened to create the illusion that the hindquarters are closest to the viewer.

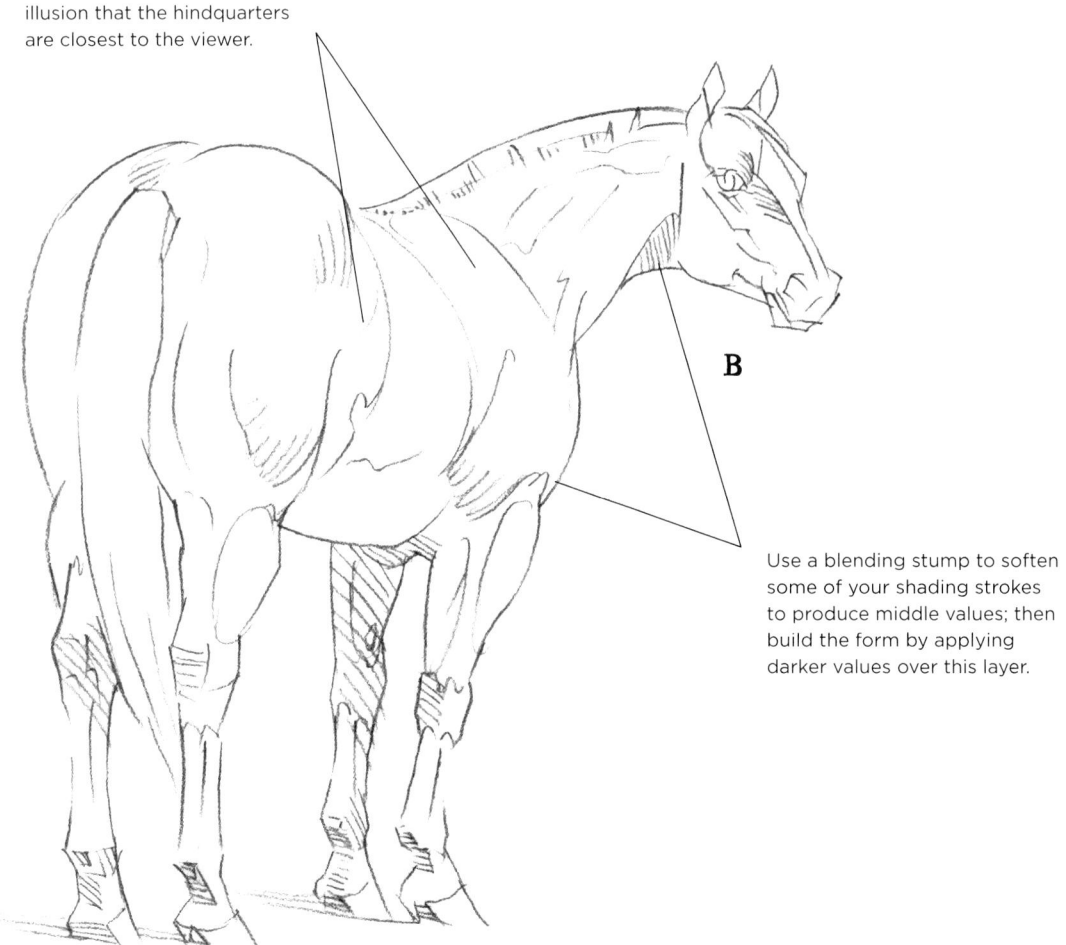

B

Use a blending stump to soften some of your shading strokes to produce middle values; then build the form by applying darker values over this layer.

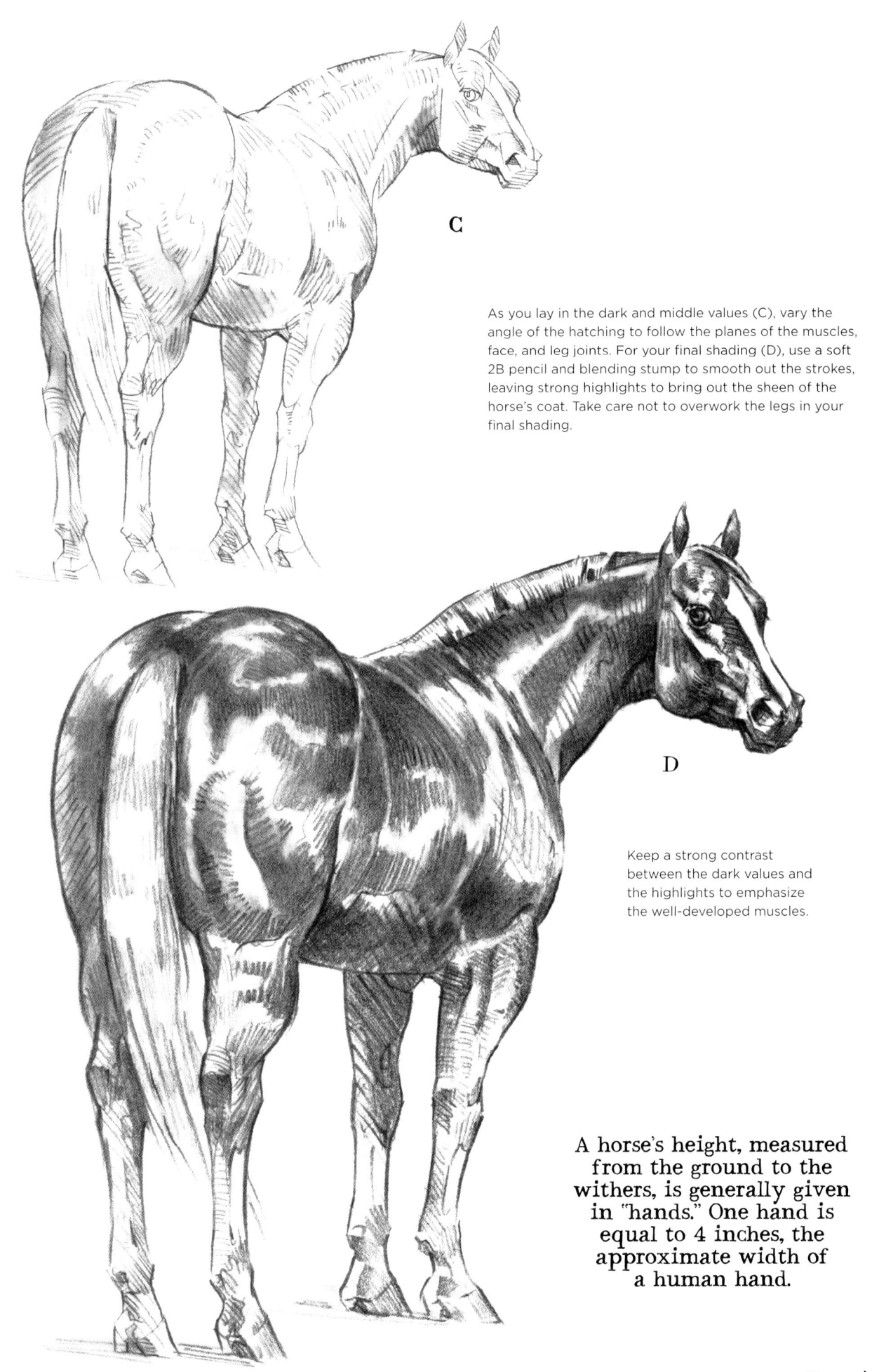

C

As you lay in the dark and middle values (C), vary the angle of the hatching to follow the planes of the muscles, face, and leg joints. For your final shading (D), use a soft 2B pencil and blending stump to smooth out the strokes, leaving strong highlights to bring out the sheen of the horse's coat. Take care not to overwork the legs in your final shading.

D

Keep a strong contrast between the dark values and the highlights to emphasize the well-developed muscles.

A horse's height, measured from the ground to the withers, is generally given in "hands." One hand is equal to 4 inches, the approximate width of a human hand.

Standardbred Trotter

The trot is a two-beat, diagonal gait with interesting footwork. The front left and rear right legs move forward simultaneously, followed by the front right and rear left legs. There are points where all four feet will be off the ground at the same time, giving the appearance of a floating horse. This project depicts a Standardbred trotter during a warmup; it is working at a moderate speed, and its body is not fully extended.

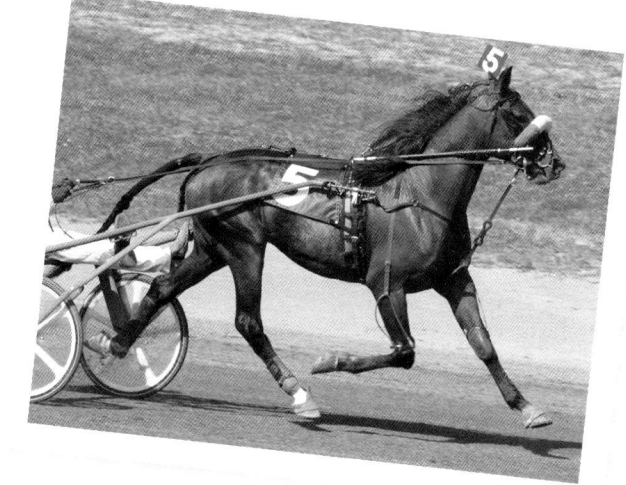

Step 1 Establish the basic outline of the horse using an HB pencil and loose strokes. In this early stage, keep the lines light, erasing and adjusting as necessary. Add a few lines to block in the forms of the muscles, indicating where the light and dark values meet.

Defining the Muscles Because this drawing depicts a competitive horse, it's important to emphasize the fine musculature. Keep the croup flat and the haunches well defined to indicate the propelling power of the hindquarters.

The Standardbred is known for its skill in harness racing. It is the fastest trotting breed of horse in the world.

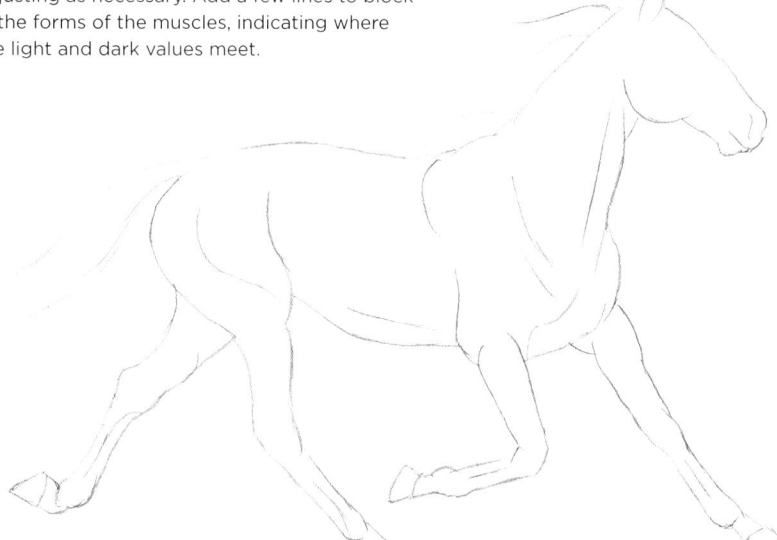

Step 2 When you're satisfied with the basic outline, refine the lines to carefully depict the subtle curves and angles. Use long, tapering strokes to begin rendering the mane and tail. Develop the outline to show the muscles, tendons, ligaments, and facial features. Note the details in the reference that make this active pose unique. Notice how one ear is tipped back to listen for cues from the driver, whereas the other is facing forward to listen ahead. Also, the visible nostril is slightly flared from the physical activity.

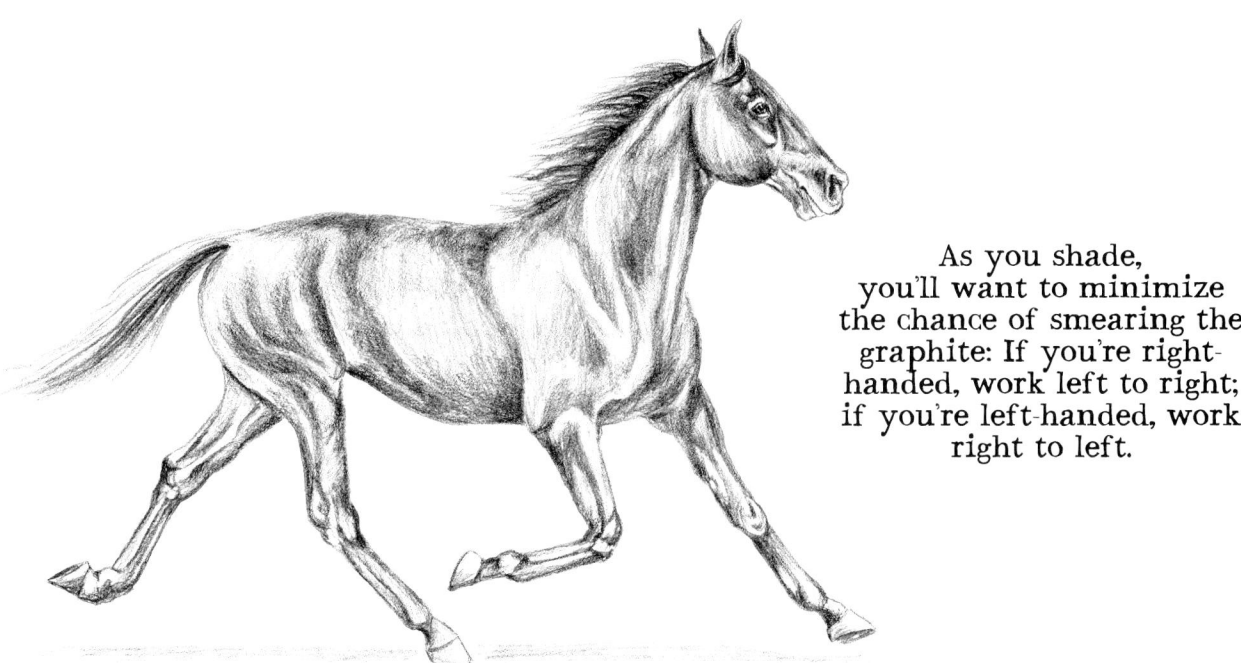

As you shade, you'll want to minimize the chance of smearing the graphite: If you're right-handed, work left to right; if you're left-handed, work right to left.

Step 3 At this point, switch to a 3B and begin shading the horse to add form. Build up the tone evenly over the horse, starting with the shadows and gradating to the lighter areas. To suggest movement in the horse, avoid blending to keep the shading rough and sketchy.

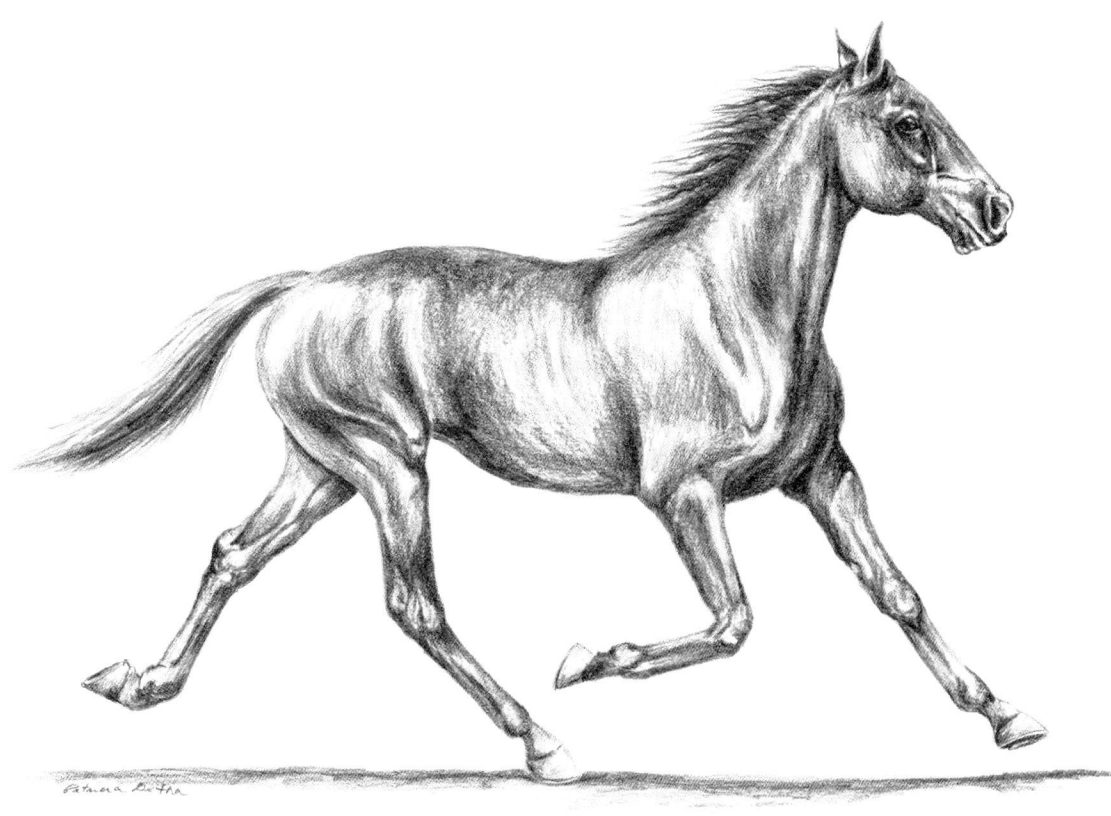

Step 4 In this final step, focus on punching up the values. Stick with the HB and 2B pencils to shade within the lighter areas, but change to a 6B for darker values. It's important to use the softest pencils for the darkest areas, as harder pencils can burnish the graphite, causing odd reflections or even damage to the paper's surface.

Horses & Riders

When you depict a horse with a rider, the two should be drawn as if they are one entity. Develop them both at the same time as you draw. The rider's body, leg, and hand position are important elements that, when drawn correctly, will make your drawings realistic.

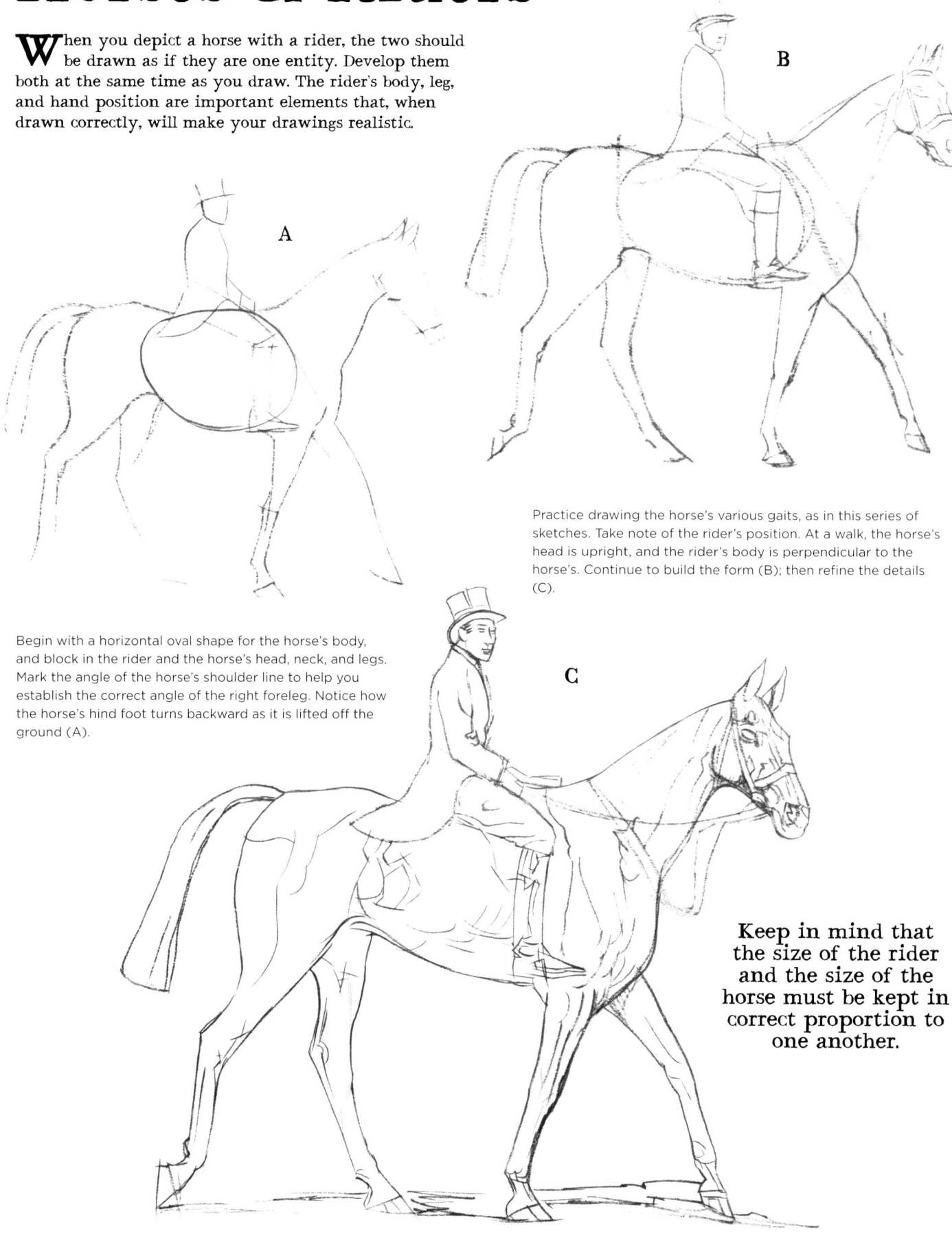

A

B

Practice drawing the horse's various gaits, as in this series of sketches. Take note of the rider's position. At a walk, the horse's head is upright, and the rider's body is perpendicular to the horse's. Continue to build the form (B); then refine the details (C).

Begin with a horizontal oval shape for the horse's body, and block in the rider and the horse's head, neck, and legs. Mark the angle of the horse's shoulder line to help you establish the correct angle of the right foreleg. Notice how the horse's hind foot turns backward as it is lifted off the ground (A).

C

Keep in mind that the size of the rider and the size of the horse must be kept in correct proportion to one another.

The slow, loping gait of a horse is called a canter. At this moderate pace, the horse's center of gravity is shifted slightly forward, evident in the forward thrust of the head and body. Notice that the rider is leaning forward toward the horse's head, following the horse's motion with his own body. Keep your lines fluid and loose to convey the sense of movement.

Don't forget that the most important thing about drawing is having fun.

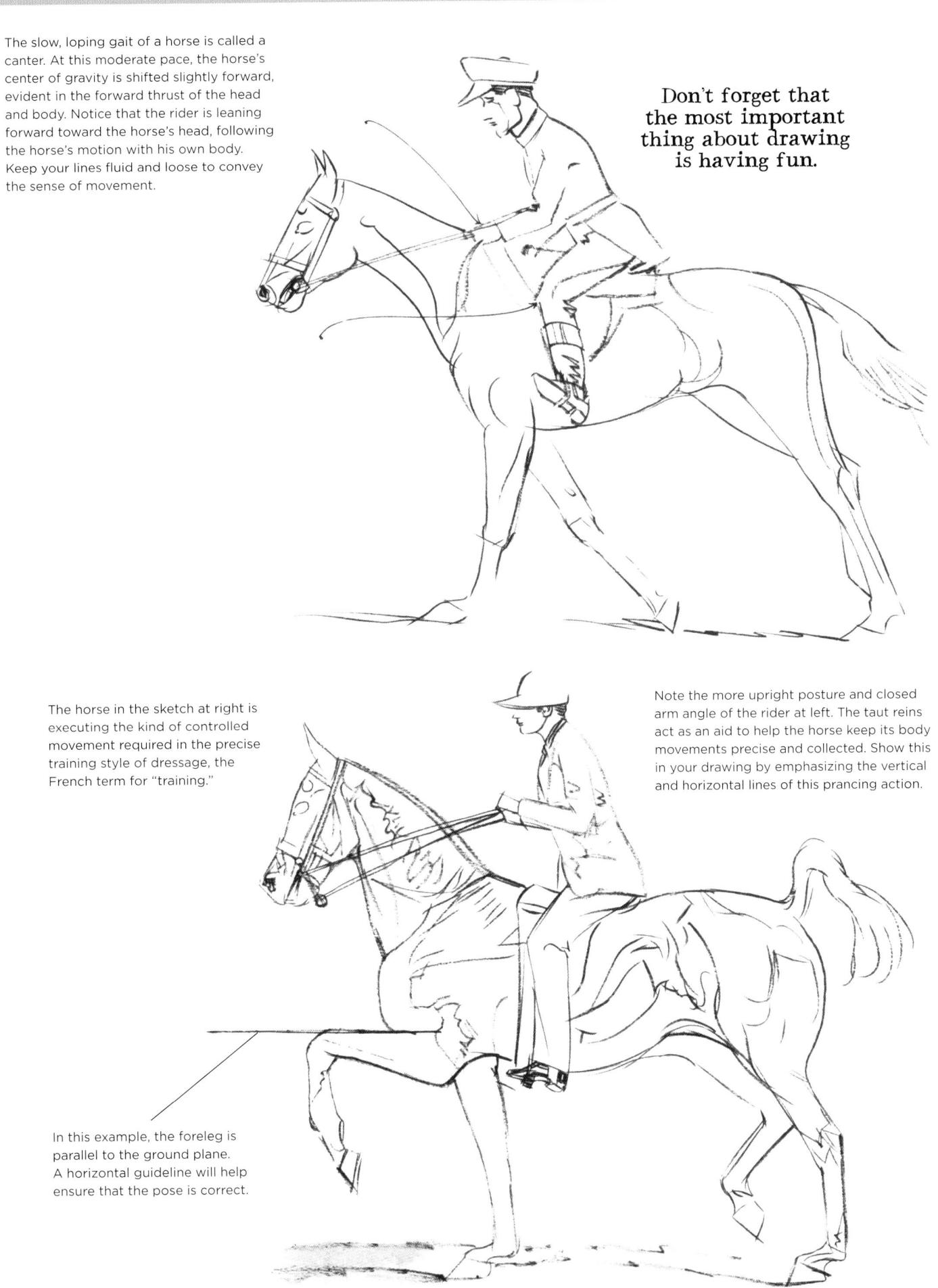

The horse in the sketch at right is executing the kind of controlled movement required in the precise training style of dressage, the French term for "training."

Note the more upright posture and closed arm angle of the rider at left. The taut reins act as an aid to help the horse keep its body movements precise and collected. Show this in your drawing by emphasizing the vertical and horizontal lines of this prancing action.

In this example, the foreleg is parallel to the ground plane. A horizontal guideline will help ensure that the pose is correct.

Jumping is an exciting horse sport, whether it's stadium show jumping, cross-country racing, or steeplechasing. Notice how dramatically the rider shifts body position to follow the horse's movement. The rider must remain over the horse's center of gravity to help the horse maintain its balance and to keep from hindering the horse's effort. Being aware of these details will help keep your drawings accurate.

A

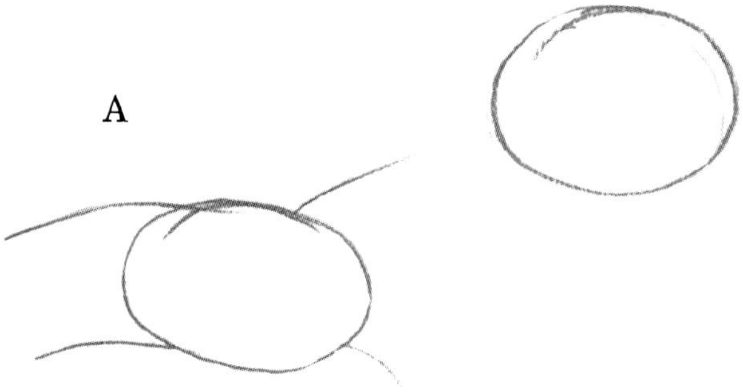

A

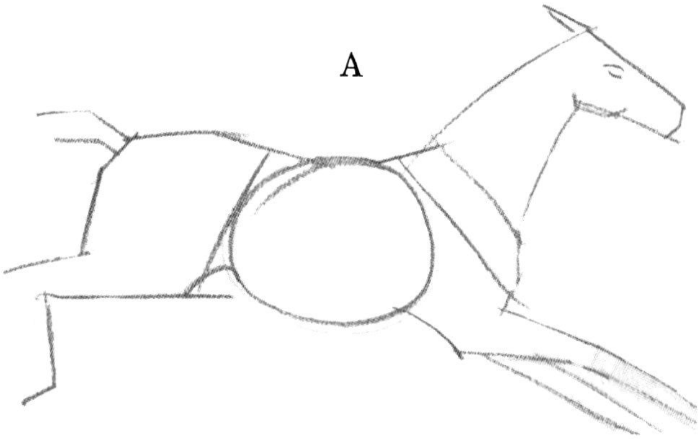

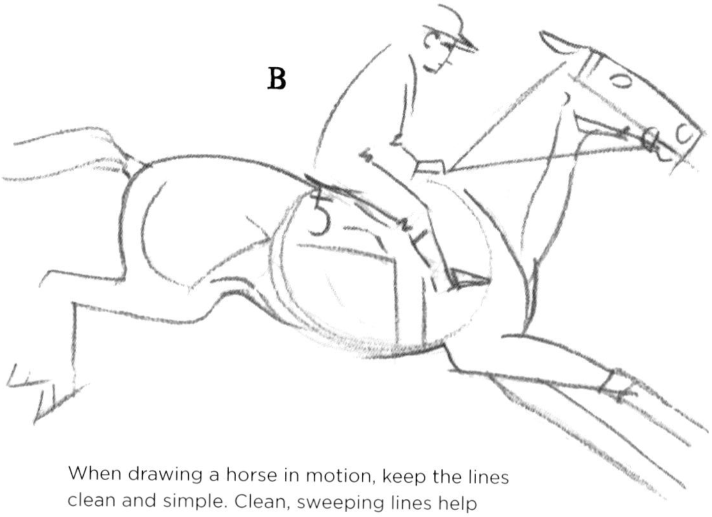

Use either an HB or a 2B pencil for these sketches.

B

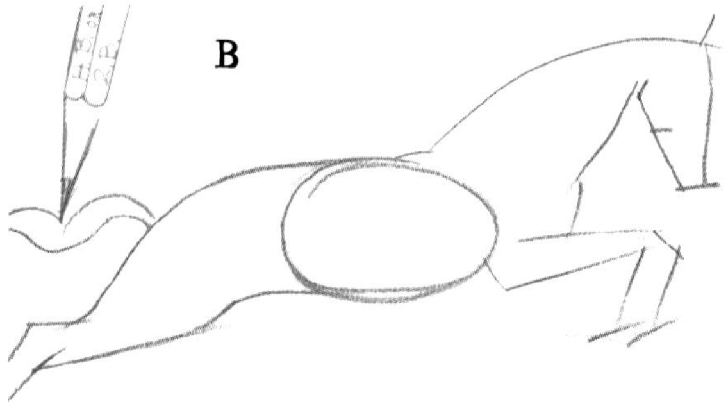

B

When drawing a horse in motion, keep the lines clean and simple. Clean, sweeping lines help convey a sense of the action. Make a lot of rough sketches like these to practice capturing the feeling of movement in your drawings.

Remember to work from photographs of horses in various activities. This will help you check the accuracy of the horse's leg movement and the rider's position.

C

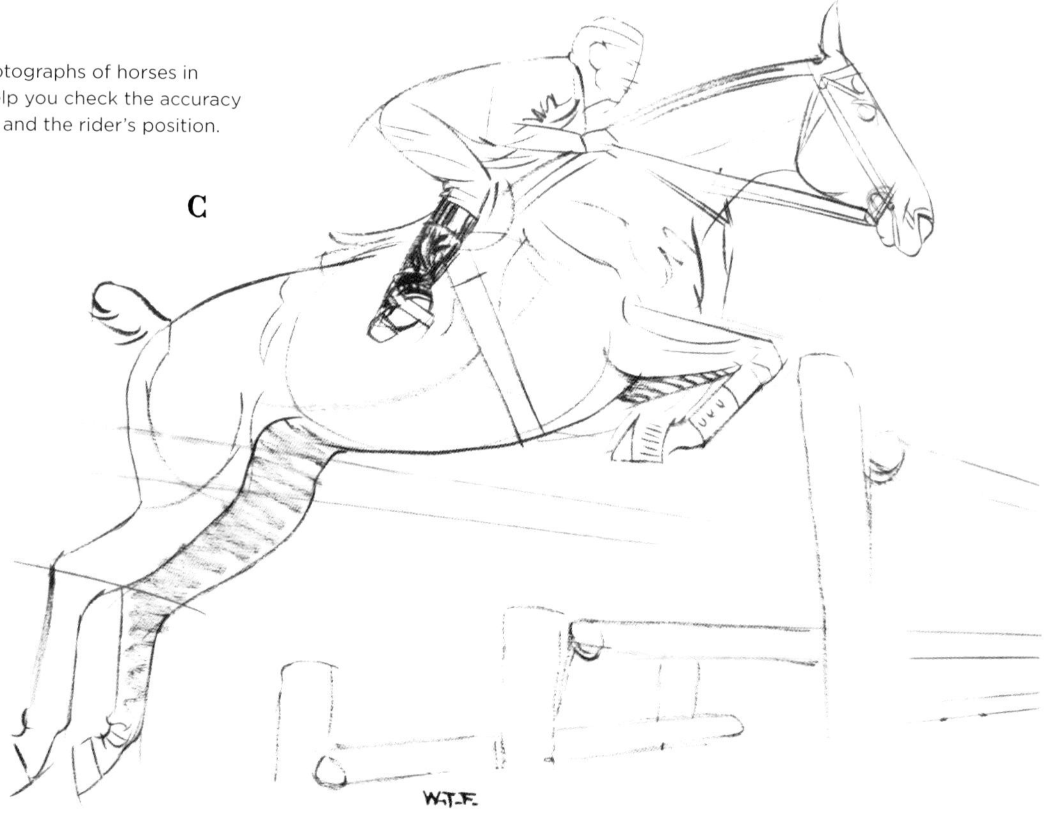

W.T.F.

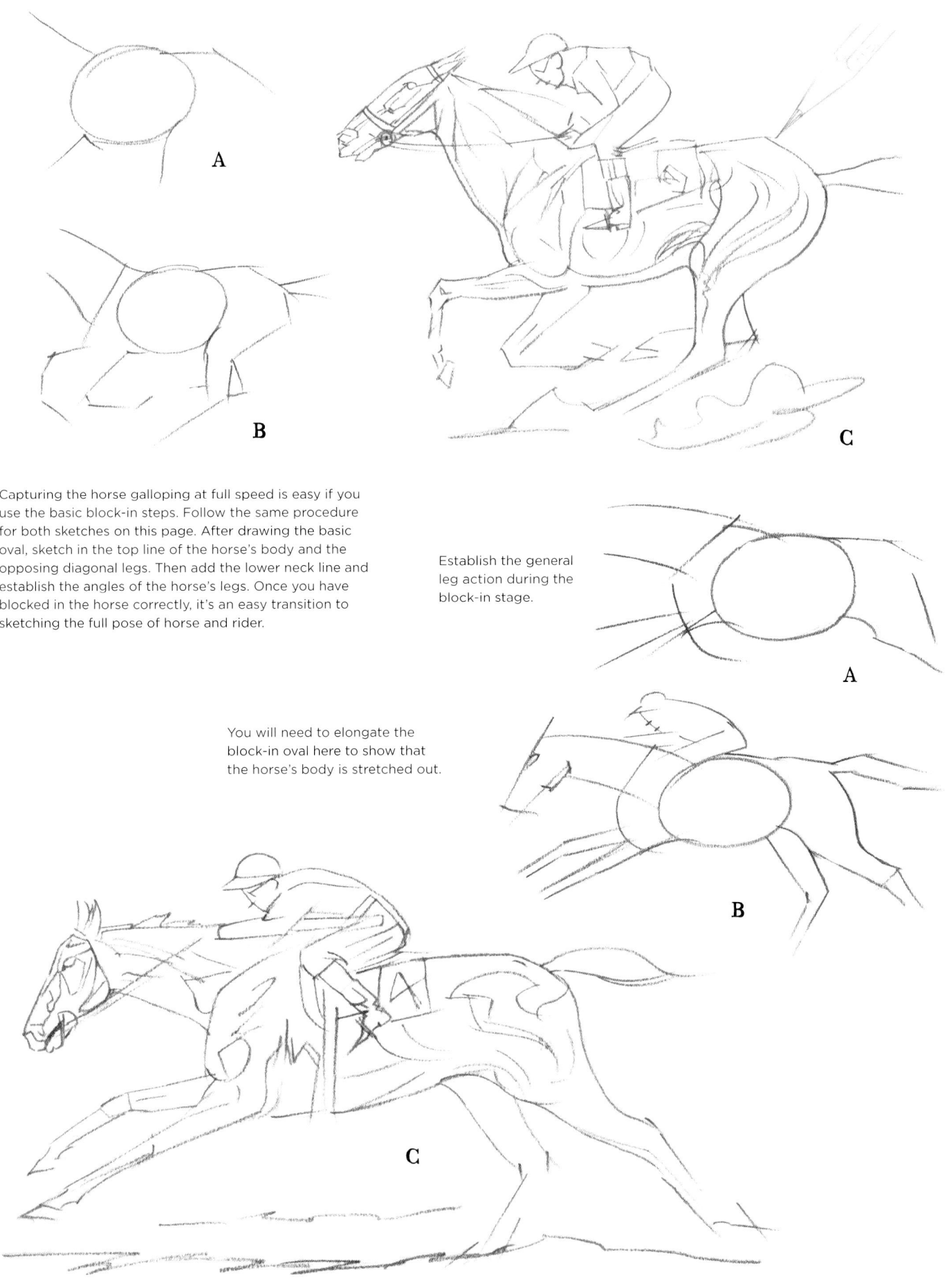

A

B

C

Capturing the horse galloping at full speed is easy if you use the basic block-in steps. Follow the same procedure for both sketches on this page. After drawing the basic oval, sketch in the top line of the horse's body and the opposing diagonal legs. Then add the lower neck line and establish the angles of the horse's legs. Once you have blocked in the horse correctly, it's an easy transition to sketching the full pose of horse and rider.

Establish the general leg action during the block-in stage.

A

You will need to elongate the block-in oval here to show that the horse's body is stretched out.

B

C

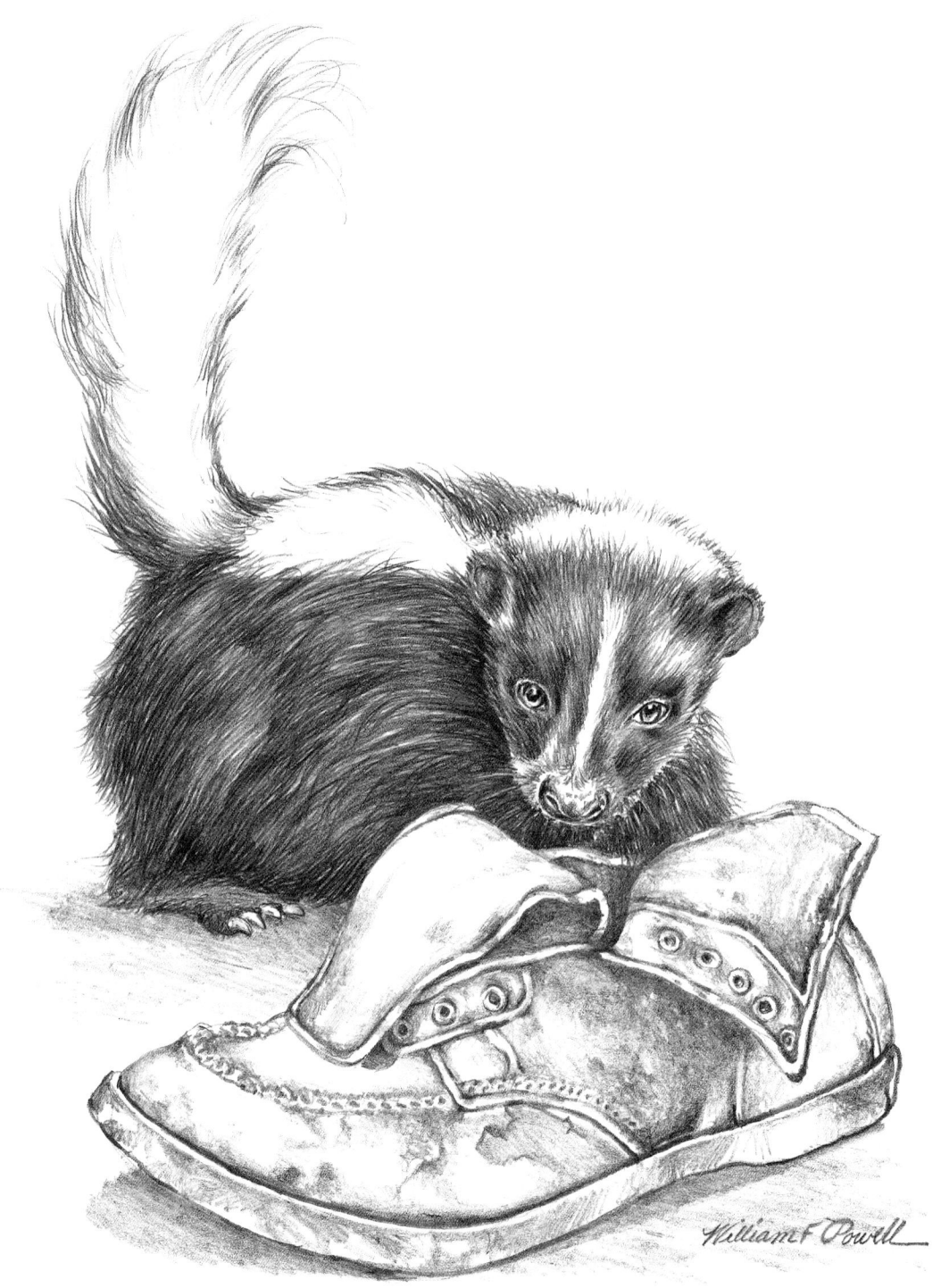

Animal Portraits

Planning a piece around an animal subject is one of the best ways to express yourself as an artist. It gives you a unique opportunity to use your animal subject to tell a story in your artwork. You can also create a statement piece because the goal is to convey not just the physical features of the animal, but also the essence of the animal's spirit. Through careful observation and skillful rendering, artists can create works that evoke emotion and connection with the viewer. Each portrait is an opportunity to celebrate the individuality of animals, capturing their presence in a way that feels both personal and timeless.

In this chapter, you will discover how to create a successful composition, compose scenes, combine photographs, and achieve a realistic animal likeness. Step-by-step projects are designed to reinforce your learning; soon you will be able to create your own animal portraits with ease.

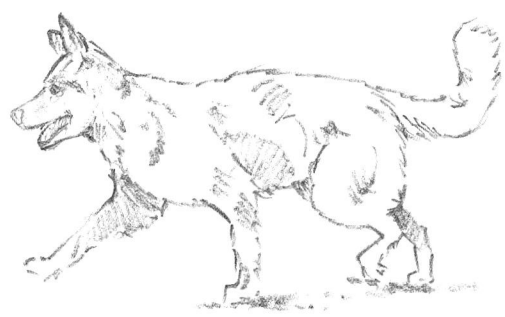

Composition

Composition, or the arrangement of elements in a scene, can make or break a work of art. All the skill alone will not help you if your composition is dull and uninteresting. Some artists just seem to have a natural "talent" for composition, but in actuality, this talent stems from learning basic principles and trial and error. Be sure to think about your drawing and plan it before you start. Make quick thumbnail sketches to work out any compositional issues ahead of time.

COMPOSITION TECHNIQUES

If you feel uncomfortable with a drawing, try looking at it upside down or in a mirror; whatever is bothering you will be more easily apparent. Keep everything you draw. You can learn from your mistakes by reviewing your less successful drawings every now and then.

ODD NUMBERS AND ASYMMETRY

Generally, subjects are more appealing when grouped in odd numbers rather than even numbers. Consider this when planning your composition. You can use even numbers in your compositions, of course, but you'll want the subjects to differ in size—for instance, you could draw three baby birds in a nest with their mother. Or you can introduce some asymmetry, like drawing three frogs on one end of a log looking at a solitary frog on the other end.

THE RULE OF THIRDS

Another method for creating a pleasing composition is to divide the picture into thirds (vertically, horizontally, or both) and place your center of interest at or near one of the points where the lines intersect. This keeps your focal point away from the extremes—corners, dead center, or at the very top or bottom of the composition. In the drawing at right, the tiger's right eye is placed where two of the lines intersect, creating a pleasing composition.

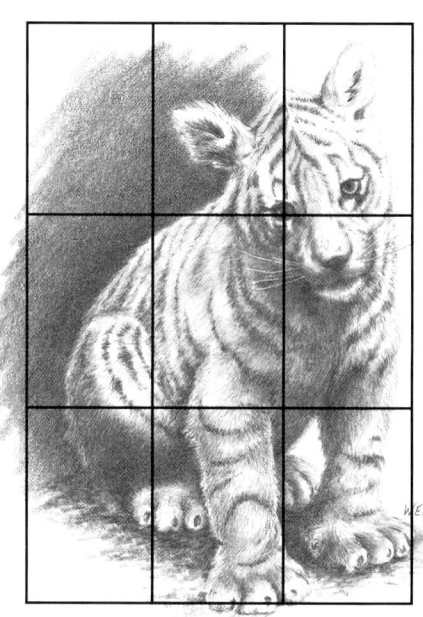

GEOMETRIC COMPOSITION

Divide your composition into geometric shapes (rectangles, triangles, or circles), and place the elements of the drawing where these lines divide and intersect, as well as within the areas created by the intersections. Look at the geometric shapes that form in your drawing. Is there a strong triangular formation? Or have you created a centrally balanced work? Notice how the internal shapes lead your eye around the page. Be aware of any compositional subtleties that can create divisions in your drawing.

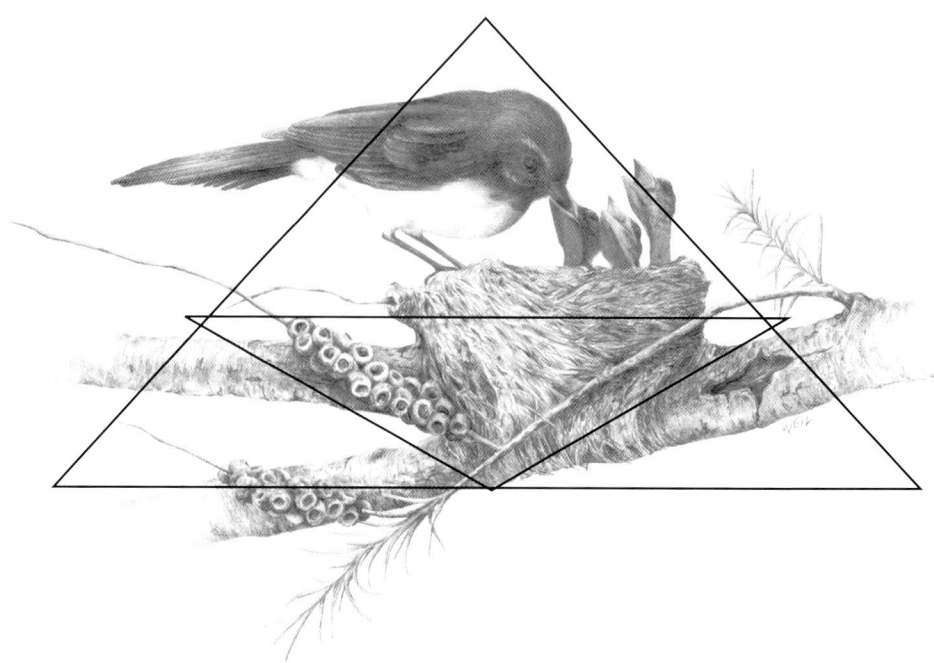

USING REFERENCES

When planning a composition, gather as many references as you can to explore your subject. Sketches and photos of your own are the best sources, but you can also search books, magazines, and other sources that inspire you. Be aware that photos taken with a flash will be tonally flat and contain flash highlights, especially in the eyes. For this reason, don't copy a photograph exactly; just use it as a guide.

Whenever you use material that is not your own, you must be aware of copyright restrictions. If you have used another's work to create your drawing, you cannot sell or publish that work as an original. When in doubt, ask the original creator's permission. Many photographers and artists will grant permission, but some will require that you pay a fee or that you purchase a licensing agreement.

USING PHOTO-EDITING SOFTWARE

If you want to combine elements from multiple photographs into one image, you can use photo-editing software to piece together the photographs. In the demonstration below, several different reference images were combined to create a single composition. All of these shots of a group of meerkats were good, but none have the animals all looking in one direction. Elements from three photos were pieced together to show all the animals huddled together, making eye contact with the viewer.

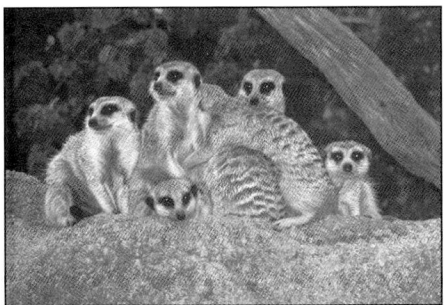

Step 1 In this first photo, the body positions are strong, but only two of the animals are looking directly at the camera.

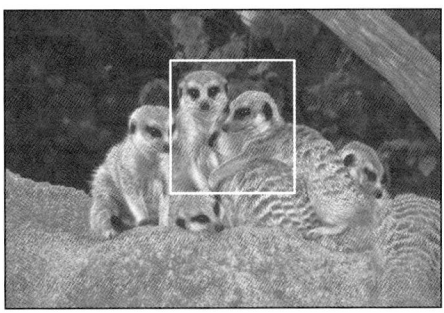

Step 2 In the second photo, these two heads are suitable to a strong composition, so they are selected and copied.

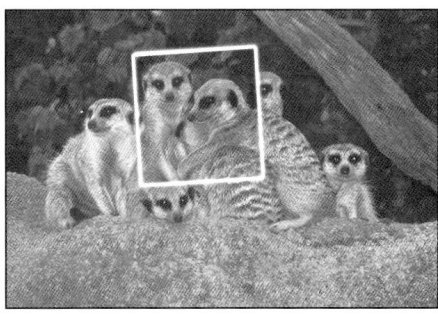

Step 3 The new heads are pasted onto a new layer in the photo file. This obscures the head of the back meerkat, which is easily fixed by returning to the first layer and selecting and copying the meerkat's head.

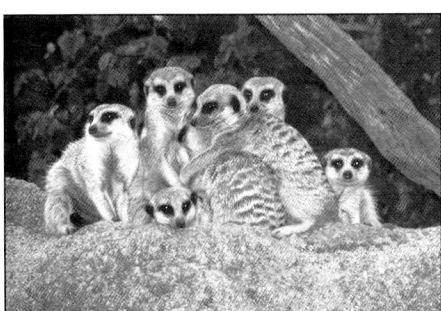

Step 4 The head is added onto a new layer in the working file.

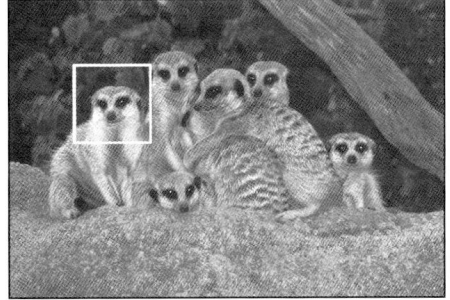

Step 5 In the third photo, the head of the far-left meerkat is copied and pasted onto a new layer.

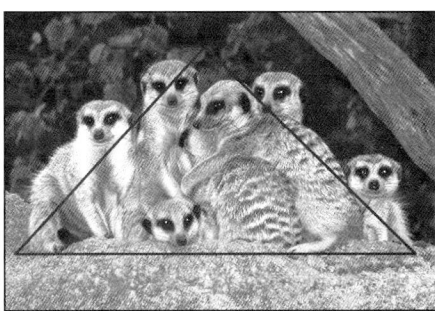

Step 6 With all the elements in place, you can now work out a pleasing composition like the one shown here.

Perspective Basics

For a drawing to be considered realistic, it needs to give the impression that it inhabits a three-dimensional space with depth and distance. To do this, employ the rules of perspective in your drawings. The first (and most important) rule of perspective is that objects that are closest to the viewer are larger than objects that are farther away. Here you'll find demonstrations of one- and two-point perspective.

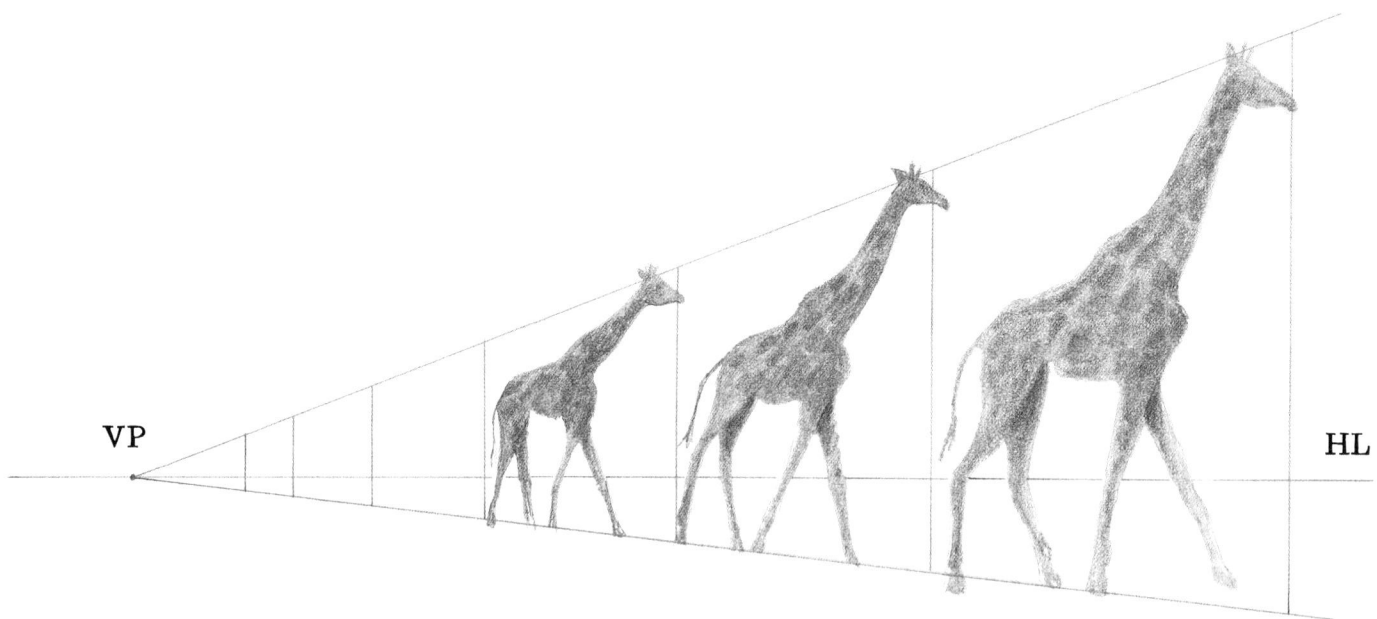

One-Point Perspective In one-point perspective, there is only one vanishing point (VP), or the point at which all perspective lines converge and seem to vanish. First draw a horizontal line on your paper to represent the horizon line (HL), or eye level. Then place a dot to the far left on the HL for the VP. Next, draw a vertical line to the far right that intersects the HL at a 90-degree angle. About three-quarters of this line should be above the HL, and about one-quarter should be below it. Imagine that this vertical line is a fence post (or your subject, like this standing giraffe). Now draw a line from the top of this post to the VP, and another from the bottom of the post to the VP. This V-shaped guide allows you to see exactly where the top and bottom of each successive post (or giraffe) is located.

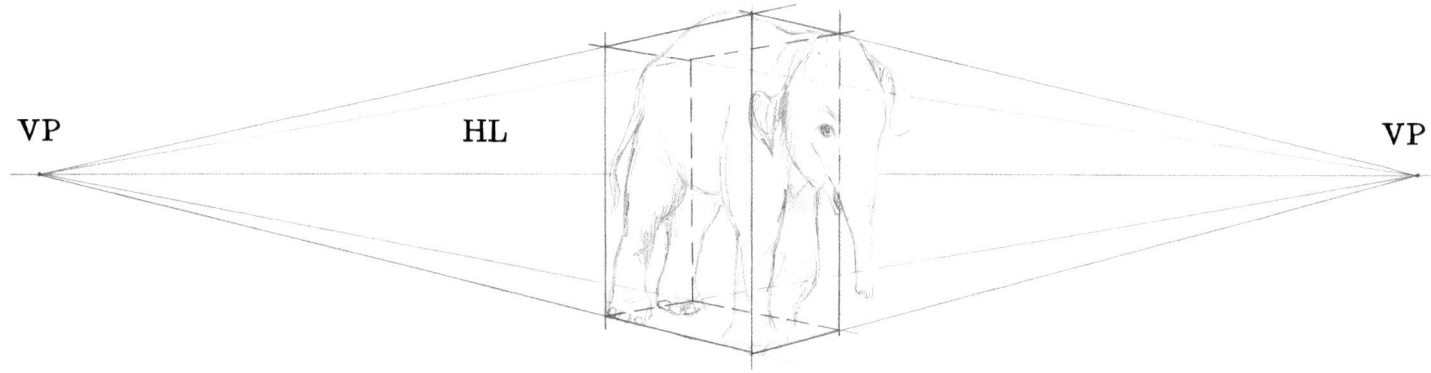

Two-Point Perspective In two-point perspective, there are two vanishing points. The best way to demonstrate this is by drawing a three-dimensional cube. First draw the HL, and place one VP on the far left and another VP on the far right. Draw a 90-degree line that bisects the HL at about the halfway point for the center "post." This line should extend above and below the HL at an equal distance. Draw lines from the top and bottom of the post that extend to each VP. Draw two more vertical lines to the left and right of the center post. These two new posts represent the corners of your cube. At the point where each corner post intersects the VP lines, draw a new line back to the opposite VP. These lines form the back edges of your cube, and the place where they intersect guides you to the position of the final back corner post, completing your cube. The baby elephant in the cube demonstrates how animals are affected by perspective. The elephant's feet are positioned on the bottom corners of the cube, and the perspective of the VPs directly affects their positions.

Foreshortening

Foreshortening is an important method of creating the illusion of depth in a drawing, and it works hand in hand with perspective. In foreshortening, the part of the subject that is closest to the viewer appears larger than the parts that are farther away. To create this illusion when drawing, just shorten the lines on the sides of the object that is closest to the viewer.

Visual Example To see foreshortening in action, hold a dinner plate straight out in front of you. It appears as a circle. Now tilt the plate slowly away from you. The plate now appears much shorter. This shape is called an "ellipse."

Recognizing Foreshortening This sketch of an iguana is a good example of foreshortening. Notice the difference in the size of the iguana's right foot compared to its left foot. The left foot was drawn much larger because it's closer to the viewer.

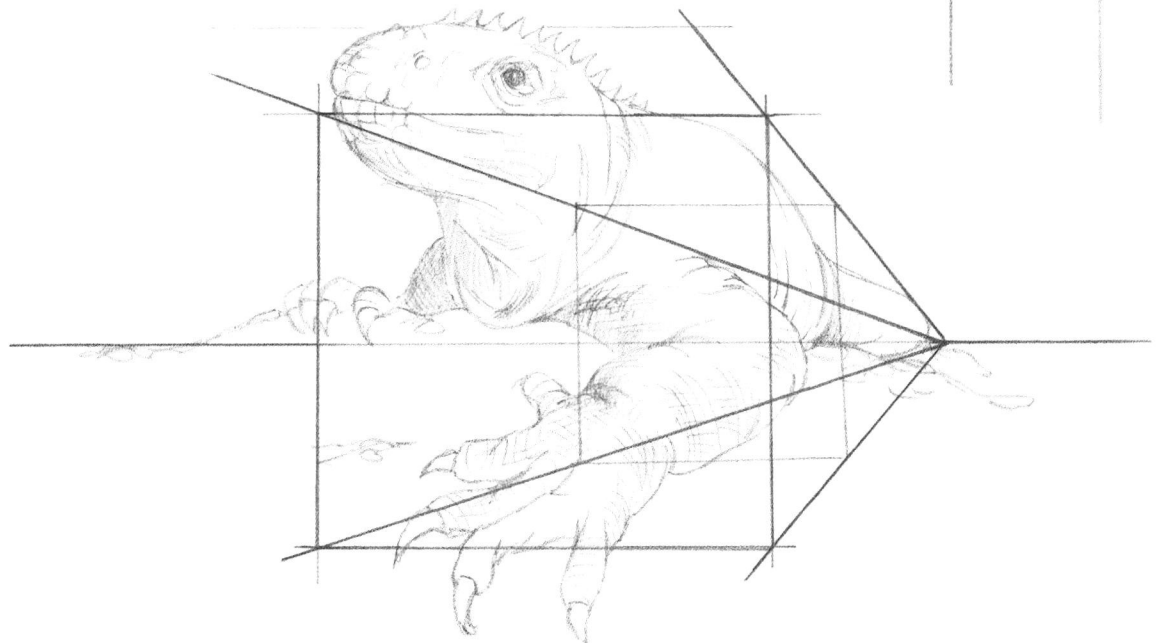

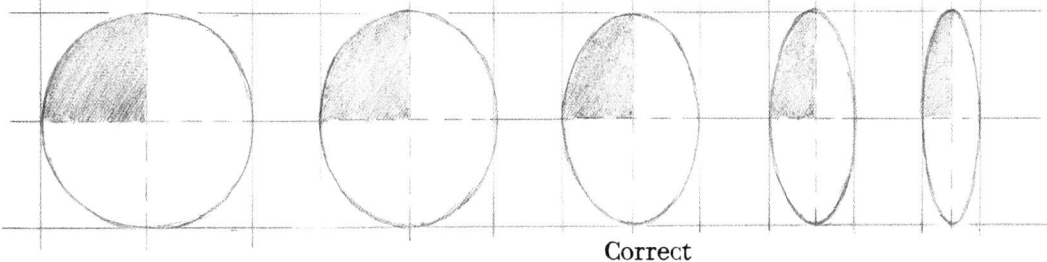

Correct

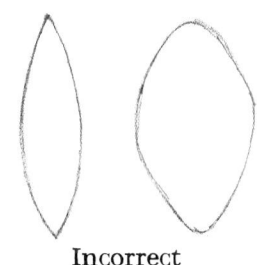

Incorrect

Drawing Ellipses An ellipse is merely a circle that has been foreshortened, as discussed above. It's important for artists to be able to correctly draw an ellipse, as it is one of the most basic shapes used in drawing. Try drawing a series of ellipses, as shown here. Start by drawing a perfect square; then bisect it with a horizontal line and a vertical line. Extend the horizontal lines created by the top and bottom of the square; also extend the center horizontal line to the far right. Create a series of rectangles that reduce in width along the horizontal line. Go back to the square and draw a curve from point to point in one of the quarters, as shown here. Repeat this same curve in the remaining quarters (turn the paper as you draw if it helps), and you will have created a perfect circle within the square. Repeat this process in each of the narrowing rectangles to produce a range of ellipses. Use this exercise whenever you have difficulty drawing a symmetrical ellipse or circle.

Creating a Focal Point

A key element in creating a successful composition is including more than one area of interest, without generating confusion about the subject of the drawing. Compositions are often based on one large object, which is balanced by the grouping, placement, and values of smaller objects. Directing the viewer's eye with secondary focal points helps move the viewer through a scene, so that it can be enjoyed in its entirety.

The primary focal point should immediately capture the viewer's attention through size, line quality, value, placement on the picture plane, and the proximity of other points of interest which call attention to it. The secondary focal point is the area that the eye naturally moves to after seeing the primary focal point; usually this element is a smaller object or objects with less detail. Another secondary focal point may be at some distance from the viewer's eye, appearing much smaller, and showing only minor detailing, so that it occupies a much less important space in the drawing. This distant focal point serves to give the viewer's eye another stop on the journey around the composition before returning to the primary focal point.

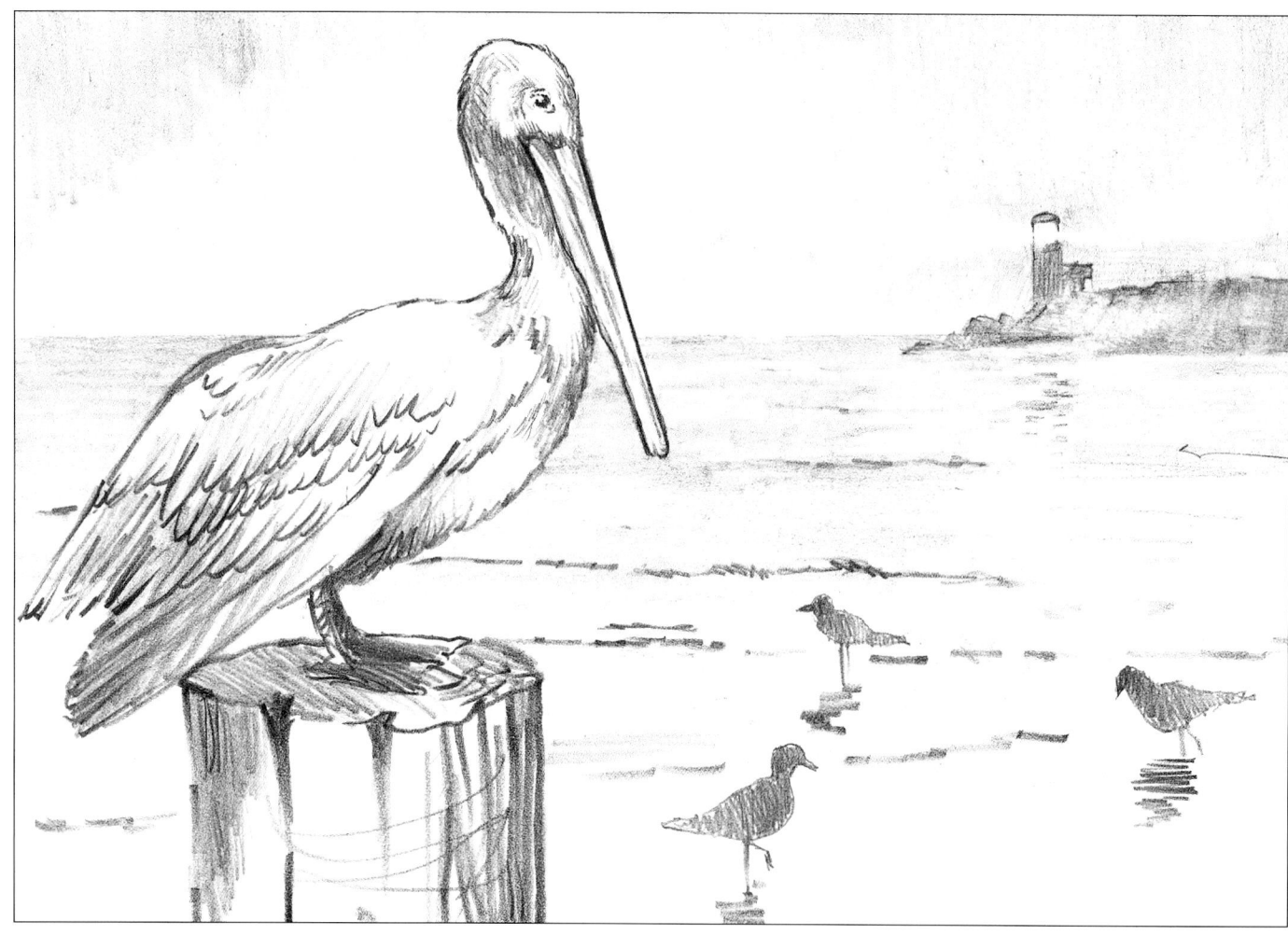

Primary, Secondary, and Distant Focal Points The size and detail on the pelican designates it as the primary focal point, so it immediately catches the viewer's eye. The pelican's gaze and the point of its bill shifts the attention to the small birds in the foreground (the secondary focal point). By keeping the texture and value changes subtle in the middle ground, the eye moves freely to this point. These three small birds are shaded fairly evenly so that they don't detract from the primary focal point. The triangle created by the birds, along with the water's edge and the point of land, leads the viewer's eye to another, more distant focal point—the lighthouse. At the lighthouse, the two subtle rays of light against the shaded background suggest a visual path. The rays of light, the point of land, and the horizon line all work together to bring the viewer's eye back to the pelican, and the visual journey begins again.

Vertical Landscapes

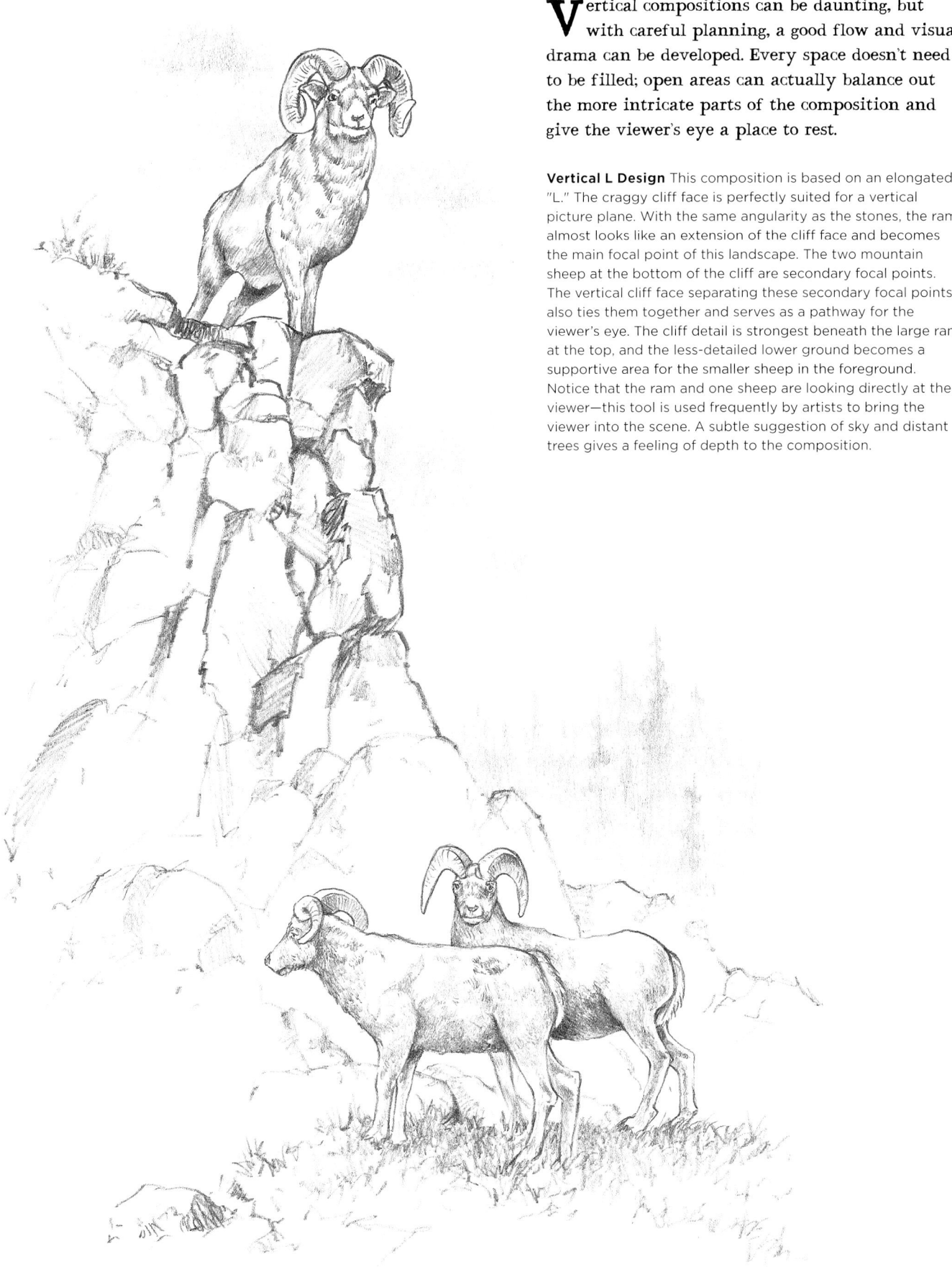

Vertical compositions can be daunting, but with careful planning, a good flow and visual drama can be developed. Every space doesn't need to be filled; open areas can actually balance out the more intricate parts of the composition and give the viewer's eye a place to rest.

Vertical L Design This composition is based on an elongated "L." The craggy cliff face is perfectly suited for a vertical picture plane. With the same angularity as the stones, the ram almost looks like an extension of the cliff face and becomes the main focal point of this landscape. The two mountain sheep at the bottom of the cliff are secondary focal points. The vertical cliff face separating these secondary focal points also ties them together and serves as a pathway for the viewer's eye. The cliff detail is strongest beneath the large ram at the top, and the less-detailed lower ground becomes a supportive area for the smaller sheep in the foreground. Notice that the ram and one sheep are looking directly at the viewer—this tool is used frequently by artists to bring the viewer into the scene. A subtle suggestion of sky and distant trees gives a feeling of depth to the composition.

Landscape Elements

When developing a sense of depth in your compositions, remember what attracts the viewer's eye. Larger elements and those that overlap other elements demand attention. Also, extensive detail and darker values will draw attention to even a small element. Consider these principles in your landscape compositions. Look for them in the landscapes on the previous pages and below.

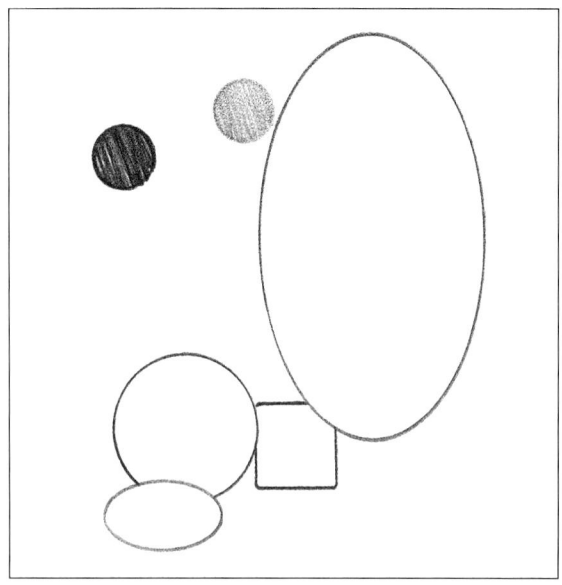

Commanding Attention Notice that the very large oval occupies as much space as all the other elements in this sketch combined and is therefore very important, but the shaded circles, which are a fraction of the oval's size, vie for the viewer's attention. The outlined shapes at the bottom draw the eye last, but their overlapping edges give a feeling of some depth.

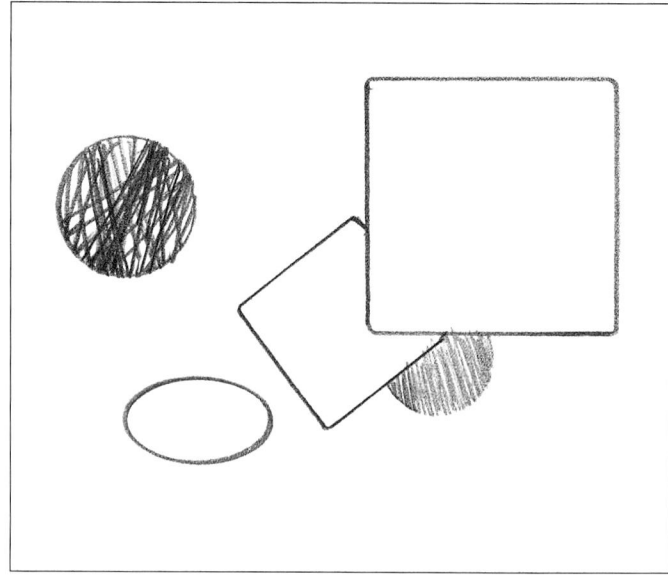

Focal Points The complexity of the underlapping placement and shading on the partially hidden circle compels the eye, even though it is smaller than most of the other elements. However, the dark circle with interior lines (showing detail) is still the strongest focal point, and the viewer's gaze will be repeatedly drawn to that spot.

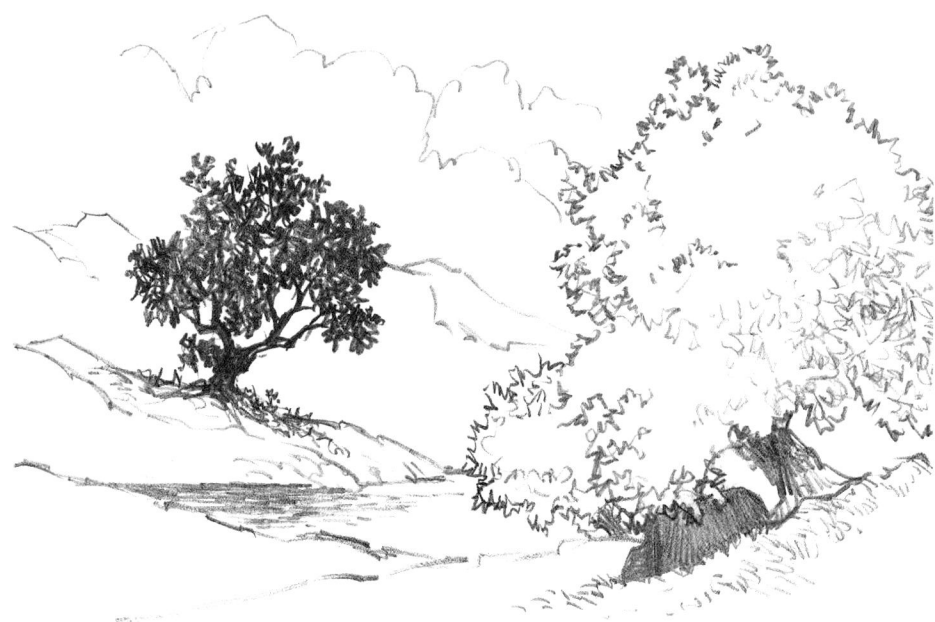

Attracting the Viewer's Eye As shown in the "Focal Points" thumbnail sketch (above right), the darker values of the shaded rock beneath the tree attract the viewer's eye, even though it is smaller than the rest of the elements. By drawing the foreground tree so that it overlaps the small rock, a sense of depth and dimension is produced (as illustrated in the thumbnail where the two squares overlap the small shaded circle). The dark background tree attracts the most attention, as seen in the same thumbnail, because it so strongly contrasts the light values of the foreground tree.

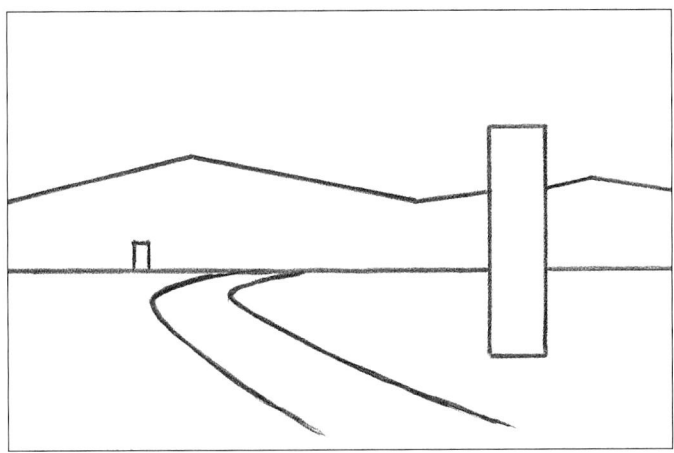

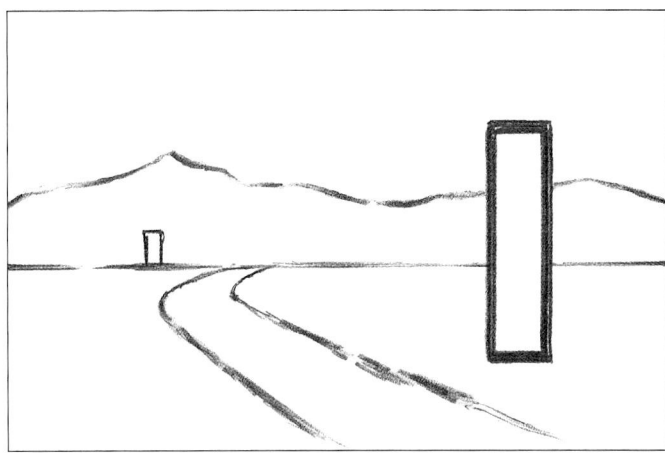

Lack of Focal Point When all lines in a composition are drawn with the same depth of intensity (value) and width, the entire design appears flat and uninteresting, with no focal point.

Focal Depth and Flow By simply changing the weight of the lines of the foreground rectangle, and by varying the quality of lines in the road and mountain, the scene has more focal interest.

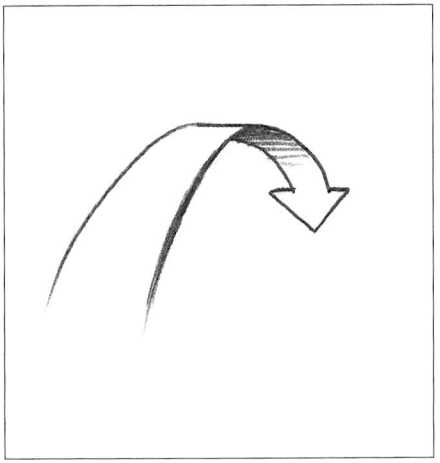

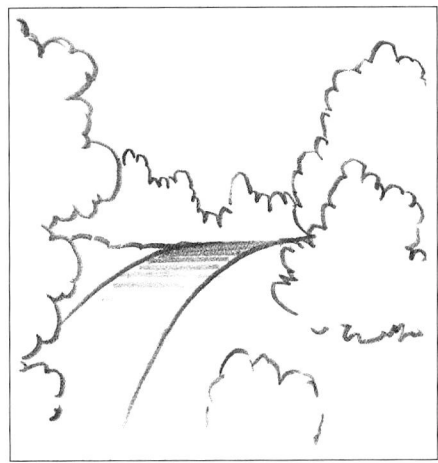

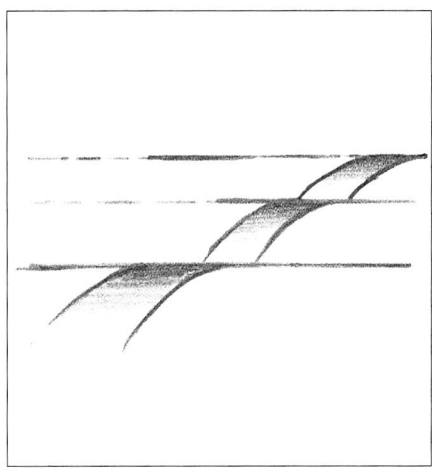

Focal Curve A graceful curve leads the eye into the composition. This can be used for roads and pathways (to create the illusion of hills and valleys) as well as subjects, such as floral arrangements to direct the viewer's eye.

Focal Depth The focal curve is one way of creating depth in a composition. Here it serves as a road in a natural setting, leading the viewer into the scene. The use of overlapping elements—the trees—also adds to the illusion, creating focal depth.

Multiple Focal Curves To further accentuate the feeling of distance, more than one curve can be used, along with multiple elevation lines. Notice that the curve segments are displaced and become smaller as they recede in the distance.

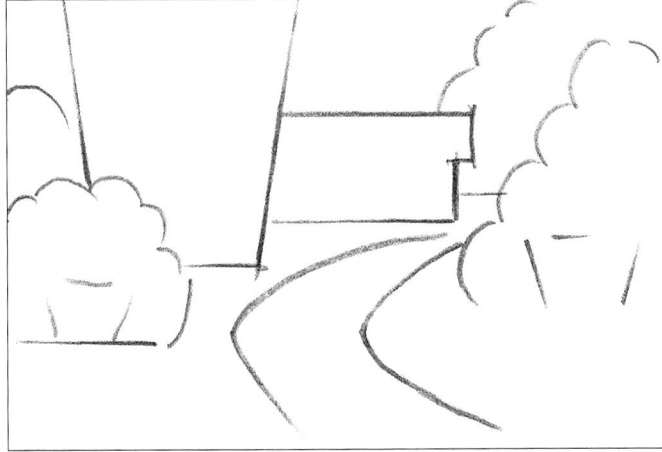

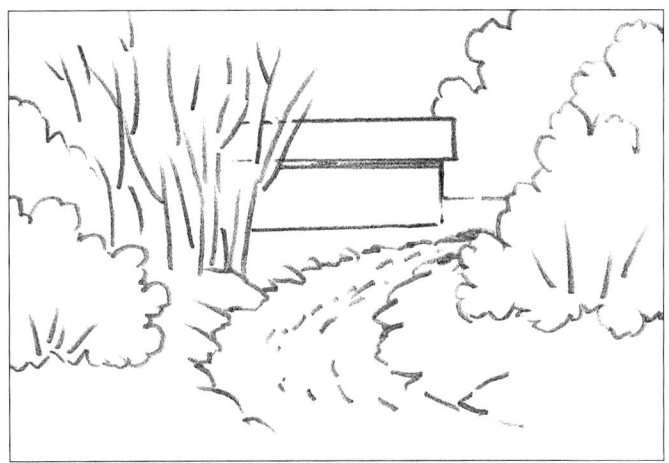

Sketching Focal Patterns Sketch a preliminary, simple pattern plan to show the general placement of elements without the distraction of internal details, value, or line quality. Look for the focal pattern—how the eye moves around the picture and what is important—and adjust as needed.

Develop the Pattern After sketching and adjusting a preliminary pattern plan, lightly add details to build the feeling of rhythmic movement and depth. Begin varying the weight of the lines and refining the shapes of the elements. As you continue, use value to further accentuate the focal pattern.

Composing Animal Scenes

Thoughtful planning of size and placement is almost as important as your choice of animal subject. Animals usually are portrayed in "classic" or natural poses for the kind or breed. Backgrounds should be minimal or include just a few habitat clues to place the focus on the animals. Multiple photographic references often are the best way to capture the animal pose you want to draw.

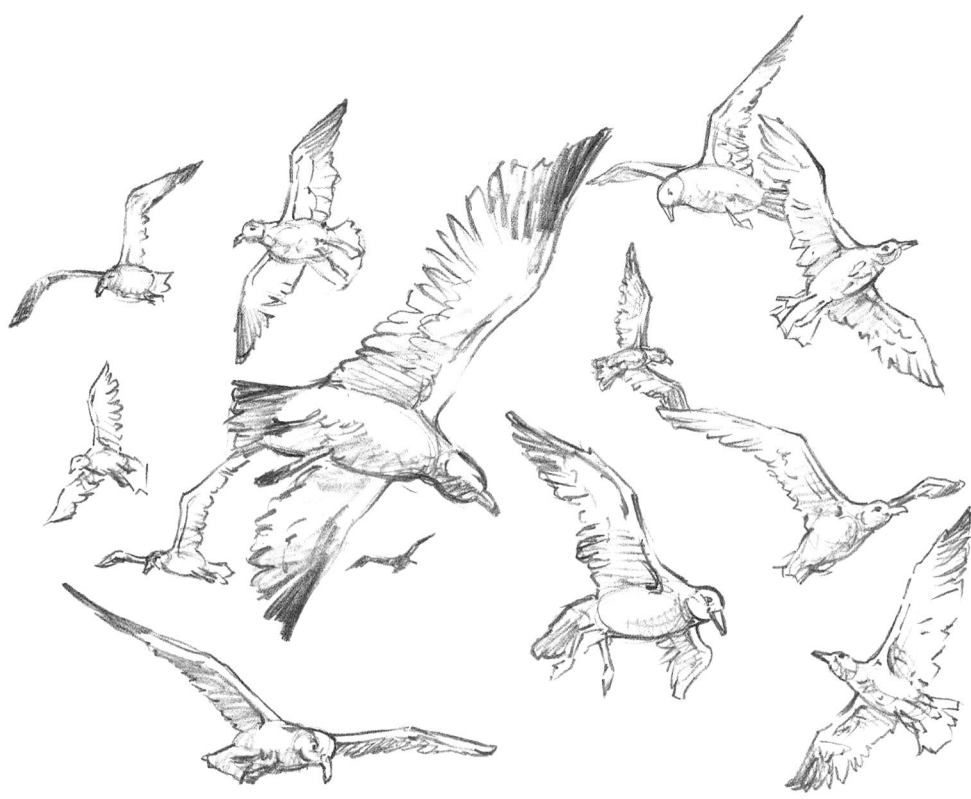

Groups of Animals Seagulls feeding in flight provide an interesting subject. The statement of this composition is their fluid movements while showing the flurry of activity in their search for morsels of food. The X- and O-composition methods shown below were combined to create this drawing, which was assembled from several photos. Slight overlapping adds to the action and creates depth.

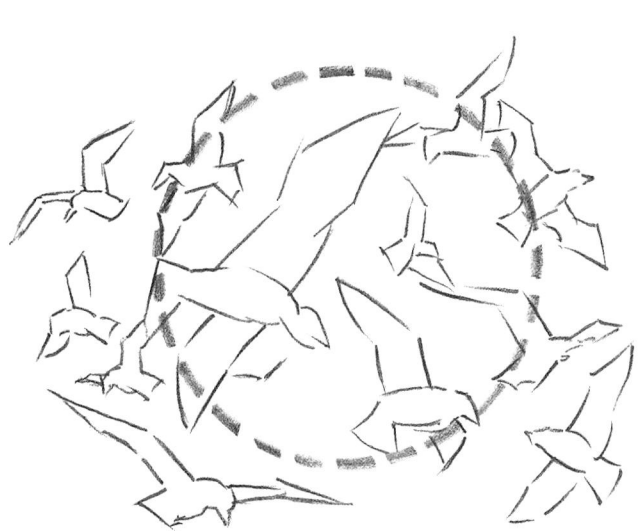

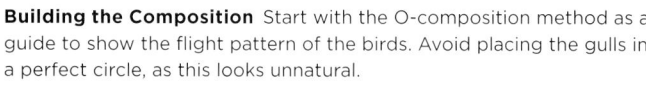

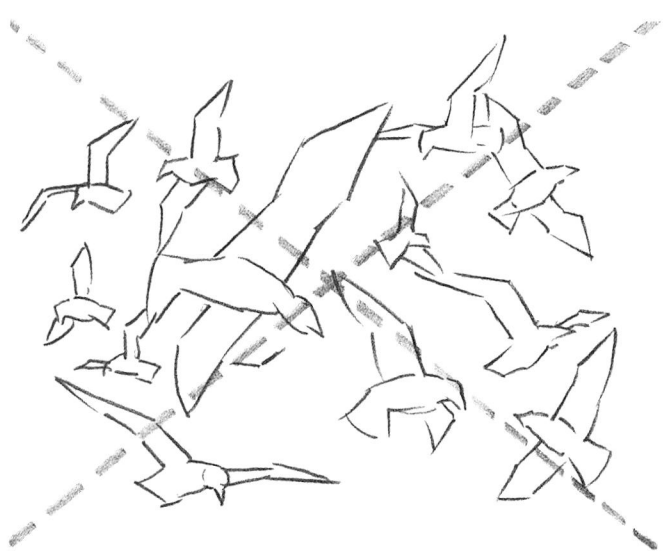

Building the Composition Start with the O-composition method as a guide to show the flight pattern of the birds. Avoid placing the gulls in a perfect circle, as this looks unnatural.

Balancing the Composition By overlaying the X composition, more balance is added. Escape monotony by using the X only as a guide and not placing the gulls directly on the lines.

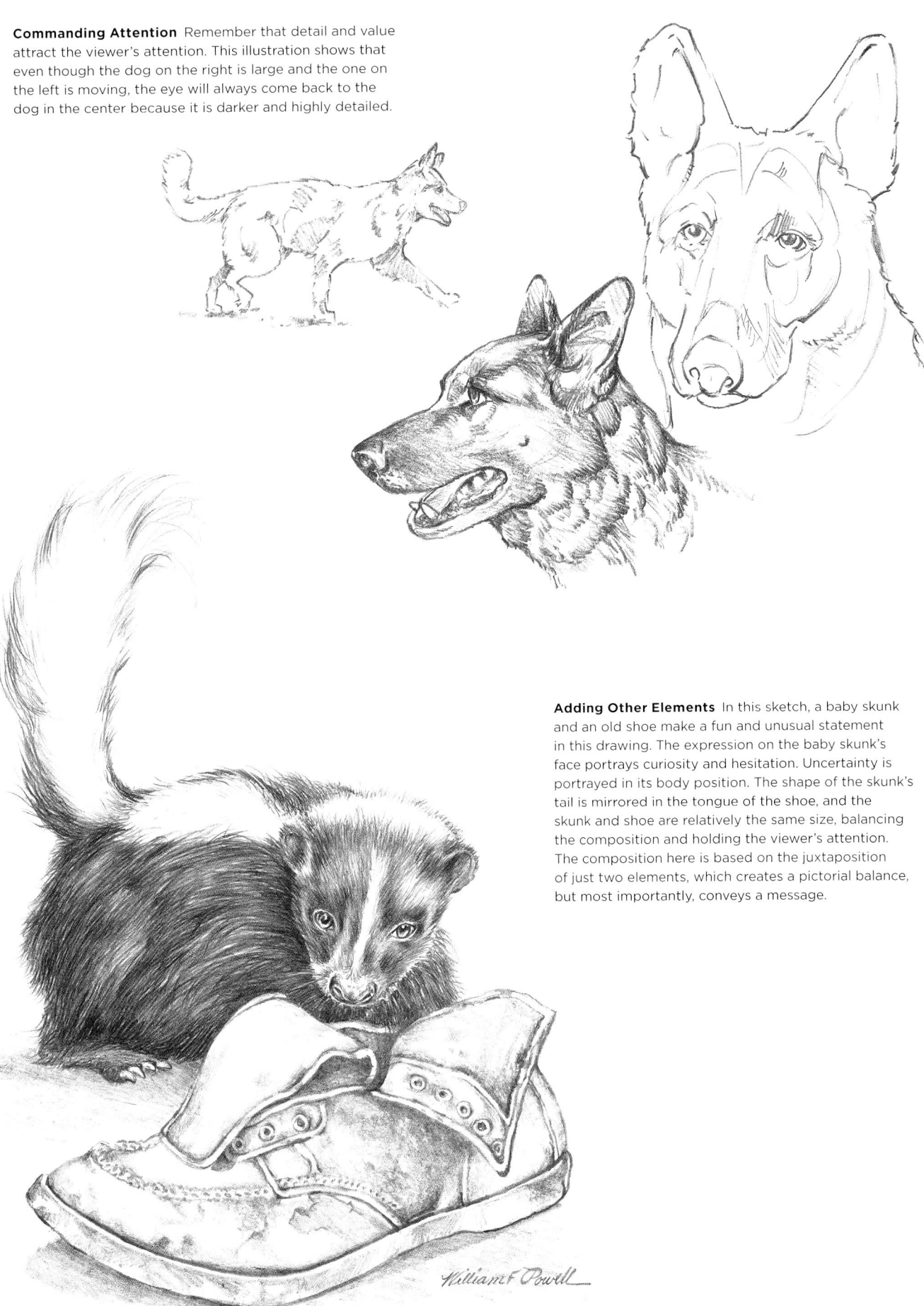

Commanding Attention Remember that detail and value attract the viewer's attention. This illustration shows that even though the dog on the right is large and the one on the left is moving, the eye will always come back to the dog in the center because it is darker and highly detailed.

Adding Other Elements In this sketch, a baby skunk and an old shoe make a fun and unusual statement in this drawing. The expression on the baby skunk's face portrays curiosity and hesitation. Uncertainty is portrayed in its body position. The shape of the skunk's tail is mirrored in the tongue of the shoe, and the skunk and shoe are relatively the same size, balancing the composition and holding the viewer's attention. The composition here is based on the juxtaposition of just two elements, which creates a pictorial balance, but most importantly, conveys a message.

William F Powell

Animal Portraits | 137

Kangaroo

Australia's iconic marsupial is an ideal subject to photograph, as it often is found in a stationary pose, either grazing or watching. This kangaroo, with its head gazing directly at the viewer and its large tail resting on the ground, is a good example of the quiet nature of these graceful animals.

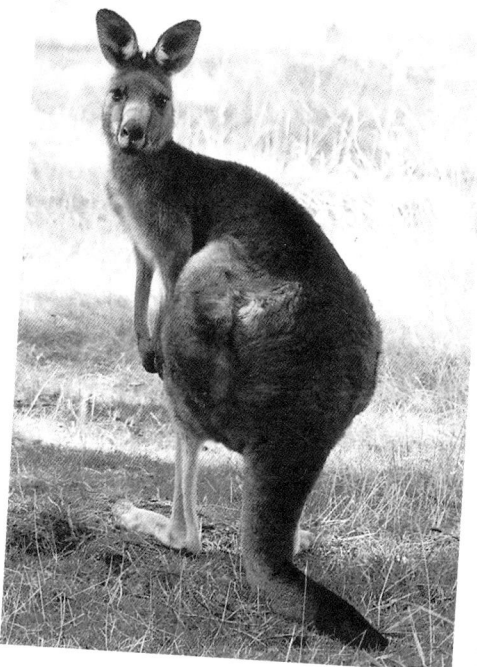

Experimenting with Texture A kangaroo's coat is thick and dense, with an even color and texture. It's fun to explore the swirls and flow of their fur texture in your drawings.

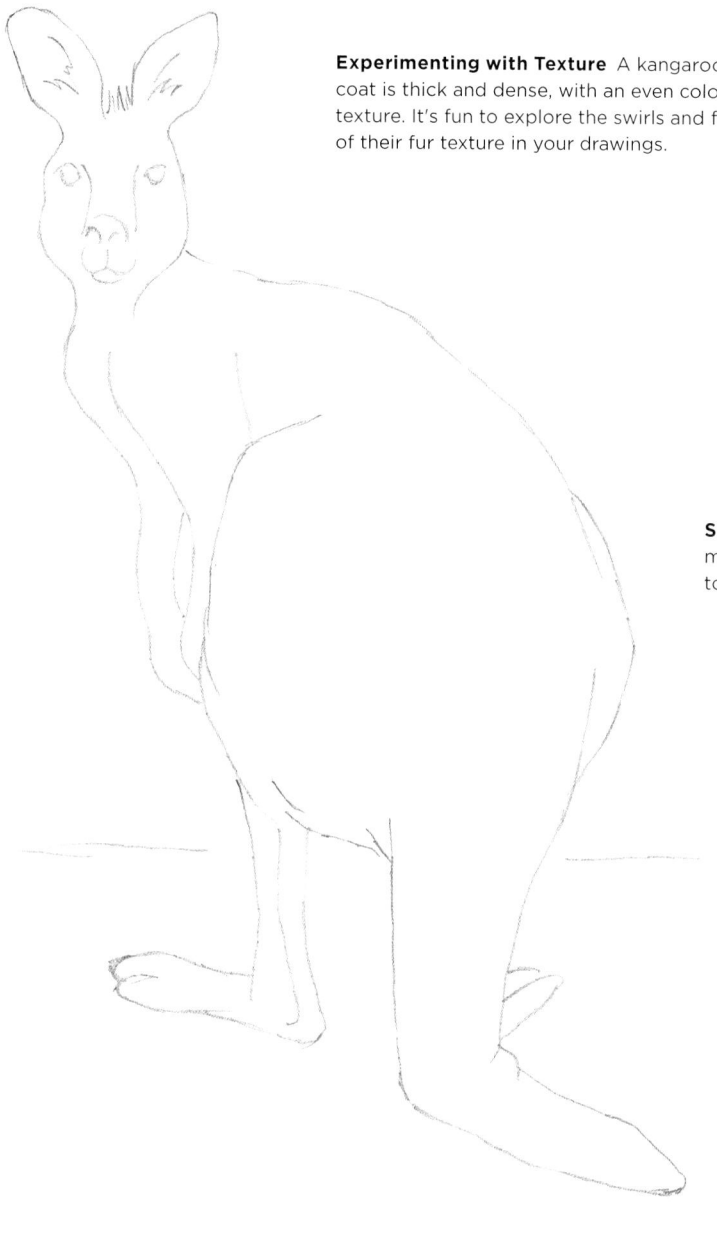

Step 1 Draw the outline of the kangaroo, including the eyes, muzzle, nose, mouth, and a few small fur details. Add a line or two to indicate the ground.

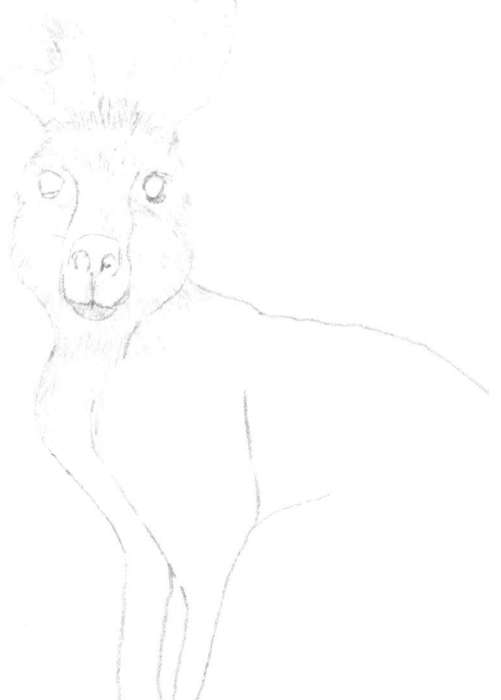

Step 2 Starting with the ears and working down the head, use a sharp 2H clutch lead to draw quick, short strokes for the undercoat, which will act as a directional guide for the rest of the fur. Leave the eyes and highlights of the cheeks, muzzle, and ears white.

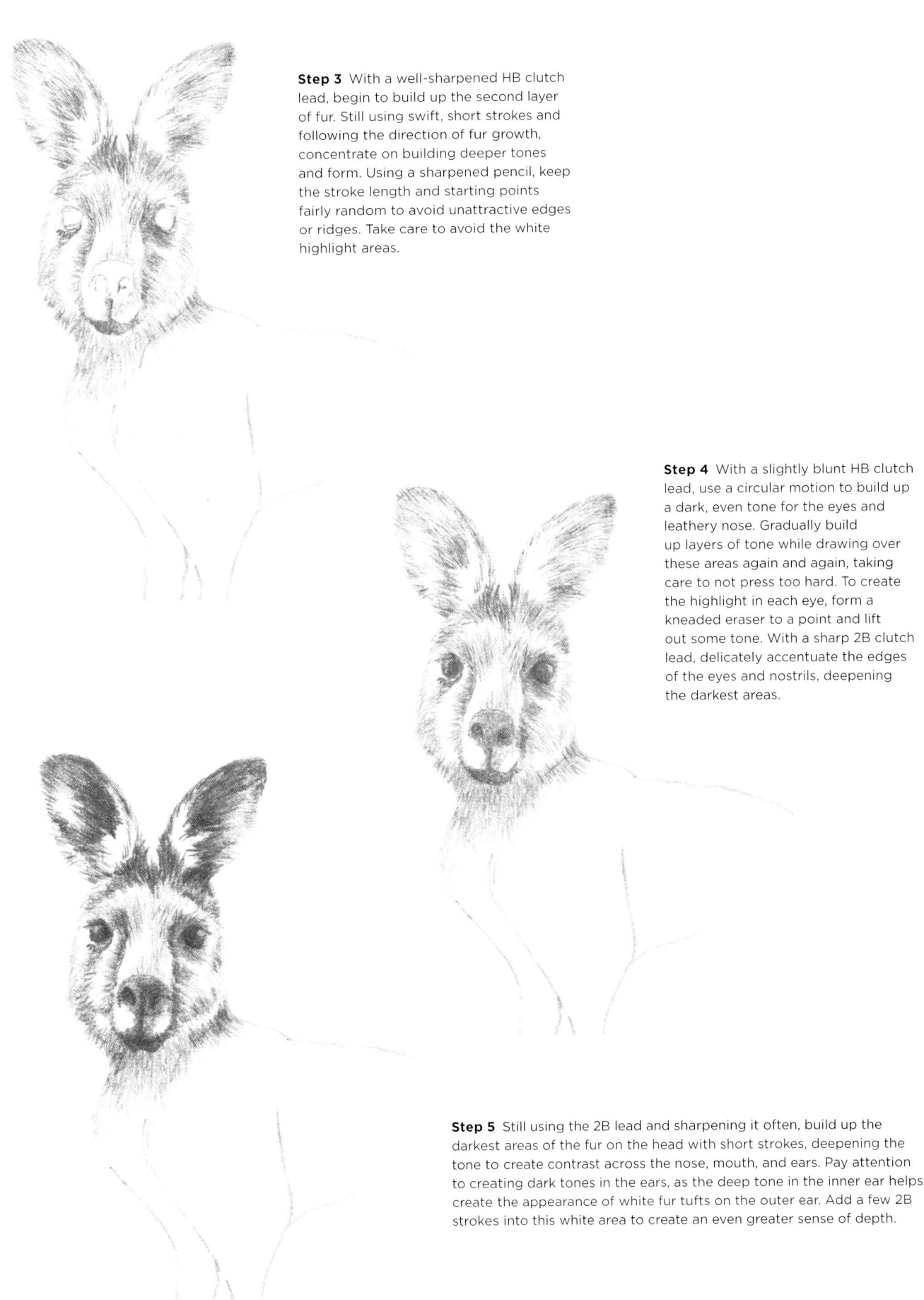

Step 3 With a well-sharpened HB clutch lead, begin to build up the second layer of fur. Still using swift, short strokes and following the direction of fur growth, concentrate on building deeper tones and form. Using a sharpened pencil, keep the stroke length and starting points fairly random to avoid unattractive edges or ridges. Take care to avoid the white highlight areas.

Step 4 With a slightly blunt HB clutch lead, use a circular motion to build up a dark, even tone for the eyes and leathery nose. Gradually build up layers of tone while drawing over these areas again and again, taking care to not press too hard. To create the highlight in each eye, form a kneaded eraser to a point and lift out some tone. With a sharp 2B clutch lead, delicately accentuate the edges of the eyes and nostrils, deepening the darkest areas.

Step 5 Still using the 2B lead and sharpening it often, build up the darkest areas of the fur on the head with short strokes, deepening the tone to create contrast across the nose, mouth, and ears. Pay attention to creating dark tones in the ears, as the deep tone in the inner ear helps create the appearance of white fur tufts on the outer ear. Add a few 2B strokes into this white area to create an even greater sense of depth.

Animal Portraits | 139

Step 6 Go over the entire head once again with fine strokes of a sharp HB clutch lead, further refining the details. This final layer helps blend the underlying layers and creates an even, smooth texture. Continue the linework down the neck, alternating HB and 2H leads. This blends the finished area of the head into the body. Lighten the outline with a kneaded eraser. Then, with a sharp 2H clutch lead, work down the forearms and the back of the kangaroo, following the direction of the fur.

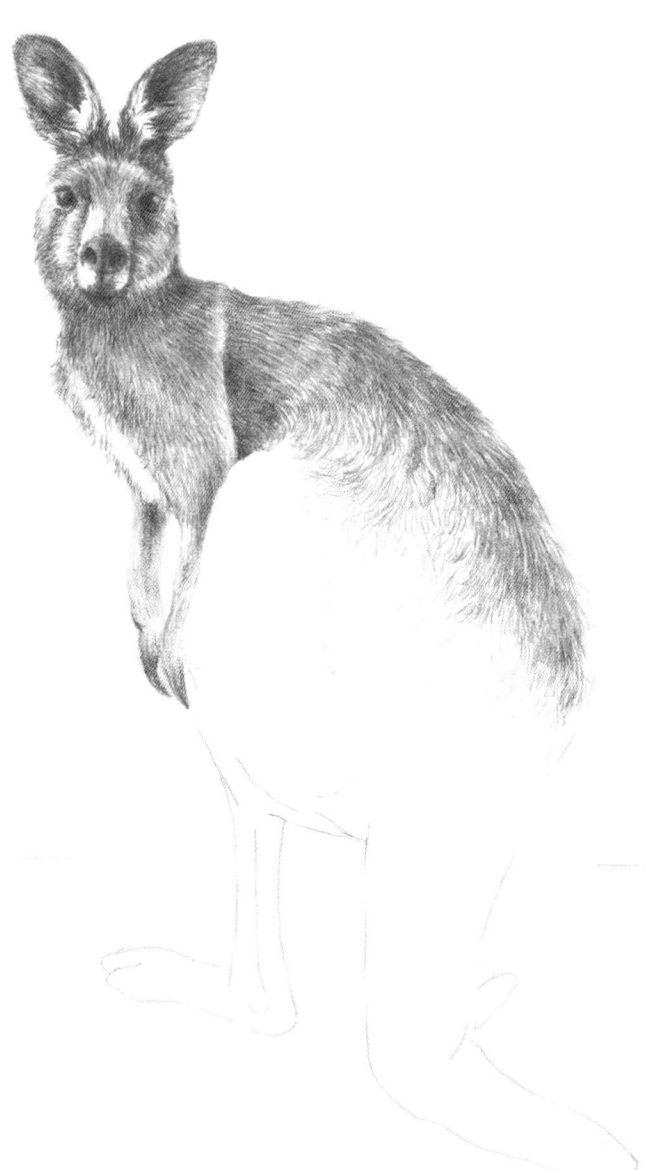

Step 7 Use a sharp HB clutch lead to add a second layer of fur over the undercoat. Where the fur is darker, the strokes are closer together; where the fur is lighter, the strokes are farther apart. The fur is longer and wavier on the kangaroo's back, so your pencil strokes should reflect this. For the fur over the back and sides, keep the strokes short and close together, allowing the HB to blend into the 2H layer. Then use a sharp 2B lead to darken the fur, adding form and tone. Use a 2B lead to darken the areas above the animal's right arm and along the front of its shoulders to create the patch of white fur on the chest.

Step 8 To give the impression of sunlight shining across the body, leave some white showing in the highlight areas of the leg and hip. Leave a small area of white on the tail where you eventually will add some blades of grass. This overlap helps show that the tail is resting on the ground. Build the undercoat into the rest of the torso and tail with a 2H clutch lead. Then apply a second layer with an HB lead, taking care to leave some white areas showing on the leg, hip, and tail. Keep your strokes a little looser around the hip, giving them a bit more length and wave, and make tighter strokes on the tail to reflect its shorter, denser fur.

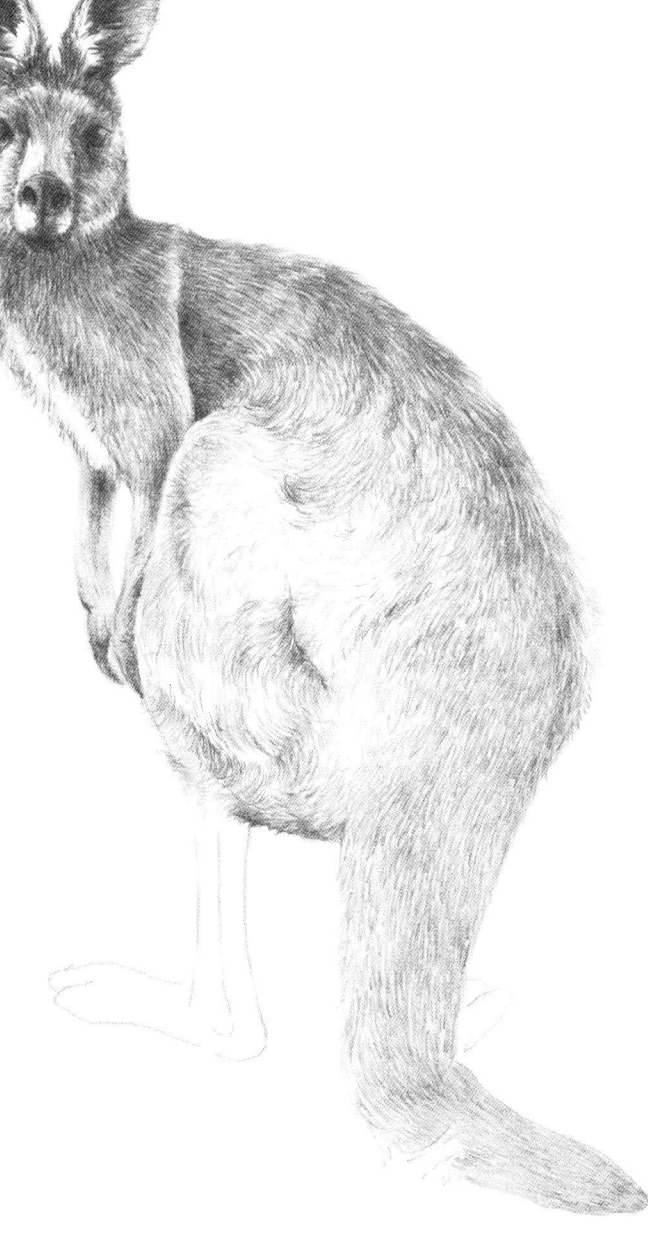

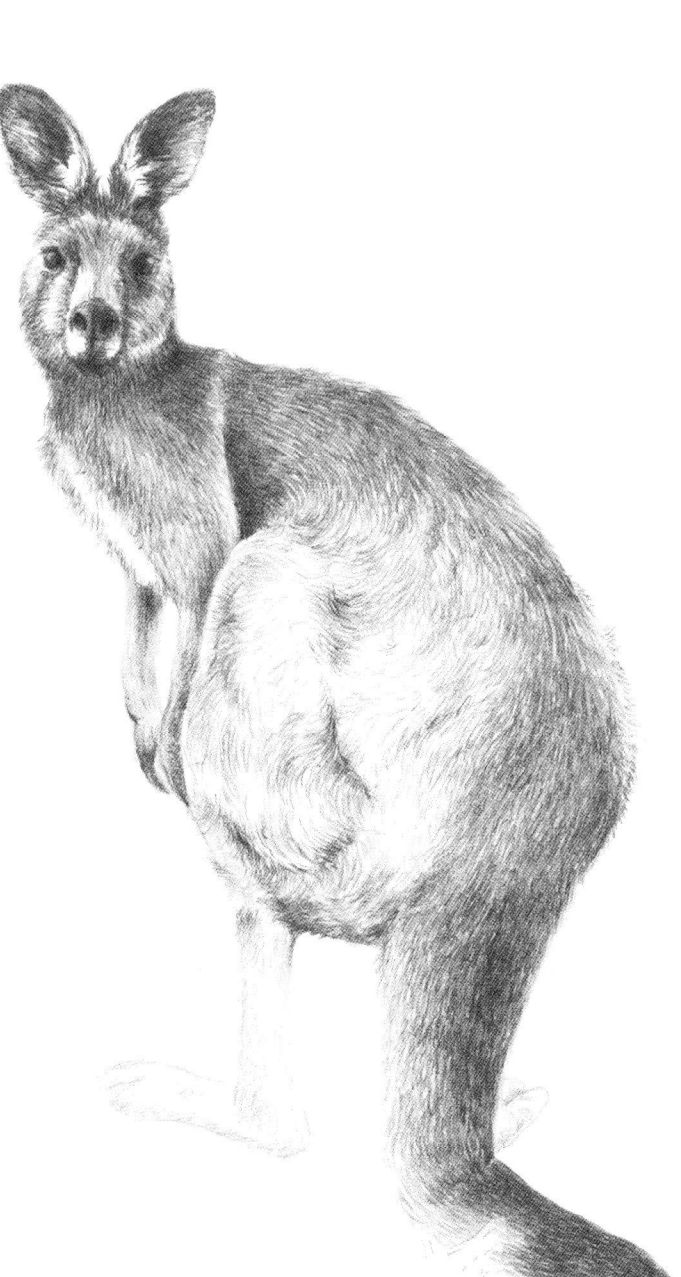

Step 9 Use a 2B clutch lead to create darker fur over the back and down the tail. The tail is quite dark and needs a bit of layering to build up the correct tone. Leave the tone lighter along the edge of the back and tail to create the illusion of a rounded, three-dimensional form. Moving to the legs, soften the guidelines with a kneaded eraser; then use an HB lead and light pressure to create the fine fur. There is reflected light on the sides and backs of the legs, so keep these areas lighter in tone. Use only a sharp HB lead here, as there is not a great tonal range in the legs, but apply several layers to build up the texture. Add a few strokes of a sharp 2B lead to deepen the tone around the ankle and under the hip.

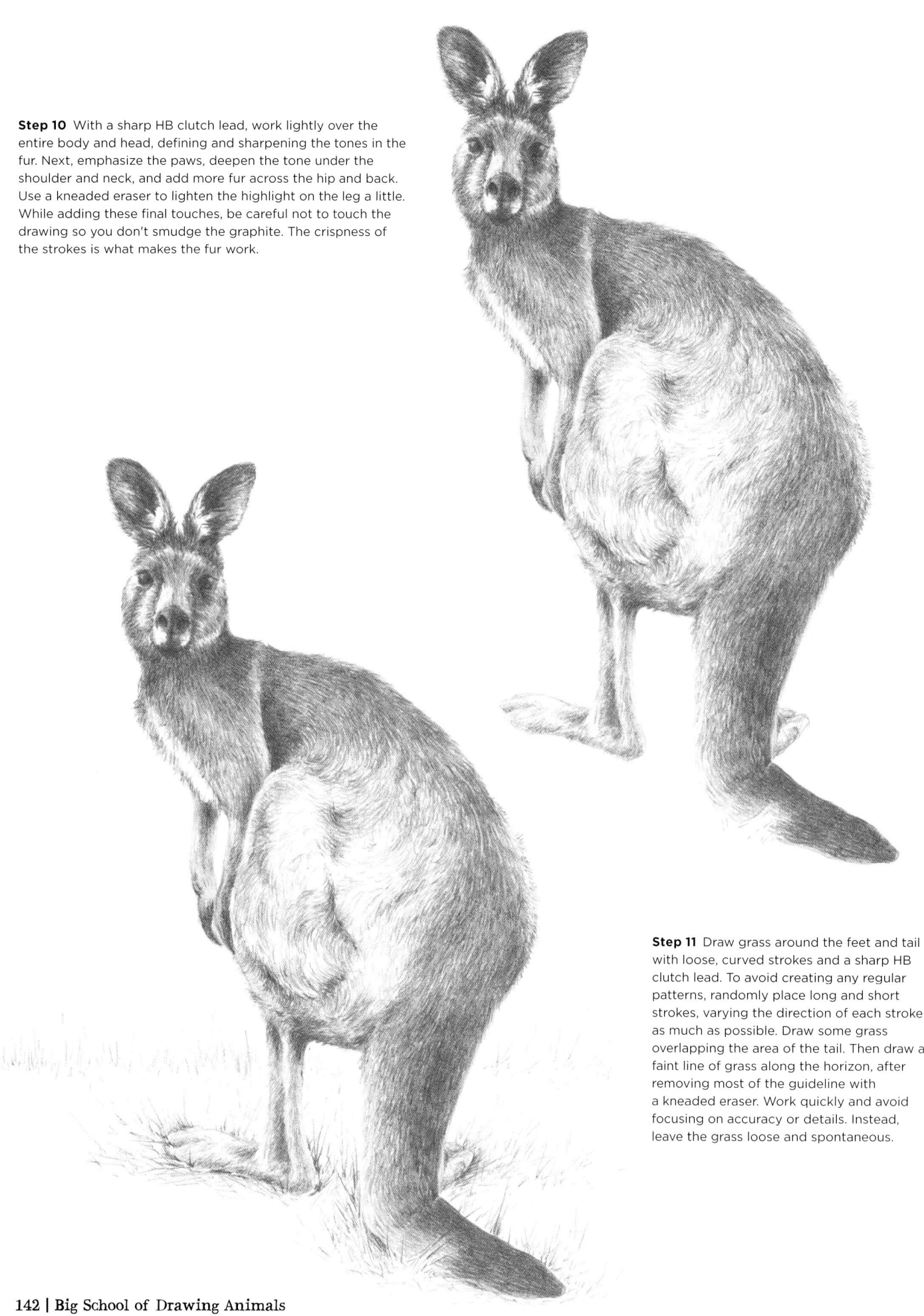

Step 10 With a sharp HB clutch lead, work lightly over the entire body and head, defining and sharpening the tones in the fur. Next, emphasize the paws, deepen the tone under the shoulder and neck, and add more fur across the hip and back. Use a kneaded eraser to lighten the highlight on the leg a little. While adding these final touches, be careful not to touch the drawing so you don't smudge the graphite. The crispness of the strokes is what makes the fur work.

Step 11 Draw grass around the feet and tail with loose, curved strokes and a sharp HB clutch lead. To avoid creating any regular patterns, randomly place long and short strokes, varying the direction of each stroke as much as possible. Draw some grass overlapping the area of the tail. Then draw a faint line of grass along the horizon, after removing most of the guideline with a kneaded eraser. Work quickly and avoid focusing on accuracy or details. Instead, leave the grass loose and spontaneous.

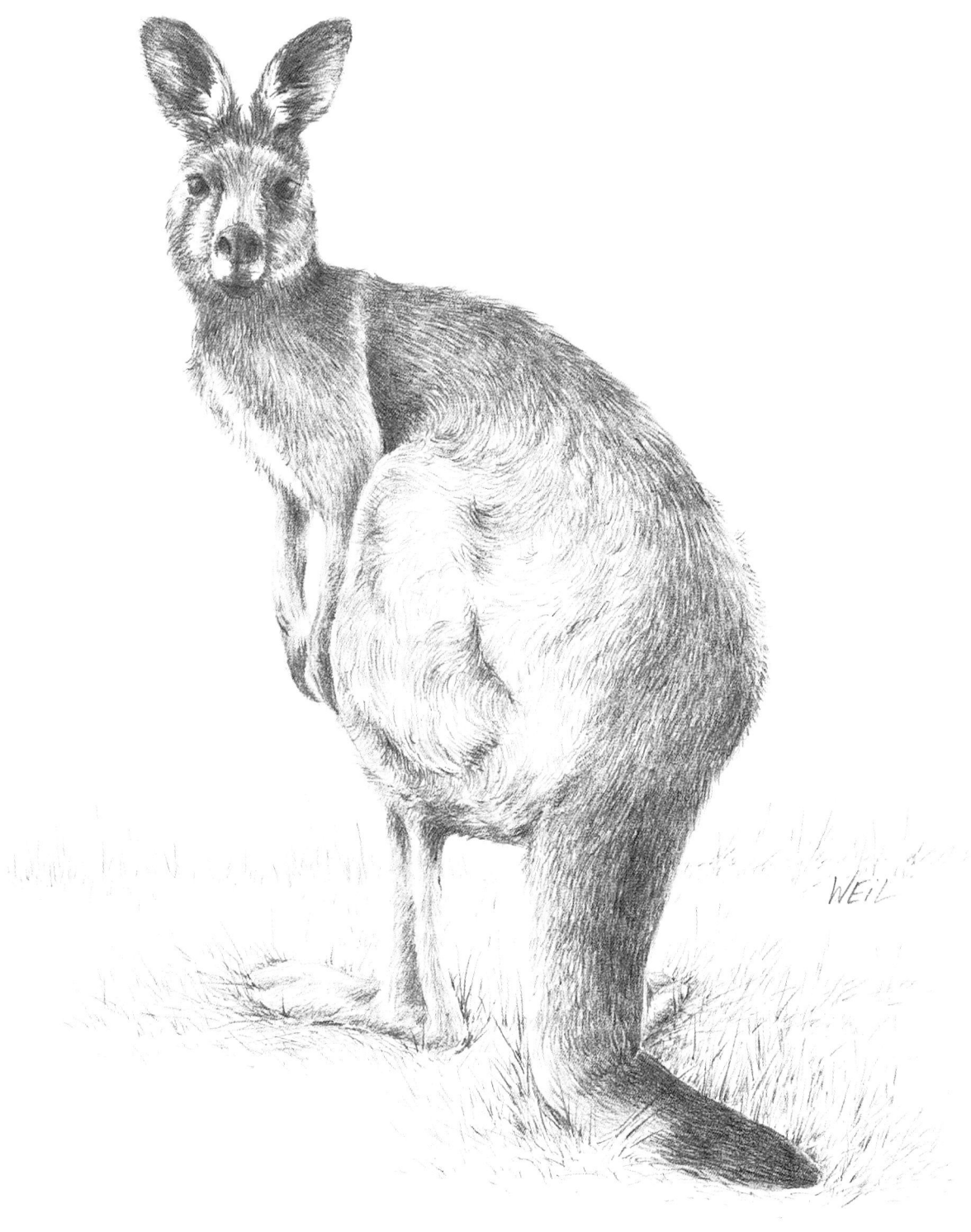

Step 12 Continue to develop the grass, darkening the tone under the kangaroo's feet to further ground the animal. When you're finished, sign the work and lightly spray the entire drawing with workable fixative to help prevent smudging.

Asian Elephant

Large animals such as elephants are great subjects for your first attempts at drawing wildlife. The big, round forms are easy to understand, and the texture of the skin is less daunting than fur. This project features an Asian elephant, which differs slightly from an African elephant in that it has a smaller body and ears, as well as a more rounded back. It also has a fourth toenail on its rear feet and only one "finger" at the end of its trunk. The head and body are sparsely covered in wiry hair. Because they are working animals, their tusks often have been cut short to prevent damage to their surroundings. Noting these characteristics will help you to accurately portray this type of elephant.

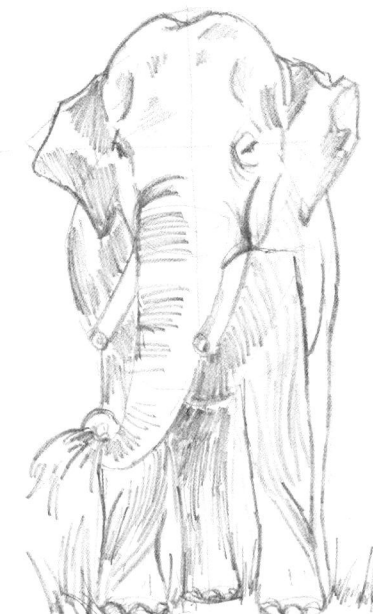

Rough Sketch Start with a rough sketch. Using a soft 2B pencil, define the general forms of the elephant. Next, indicate the light and dark areas, keeping in mind that the light is coming from above right.

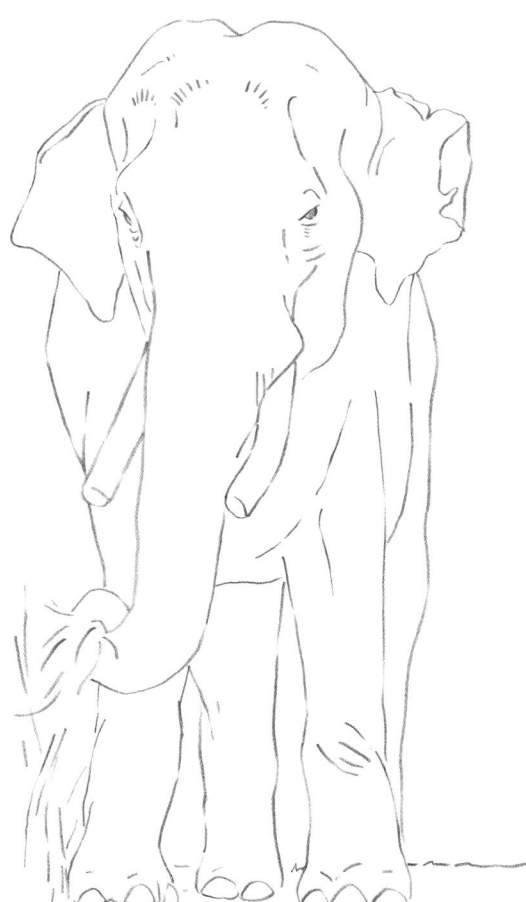

Step 1 Use an HB pencil to refine your outline. Do not include any details or the background at this time.

Step 2 Create a very soft, smooth tone to represent the underlayer of skin prior to adding the rough, cracked texture. Using a 2B pencil, make small circular strokes to fill in the darkest shadow areas. Leave large areas of white for now. You will blend the graphite into these areas in the next step.

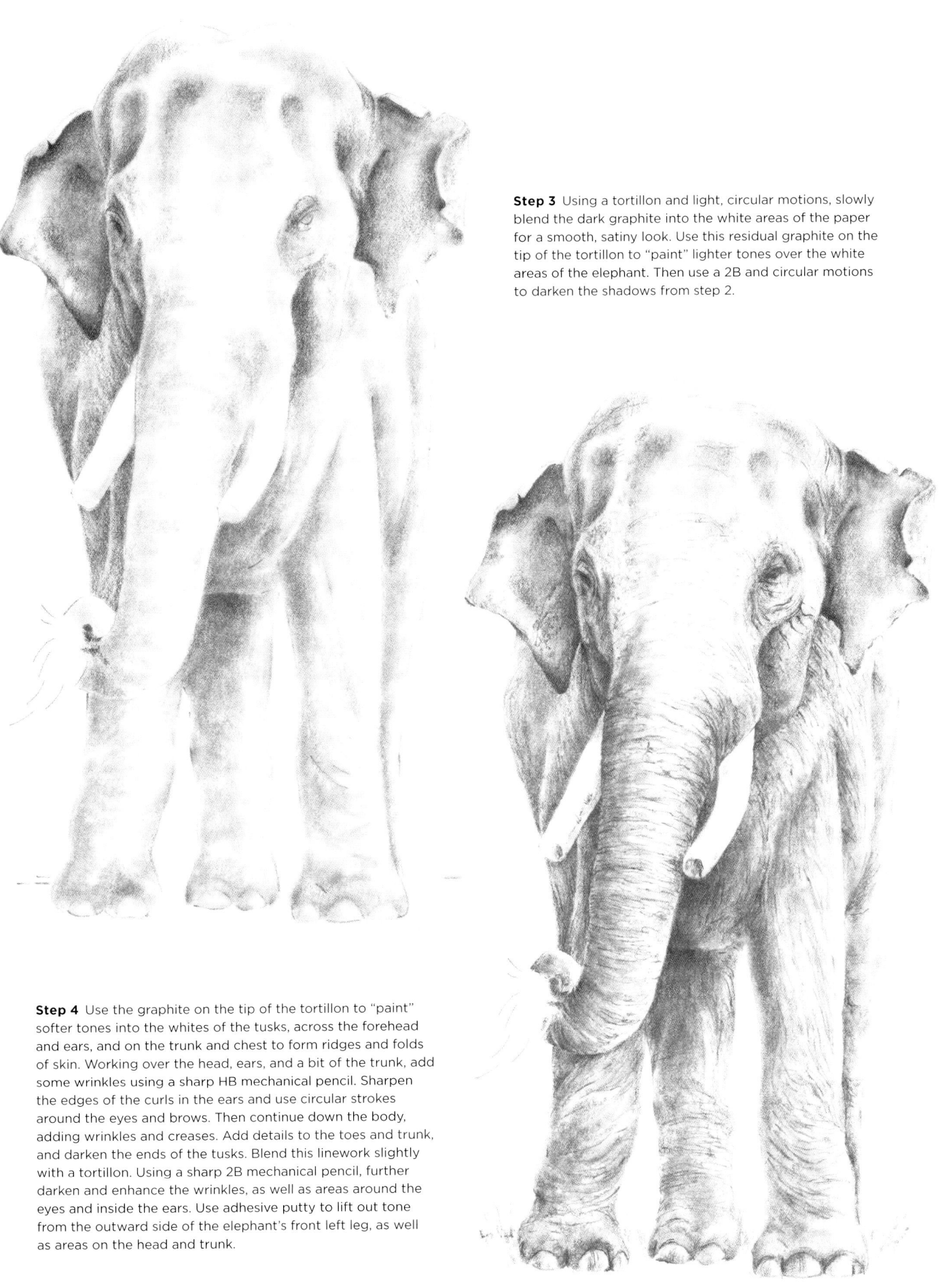

Step 3 Using a tortillon and light, circular motions, slowly blend the dark graphite into the white areas of the paper for a smooth, satiny look. Use this residual graphite on the tip of the tortillon to "paint" lighter tones over the white areas of the elephant. Then use a 2B and circular motions to darken the shadows from step 2.

Step 4 Use the graphite on the tip of the tortillon to "paint" softer tones into the whites of the tusks, across the forehead and ears, and on the trunk and chest to form ridges and folds of skin. Working over the head, ears, and a bit of the trunk, add some wrinkles using a sharp HB mechanical pencil. Sharpen the edges of the curls in the ears and use circular strokes around the eyes and brows. Then continue down the body, adding wrinkles and creases. Add details to the toes and trunk, and darken the ends of the tusks. Blend this linework slightly with a tortillon. Using a sharp 2B mechanical pencil, further darken and enhance the wrinkles, as well as areas around the eyes and inside the ears. Use adhesive putty to lift out tone from the outward side of the elephant's front left leg, as well as areas on the head and trunk.

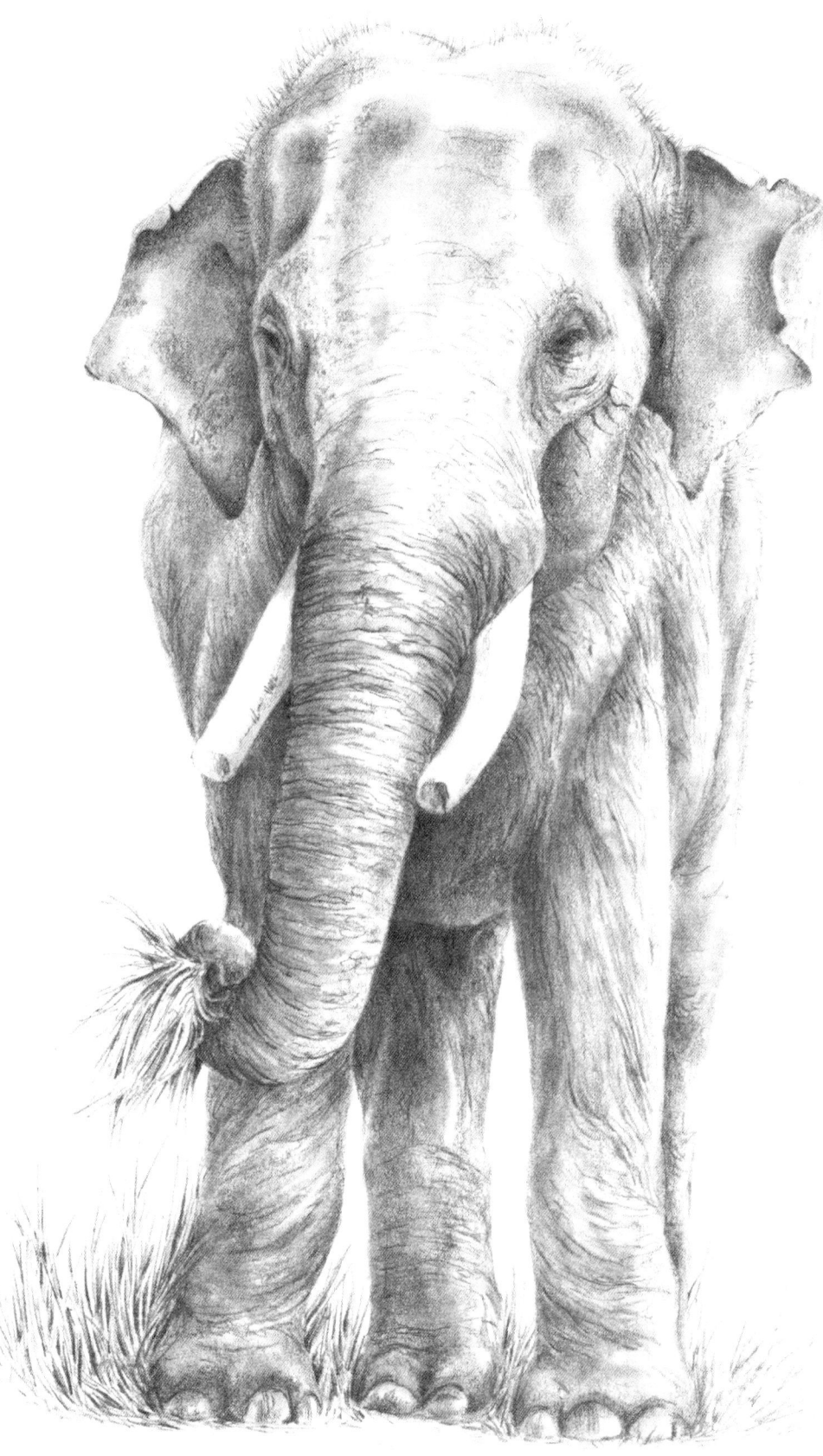

Step 5 With the 2B pencil, continue to build up the form of the tough, wrinkled skin. Deepen the tones in the darkest shadows, and add some dark hairs on the elephant's head and back. With a very sharp HB pencil, draw strokes of various lengths to represent the grass on the ground as well as at the end of the elephant's trunk. Then use a sharp 2B to fill in dark areas between the strokes, giving the grass some depth. Add further detail in the feet and toes.

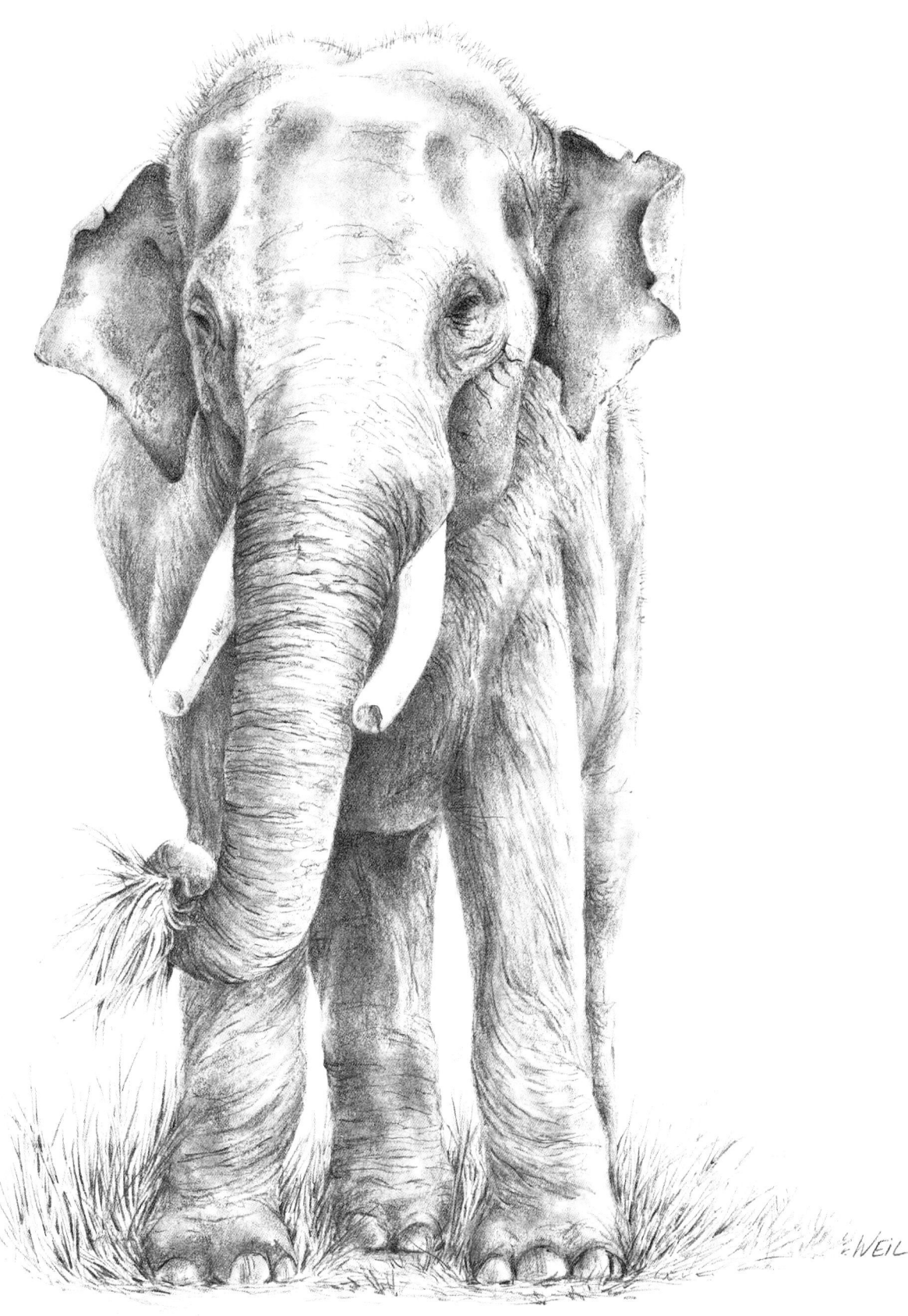

Step 6 After adding more dark values to the grass, switch to an HB pencil and return to the elephant, emphasizing darks and adding more wrinkles where needed. Fill in the foreground with grass, using an F pencil to draw the blades in freehand. Add shading where needed and finish the details.

Koala

Koala bears have such character, and their simple, round bodies are easy to draw freehand. Koalas don't move around much. In fact, they sleep more than 18 hours a day! So if you see a koala awake, be sure to take a photo because it is a rare opportunity. When drawing a koala, you will need to use a number of pencil techniques to create short and long fur, white and dark fur, and the varied textures of the nose, claws, and eyes.

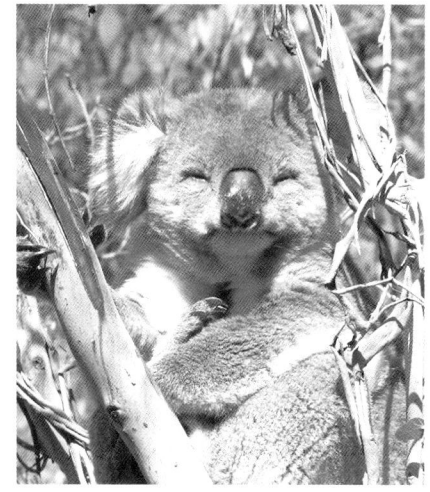 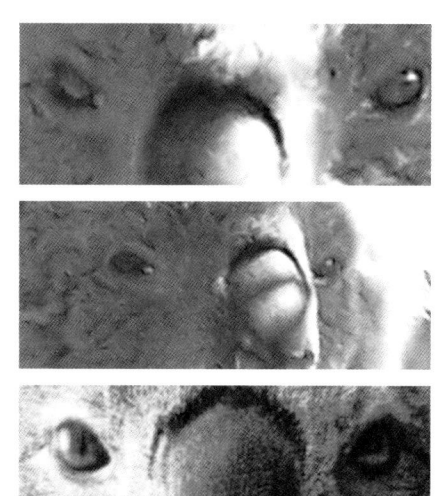

Using Multiple Photos Feel free to use a variety of photo references to create a composition that you like.

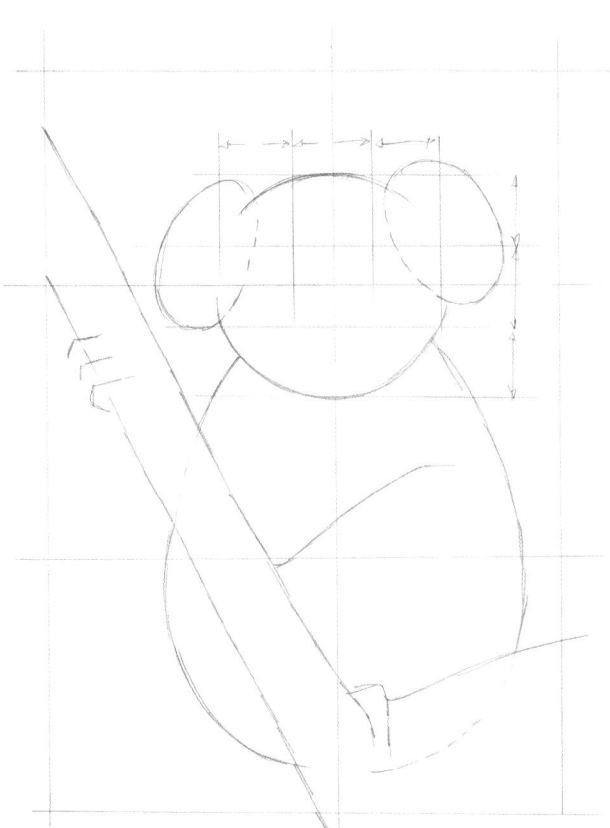

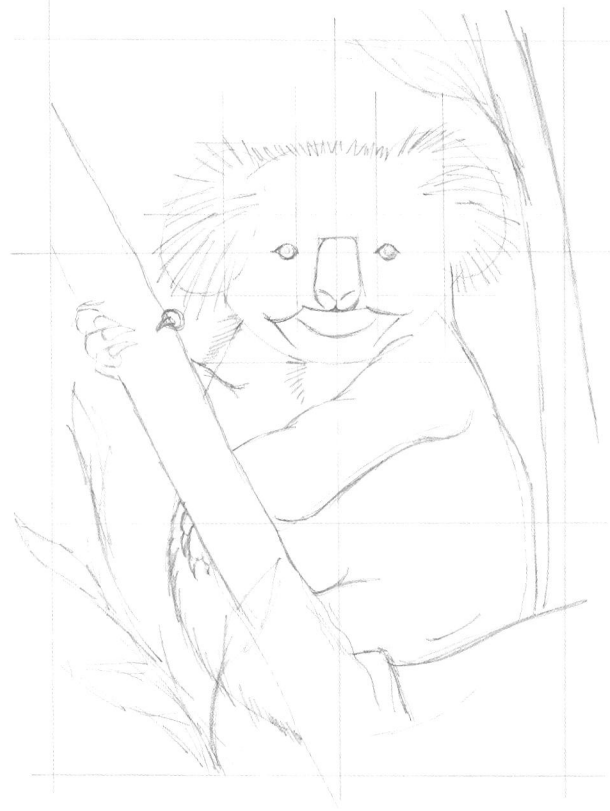

Finding the Proportions To figure out the correct proportions of the koala, draw a 6.5″ x 9″ rectangle on a sheet of tracing paper and divide this shape horizontally into thirds; then draw a vertical plumb line that is slightly off-center down the length of the rectangle. Center the head circle exactly where the plumb line and the first horizontal line meet. Then divide the head circle into thirds horizontally and vertically—this will position the facial features. Use simple oval shapes to block in the round shapes of the body and ears. Sketch the arms, fingers, and tree branches.

Blocking in the Features Block in the nose, noting where it starts and finishes in relation to the grid. Next, position the open eyes almost exactly on the top horizontal line of the grid. Now place the mouth and cheeks, which are a series of arcs within the bottom third of the head circle. Build up some fur in the ears, on top of the head, and on the chest; then develop the arms and legs, adding the long claws and noting where the heel of the foot rests against the upright branch. Finally, add a few tree branches and leaves.

Step 1 Start developing the ear on the left. Then use a sharp 2H clutch pencil to draw long, smooth lines for the undercoat, varying their lengths and directions.

Step 2 Switch to an HB clutch pencil and draw more long, broken strokes around the 2H strokes, carefully leaving the paper white in areas. As you work in the dark strokes, the white of the paper begins to form the white hairs. (This is a form of negative drawing.)

Step 3 Using a sharp 2B clutch pencil, intensify the shadowed areas of the fur under and on the edge of the ear. This dark tone creates a high contrast and makes the white areas stand out, increasing the impression of long, white fur. With the 2H clutch pencil, refine and smooth out the detail.

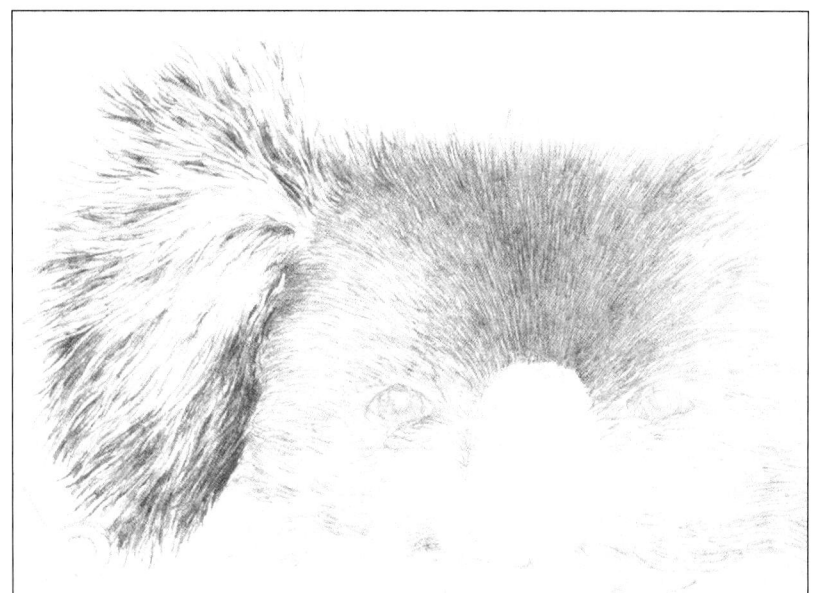

Step 4 After lightening the outline of the rest of the head with a kneaded eraser, use a 2H clutch pencil to create short, quick strokes all over the head, avoiding the eyes and the nose. Draw in the direction of fur growth, placing the strokes close together using a tight, controlled movement. After covering the face, go back in with an HB pencil and darken the areas across the forehead and above the nose, using the same short strokes as before. Then use a 2H to add a quick layer of fur to the ear on the right, as well as to build up the fur around the cheeks, chin, and mouth. Draw the iris in each eye with a light layer of 2H, and add some tone to the nose.

Step 5 With a dull HB pencil, add circular strokes to the nose, leaving some areas white. Switch to a 2B and use short strokes above and below areas of the nose to create more contrast and to darken the nostrils. Switching back to the HB, create short lines in the mouth and under the nose. Sharpen the HB and use it to refine and darken the pupils. Use the HB to form the eyelids and brows with short, directional strokes. Use the 2B to darken the irises and areas around the eyes.

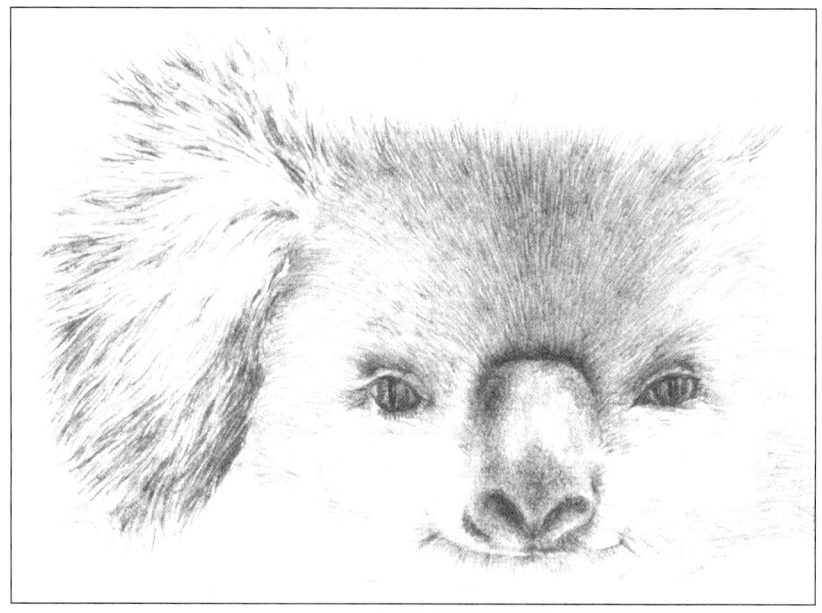

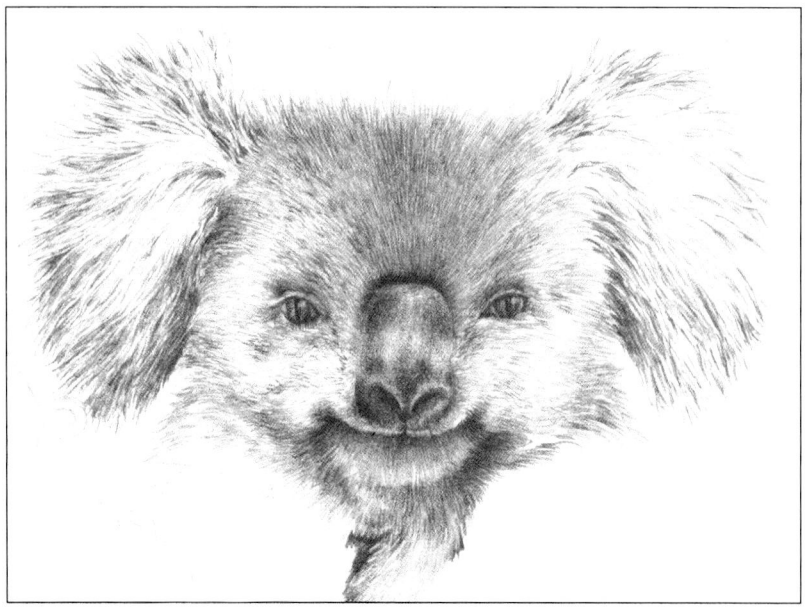

Step 6 Alternating between sharp HB and 2B pencils, build up the fur all over the face and chin. Use the 2B to create dark shadows around the mouth, nose, chin, and cheeks; then use the HB like a tortillon to blend the tone. Using both pencils and circular strokes, further develop the tone on the nose, creating a dark, leathery texture. Turning to the eyes, define the darks with the 2B and accentuate the shape and form with the HB. Next, darken the lower lids. Then carefully lift out a highlight in each eye with adhesive putty. Now concentrate on the ear on the right, repeating steps 2 and 3.

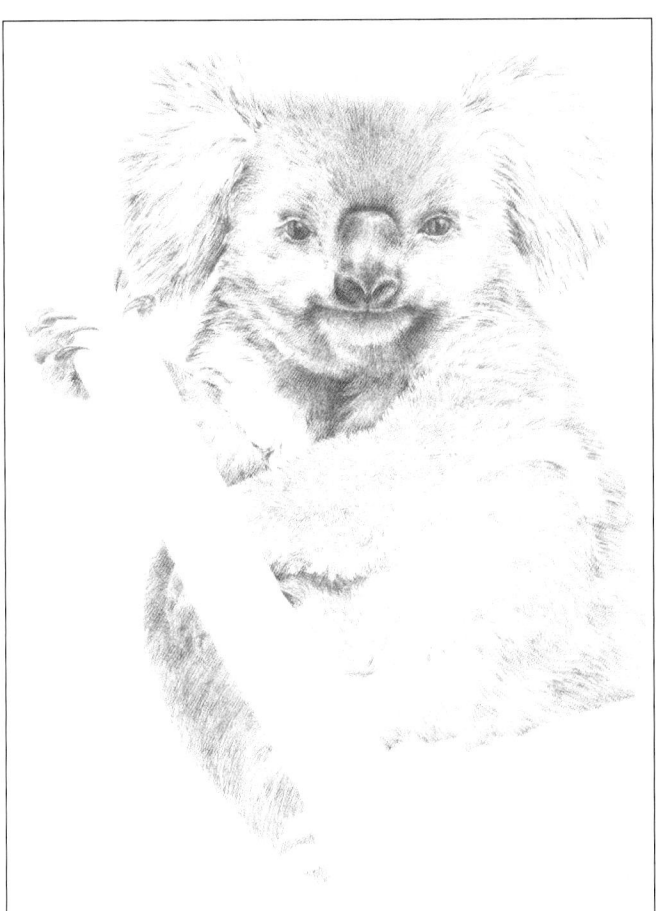

Step 7 After lightening the outline of the body with a kneaded eraser, use short, light strokes with a 2H pencil to create the undercoat for the entire body. Remember to draw in the direction of the fur growth and avoid creating patterns. Leave the chest and underarms white, but cover the rest of the body with a light network of interlacing 2H strokes. Add tone to both paws with the HB pencil, and draw the long claws.

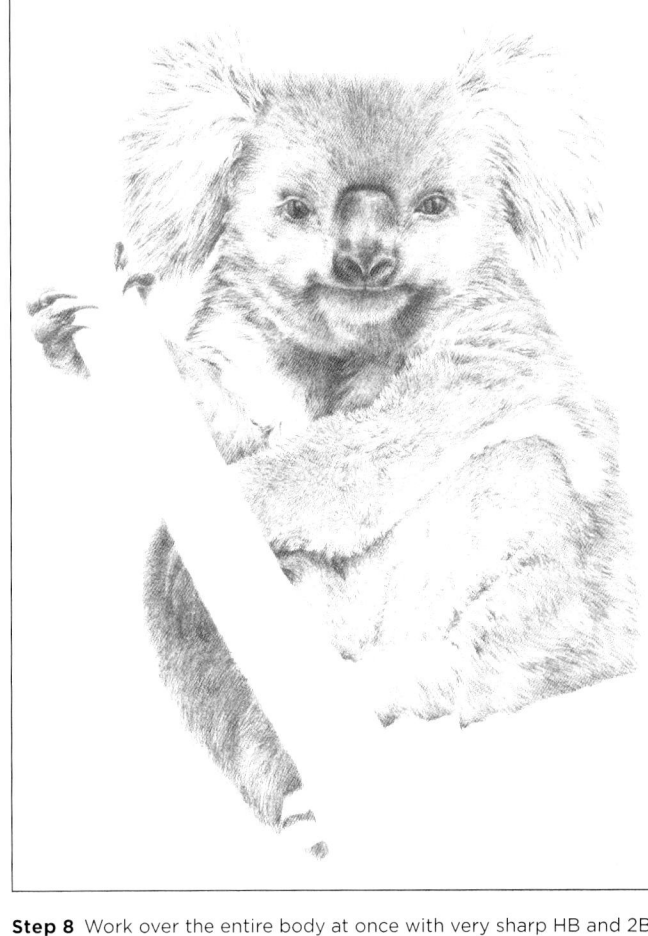

Step 8 Work over the entire body at once with very sharp HB and 2B pencils. Use the 2B to create the darkest areas near the white fur. Add some overlapping strokes on the left side of the body.

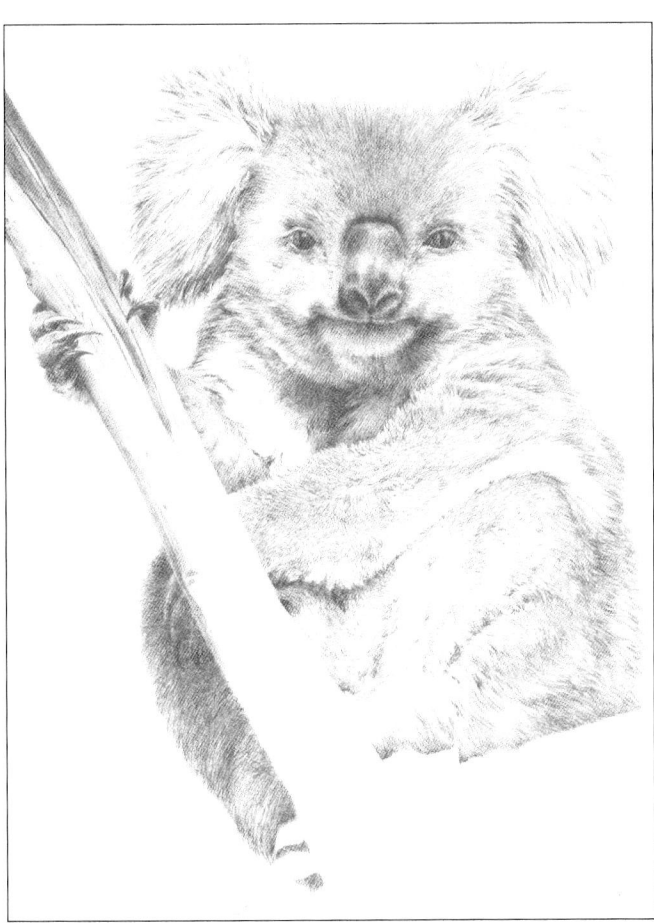

Step 9 Create a light background at the top of the image with a dull F wood-cased pencil. Add tone to the main tree branch with 2H and HB pencils, using long, smooth strokes. Build up the tone of the branch as a series of long lines of different values, creating the lined texture of a eucalyptus tree. Add some nicks with the HB for more texture.

Animal Portraits | 151

Step 10 Use an HB pencil to add the slightly curved shadows cast on the branch by the koala's fingers and claws. Then use the 2B to deepen the tone of the shadows, as well as darken and intensify the hand and claws to create more form. Continue working down the branch, alternating between the 2H and 2B pencils. Add tone to the fattest part of the branch, where the koala rests, and create the three strips of bark hanging over this wide section. The tree branches in this drawing frame the work nicely; they also keep the viewer's eye from straying out of the picture by forming a visual "wall" that leads the eye back into the center of the work.

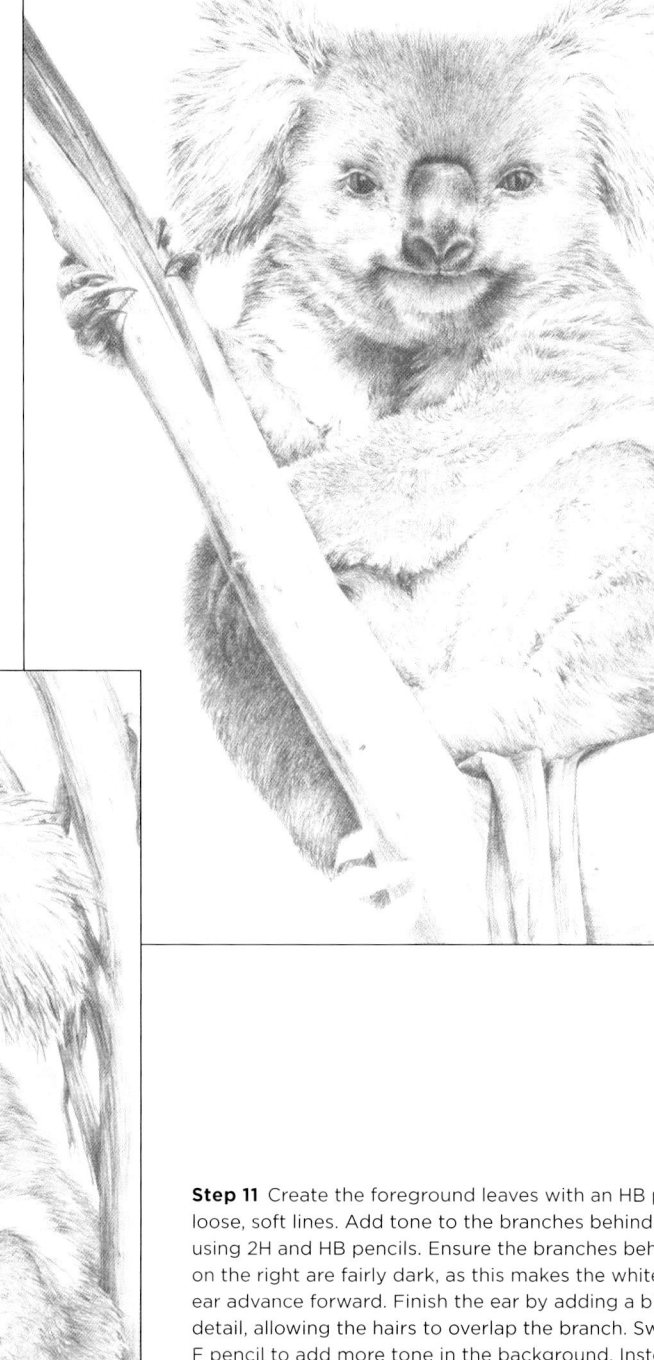

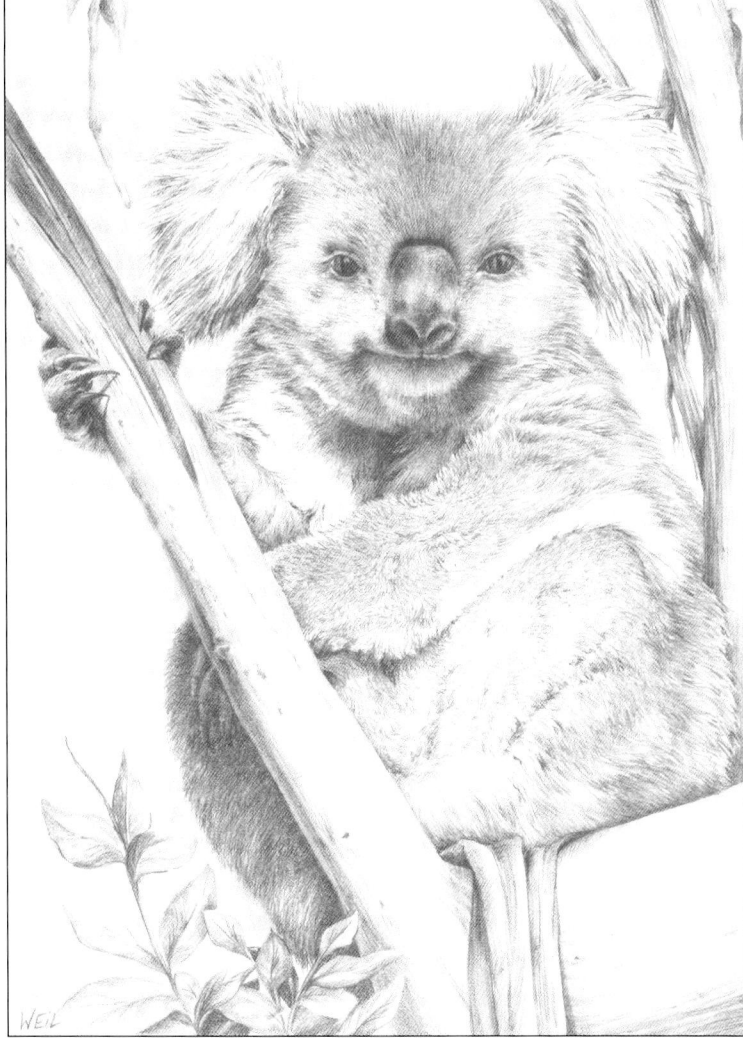

Step 11 Create the foreground leaves with an HB pencil and loose, soft lines. Add tone to the branches behind the koala, using 2H and HB pencils. Ensure the branches behind the ear on the right are fairly dark, as this makes the white fur of the ear advance forward. Finish the ear by adding a bit more detail, allowing the hairs to overlap the branch. Switch to an F pencil to add more tone in the background. Instead of creating defined shapes, use circular strokes. Add a short, hanging branch in the upper-left corner. This branch has less contrast than the others, making it recede behind the koala and providing a sense of depth; it also adds to the framing effect and helps complete the composition.

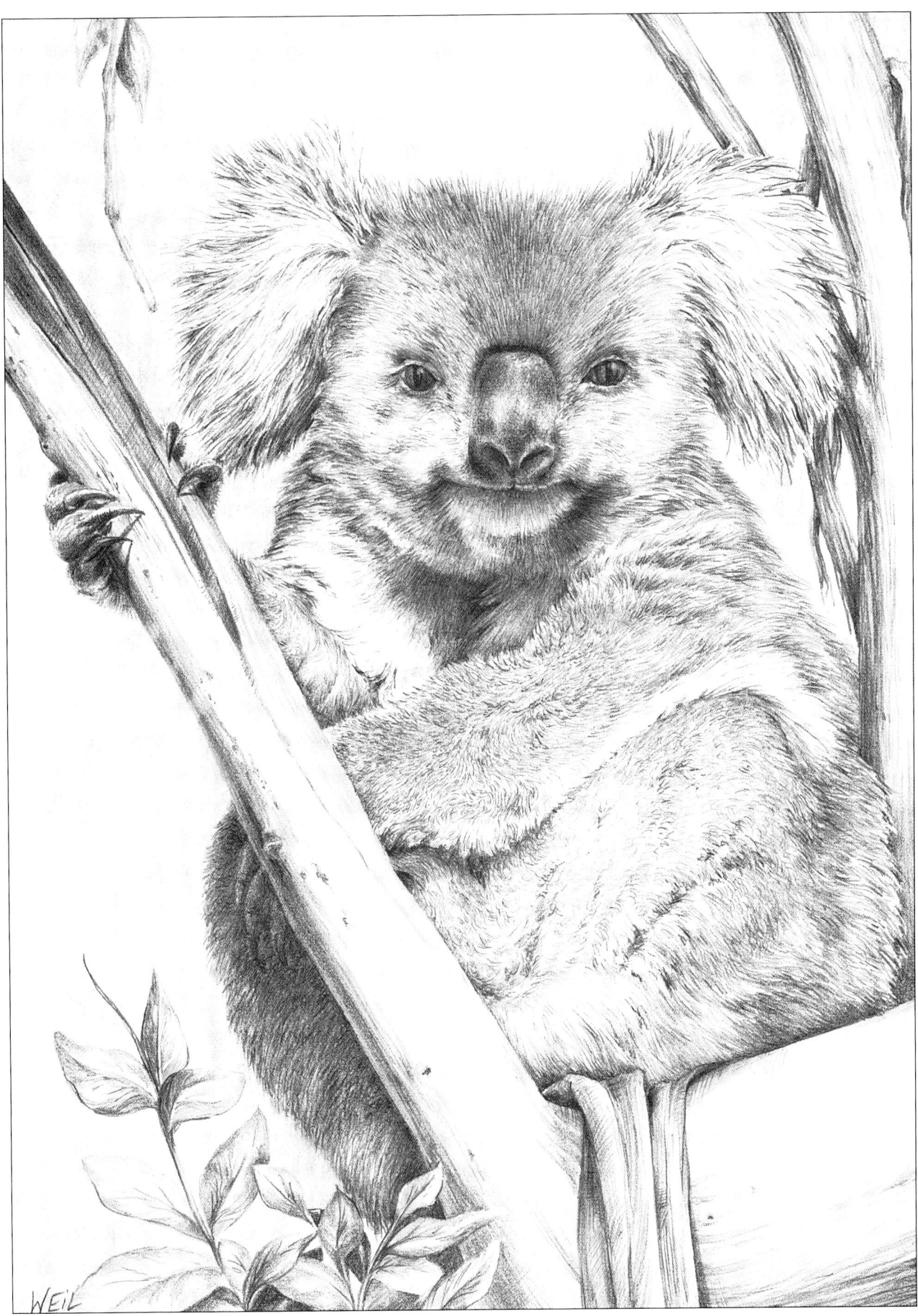

WEIL

Step 12 Add the final touches with an HB pencil: Deepen some tones for more contrast, add detail lines in the eyes and nose, and build up just a bit more fur texture all over the body.

Achieving a Likeness

Capturing a likeness can be one of the greatest challenges for an artist, yet it also can be incredibly rewarding. The foundation of a successful portrait is careful observation coupled with a thorough understanding of the head's form. Take time to study the subject's shapes and proportions. The German Shepherd's high-set ears take up almost half of the vertical area of the face. The large muzzle narrows gradually toward the blunt tip of the nose, with a gentle sloping along the bridge. The short hair of the face closely follows the form of the head and neck. In addition to breed characteristics, take notice of any elements that make this particular dog unique, such as the mole next to its mouth.

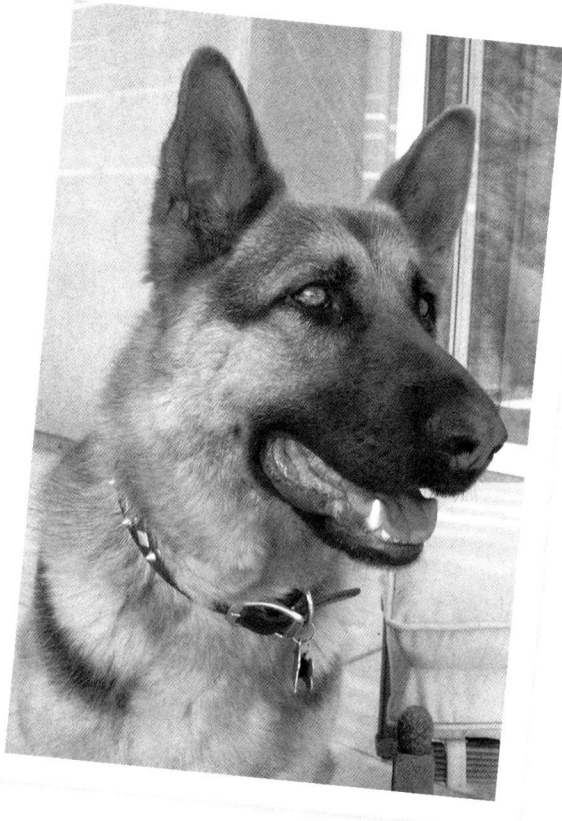

Focusing on Details Including a dog's accessories, such as a collar and tag, can help you personalize a portrait even more!

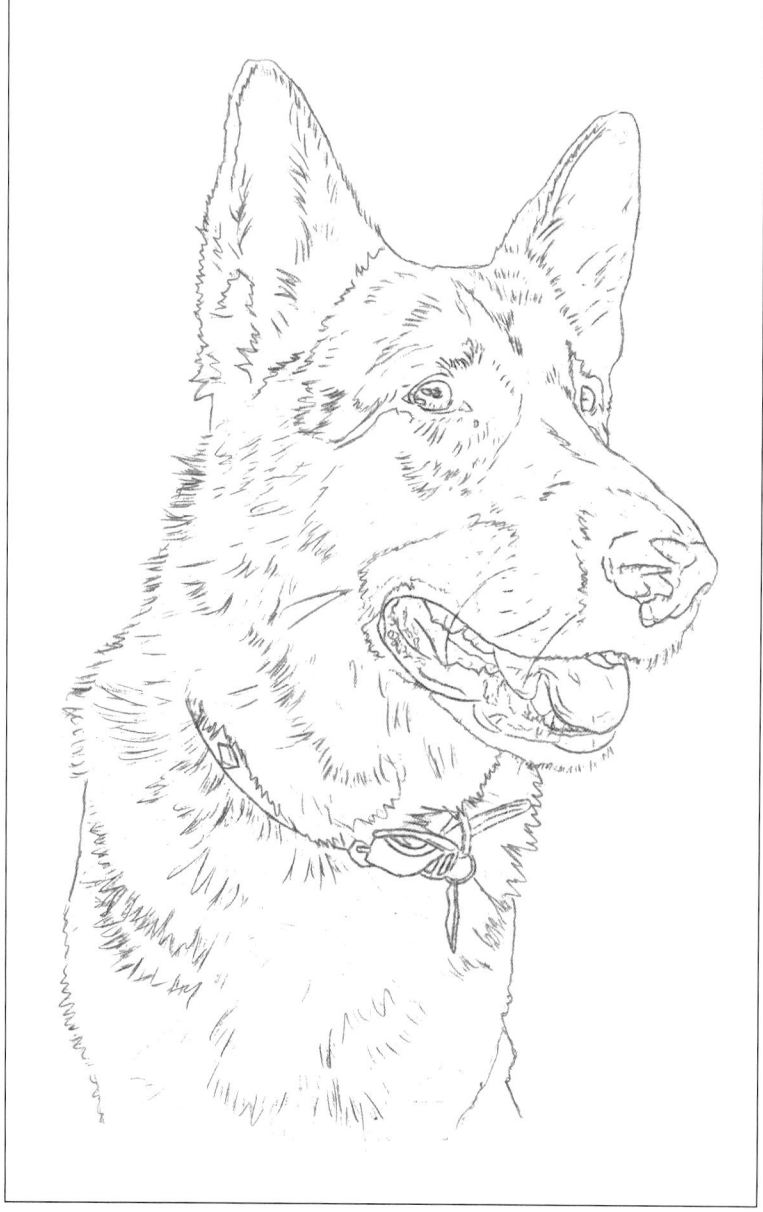

Step 1 Use a sharp HB pencil to create a freehand outline. Begin with basic shapes and then hone them into a detailed outline. Draw short lines to indicate the growth direction of the hair, and map out the areas of greatest contrast.

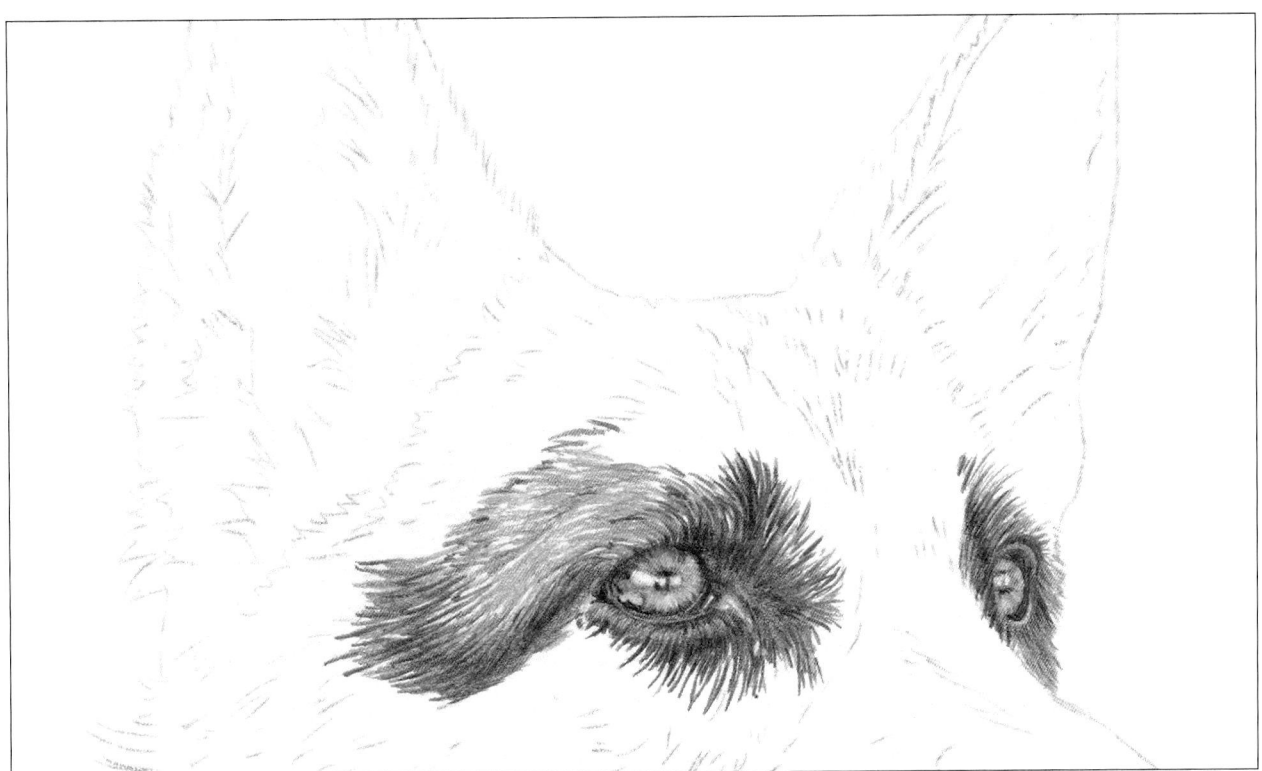

Step 2 Shade the darkest parts of each eye using a 2B pencil, leaving a highlight across the pupil and iris. Then add midtone lines radiating from the pupil for the iris. Working around the highlight, use an H pencil to cover the eye with a layer of shading. Indicate the hair surrounding the eyes with lines curving outward, switching to an HB for the lighter areas of the eyebrow. The gaps between the lines provide highlights.

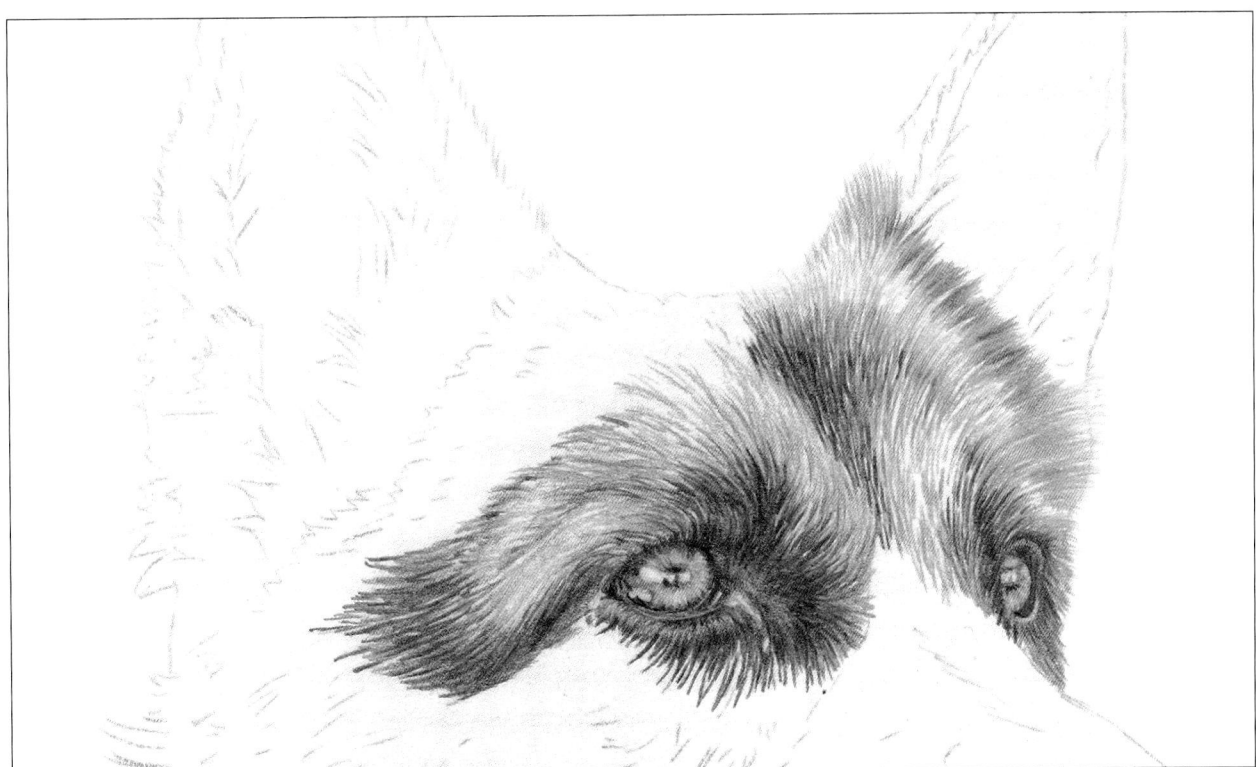

Step 3 Progress outward from the eyes, working up and over the forehead and into the dog's left ear. There is a darker patch of hair in the middle of the forehead, so apply this first, using a 2B pencil to draw the lines in the direction of hair growth. Then switch to an HB for middle-value areas of the hair, and use an H to create the lightest sections. For the lightest highlights, let the white of the paper show through.

Animal Portraits | 155

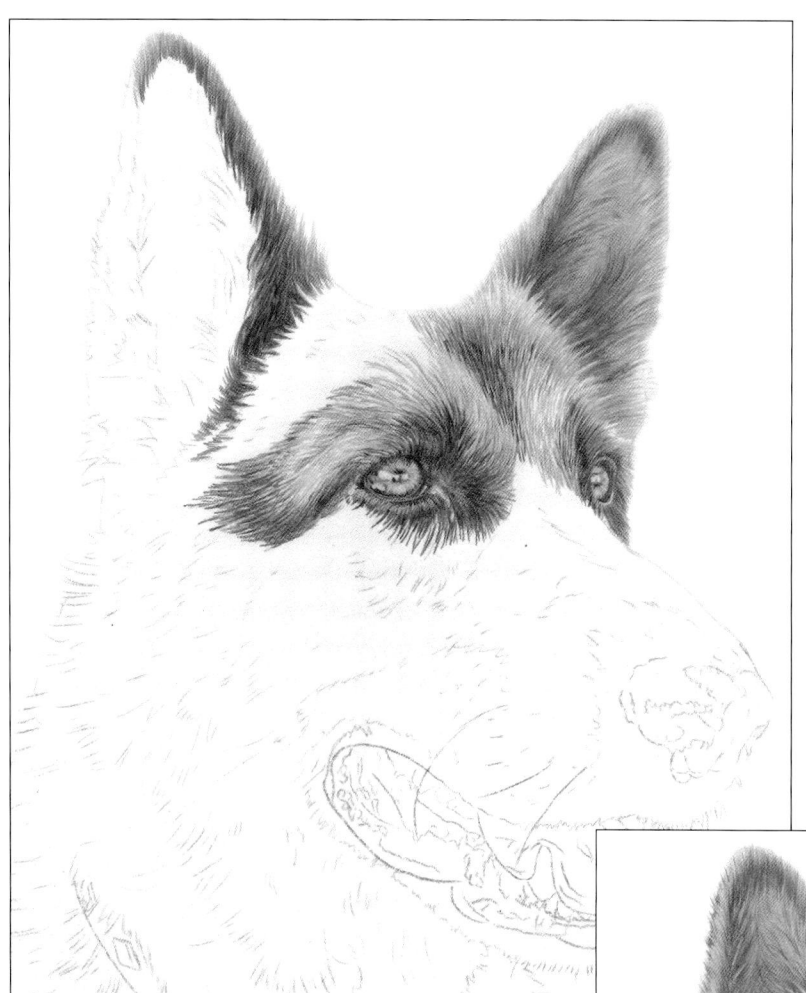

Step 4 The outer edge of the dog's right ear is very dark, so use heavy pressure and a 2B pencil to apply tapering strokes that suggest small tufts of hair. Switch to an HB pencil to render the left ear, which is lighter in value.

Step 5 For the smooth skin inside the ears, shade with an HB pencil and then blend with a tortillon. Then draw the hair over this shading, varying the values within the hair and adding shadows between the clumps of hair. Progress down the side of the head using an HB pencil, letting some of the paper show through for lighter areas.

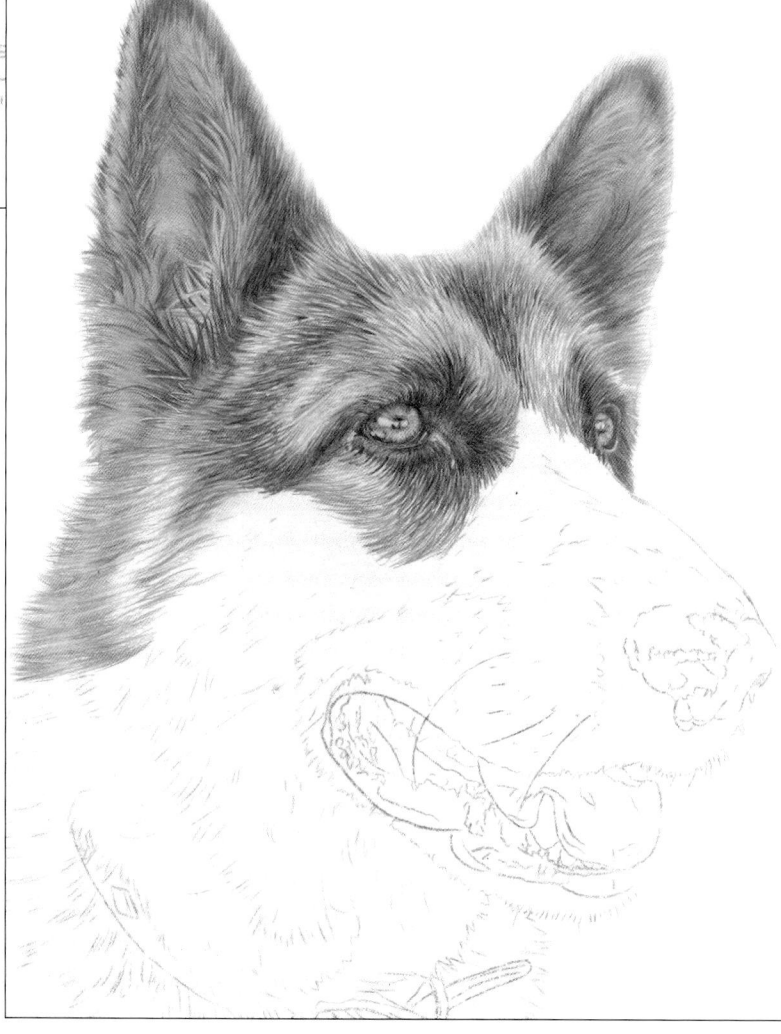

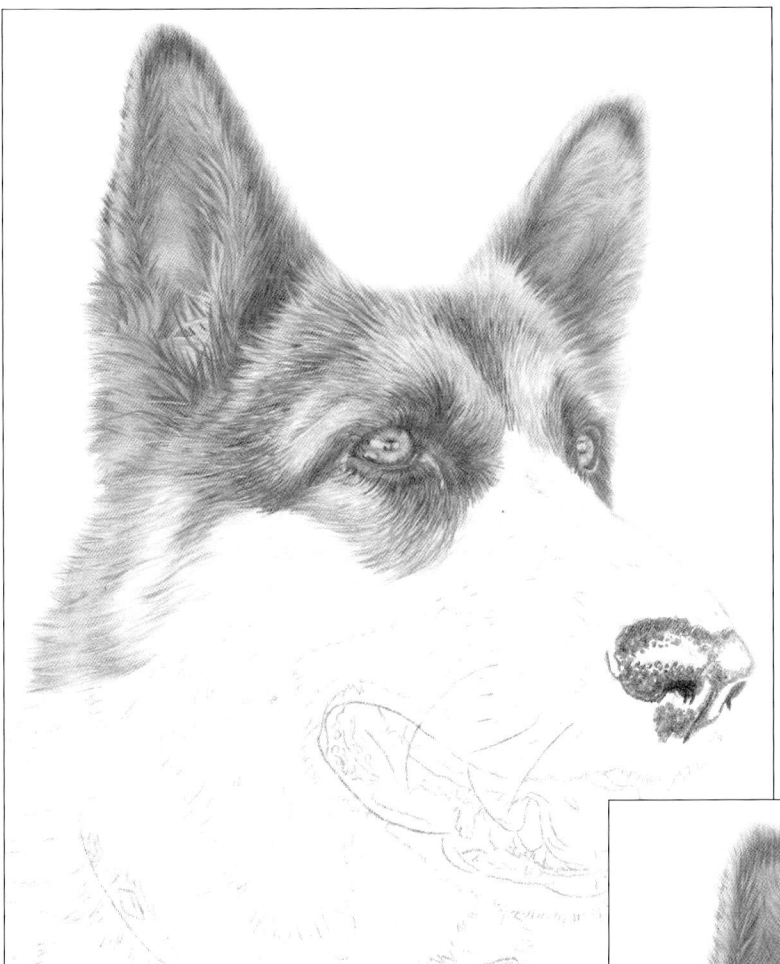

Step 6 Use a 2B pencil to draw the nose, making a series of small, dark circles to create the unique texture. Leave the highlight areas white. Next, darken the nostrils and the crease down the middle of the nose. Then finish the nose by applying some lighter circles to the "white" sections on top and under the nostrils. Use a blunt tool to indent some whiskers and coarse, longer hairs below the nose.

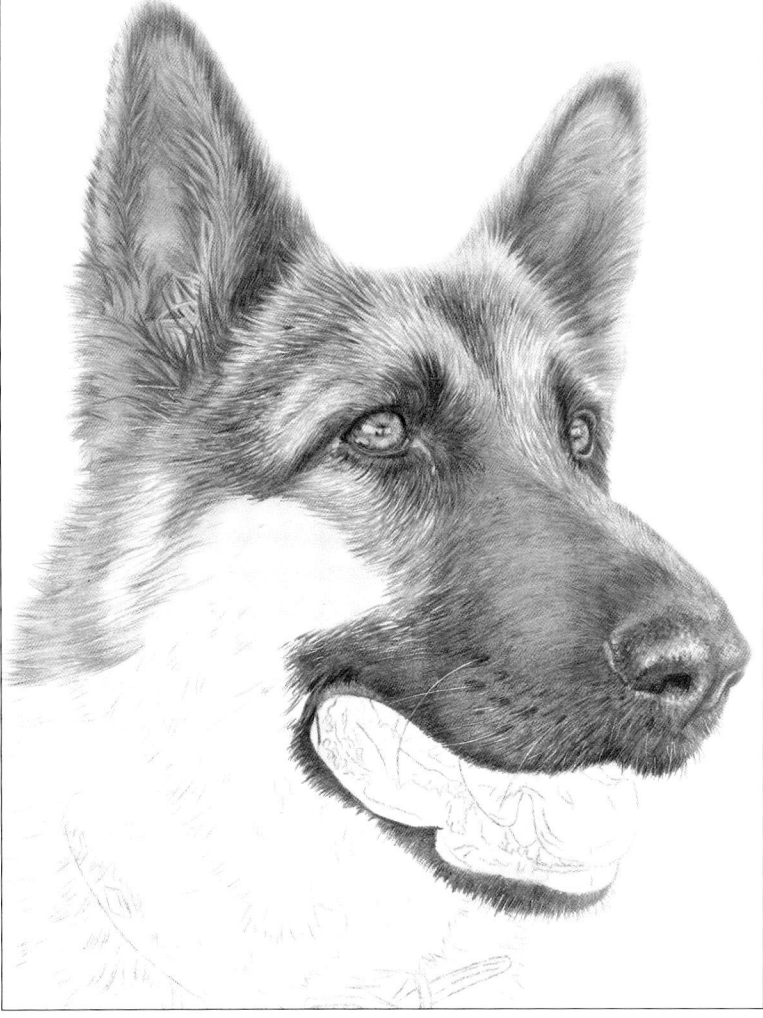

Step 7 Using close, short strokes that move away from the nose, fill in the muzzle, changing the direction of strokes near the mouth. There is actually little detail involved in the hair; accurately depicting the direction of hair growth is the key. Now use a 5B pencil to darken the hair along the edge of the mouth.

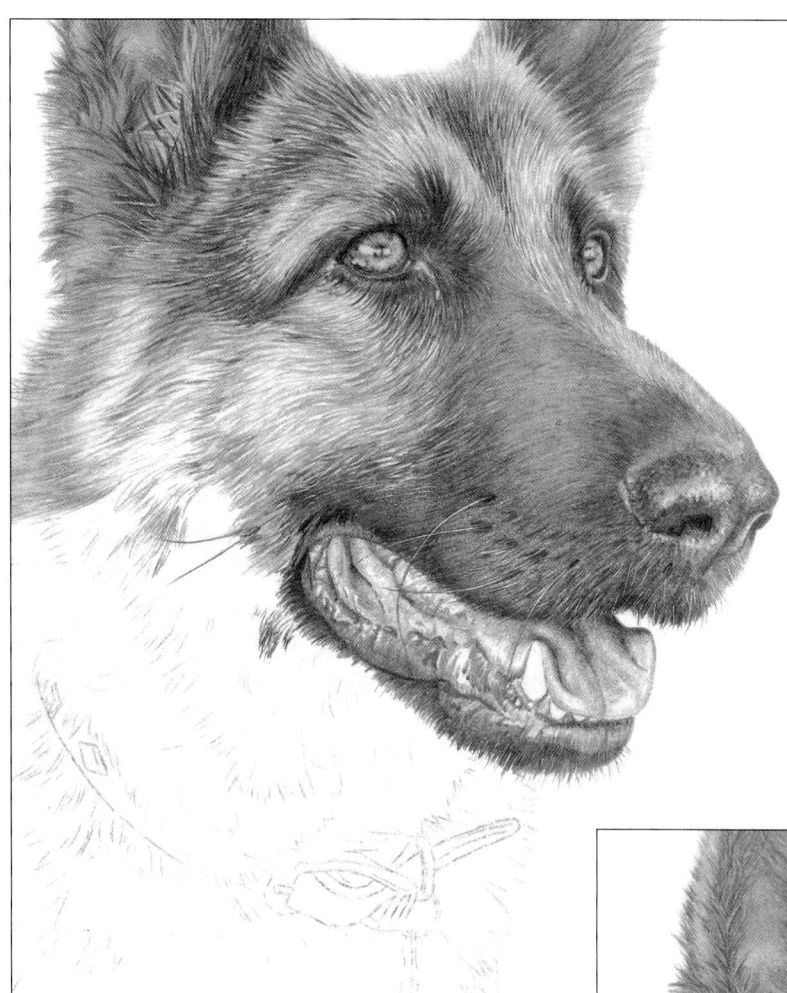

Step 8 With the muzzle defined, move on to the inside of the mouth, shading the tongue with an HB pencil and blending with a tortillon for smooth transitions. Add tone to the gums and lips using a 2B pencil, taking care to leave patches of white for strong highlights that suggest wetness. Darken the whiskers where they overlap the mouth for continuity, but leave the teeth free of graphite. Still using an HB pencil, fill in more hair on the cheek, darkening two lines to form a V shape near the corner of the mouth. (This suggests whiskers sprouting from the mole seen in the reference photo.)

Step 9 Finish filling in the hair on the cheek with an HB pencil, lightly shading over the V shape so it's visible underneath. Continue the hair pattern down the neck, drawing sections of hair that roughly follow the direction of growth. As the hair is longer here, it's important to show its flowing nature by making the strokes less uniform. The German Shepherd's collar adds a bit of interest to the lower area of the drawing. Use a 2B to shade it, working around the hair that flows over the top of the collar. Then switch to an H pencil for the shiny metal pieces.

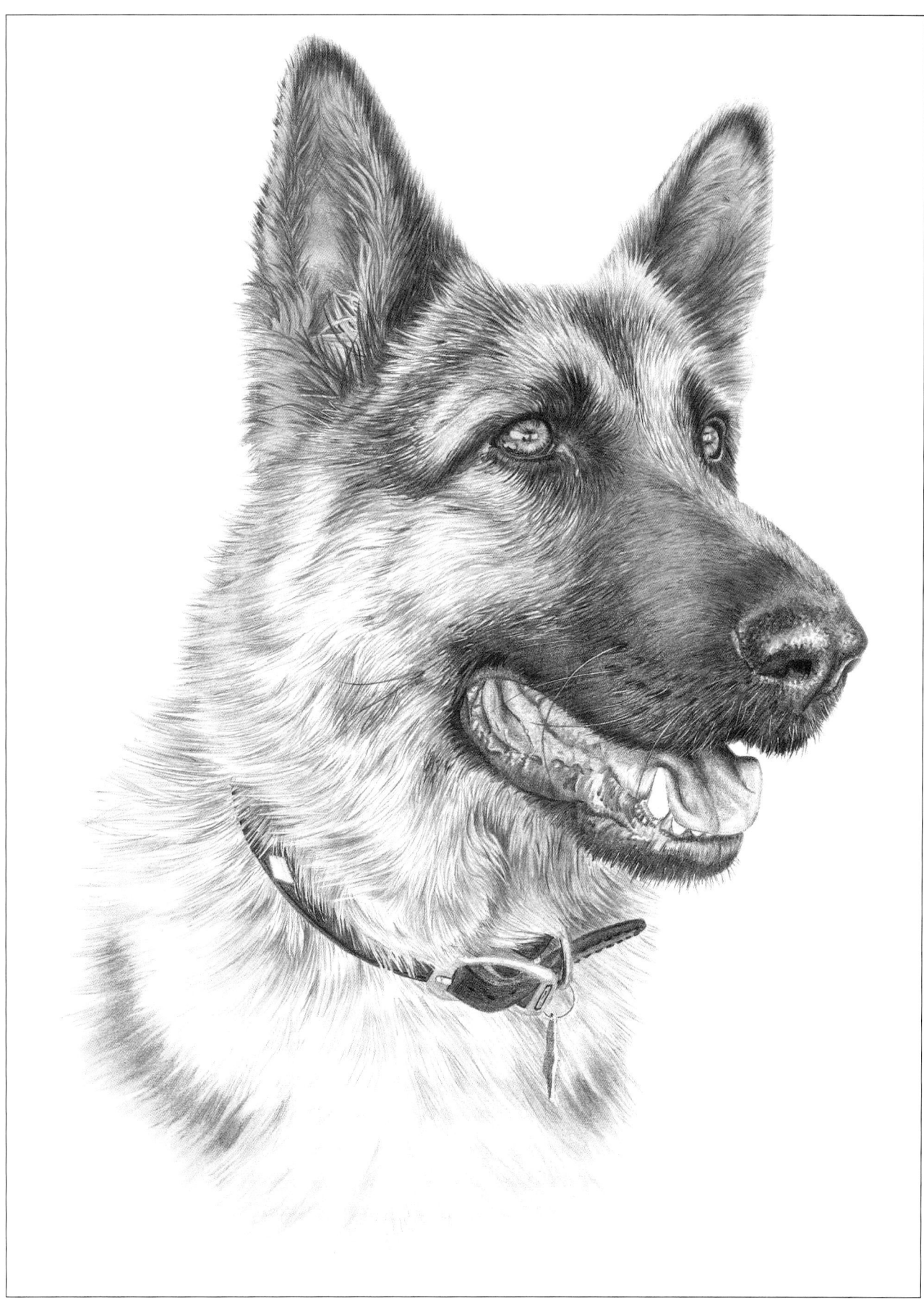

Step 10 Complete the drawing by blending the pencil strokes along the base of the neck, creating a soft transition from the hair to the white background. The bottom section actually is more paper than it is pencil—there are just enough pencil strokes to imply the shape and direction of the hair.

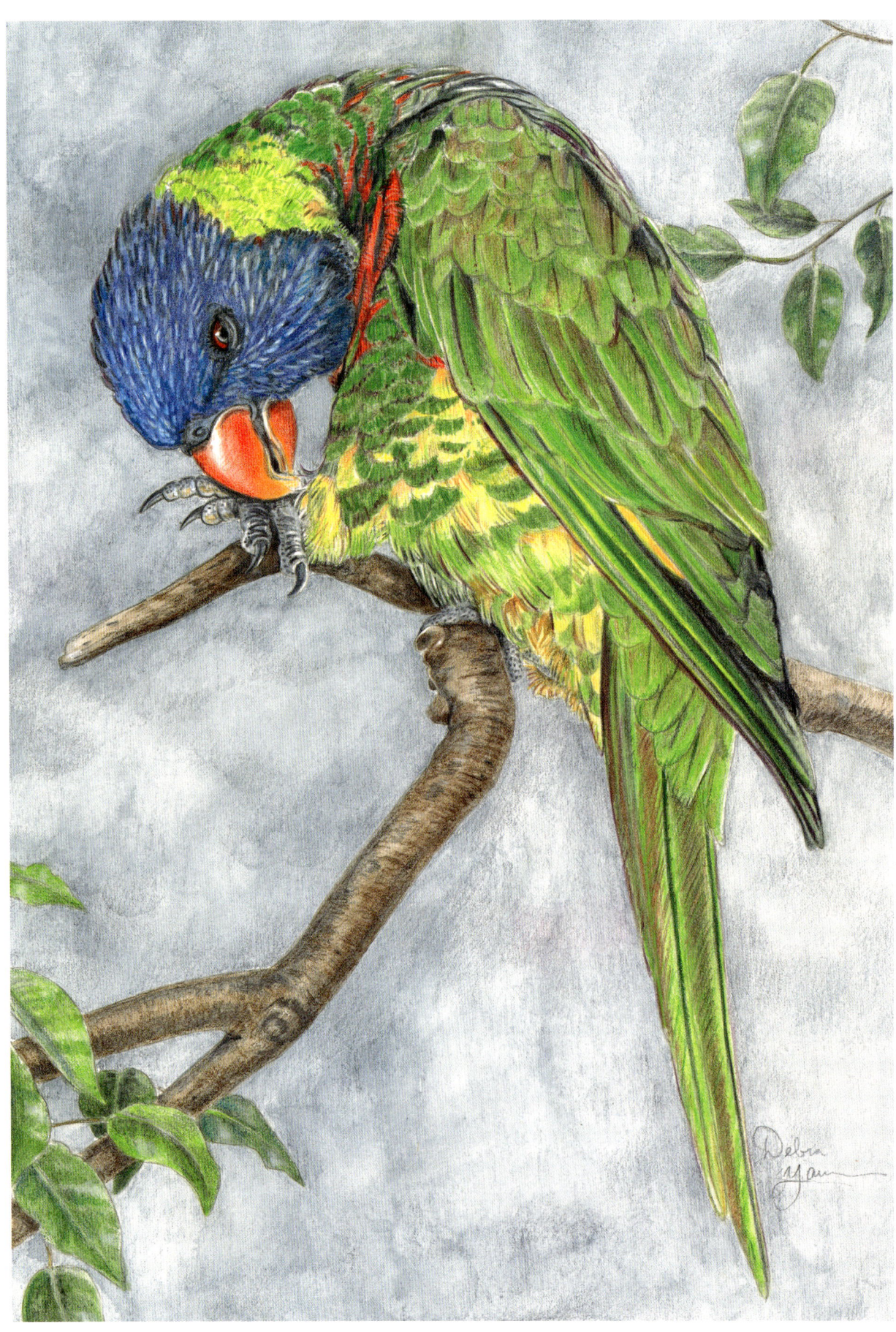

Animals in Colored Pencil

Drawing in colored pencil offers a rich, versatile medium that allows for both fine detail and vibrant expression. The layered application of color gives artists the ability to build depth and texture, creating realistic gradients or bold, striking contrasts. Colored pencils can be used to achieve delicate shading, smooth transitions, or saturated hues, depending on the pressure and techniques used. When it comes to animals, colored pencil can add a range of effects, from soft and subtle to vivid and dynamic. The control offered by colored pencils makes them ideal for intricate work, allowing artists to blend colors and fine-tune their art with precision.

In this chapter, you will learn about the tools and materials you'll need to get started in colored pencil drawing. A brief introduction to basic color theory and a variety of techniques will help you as you complete the step-by-step projects included.

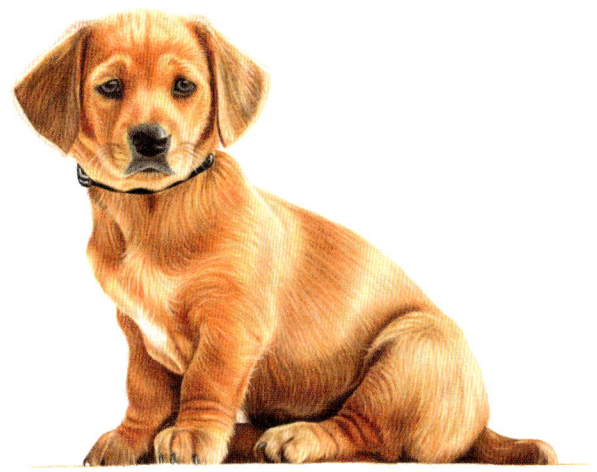

Tools & Materials

Colored pencil artwork requires few supplies. Many pencil brands are sold at reasonable prices in art stores and online; however, it's best to purchase artist-grade, professional pencils whenever possible. Student-grade pencils will not produce lasting works of art because the colors tend to fade quickly.

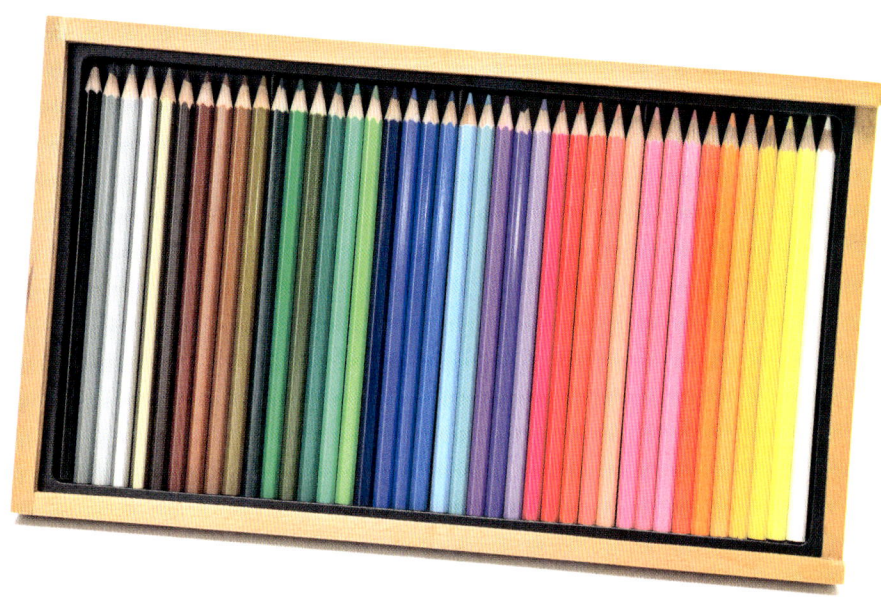

COLORED PENCILS

There are three types of colored pencils: wax-based, oil-based, and water-soluble. You should purchase a few of each and test them to see what looks great on paper.

WAX-BASED

Wax-based pencils are known for their creamy consistency and easy layering. However, they wear down quickly, break more frequently, and leave pencil crumbs behind. This is easily manageable with careful sharpening, gradual pressure, and the use of a drafting brush to sweep away debris. Wax bloom, a waxy buildup that surfaces after numerous layers of application, may also occur. It is easy to remove by gently swiping a soft tissue over the area.

OIL-BASED

These pencils produce generous color with little breakage. There is no wax bloom and little pencil debris. They sharpen nicely and last longer than wax-based pencils. They can be harder to apply, but they are manageable when establishing color and building layers.

WATER-SOLUBLE

These pencils have either wax-based or oil-based cores, which allow for a watercolor effect. Use them dry like a traditional colored pencil, or apply water to create a looser, flowing effect. This is especially nice for slightly blurred backgrounds.

UNDERSTANDING PAPER TOOTH

Choose paper based on the tooth, or paper texture. Rough paper contains more ridges than smooth paper. The paper's tooth will determine how many layers you can put down before the paper rips. Hot-pressed paper has less tooth and a smoother texture. Cold-pressed paper has more tooth and a rougher texture, which is excellent for water-soluble pencils.

Textured paper has defined ridges that accept many layers without compromising the paper.

Smooth paper is less likely to accept multiple applications of color without ripping.

CHOOSING PAPER

Smooth Bristol paper is a hot-pressed paper that accepts many layers of color. It allows you to build up your colors with a lot of layering and burnishing, which involves using strong pressure to create a polished, painterly surface. Additional surfaces include velour paper, museum board, suede mat board (great for animal fur), illustration board, wood, and sanded paper, which eats up pencils quickly but presents a beautiful, textured look. Experiment with different surface types, colors, and textures until you find what works for you.

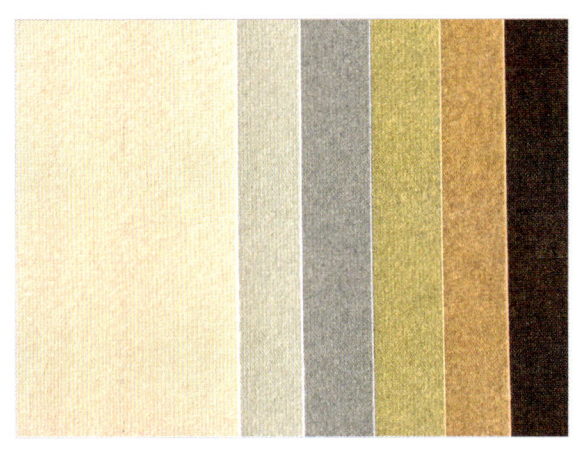

ADDITIONAL TOOLS

Pencil Sharpener
An electronic pencil sharpener with a sturdy base is great for sharpening pencils quickly, but a hand-held sharpener will do just as well.

Drafting Brushes
Use two drafting brushes to keep your paper clean. Keep one next to the pencil sharpener and wipe newly sharpened pencil points across its bristles. Use the second one to sweep pencil crumbs off your work surface. Both are valuable to minimize pencil debris.

Artist Tape
Artist tape is white and peels off surfaces easily without leaving residue behind. It provides insurance against removing the top layer of paper or color.

Spray Fixative
Spray fixatives seal your artwork but still allow you to make color changes. They prevent smudging and wax bloom from occurring. Before using, gently remove any wax bloom with a tissue or soft cloth. Step outside and make a few test sprays to eliminate any spitting. Then hold the can approximately 6 inches away from your artwork and spray in a smooth horizontal motion. Repeat in a vertical motion. Be sure to do this outside, as the fixatives are toxic.

Erasers
Unlike graphite, colored pencil pigment is not easy to erase; however, you may use several types of erasers to eliminate unwanted marks and lighten dense color. The Pink Pearl eraser gets rid of initial graphite sketch lines and helps clean up edges and borders of a finished piece. Kneaded erasers are great for lifting color. Just stretch off a piece, roll into a ball, and press down on the overly saturated color. Battery-powered erasers are great for eliminating color altogether, but can easily rip through paper or wear down the tooth.

Drawing Board
You can find drawing boards at any art store or online. To prep the drawing board, tape down a blank piece of paper to create a cushion between your work surface and the board for a smoother color application. Drawing boards with a handle are easy to transport.

Color Basics

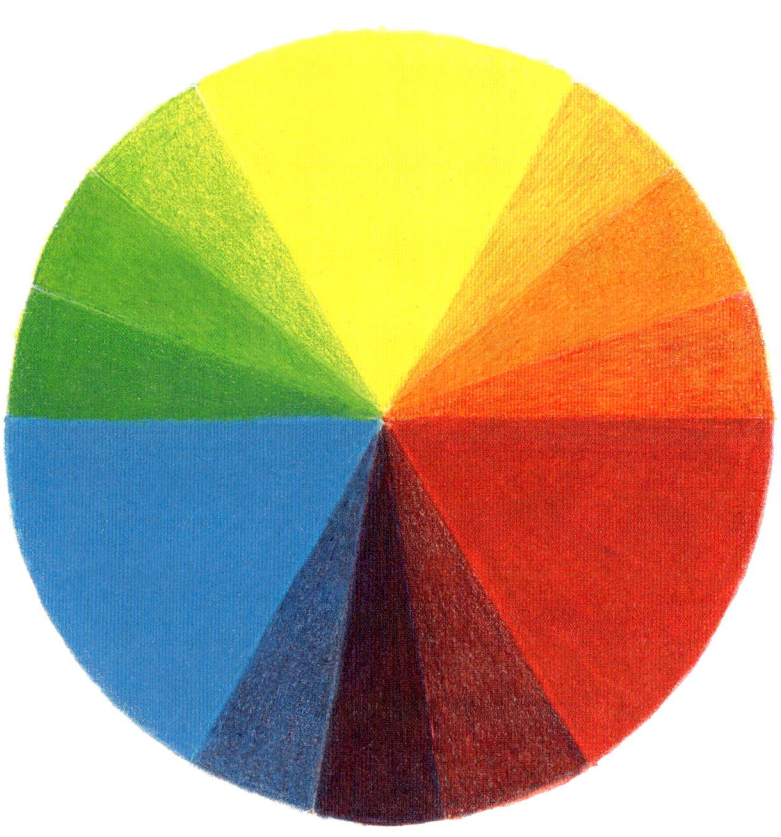

Colored pencils are transparent by nature, so instead of "mixing" colors as you would for painting, you layer colors on top of one another to create blends. Knowing a little about basic color theory can help you tremendously in drawing with colored pencils. The *primary colors* (red, yellow, and blue) are the three basic colors that can't be created by mixing other colors; all other colors are derived from these three. *Secondary Colors* (orange, green, and purple) are each a combination of two primary colors. *Tertiary colors* (red-orange, red-purple, yellow-orange, yellow-green, blue-green, and blue-purple) are a combination of a primary color and a secondary color.

Color Wheel A color wheel is a useful reference tool for understanding color relationships. Knowing where each color lies on the color wheel makes it easy to understand how colors relate to and react with one another.

COMPLEMENTARY COLORS

Complementary colors are any two colors directly across from each other on the color wheel (such as red and green, orange and blue, or yellow and purple). You can actually see combinations of complementary colors in nature—for instance, if you look at white clouds in a blue sky, you'll notice a hint of orange in the clouds.

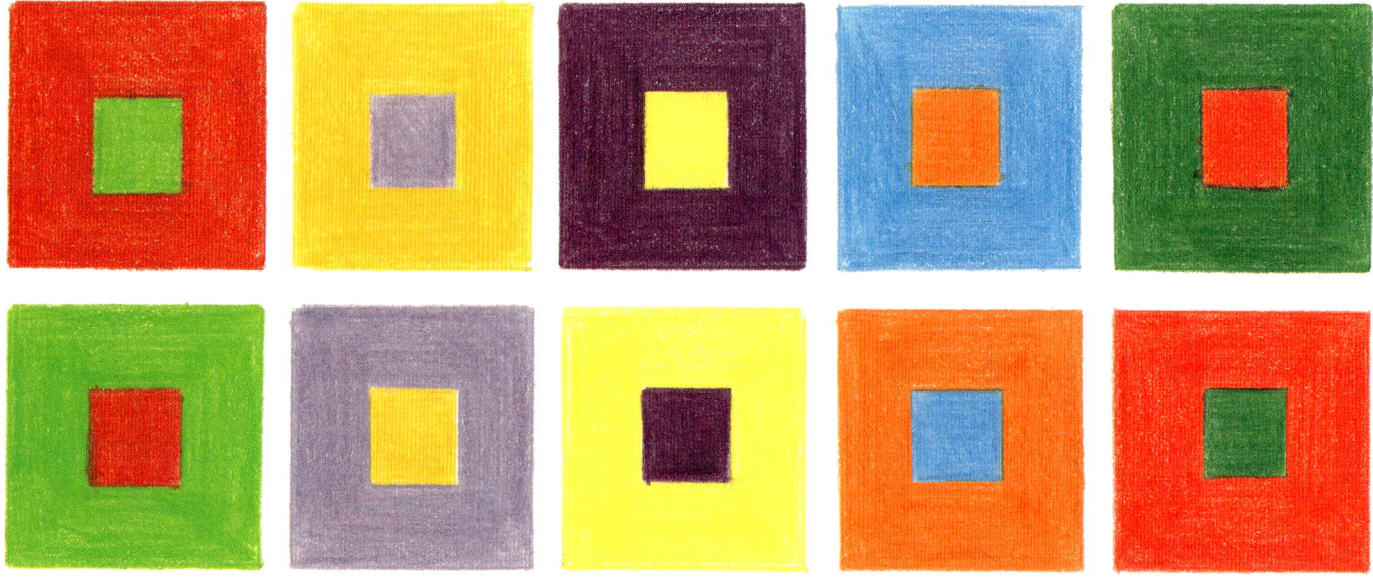

Using Complements When placed next to each other, complementary colors create lively, exciting contrasts. Using a complementary color in the background will cause your subject to seemingly "pop" off the paper. For example, you could place bright orange poppies against a blue sky or draw red berries amid green leaves.

Colored Pencil Techniques

Colored pencil is an amazingly satisfying medium to work with because it's so easily manipulated and controlled. The way you sharpen your pencil, the way you hold it, and the amount of pressure you apply all affect the strokes you create. With colored pencils, you can create everything from soft blends to brilliant highlights to realistic textures. Once you get the basics down, you'll be able to decide which techniques capture your subject's unique qualities. There are as many techniques in the art of colored pencil as there are effects, and the more you practice and experiment, the more potential you will see in the images that inspire you.

PRESSURE

Colored pencil is not like paint: You can't just add more color to the tip when you want it to be darker. Because of this, your main tool is the amount of pressure you use to apply the color. It is always best to start light so that you maintain the tooth of the paper for as long as possible. Eventually, you will develop the innate ability to change the pressure on the pencil to create your desired effect.

Light Pressure Here, color was applied by just whispering a sharp pencil over the paper's surface. With light pressure, the color is almost transparent.

Medium Pressure This middle range creates a good foundation for layering. This is also the pressure you might want to use when signing your drawings.

Heavy Pressure Really pushing down on the pencil flattens the paper's texture, making the color appear almost solid.

STROKES

The direction, width, and texture of each line you draw will contribute to the effects you create. Practice making different types of strokes. You may have a natural tendency toward one or two strokes in particular, but any stroke can help convey texture and emotion in your work.

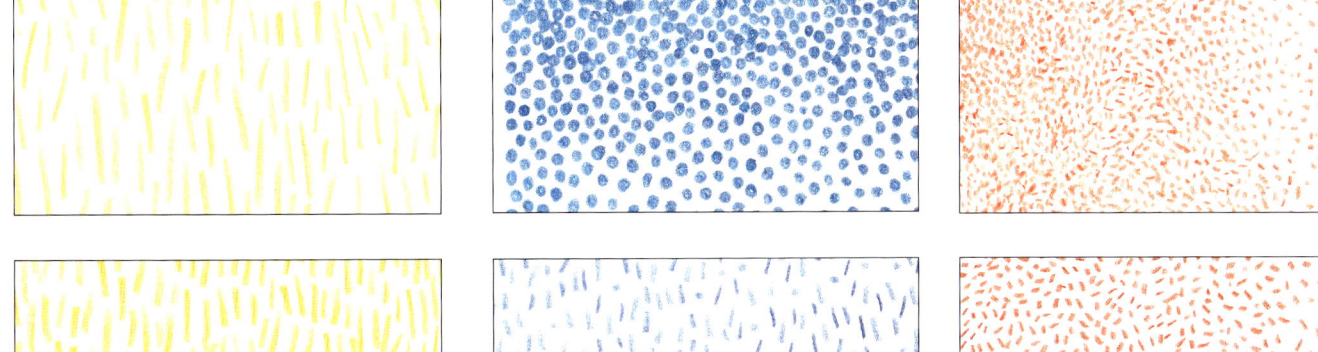

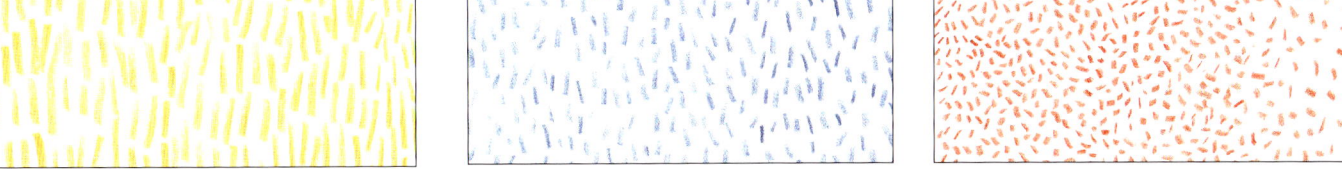

Strokes and Texture You can imitate a number of different textures by creating patterns of dots and dashes on the paper. To create dense, even dots, twist the point of your pencil on the paper.

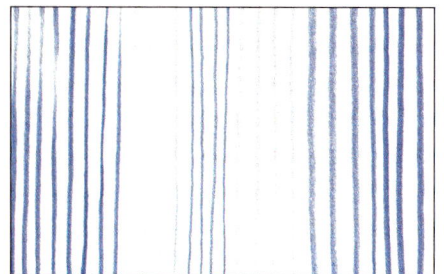 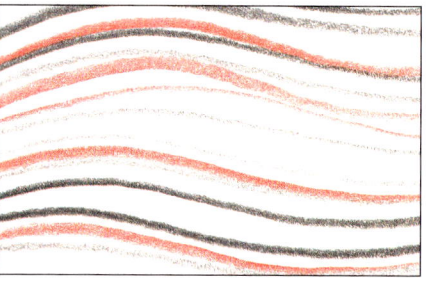 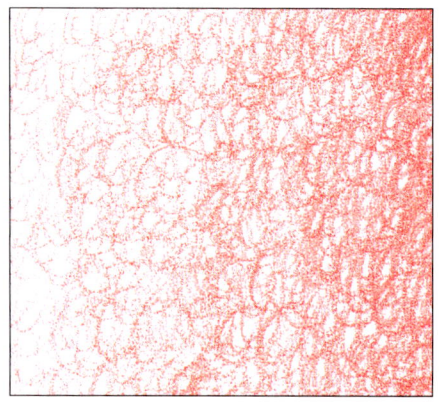

Strokes and Movement While a group of straight lines can suggest direction (above left), a group of slightly curved lines (above right) conveys a sense of motion more clearly. Try combining a variety of strokes to create a more turbulent, busy design. These exercises can give you an idea of how lines and strokes can be expressive as well as descriptive.

Varied Line Vary the width and weight of the lines you create to make them more textured and interesting. These calligraphic lines can create a feeling of dimension in your drawing.

TYPES OF STROKES

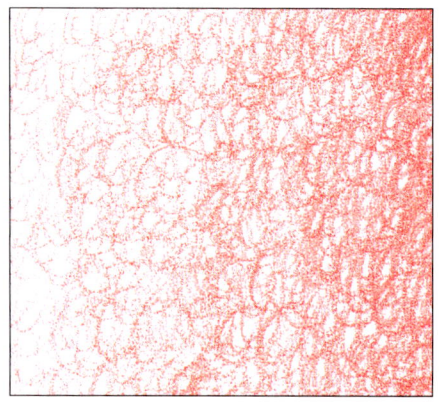 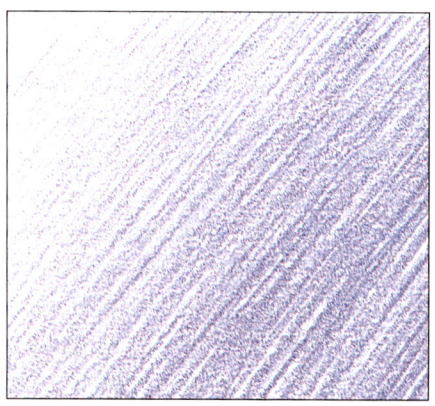 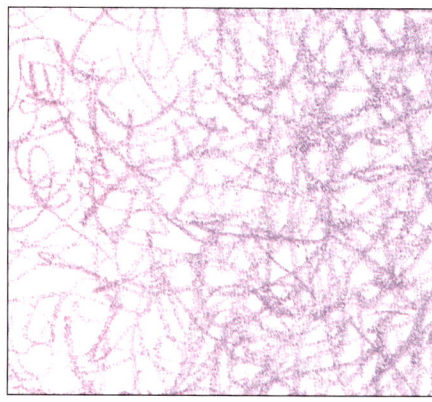

Circular Move your pencil in a circular motion, either in a random manner as shown here or in patterned rows. For denser coverage as shown on the right side of the example, overlap the circles. You can also vary the pressure throughout for a more random appearance.

Linear Work in a linear fashion, depending on your preference: vertically, horizontally, or diagonally. Your strokes can be short and choppy or long and even, depending on the texture desired.

Scumbling Create this effect by scribbling your pencil over the surface of the paper in a random manner, creating an organic mass of color. Changing the pressure and the amount of time you linger over the same area can increase or decrease the value of the color.

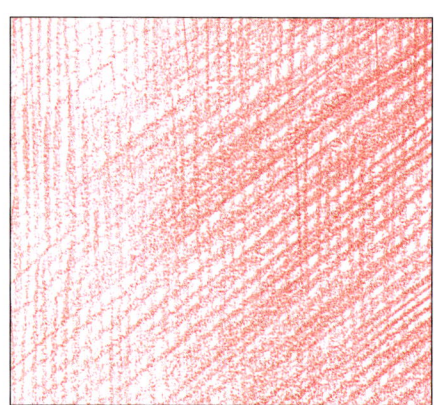  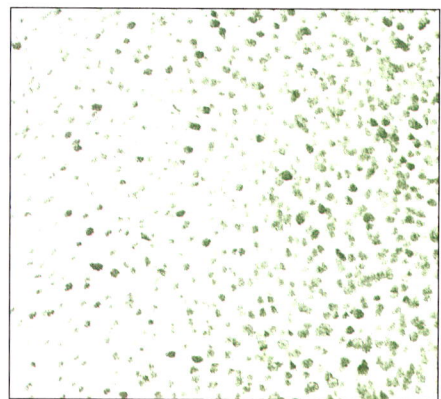

Hatching This term refers to creating a series of roughly parallel lines. The closer the lines are together, the denser and darker the color. Crosshatching is laying one set of hatched lines over another but in a different direction. You can use both of these strokes to fill in an area of color or to create texture.

Smooth No matter what your favorite stroke is, strive to control the pencil and apply a smooth, even layer of color. Use small circles, as shown in this example. Note that the color is so smooth you can't tell how it was applied.

Stippling This is a more mechanical way of applying color, but it creates a very strong texture. Simply sharpen your pencil and create small dots all over the area. Make the dots closer together for denser coverage.

LAYERING & BLENDING

Painters mix their colors on a palette before applying them to the canvas. With colored pencil, all color mixing and blending occurs directly on the paper. By layering, you can either build up color or create new hues. To deepen a color, layer more of the same over it; to dull it, use its complement. You can also blend colors by burnishing with a light pencil or using a colorless blender.

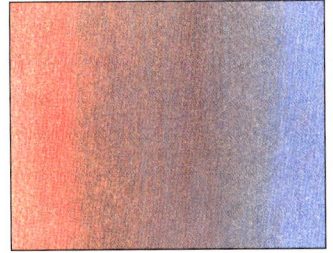

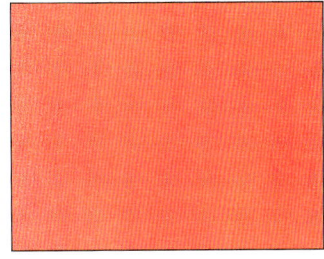

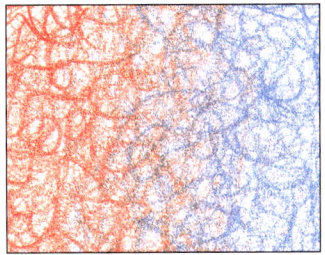

Layering The simplest approach to blending colors together is to layer one color directly over the other. This can be done with as many colors as you think necessary to achieve the color or value desired. The keys to this technique are to use light pressure, work with a sharp pencil point, and apply each layer smoothly.

Burnishing with a Colorless Blender Burnishing requires heavy pressure to meld two or more colors together for a shiny, smooth look. Using a colorless blender darkens the colors, whereas using a white or light pencil lightens the colors and gives them a hazy appearance.

Burnishing Light Over Dark You can also burnish using light or white pencils. To create an orange hue, apply a layer of red and then burnish over it with yellow. Always remember to place the darker color first; if you place a dark color over a lighter color, the dark color will overpower and no real blending will occur. Also try not to press too hard on the underlayers of the area you intend to burnish; if you flatten the tooth of the paper too soon, the resulting blend won't be as effective.

Optical Mixing In this method, commonly used in pastel work, the viewer's eye sees two colors placed next to each other as blended. Scumble, hatch, stipple, or use circular strokes to apply the color, allowing the individual pencil marks to look like tiny pieces of thread. When viewed together, the lines form a tapestry of color that the eye interprets as a solid mass. This is a lively, fresh method of blending that will captivate your audience.

CREATING FORM

Value is the term used to describe the relative lightness or darkness of a color (or of black). By adding a range of values to your subjects, you create the illusion of depth and form. Color can confuse the eye when it comes to value, so a helpful tool can be a black-and-white copy of your reference photo (if you're using one). This will take color out of the equation and leave only the shades of gray that define each form.

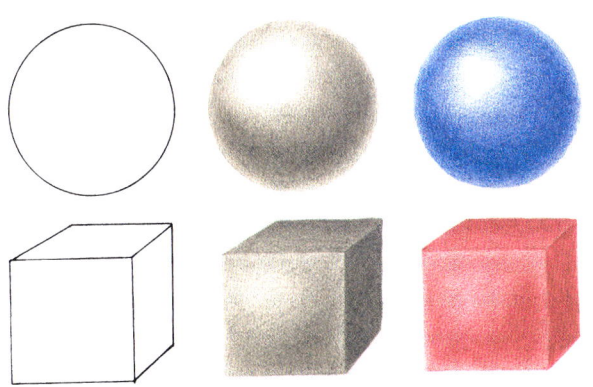

Creating Form with Value In this example, you can see that the gray objects seem just as three-dimensional as the colored objects. This shows that value is more important than color when it comes to creating convincing, lifelike subjects. To practice before you begin the projects, first draw the basic shape. Then, starting on the shadowed side, begin building up value, leaving the paper white in the areas where the light hits the object directly. Continue adding values to create the form of the object. Add the darkest values last. As the object gets farther away from the light, the values become darker, so place the darkest values on the side directly opposite the light.

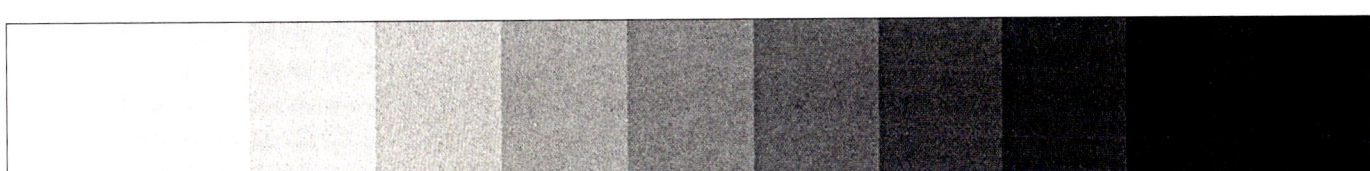

Value Scale Another helpful tool for understanding value is a scale showing the progression from white (the lightest value) to black (the darkest value). Most colored pencil brands offer a variety of grays, distinguished with a name of either "warm" or "cool" and a percentage to indicate the concentration of color, such as "cool gray 20%." (Lower percentages are lighter.)

Toucan

This project is all about bright, fabulous color! Nearly every color of the rainbow is represented in this tropical image. There is certainly a place for soft, muted pastel colors in art; however, when an artist seeks drama in a composition, strong, pure colors do not disappoint. Use colors from the secondary palette to add more color, if you like.

PALETTE

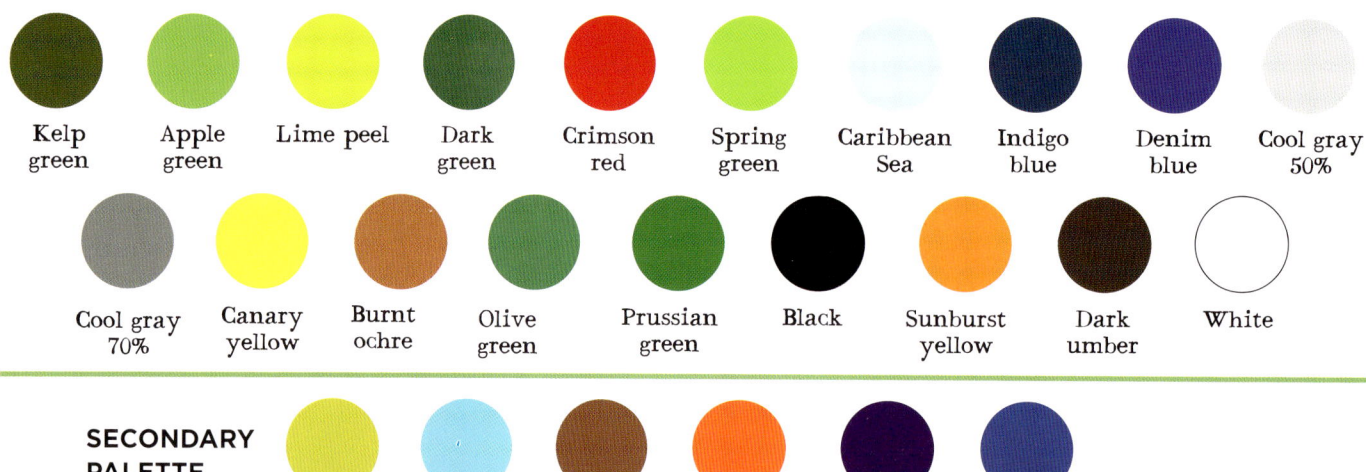

Kelp green | Apple green | Lime peel | Dark green | Crimson red | Spring green | Caribbean Sea | Indigo blue | Denim blue | Cool gray 50%

Cool gray 70% | Canary yellow | Burnt ochre | Olive green | Prussian green | Black | Sunburst yellow | Dark umber | White

SECONDARY PALETTE

Chartreuse | Non-photo blue | Burnt sienna | Orange | Black grape | Ultramarine

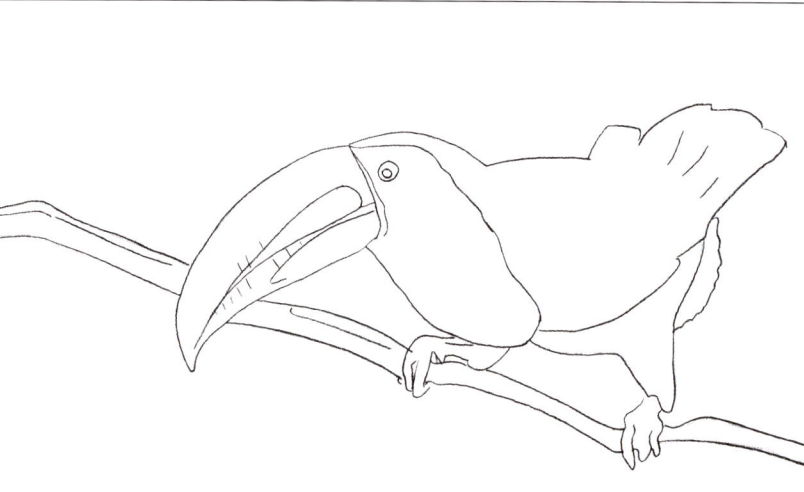

Step 1 Sketch the basic outlines of this simple composition with cool gray 50%, a neutral color that will blend with colors applied in later steps. Block in the dark areas of the background with black, using light to medium pressure. Then add another layer to the darkest areas around the perimeter. Using moderate pressure, apply olive green over the entire background with horizontal strokes.

Step 2 Next, use medium pressure and horizontal strokes to layer apple green over olive green, followed by another layer of olive green. To burnish the background for a polished, glossy look, use white followed by dark green. Then burnish the lightest, warmest areas with canary yellow and darken the lower left quadrant with dark green.

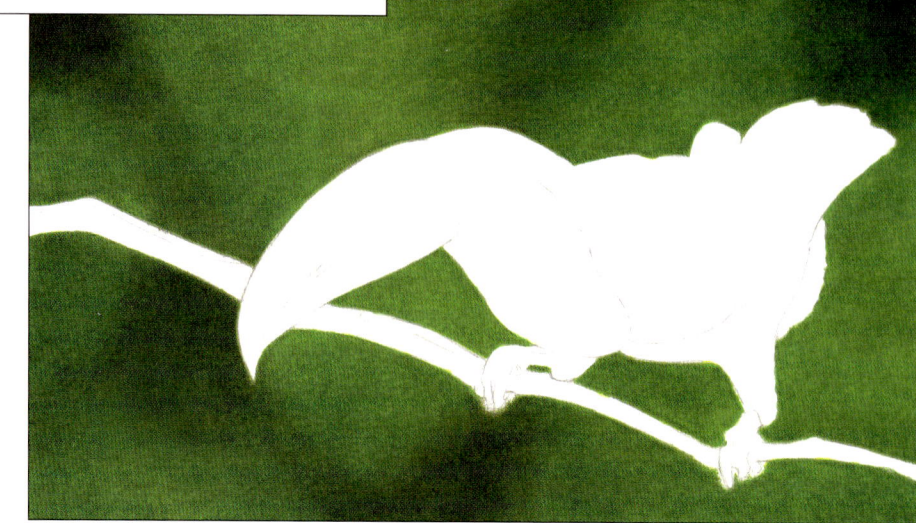

ARTIST'S TIP
Smooth, blended backgrounds contrast the sharp detail of the main subject.

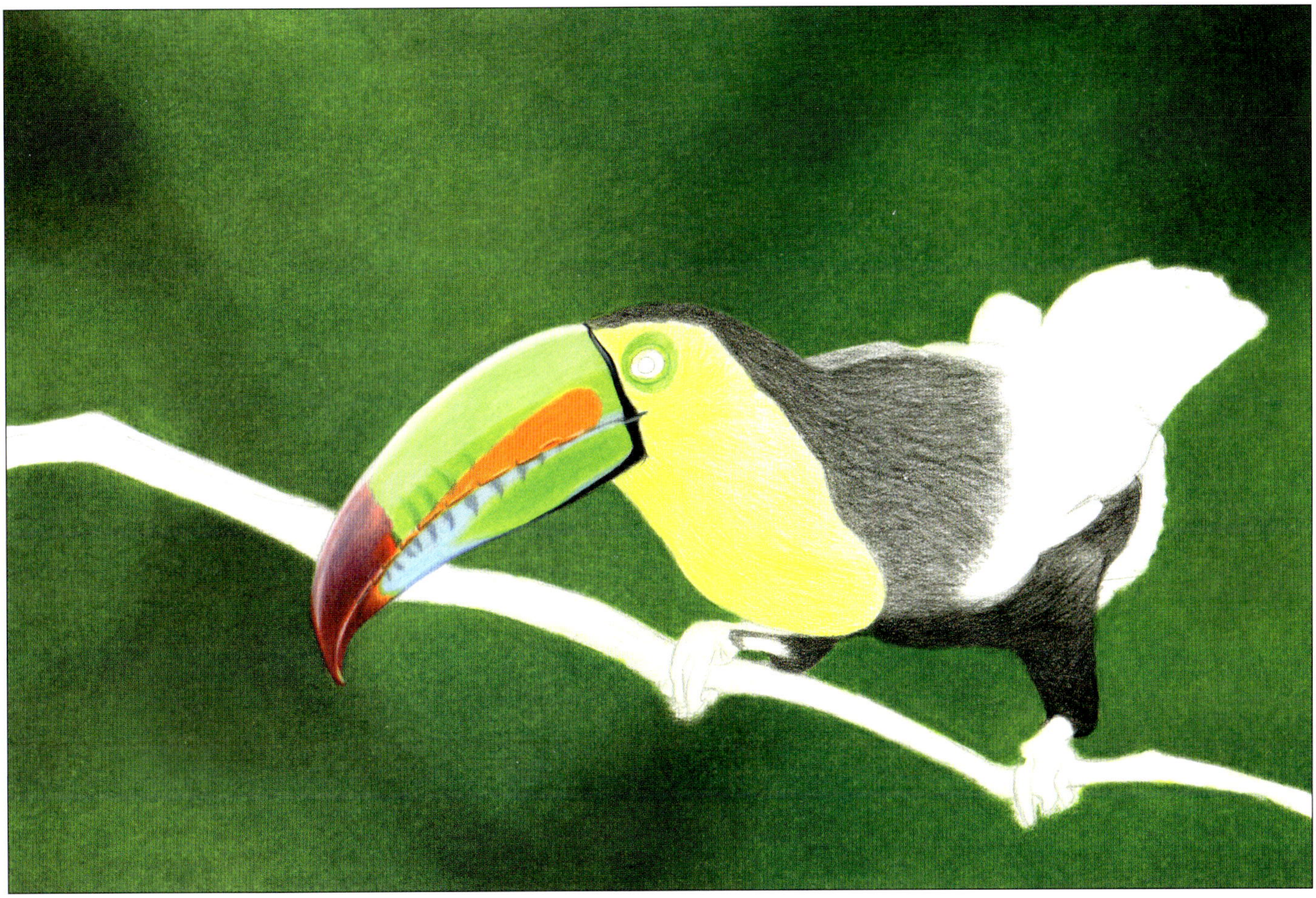

Step 3 Use black to draw the thin, vertical strip between the toucan's eye and beak, applying two layers. Then focus on the beak, completing it before moving on to other areas of the bird. (See detail below.) Outline the eye with cool gray 70%, encircle this with dark green, and color the resulting ring with apple green. Layer the toucan's chest with canary yellow, and give the back and leg areas a basecoat of black.

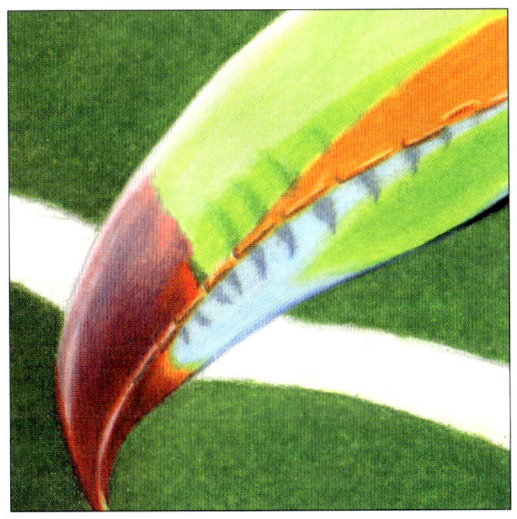

BEAK DETAIL

Apply two layers of spring green above and below the orange marking on the beak. Add two layers of chartreuse over the brighter green areas, burnishing with white above the orange marking and layering apple green below. For the orange marking, fill the area with two coats of sunburst yellow and then two coats of orange. For the blue area, apply two coats of non-photo blue and burnish with white. Draw the triangular streaks with cool gray 70%, and then cover them with ultramarine and white. Layer the red area of the beak first with crimson red, burnishing with white. For the darkest areas of red, stroke in black grape and burnish again with white, working around the two thin white streaks that extend to the beak's tip. Use cool gray 70% to draw the dark lines on the mouth and add canary yellow to the tip of the beak.

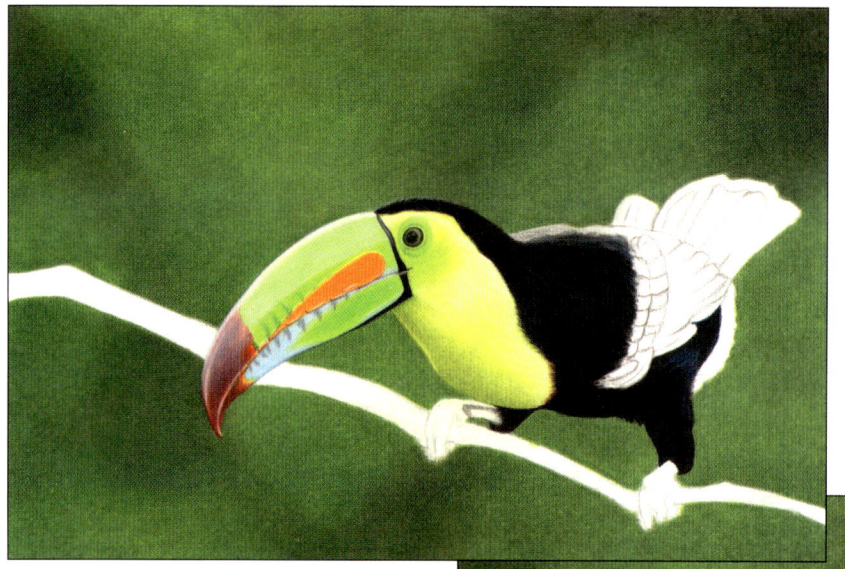

Step 4 To finish the toucan's yellow chest, add two more layers of canary yellow, leaving a small space between the yellow and black areas. Use limepeel to lay in the shadowed area on the far left side, and then apply kelp green in the darkest area (above the foot). Blend down with white and reapply canary yellow, limepeel, and kelp green. Use limepeel as a transition color from the dark green at left into the bright yellow at right. Around the eye, use sunburst yellow and spring green. Finish by burnishing with white in the lightest area alongside the dark feathers. Pull white streaks into the yellow area to blend. Next, add black to the toucan's body and complete the eye. (See "Eye Detail" below.)

Step 5 Define the two rows of feathers with black, followed by indigo blue. Add denim blue to the dark blue areas, and Caribbean Sea to the light blue areas. Then burnish with white for smoothness and reapply the three blue colors until you are satisfied. For defined lines and extreme darks, streak and blend with black. For the red area below the tail, apply crimson red and then burnish and blend with white. Repeat this process to intensify the red. Then color the feet. (See "Feet Detail" below.)

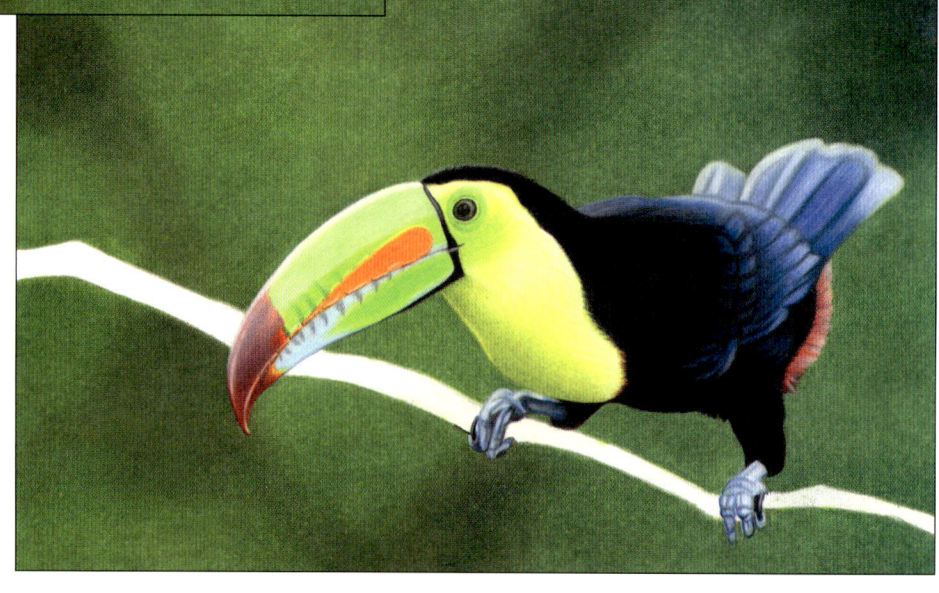

EYE DETAIL
For the bird's eye, outline the pupil with a 2B graphite pencil and draw three small highlights. Use black to fill in the pupil, working around the highlights, and then outline the exterior eyeball. Fill in the remainder of the eye with dark green, and use white to lighten the top right area. Use dark green, spring green, and canary yellow to finish the furry area around the eye.

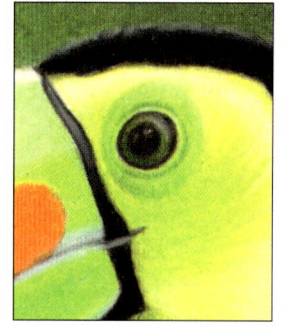

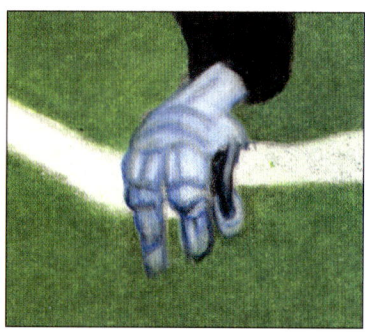

FEET DETAIL
For the feet, add the markings with cool gray 70%, followed by denim blue. Layer both feet with Caribbean Sea, and then blend and burnish with white. For the extreme darks and the claws, use black. Finish with an overall softening layer of white.

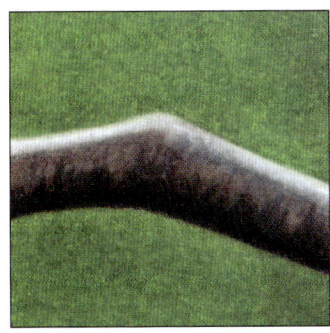 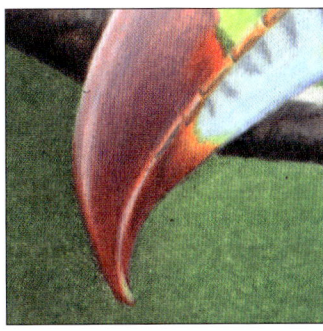 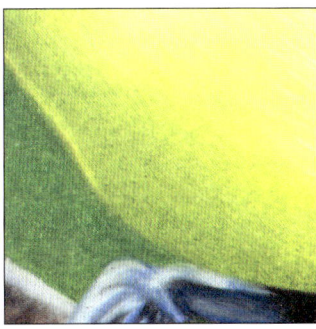

ARTIST'S TIP

Notice how the direction of the strokes are drawn to describe the form of each object. Instead of applying straight, uniform strokes within an area of color, think about the curves of the surface and lay in colors accordingly. Stroke around the curvature of the branch, along the curve of the beak, and along the toucan's chest to suggest its roundness. Using this technique will bring dimension and depth to your artwork.

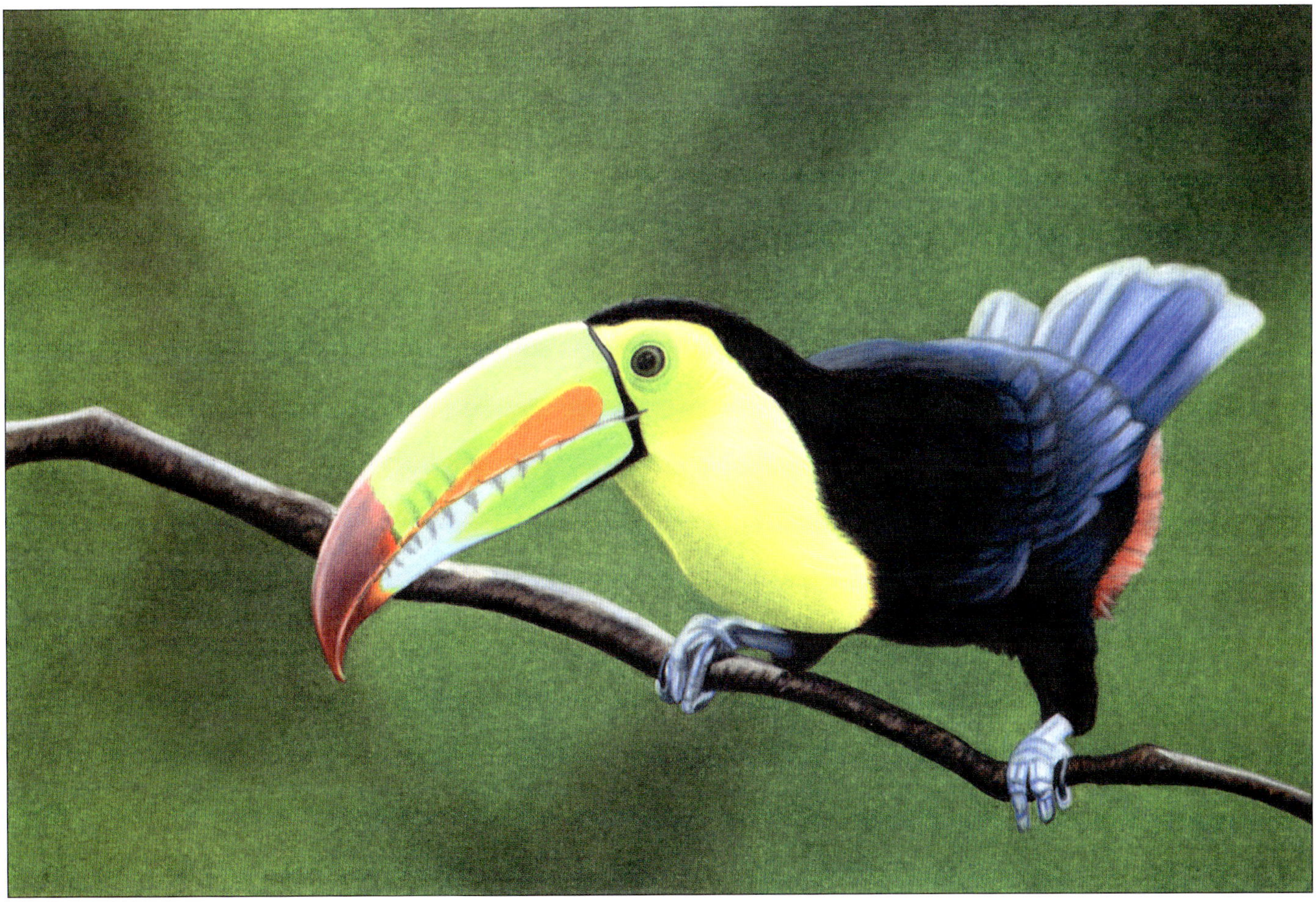

Step 6 Layer black in the darkest areas of the branch, followed by dark umber with vertical and jagged strokes. Leave the white areas alone for now, and use dark umber and burnt ochre to lay in the light and dark browns. Then reapply black over the existing black areas and line the branch with black, avoiding the highlighted areas. Lightly apply Caribbean Sea over the white areas and then burnish with white. To fill in the background near the branch and bird, use a sharp Prussian green pencil. Clean up the edges and spray with workable fixative to finish.

Kitten

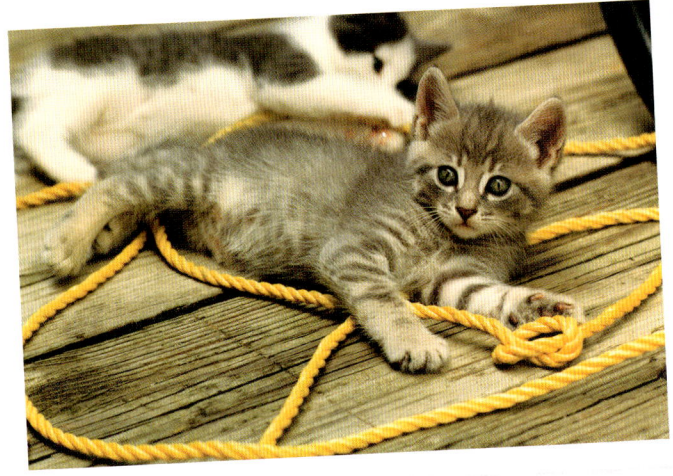

Animals make wonderful subjects to draw because there are so many different kinds to choose from. They all have their own distinctive features and textures, whether they are smooth and scaled, fluffy and feathered, or soft and furry. The artist of this piece uses blending and layering techniques to convey the distinctive patterns in the soft, silky fur of this playful kitten.

PALETTE

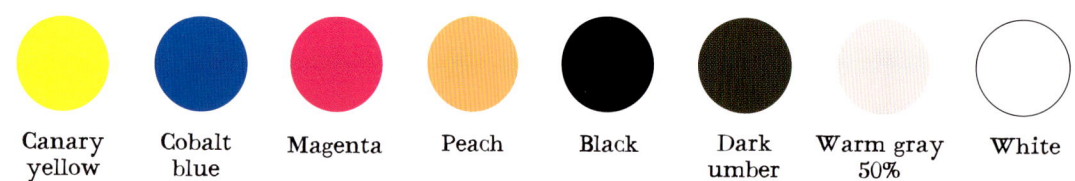

Canary yellow | Cobalt blue | Magenta | Peach | Black | Dark umber | Warm gray 50% | White

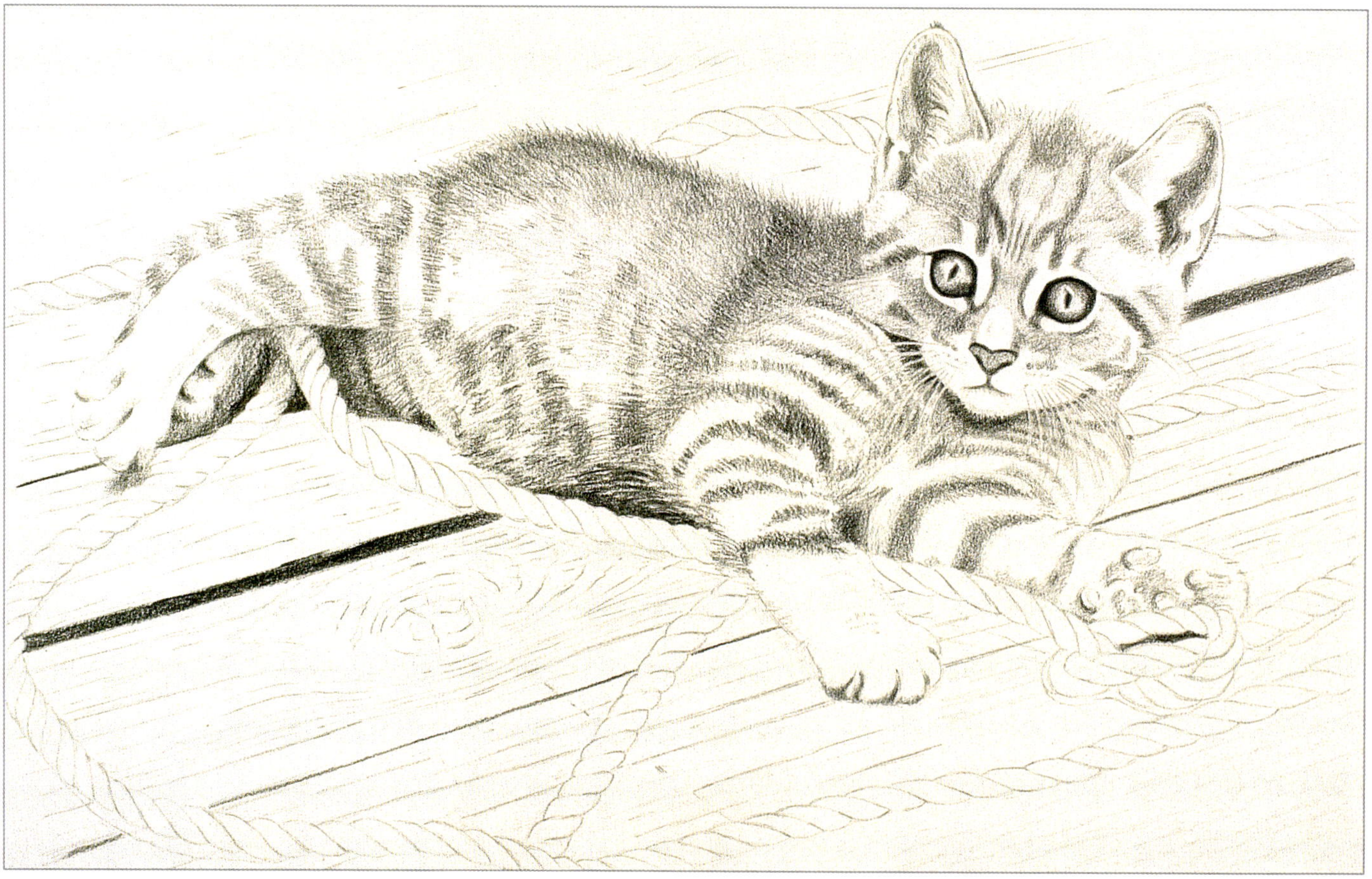

Step 1 Start with a simple sketch. When you are happy with your drawing, apply black to the darkest areas around the kitten and lightly layer over the gray areas of the fur. Continue to apply various values of warm gray 50% with a fairly sharp pencil, using a circular motion. Next, use gray to fill in around the areas of lighter fur and the area around the whiskers, leaving the whiskers white.

Step 2 Apply a light layer of peach to the insides of the ears, to the nose, the belly, and around the mouth, using circular strokes. The upturned paw pads receive a layer of peach, but leave the highlights white. Add a light layer of dark umber to the rope and then add a heavier layer on the shadowed side. Work a light layer of dark umber into the fur and over the paw pads. Detail the wood with black, making sure all the strokes follow the direction of the wood grain.

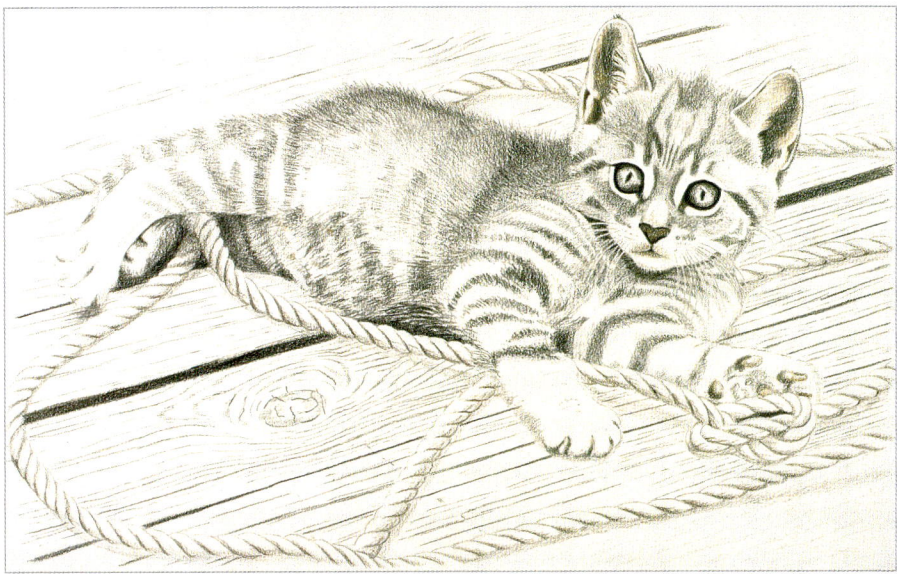

ARTIST'S TIP

As you work, check your drawing for accuracy by turning it and the reference photo upside down and comparing the two. This makes it easier to spot any problems because you're forced to really see the actual object, rather than relying on any preconceptions you may have about what the subject should look like.

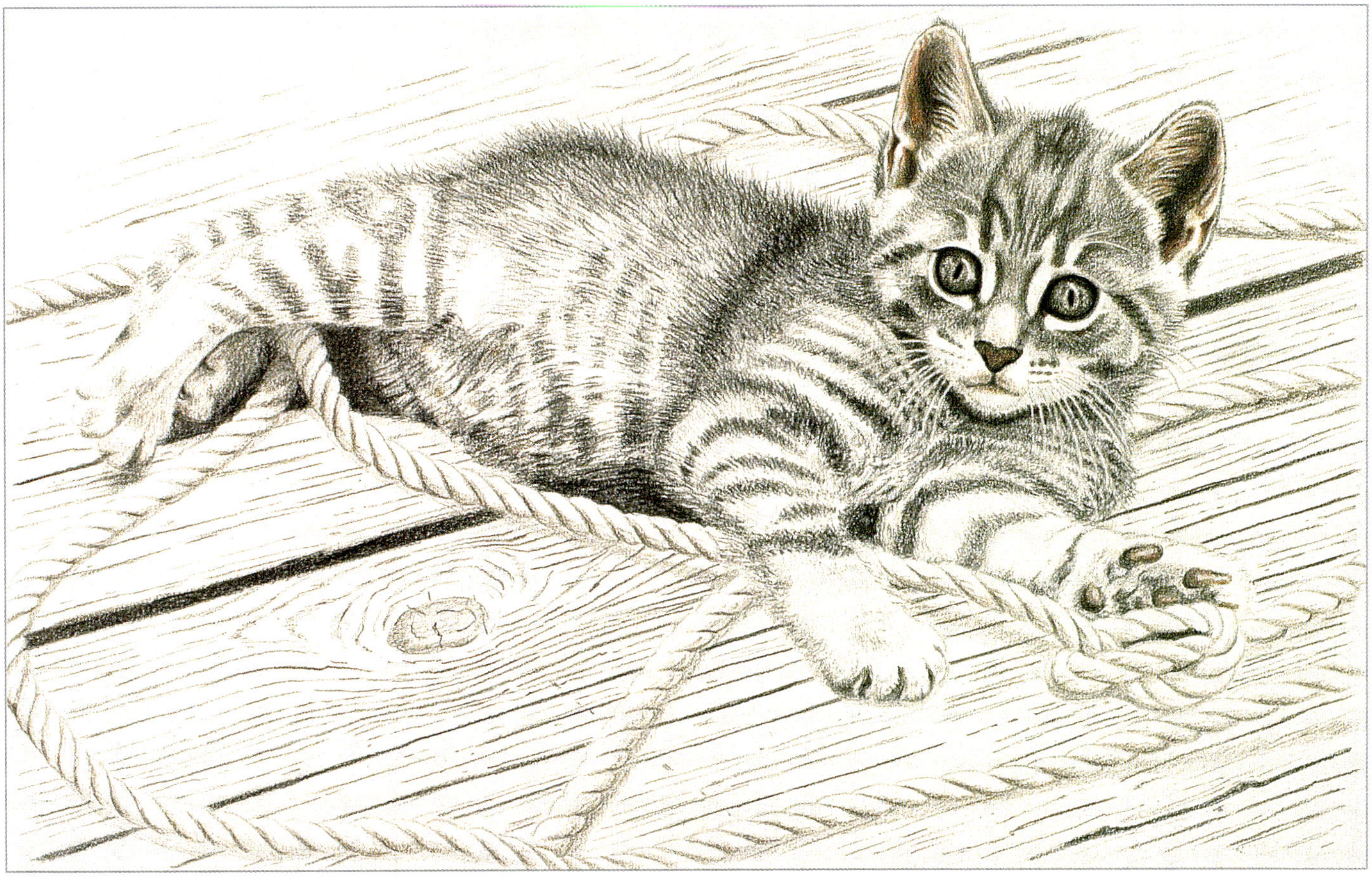

Step 3 Lightly apply magenta over the insides of the ears. Add light layers of magenta and dark umber to the paw pads, using circular strokes for a soft blend. Soften the black rims around the eyes with dark umber and also add dark umber to the stripes in the fur. Add some more black to the dark grays in the fur and darken some areas of the chest and front legs, using short, tapered strokes that follow the direction of fur growth. Then add dark umber to the stripes and the darker areas of the hind legs, using a blending stump to soften the colors. Add a ring of dark umber to the eyes around the pupils, and then use dark umber to draw over the black detail lines in the wood.

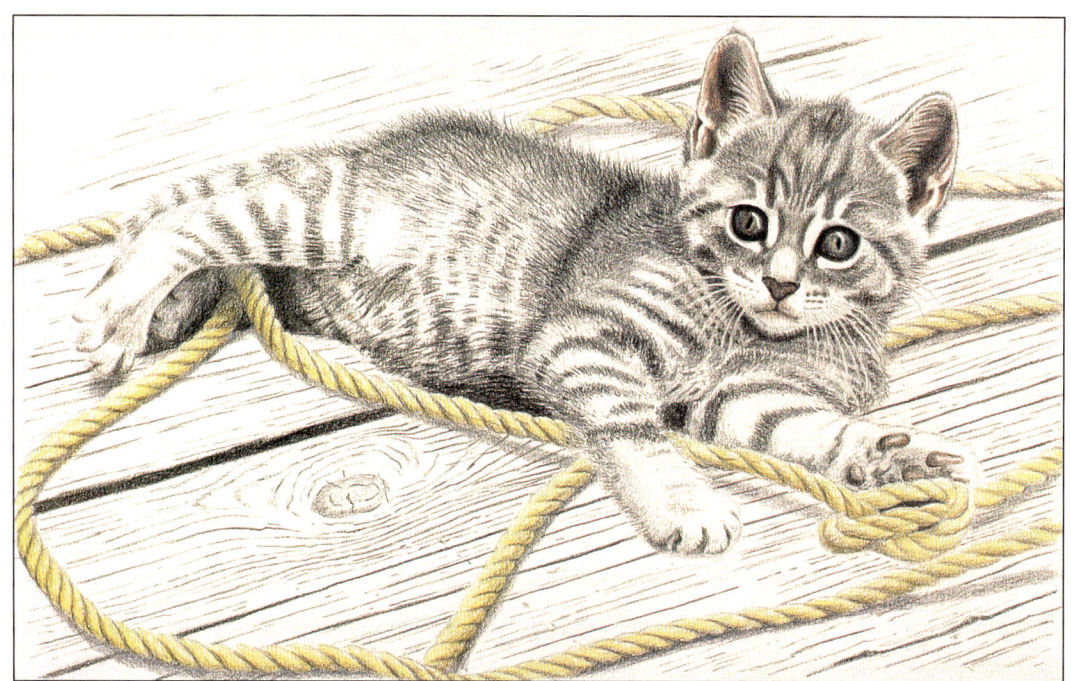

Step 4 Layer cobalt blue over the irises in the eyes, saving the white highlights. To deepen the shadows, apply some blue over the chin, under the neck, along the shadow of the front legs, and in all of the shadowed areas of the rope. Add blue to the back leg and the tail to "push" them back a bit. Add a touch of canary yellow to the eyes between the iris and the pupil. Apply yellow to the rope, putting a slightly heavier layer on the strand in the foreground. Then layer a little black over the rope's blue cast shadow to darken it.

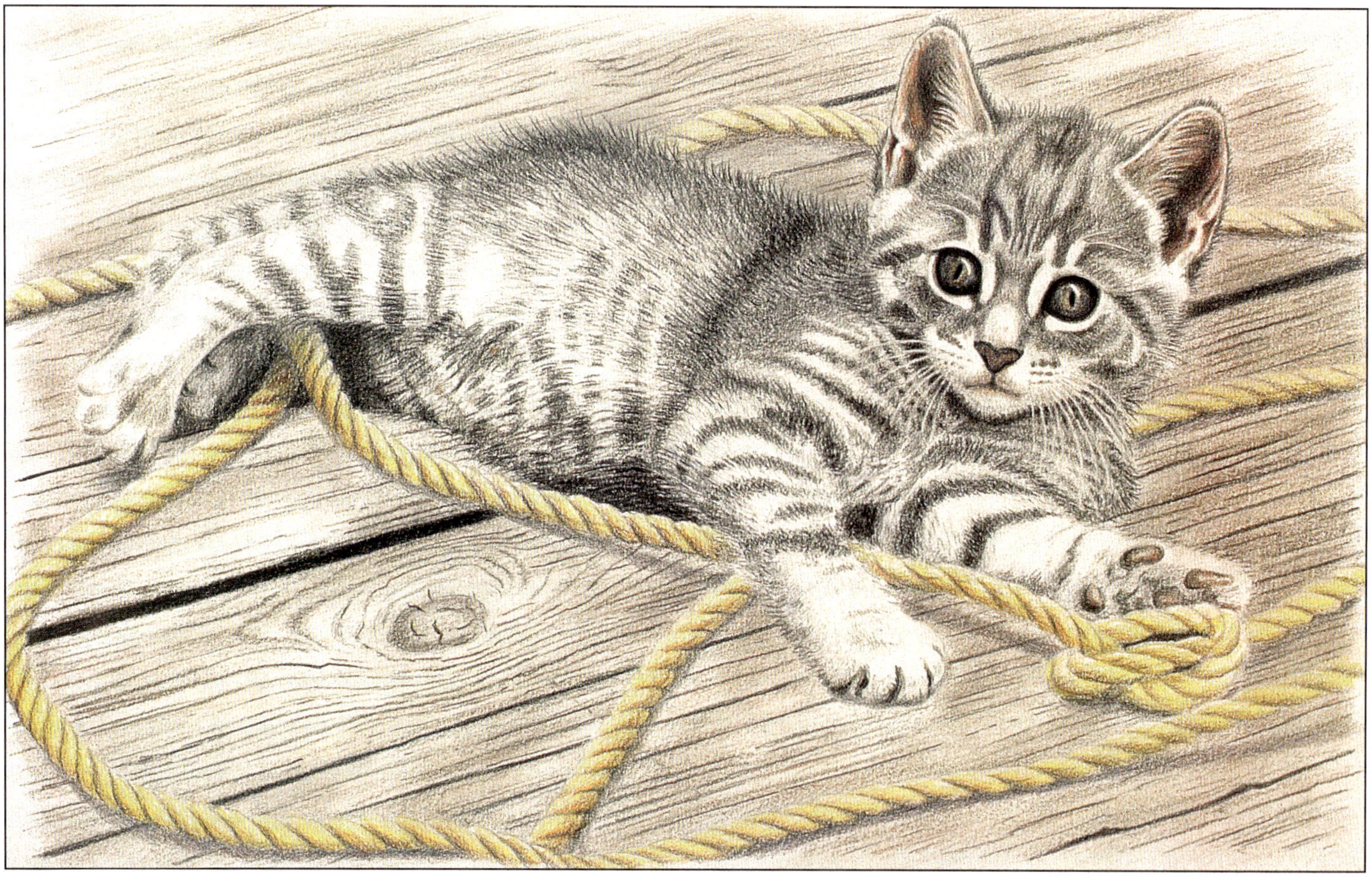

Step 5 Apply cobalt blue to the dark cracks of the deck and add a few light strokes of magenta in front of the kitten. Add magenta to the shadow under the rope, creating a purple hue. Add a shadow under the knot in the rope and then apply another light layer of dark umber to darken the wood. Lightly add a few spots of canary yellow and use a blending stump to soften the colors. Draw the kitten's fur over the wood with black, making short strokes that start at the body and go out in slightly different directions.

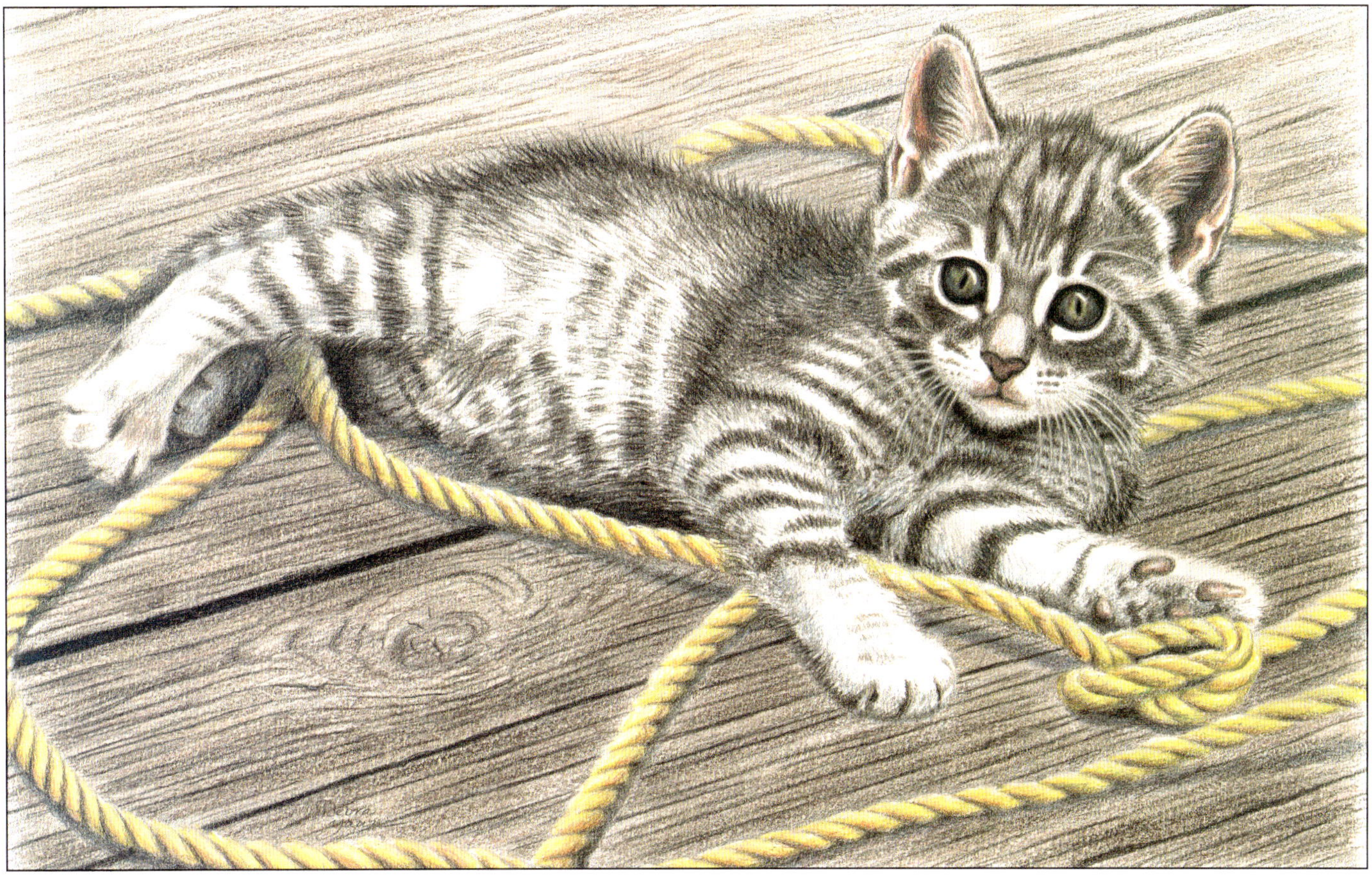

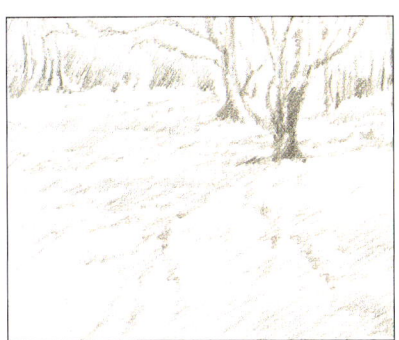

Step 6 Soften the fur even more by blending short strokes of white over some of the black. Draw white over the whiskers and create a few hard strokes of white through some of the darker areas (such as the belly) to show the texture of the fur. Add a little more cobalt blue, dark umber, and canary yellow to the eyes. Then finish with a layer of white to soften and blend the colors. Add white to the tiny tufts of fur in the ears, and use short black strokes to widen the stripes on the legs. Darken the shadows under the ropes in a few places with a little more blue and black, but keep the shadows light to keep the focus on the kitten. Use white to soften the colors in the rope. Darken the wood a little more, by adding black and dark umber to the foreground. Finally, apply a light layer of yellow to warm the color of the wood.

THE PENCIL SKETCH

Many colored pencil artists begin with a black-and-white value drawing; this method is called "grisaille." Grisaille allows the artist to establish the darks and lights in a subject before applying color. Then, as the transparent colored pencil values are layered over the initial drawing, the dark values lend additional depth to the darkest areas. The example below demonstrates how the grisaille technique helps build volume in a simple scene.

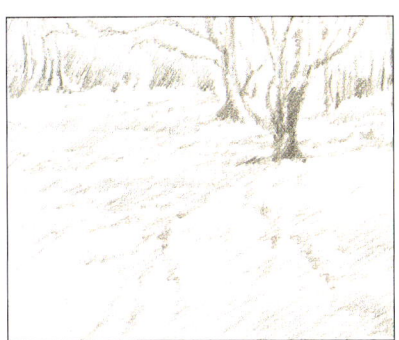
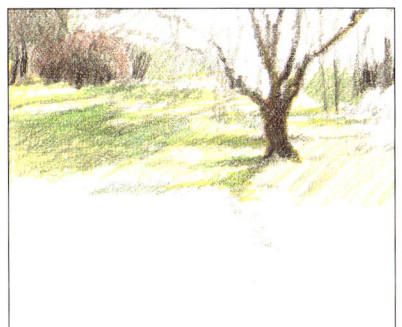
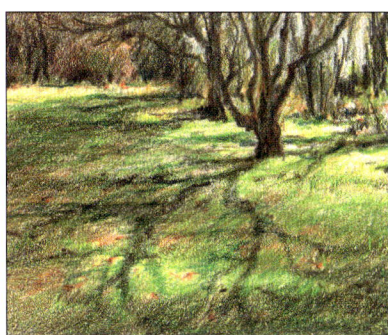

Puppy

To draw fur, first establish the color base and block in the dark areas. Midtones and highlights will follow, and blending is important. Short-haired animals will require short, quick strokes, while long-haired animals will need longer, curved strokes. Establish the initial stroke patterns and then begin to build color. Apply layer upon layer in the direction of the fur. A lovely blend of colors will develop that will resemble the animal's natural coat.

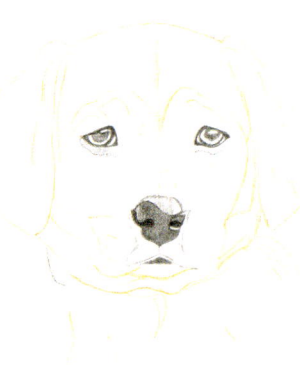

PALETTE

Beige	Dark brown	Tuscan red	Goldenrod
Blue violet lake	Burnt ochre	Mineral orange	Peach
Peach beige	Sand	Chocolate	Black
Terra cotta	Dark umber	Light umber	White

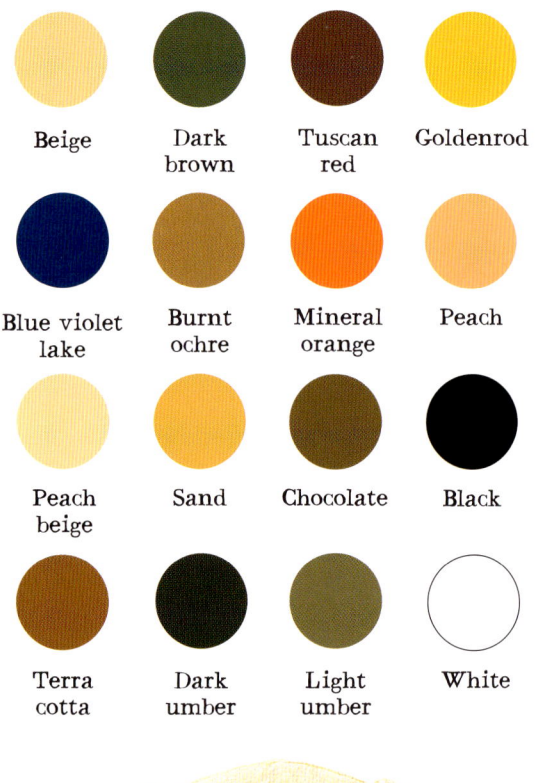

Step 1 Lightly sketch the puppy with mineral orange and use a graphite F pencil to add the eyes and nose.

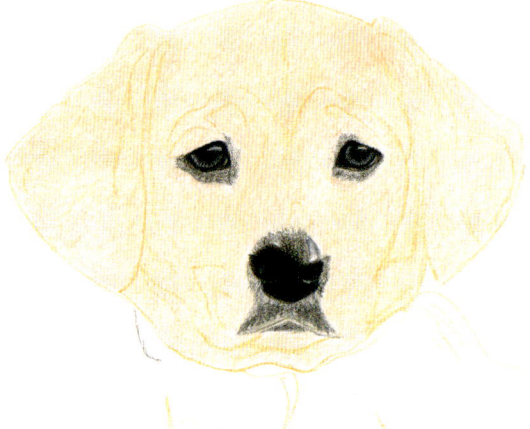

Step 2 Outline the eyes in black and use blue violet lake to color the irises. Build up the pupils with light layers of black and keep the highlights white. Finish with light black spokes around the iris, and block in the dark markings of fur around the eyes with black. Use black on the nose and white for the highlights. Begin the fur with washes of peach beige, beige, and peach using circular strokes to create a nonlinear foundation for the fur.

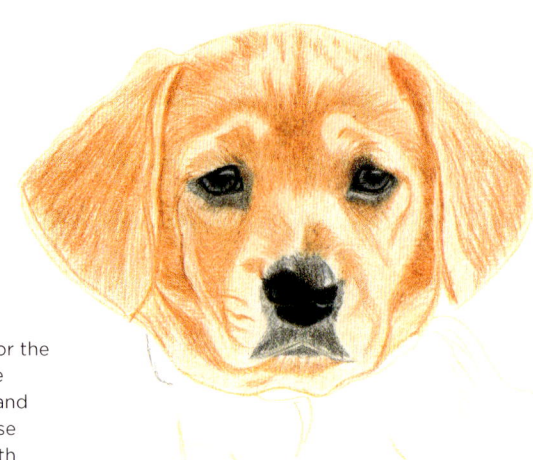

Step 3 Block in the darks of the face and ears with burnt ochre. Always move in the direction of the fur patterns. In this case, strokes are short on the face and long on the ears.

Step 4 Layer goldenrod over the face, using medium pressure in the dark areas and gentle pressure in the light areas. Use terra cotta over the dark red areas and bring out the eye area with more black. Beginning at the top of the head, use beige to blend the existing colors; then add burnt ochre and dark umber above the right eye. Use black and Tuscan red to define the area where the ears meet the face. Use terra cotta, light umber, and mineral orange for the remaining dark areas. Use beige, burnt ochre, and mineral orange for the light areas. Add Tuscan red to the outer cheek areas and draw whiskers with light umber and white. For the right ear, use Tuscan red, dark umber, goldenrod, and terra cotta; then blend with burnt ochre. Lightly add beige, light umber, terra cotta, and a small ridge of dark umber at the bottom of the left ear. Finish with a burnish of white above the brown ridge, and outline the head with burnt ochre using jagged strokes.

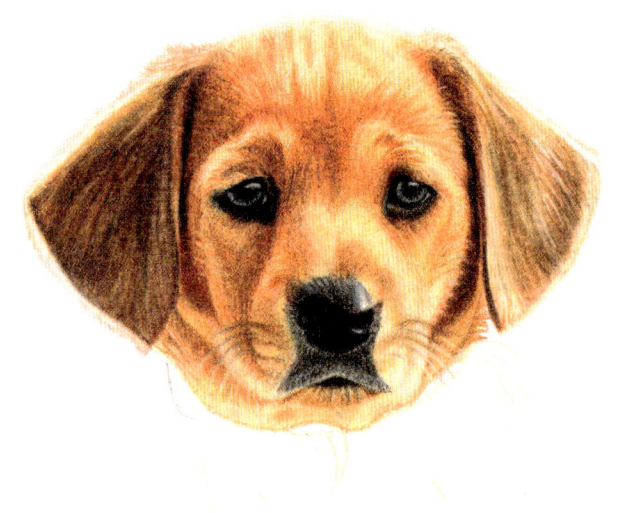

NOSE DETAIL

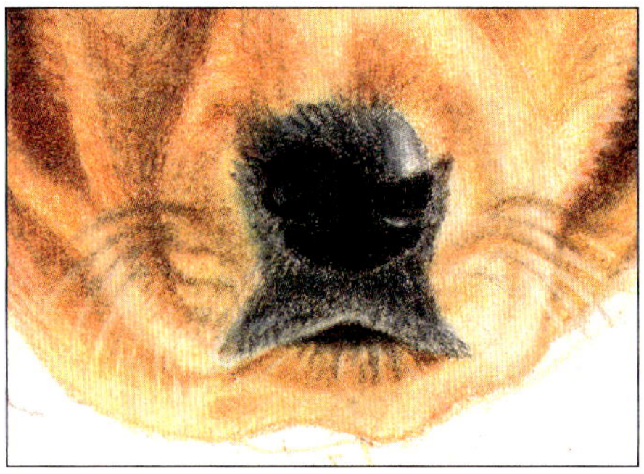

Blend the nose with white; then add more black and blend with white. Add dark umber just below the nose following the mouth line. Use white to blend the black into the lip, and use a curved line of Tuscan red below the mouth.

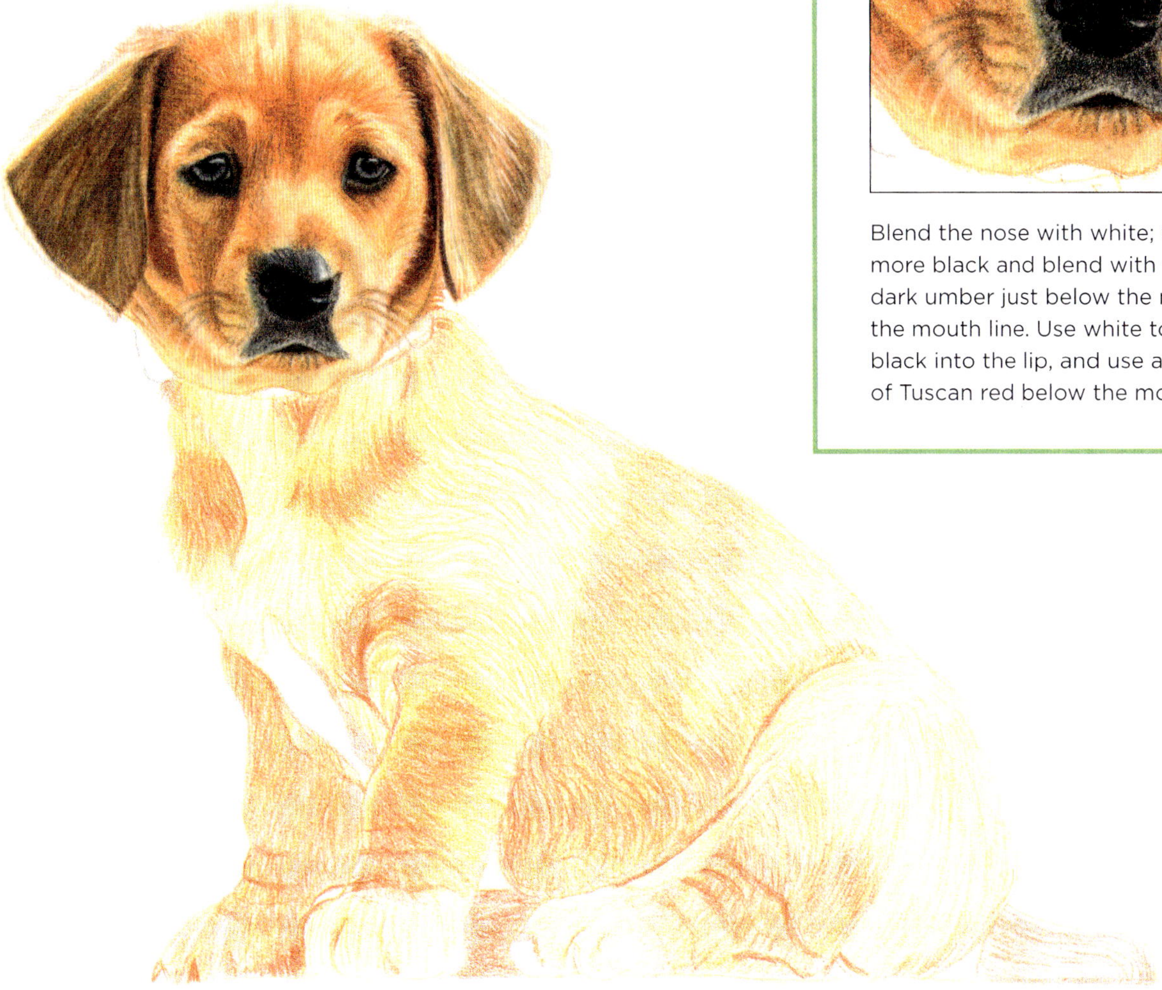

Step 5 Block in the darker body areas with burnt ochre using short to medium strokes. Cover the entire body in a goldenrod wash using light pressure.

Step 6 Beginning below the collar, draw fur strands with burnt ochre, light umber, terra cotta, and goldenrod. Blend with sand and continue to build up the chest fur with the same colors. Apply a dark umber streak over the left indentation and black and Tuscan red over the creased fur below the mouth. Use burnt ochre and terra cotta to further block in the feet and legs. Begin to lay in the torso fur with burnt ochre, light umber, terra cotta, goldenrod, and chocolate. Burnish and blend these together with white. Repeat the process with all colors as needed. Add a layer of dark umber to the lower stomach area.

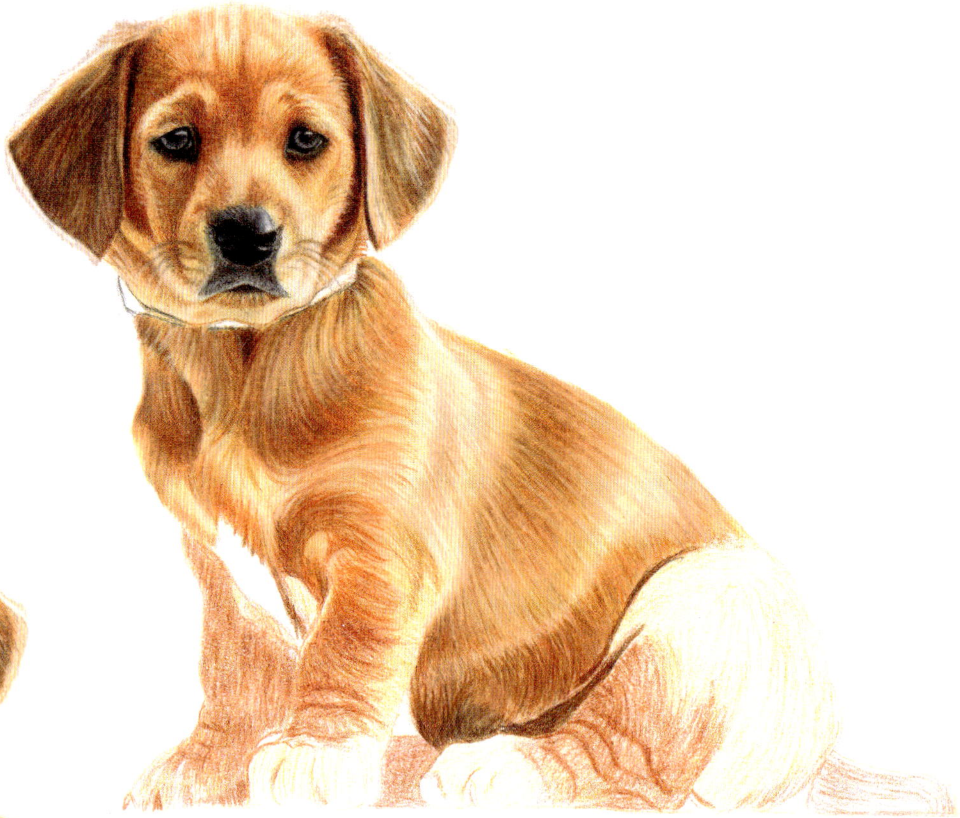

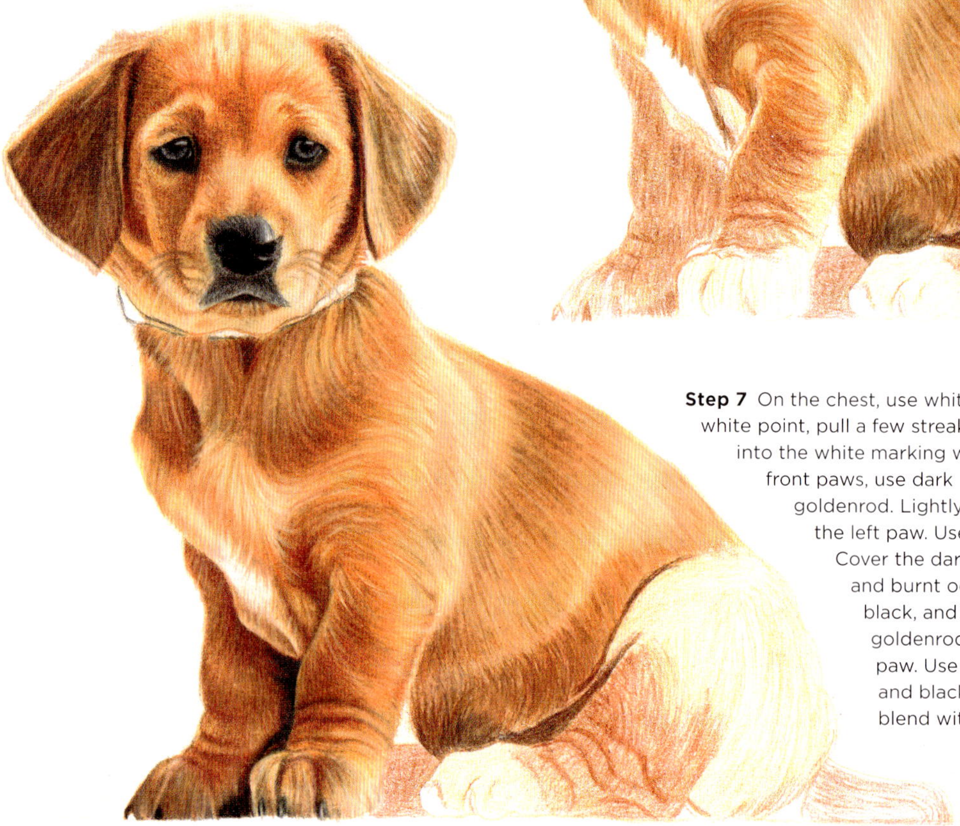

Step 7 On the chest, use white to blend above the white fur patch. With a white point, pull a few streaks of fur into the far left. Draw a few strands into the white marking with burnt ochre. For the area between the front paws, use dark brown, Tuscan red, burnt ochre, and goldenrod. Lightly blend with white and swirl the fur out over the left paw. Use dark umber and terra cotta for the wrinkles. Cover the darker areas of the right paw with dark brown and burnt ochre. Use goldenrod on top and dark umber, black, and Tuscan red for the heavy shadow. Blend with goldenrod and use chocolate and burnt ochre for the paw. Use dark umber and terra cotta for the wrinkles and black for the toe markings and dark fur. Lightly blend with white.

FUR DETAILS

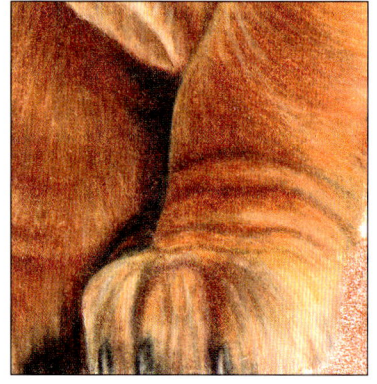

Blend the paw with mineral orange and add terra cotta and chocolate down the left side. Blend with white down the right side in the direction of the fur. Add a streak of terra cotta down the outside of the paw. Use beige, terra cotta, and burnt ochre for the toes. Add Tuscan red and dark umber in the toe areas. For the toenails, use black and blend with white.

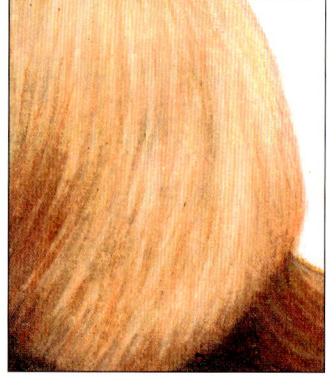

Cover the left haunch with beige and then peach beige. Use chocolate and dark brown to stroke in the fur and block in the darker areas. Burnish with white. Repeat with strokes of burnt ochre, light umber, and a burnish of white. Add goldenrod to warm the colors.

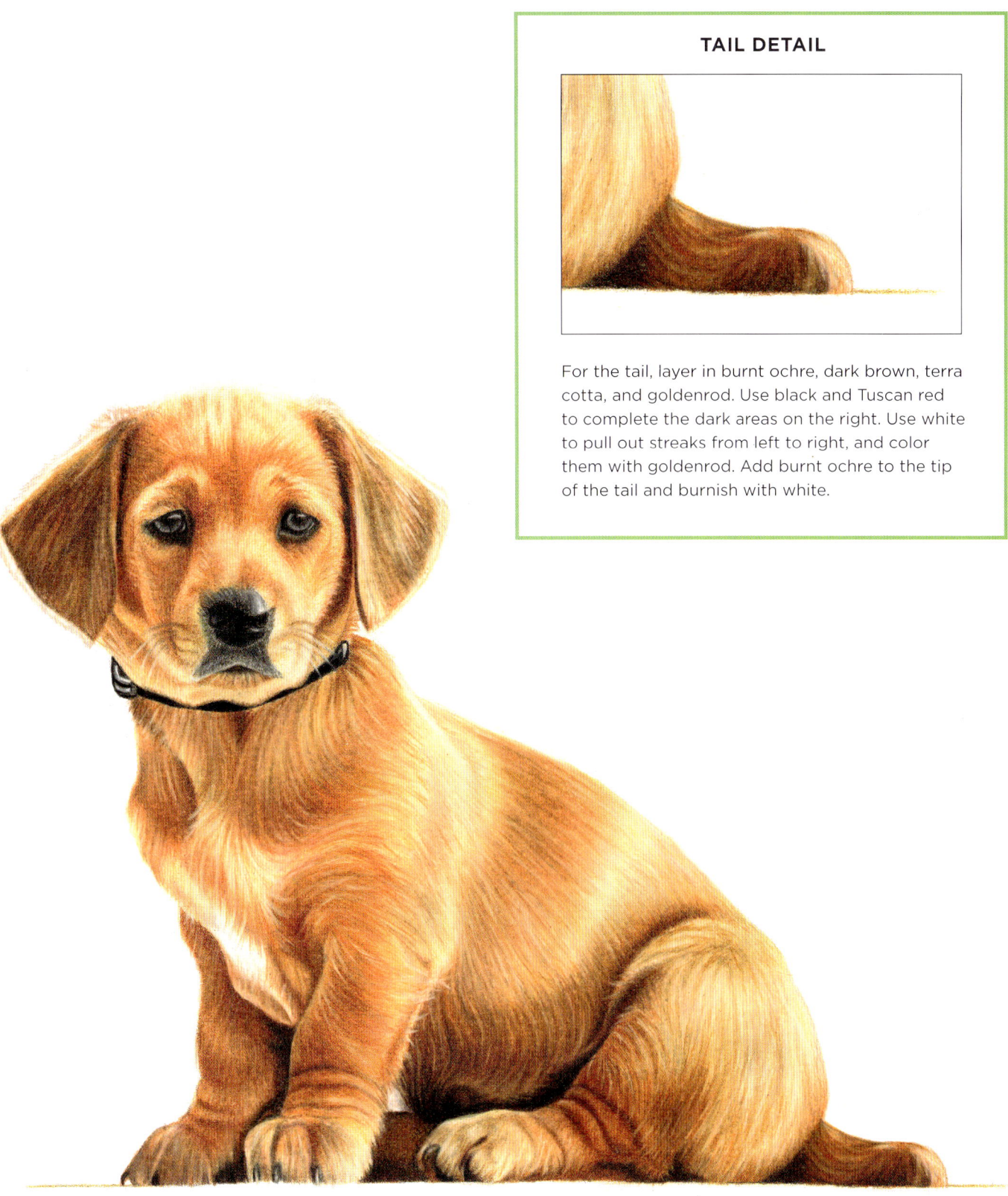

For the tail, layer in burnt ochre, dark brown, terra cotta, and goldenrod. Use black and Tuscan red to complete the dark areas on the right. Use white to pull out streaks from left to right, and color them with goldenrod. Add burnt ochre to the tip of the tail and burnish with white.

Step 8 For the rear right foot, lightly apply dark umber then burnt ochre; then layer terra cotta and black for the shadows. Block in the dark folds on the left foot with dark brown and Tuscan red, and blend with burnt ochre and terra cotta. Pull streaks of fur over the folds with a sharp white point. On the two dark shadows at the heel, use black and Tuscan red. Cover the toe area with beige, peach beige, and streaks of light umber. Use white to blend and burnt ochre for the reddish brown areas. Complete the toenails with black and Tuscan red and blend with white. Block in the underbelly's extreme darks with dark umber. From left to right, use dark umber, terra cotta, and black to create the fur and dark circular patch. Use terra cotta, black, and Tuscan red to outline and fill in the dark circular shape above the leg. Then stroke in terra cotta, dark umber, and goldenrod below the puppy's left front leg, above the haunch, and on the back. Use white to pull out streaks of fur. Color the collar with black, blend with white, and pull whiskers across it using a sharp white point. Erase all smudges and spray with workable fixative.

Shetland Sheepdog

At first glance, this Shetland Sheepdog may remind you of Lassie, the famous Collie that represented the ideal canine companion. But even for those not familiar with Lassie, the loyal and wise characteristics of this sheepdog are conveyed through its fine, soft fur and attentive, friendly expression. The dog's flowing coat is drawn with just a few colors and long, swinging movements.

PALETTE

 Henna

 Jasmine yellow

Cool gray 30%

 Cool gray 90%

 Dark umber

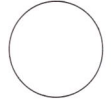 Yellow ochre

White

 Sienna brown

SECONDARY PALETTE

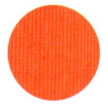 Poppy

 Burnt ochre

Warm gray 20%

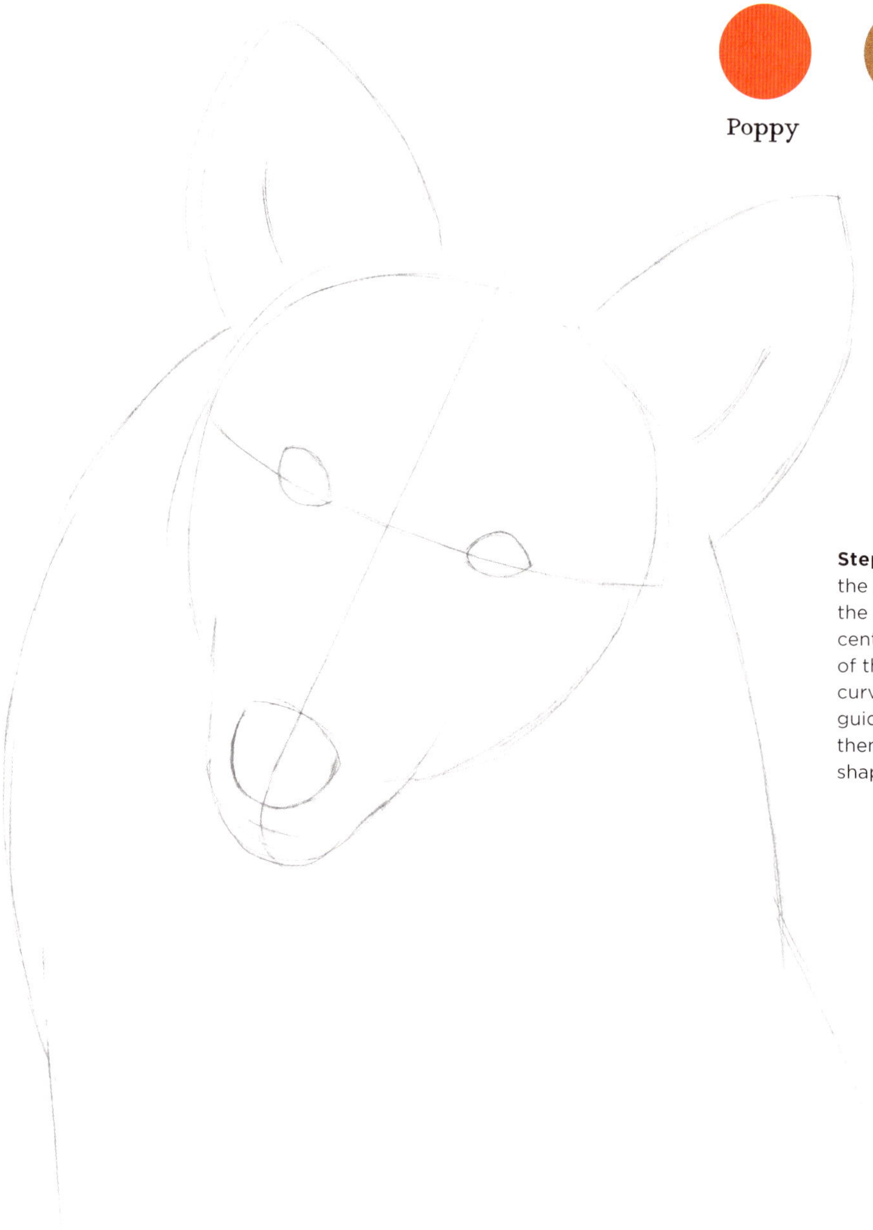

Step 1 With an HB pencil, sketch a circle for the dog's head and a rounded triangle for the muzzle. Then draw the vertical centerline so it reflects the angled position of the dog's head. Next, add the slightly curved horizontal centerline. Use these guidelines to position the eyes and nose; then draw the large ears and the basic shape of the body.

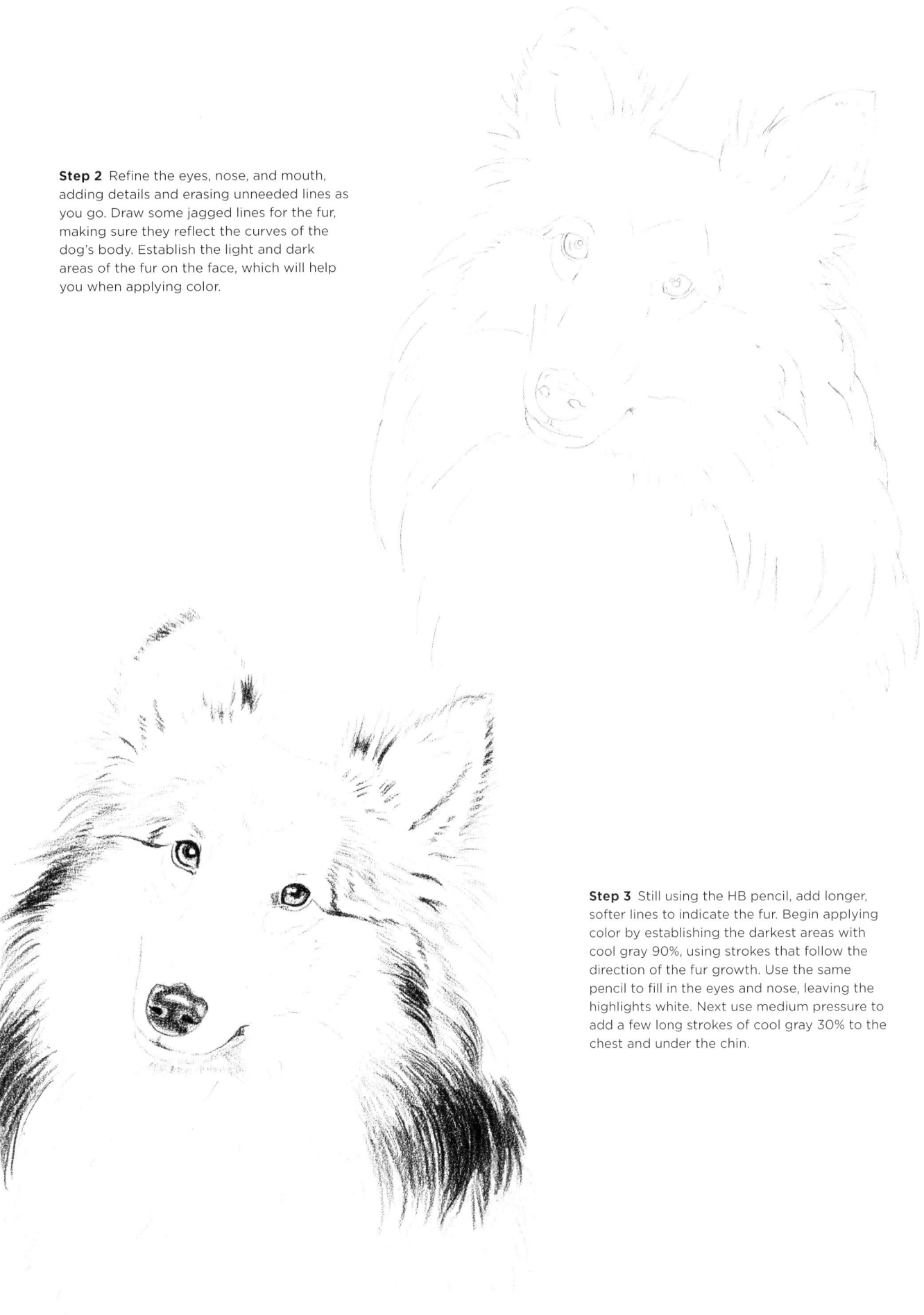

Step 2 Refine the eyes, nose, and mouth, adding details and erasing unneeded lines as you go. Draw some jagged lines for the fur, making sure they reflect the curves of the dog's body. Establish the light and dark areas of the fur on the face, which will help you when applying color.

Step 3 Still using the HB pencil, add longer, softer lines to indicate the fur. Begin applying color by establishing the darkest areas with cool gray 90%, using strokes that follow the direction of the fur growth. Use the same pencil to fill in the eyes and nose, leaving the highlights white. Next use medium pressure to add a few long strokes of cool gray 30% to the chest and under the chin.

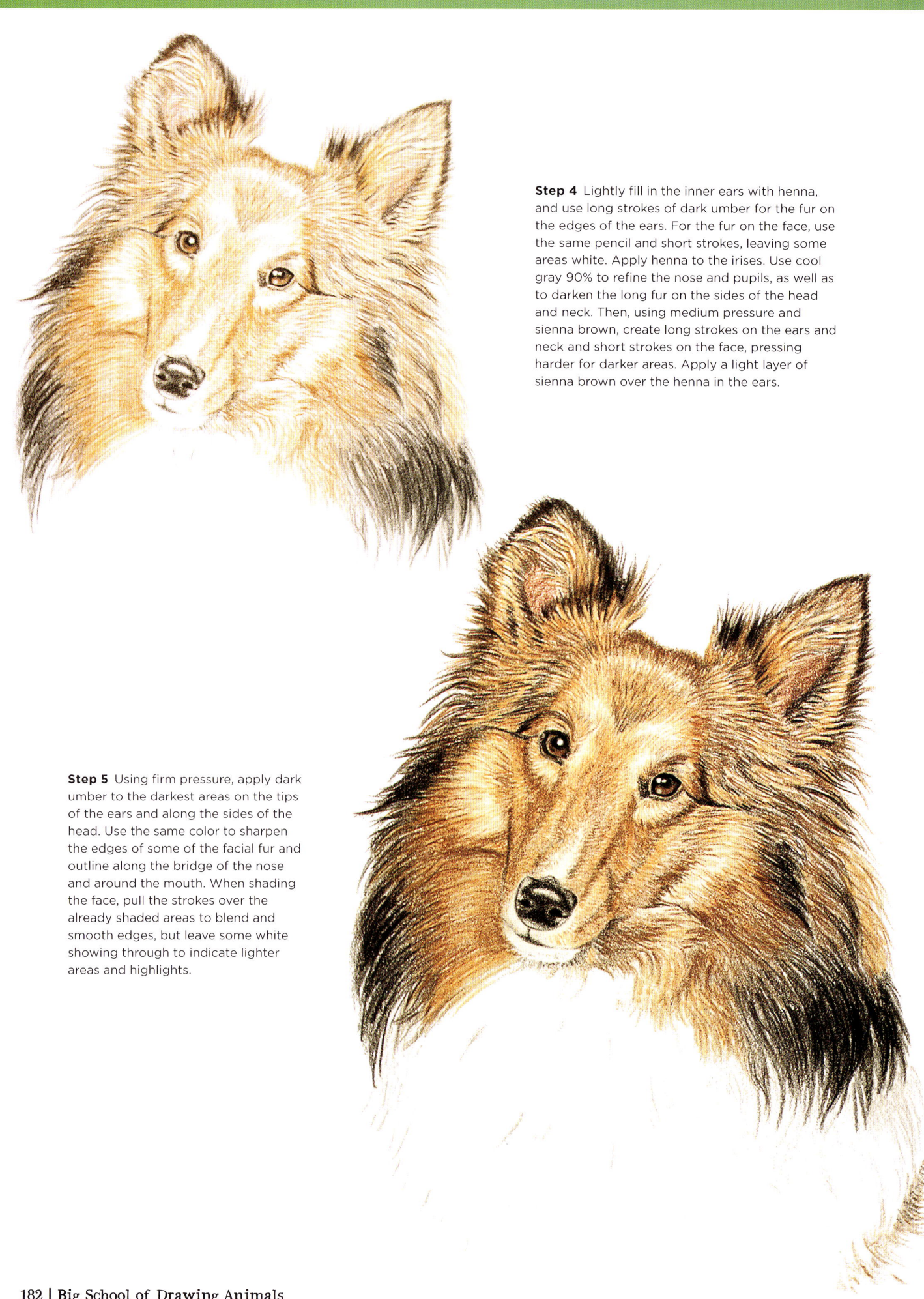

Step 4 Lightly fill in the inner ears with henna, and use long strokes of dark umber for the fur on the edges of the ears. For the fur on the face, use the same pencil and short strokes, leaving some areas white. Apply henna to the irises. Use cool gray 90% to refine the nose and pupils, as well as to darken the long fur on the sides of the head and neck. Then, using medium pressure and sienna brown, create long strokes on the ears and neck and short strokes on the face, pressing harder for darker areas. Apply a light layer of sienna brown over the henna in the ears.

Step 5 Using firm pressure, apply dark umber to the darkest areas on the tips of the ears and along the sides of the head. Use the same color to sharpen the edges of some of the facial fur and outline along the bridge of the nose and around the mouth. When shading the face, pull the strokes over the already shaded areas to blend and smooth edges, but leave some white showing through to indicate lighter areas and highlights.

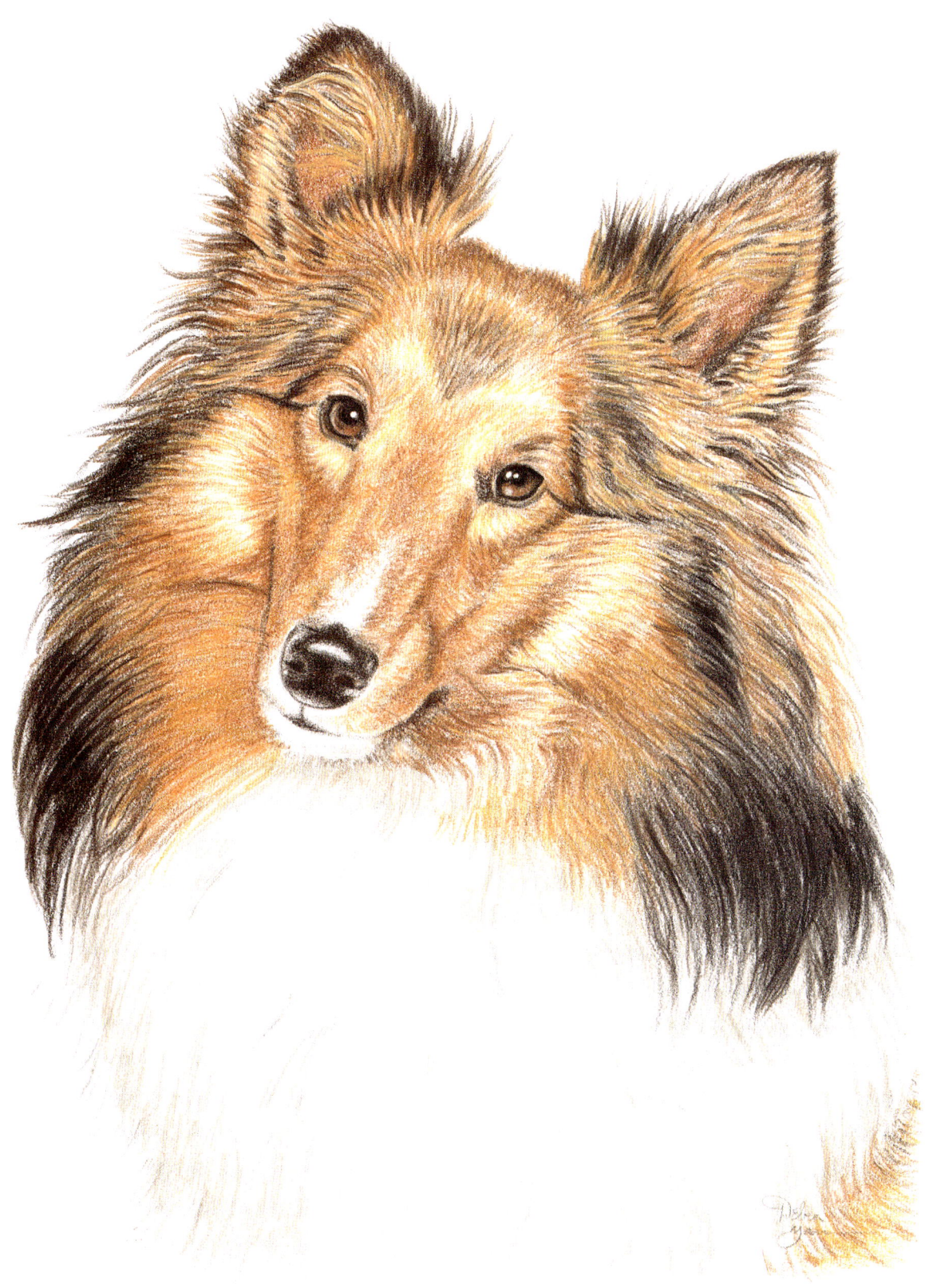

Step 6 Apply cool gray 30% to areas of the chest and under the neck, using firm pressure in the darkest areas. Then use dark umber to sharpen the eyes and the areas around them. Step back from drawing and squint your eyes to see which areas need to be darker; then refine the black edges of the fur with a few firm strokes. Using medium pressure, apply yellow ochre over areas of the face and neck, adding enough color so that all but the whitest fur is covered. Then use medium pressure to apply jasmine yellow to the lighter areas on the face, leaving the small area around the mouth and the bridge of the nose white. Next, slightly darken the nose with cool gray 90%. To finish, add strokes of sienna brown and yellow ochre to the fur on the dog's lower left side.

Leopard

Just as some animals develop an incredible display of color (such as the Toucan on page 168), there are some animals whose natural colors blend in with their surroundings. The leopard's earthy colors allow it to completely disappear on the plains of the savanna. Think of this characteristic as you draw the plants in the foreground.

PALETTE

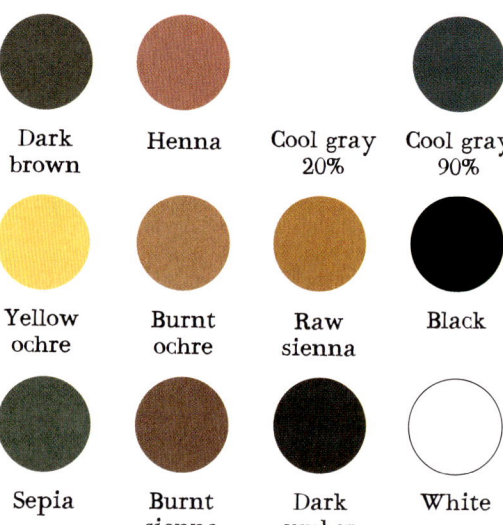

Dark brown   Henna   Cool gray 20%   Cool gray 90%

Yellow ochre   Burnt ochre   Raw sienna   Black

Sepia   Burnt sienna   Dark umber   White

Step 1 Sketch the basic shape of the head with an HB pencil. The head is turned at a three-quarter angle, so shift the vertical centerline to the right and curve it to follow the form of the face. Note that the guidelines for the eyes, nose, and mouth are also curved. Indicate the ears and nose with triangle shapes, and depict the cheeks with two half-circles. Next, draw the body, adding a small hump for the shoulders.

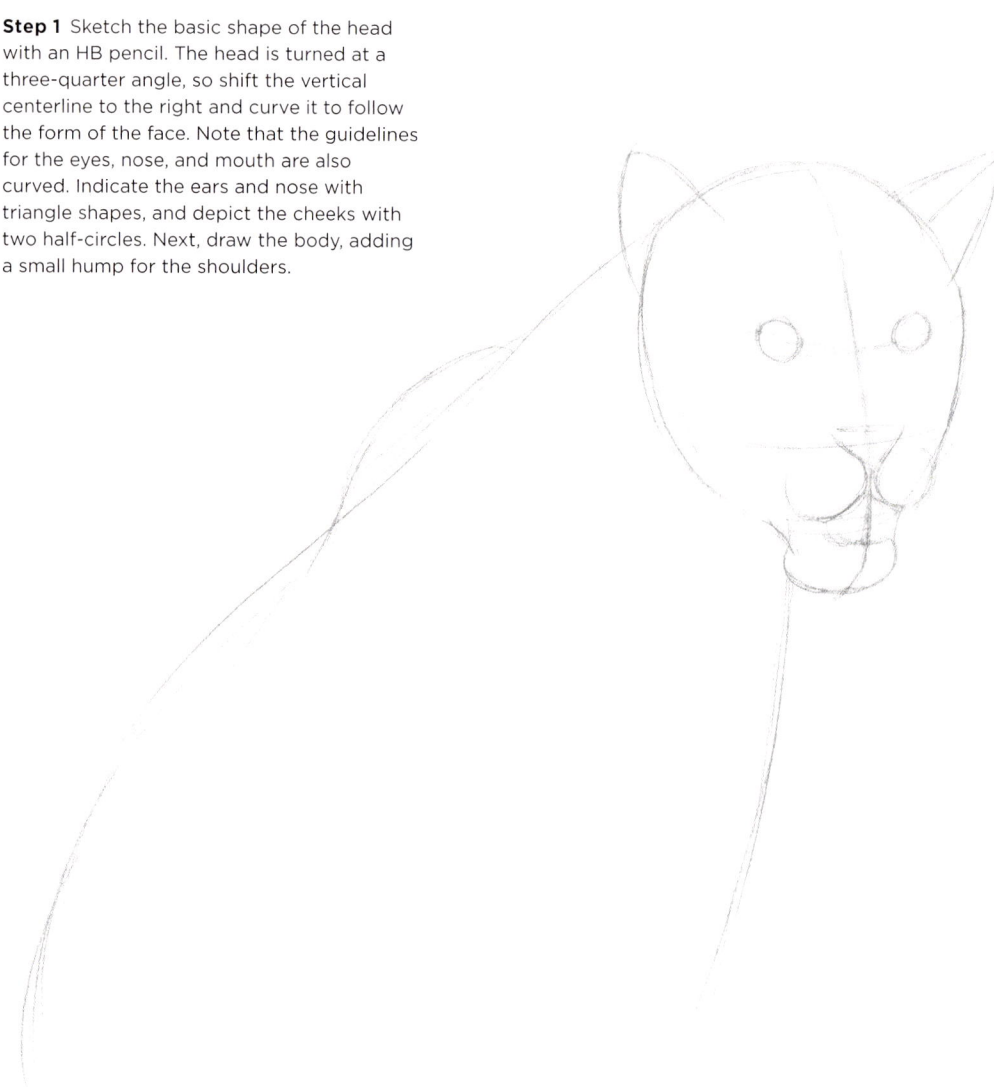

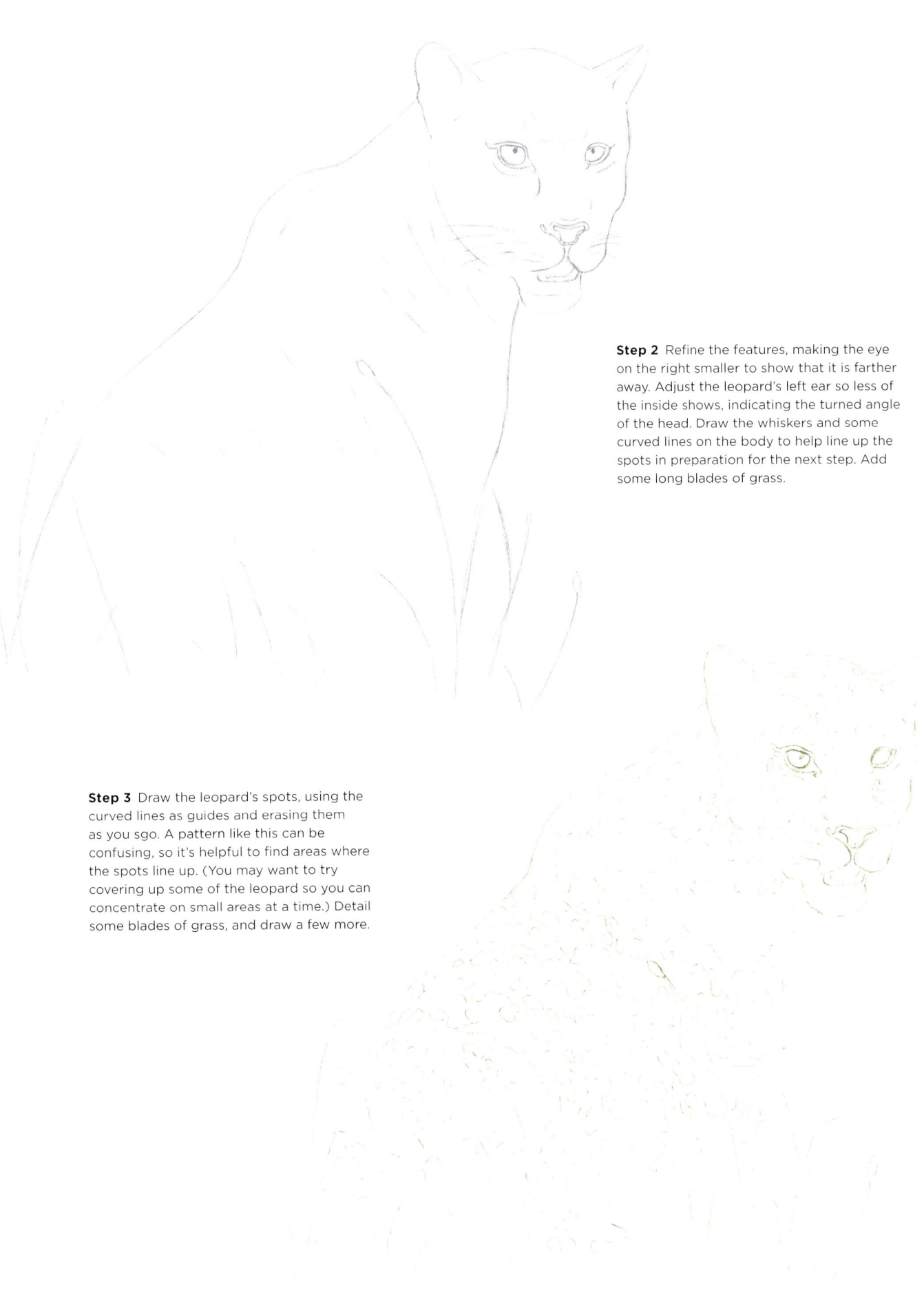

Step 2 Refine the features, making the eye on the right smaller to show that it is farther away. Adjust the leopard's left ear so less of the inside shows, indicating the turned angle of the head. Draw the whiskers and some curved lines on the body to help line up the spots in preparation for the next step. Add some long blades of grass.

Step 3 Draw the leopard's spots, using the curved lines as guides and erasing them as you sgo. A pattern like this can be confusing, so it's helpful to find areas where the spots line up. (You may want to try covering up some of the leopard so you can concentrate on small areas at a time.) Detail some blades of grass, and draw a few more.

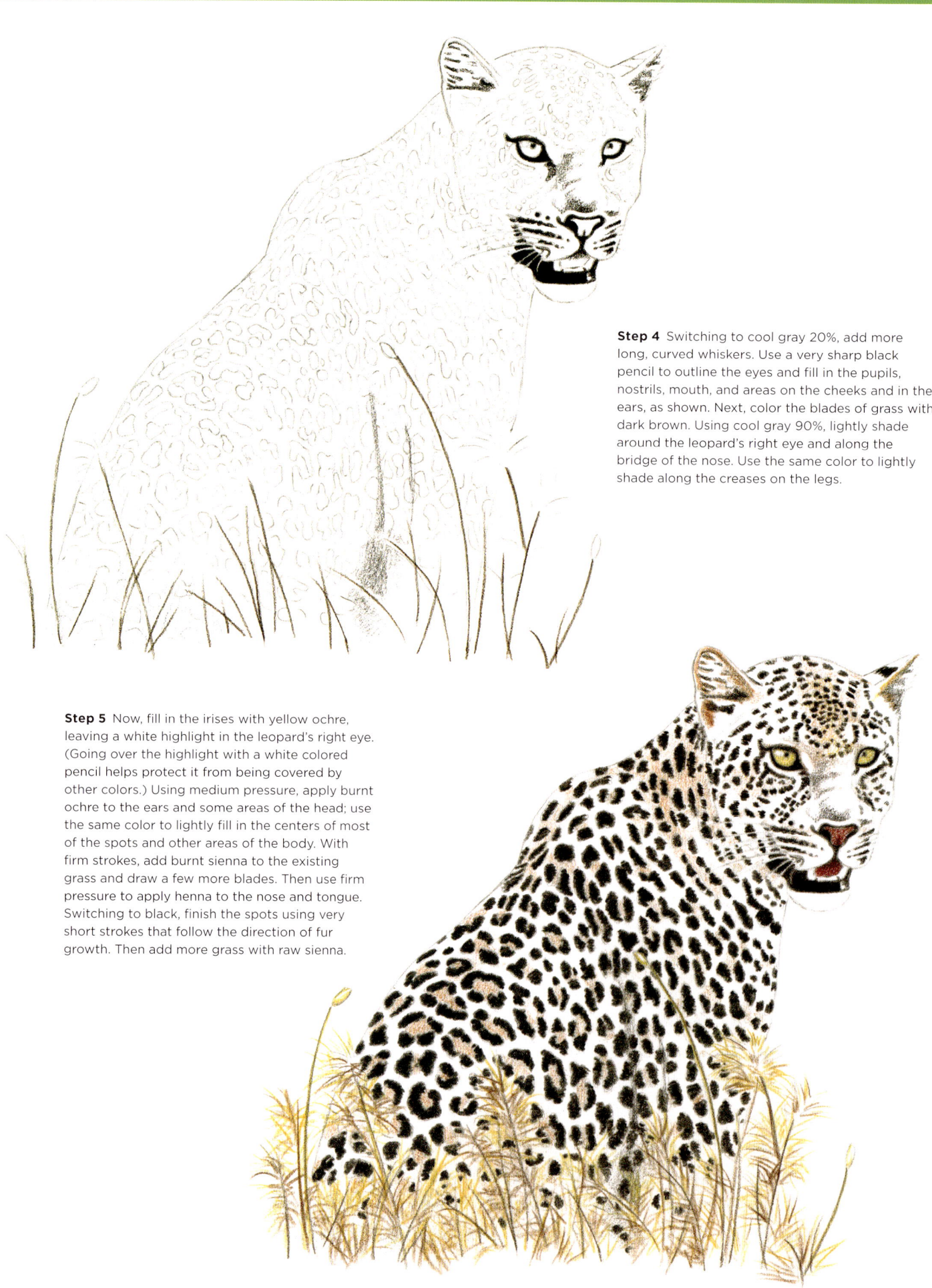

Step 4 Switching to cool gray 20%, add more long, curved whiskers. Use a very sharp black pencil to outline the eyes and fill in the pupils, nostrils, mouth, and areas on the cheeks and in the ears, as shown. Next, color the blades of grass with dark brown. Using cool gray 90%, lightly shade around the leopard's right eye and along the bridge of the nose. Use the same color to lightly shade along the creases on the legs.

Step 5 Now, fill in the irises with yellow ochre, leaving a white highlight in the leopard's right eye. (Going over the highlight with a white colored pencil helps protect it from being covered by other colors.) Using medium pressure, apply burnt ochre to the ears and some areas of the head; use the same color to lightly fill in the centers of most of the spots and other areas of the body. With firm strokes, add burnt sienna to the existing grass and draw a few more blades. Then use firm pressure to apply henna to the nose and tongue. Switching to black, finish the spots using very short strokes that follow the direction of fur growth. Then add more grass with raw sienna.

FUR DETAIL

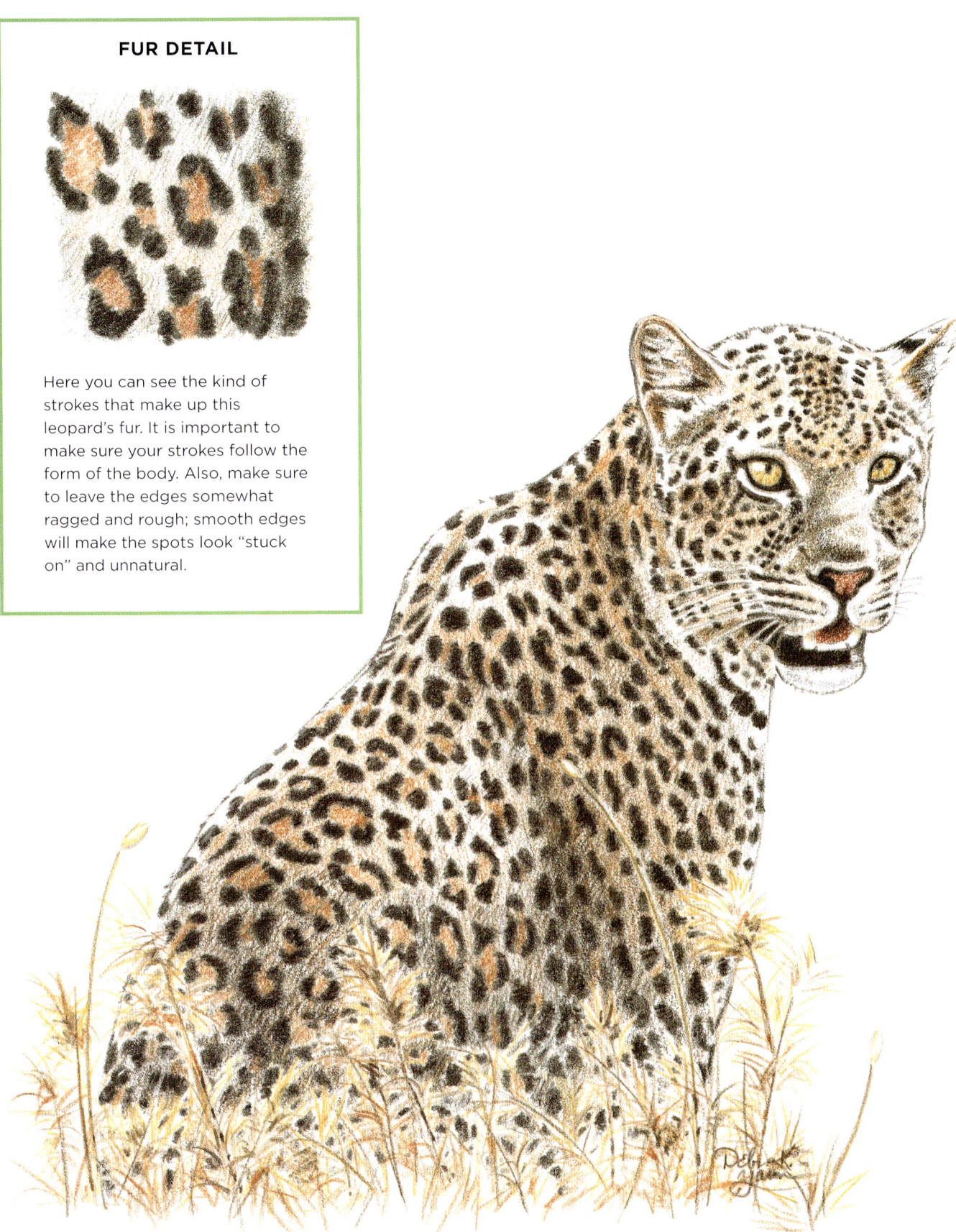

Here you can see the kind of strokes that make up this leopard's fur. It is important to make sure your strokes follow the form of the body. Also, make sure to leave the edges somewhat ragged and rough; smooth edges will make the spots look "stuck on" and unnatural.

Step 6 Apply a light layer of sepia over most of the body and lower face. Add cool gray 90% to the ears and middle of the body to emphasize the crease behind the front leg. Next, add cool gray 20% to the chin, leaving the center white. Using firm, short strokes, add some dark areas to the grass with sepia and burnt ochre. Now apply dark umber to most of the body, adding a few strokes of burnt ochre to the spots and some cool gray 90% to the leopard's rump. To finish, use a very sharp cool gray 90% to darken a few areas on the body and go over the outlines of the edges of the body and head, varying the pressure so the lines aren't solid and look more realistic.

Guinea Pig

This silky little guinea pig is so cute. To achieve the soft look of its fur, keep your pencil sharp, and work in the direction of the hair growth. Short, even strokes that are close together suggest the fur and texture without drawing in too much. Another important element in this drawing is the bright white highlight in the eyes. Be sure to leave these little dots of white free of any colored pencil so that the eyes appear nice and bright.

PALETTE

Black	Blue violet lake	Blush pink	Burnt ochre	Cool gray 30%	Espresso	Hot pink	Mineral orange	Sand

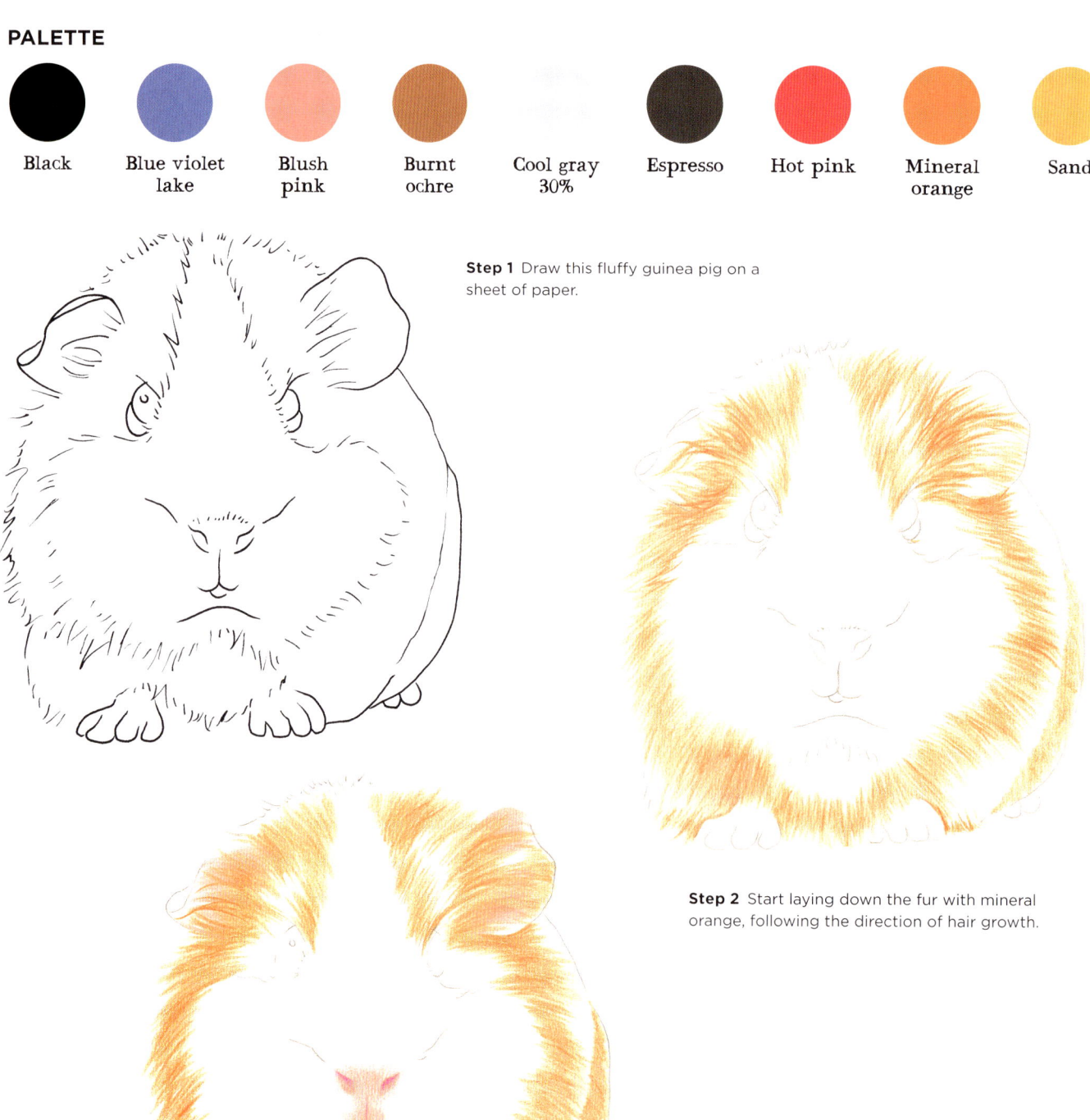

Step 1 Draw this fluffy guinea pig on a sheet of paper.

Step 2 Start laying down the fur with mineral orange, following the direction of hair growth.

Step 3 Apply blush pink to the nose, and indicate the nostrils and mouth with hot pink.
Use blush pink on the feet and areas of the ears.

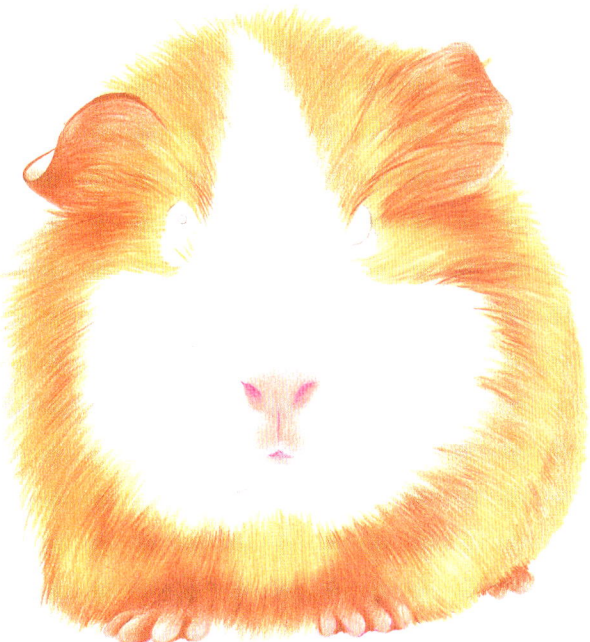

Step 4 Create darker areas of fur with burnt ochre. Then, apply this color to the edges of the ears and on the feet. Fill in lighter fur areas with sand.

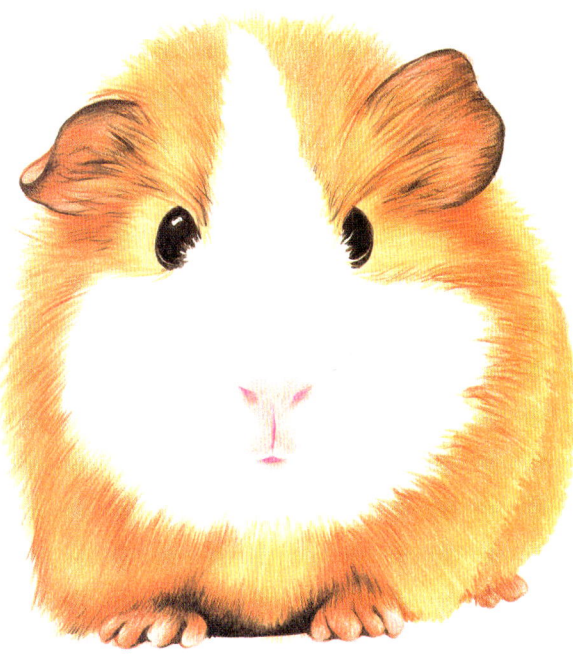

Step 5 Add dark shadows and fill in the eyes with espresso, leaving a highlight in each eye.

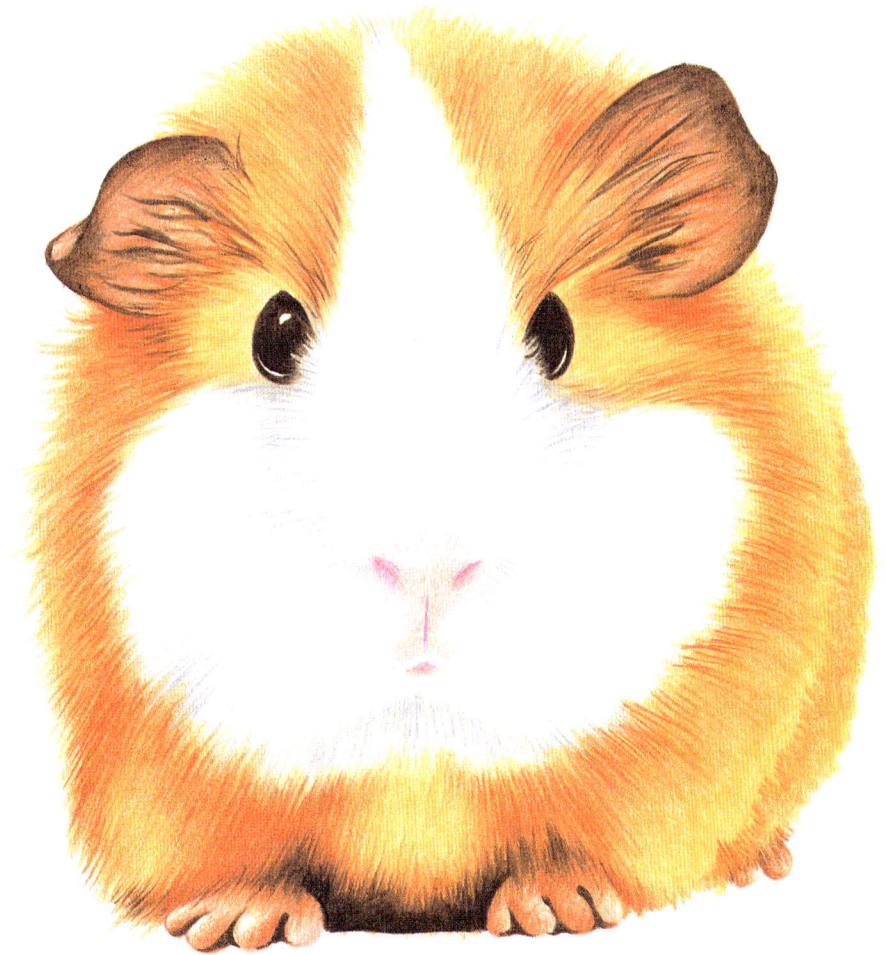

Step 6 Apply cool gray 30% and blue violet lake to create shadows in the white fur. Use blue violet lake on the nostrils and crease below the nose. Finally, deepen the outlines around the eyes and the shadows beneath the feet with black.

Index

First published in 2017 as *The Complete Beginner's Guide to Drawing Animals* (9781633221925) by Walter Foster Publishing, an imprint of The Quarto Group, 100 Cummings Center, Suite 265D, Beverly, MA 01915, USA T (978) 282-9590 F (978) 283-2742

EEA Representation, WTS Tax d.o.o., Žanova ulica 3, 4000 Kranj, Slovenia. www.wts-tax.si

Walter Foster Publishing titles are also available at discount for retail, wholesale, promotional, and bulk purchase. For details, contact the Special Sales Manager by email at specialsales@quarto.com or by mail at The Quarto Group, Attn: Special Sales Manager, 100 Cummings Center, Suite 265D, Beverly, MA 01915, USA

ISBN: 978-0-7603-9696-4

Digital edition published in 2025
eISBN: 978-0-7603-9697-1

Printed in Guangdong, China TT 062025
10 9 8 7 6 5 4 3 2 1

Produced by Coffee Cup Creative LLC
Layout by Elizabeth T. Gilbert
Copyedit by Susan H. Greer
Proofread by Stephanie Carbajal
Index by Beverlee Day

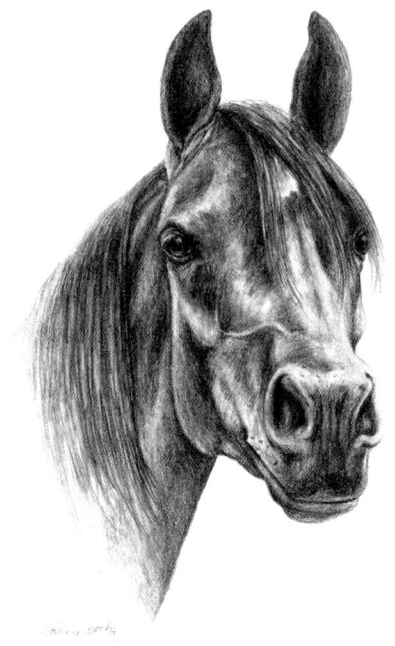